# Manchester and its Ship Canal Movement

# Manchester and its Ship Canal Movement

## Class, Work and Politics in late-Victorian England

**Ian Harford**

**Ryburn Publishing**
**KEELE UNIVERSITY PRESS**

First published in 1994
by Ryburn Publishing
an imprint of Keele University Press
Keele University, Staffordshire, England

Text © Ian Harford

Composed and printed by
Hartnolls, Bodmin, for
Ryburn Book Production
Keele University Press,
Staffordshire, England

ISBN  1 85331 075 1
Paperback
ISBN  1 85331 029 8
Souvenir edition

# Contents

# ACKNOWLEDGEMENTS

The research for this work has enabled me to meet with many people who have had some connection with the Ship Canal. From them I have learnt much both about the past and about the way that people's lives have been and are still being shaped by the changing fortunes of the Big Ditch. To all of these people I am indebted as they stimulated me to dig deeper in order to understand more about the movement which gave Lancashire its great seaway.

I would like to thank Rosemary Mellor and Patrick Joyce for their support throughout the research and writing up of the thesis, upon which this book is based. To Rosemary I owe a particular debt for she suggested that I should look at the origins of the Manchester Ship Canal and has been enthusiastic about the unfolding story. Patrick has provided me with stimulating comment and a number of avenues to explore as a result of his own work. However I must take responsibility for any mistakes and errors of interpretation.

There is a wealth of material available for the researcher and I have been given unfailing help by staff at the Greater Manchester Public Record Office, the Lancashire PRO, the John Rylands University Library of Manchester, Chetham's Library, Manchester Metropolitan University, the Working Class Movement Library and the Local Studies Units in Manchester, Salford, Oldham, Bolton, Stalybridge, Sale and Stockport. In particular I would like to mention David Taylor and Margaret De Motte at the Local Studies Unit at Manchester Central Library, where so much of the material on the Ship Canal Movement is located. The staff in all these libraries have honoured the intentions of depositors of material – that it should be widely accessible to future generations – and like all researchers I owe them especial thanks for fetching many books from the stacks and answering my questions without complaint. I am grateful also to the Manchester Ship Canal Company, Baring Brothers & Company, The Rothschild Archive (London), the Cooperative Wholesale Society, the *Manchester Evening News* and the Manchester Branch of the Graphical, Print and Media Union for generously allowing me access to their archives.

I have been helped by students in classes of the Workers' Educational Association (WEA), and many other people and friends, whose knowledge and interest in the Ship Canal have over the years given me ideas and leads for my research. For the initial typing of the earlier sections of the manuscript my thanks are due to June Atherton. Finally I am grateful to the voluntary Officers of the WEA North Western District for encouraging me to complete the research.

**Picture sources:**

| | |
|---|---|
| *MCL* | Libraries Department, Manchester City Council |
| *JRULM* | John Rylands University Library of Manchester |
| *CWS* | Cooperative Wholesale Society |
| *WCML* | Working Class Movement Library, Salford Leisure Services Department |
| *Chetham's* | Chetham's Library |
| *MSCC* | Manchester Ship Canal Company |
| *TRAFF* | Department of Environment and Leisure, Trafford Council |
| *GMPRO* | Greater Manchester Public Record Office |
| *Oldham* | Local Studies Unit, Oldham Leisure Services Department |
| *CAG* | Manchester City Art Galleries |
| *BTY* | Bridging the Years, Salford Quays Heritage Project |
| *CFS* | Compagnie Financière de Suez |
| *CM* | Chris Makepeace |

# MANCHESTER SHIP CANAL
# BRIEF CHRONOLOGY OF EVENTS

| | | |
|---|---|---|
| 1869 | | Suez Canal completed. |
| 1876 | | Hicks proposes improvements to River Irwell in letter to *Manchester Guardian*. |
| 1880 | | Construction of Panama Canal begun. |
| 1882 | May | Pamphlet "Facts & Figures..." published on proposed Tidal Navigation. |
| | June | Inaugural meeting at The Towers, home of Daniel Adamson. |
| | Nov | Mass meeting of working men in support of scheme. |
| 1883 | Jan | Critical pamphlet published by A. D. Provand. |
| | Aug | 1st MSC Bill rejected by House of Lords. |
| 1884 | Aug | 2nd MSC Bill rejected by House of Commons. |
| | Sept | Manchester merchants petition against Corporation support. |
| | Oct | Manchester Council agrees to contribute two-penny rate for Bill. |
| 1885 | June | Campaign organiser, Joseph Lawrence resigns in protest. |
| | Aug | Final MSC Bill receives Royal Assent. |
| | Sept | Promoters commence schemes to attract working men shareholders. |
| | Oct | Mass demonstration and Trades procession to Belle Vue. |
| 1886 | Feb | Rioting by unemployed in Manchester and London. |
| | July | Failure of MSC shares issue. |
| | Aug | Consultative Committee established to regain support for MSC. |
| 1887 | Feb | Adamson resigns as Chairman of MSC and is replaced by Lord Egerton. |
| | June | Rothschilds Bank underwrites £4 million of share capital. |
| | Nov | Construction of the Canal commences. |
| 1889 | Nov | Death of Ship Canal contractor, Thomas Walker. |
| 1890 | Nov | Settlement with Walker's executors, writing off £¼ million capital. |
| 1891 | Mar | Manchester Council agrees to lend £3 million; takes 5 seats on MSC Board. |
| | Dec | MSC Directors strongly criticised at City Council meeting. |
| 1892 | | Salford and Oldham Councils seek to provide loans to MSC. |
| 1893 | Apr | Manchester to lend further £2 million and have 11 directors on Board. |
| 1894 | Jan | Canal opened for traffic to Manchester. |
| | May | Formal opening by Queen Victoria. |
| | June | Appointment of full-time salaried chairman, J. K. Bythell. |

# 1

# HISTORIANS AND THE SHIP CANAL

… they would make the canal … it would be made not by a few great capitalists alone, but by large and small people all acting together, and even the poorest amongst them would find £10 or £20 to help on the work. That was the real meaning of self-government. When self-government began with self help, then there was something in it.

E. H. Pember Q.C. at the Great Trades' Procession, October 1885.

The Manchester Ship Canal, or "the People's Canal" as it has been called, was launched on a waiting world with a flurry of superlatives. The romance of Empire and foreign shores swept all before it, with the local journal of literary criticism declaring lyrically that the coming year was to be the city's Annus Mirabilis. "Manchester, the industrious Clothier of the World – that clothes the naked nations – that clothes a fourth of the inhabitants of this planet, will sail, with her varied merchandise, without let or hindrance, from Salford to the sea and so to the uttermost parts of the earth."[1] The Ship Canal project had attracted, and continued to attract more public interest and controversy than any other scheme in the region before or since, a feature which is scarcely surprising since a plan to create an inland port for ocean-going ships in a city 36 miles from the sea was a colossus by any account and the £15 million it cost reflected this.

A contemporary comparison helps to illustrate the size of the project neatly, because in 1883 – when the Manchester Ship Canal Bill was first put forward before Parliament – a Channel Tunnel was also being promoted by the Submarine Continental Railway Company at an estimated cost of £3–8 million.[2] With estimates for the Ship Canal at that stage ranging from £3–15 million, it is not unreasonable to compare the scale of the Ship Canal with the present Channel Tunnel, estimated to cost £10 billions according to the latest figures. A further feature of great significance was the role played by the City Council in providing £5 million, or one third of the capital required, for the Canal's construction – a figure which, if translated into modern figures, would not be dwarfed by the capital borrowings of many of today's "big business" municipal authorities. The immense size of the loan can be illustrated by the fact that when the Corporation first committed itself in 1891, the total annual rate levied for the whole city amounted to only just over half a million pounds, and the commitment was mainly responsible for increasing the Corporation's total debt by 65%.

The impressive scale of the enterprise and the engineering aspects of this massive project have bedazzled generations of historians and commentators who have seen the Ship Canal as epitomizing those qualities of hard work, heroism and supreme self-confidence which have been considered attributes of nineteenth century Manchester. As a contributor to the 1929 *The Soul of Manchester*[3] put it in his pithy opening sentence on the Ship Canal: "It is not an idle boast that when Manchester sets its hand to a thing that thing gets done properly".

This kind of local patriotic writing still finds its echoes in the more sophisticated literature of contemporary urban geography, as in Rodgers' more recent blithe appraisal:

The brief stresses of earlier periods were seen only as challenges to be overcome. For example it was in the deep depression of the 1880s that the Ship Canal was begun, a typically bold use of the engineer to change the facts of an inconvenient geography so that an inland city was transformed into the nation's fourth seaport.[4]

Early cartoon of big sailing ships at Throstle Nest, close to the city centre. The verse caption reads:
> But here we see the best of all,
> The masts of brigs and schooners tall,
> With cotton from the glowing West,
> Sailing up to Throstle Nest;
> With more from Egypt close behind,
> Tugged by steamers 'gainst the wind,
> While other vessels leave the quay
> And sail with merchandise away.

*MCL*

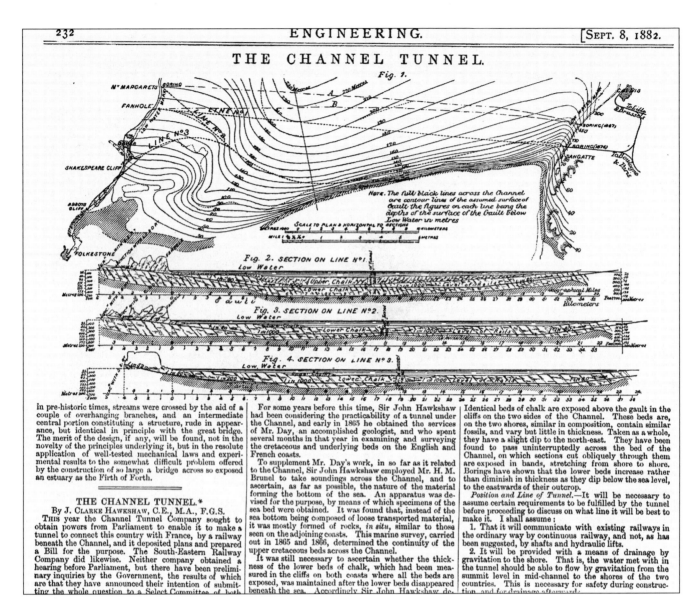

Plan of the Channel Tunnel, published in September 1882, at the start of the Ship Canal campaign.   *JRULM*

A more complete and logical examination must, however, take account of a series of prior questions concerning the origins and development of the Ship Canal. These link into major theoretical and historical debates about the nature of transformations taking place in British society in the last quarter of the nineteenth century and in the early years of the twentieth century prior to 1914. Generally these issues of class, state and economy have received inadequate treatment in this period, and certainly they have not been well-documented at the local level. Where they have been covered they have been seen as the separate provinces of the labour, political or economic historian.[5]

In contrast this study of power and class relationships in Manchester argues the interrelatedness of these themes and the need to examine issues of decline and modernization in the British economy in the context of major social and political changes. These included the emergence of a trade union movement with a labourist perspective, the widespread dissemination of socialist ideas, the development by the industrial bourgeoisie of new strategies in response to the extension of democratic representation, and the adoption of more interventionist roles by the State to solve certain social and political problems which *laissez-faire* capitalism failed to address effectively. The period of the Ship Canal movement from the early 1880s until the mid 1890s coincided with both an extension of the franchise and with a build up of extra-parliamentary working class political action at national and local level, which posed a destabilizing threat to existing political structures and power-holders. The Ship Canal project was initially seen and discussed as a commercial venture to be implemented for economic reasons, but as it progressed and drew in a variety of new interests – trade union and cooperative representatives, politicians, radicals and reformers – it took on the characteristics of a mass movement which quite explicitly aimed to attract the working class of the region. Indeed, in this respect, it can be viewed as prefiguring Chamberlain's Tariff Reform League formed twenty years later.

This feature of the Ship Canal's development, which has been ignored by historians, was to be of considerable significance in 1885–86 when, with the Canal's future seriously at risk, demonstrations and rioting over the unemployment question, promoted by Social Democratic Federation agitators, spread from London to many of the provincial cities including Manchester. Within days the Ship Canal project was being promoted by Adamson and other leading figures as a cure for the labour problems of the region. Although there had been opposition earlier to the scheme from Manchester's commercial and industrial bourgeoisie, there was no antagonism in Manchester to this significant change of emphasis. The depression and the problems of social unrest and unemployment had emerged firmly as political issues. The working class voter had become a force to be reckoned with, and most certainly not to be overlooked. As Beatrice Webb was to confide in her diary as she looked back to this period:

> We forget that it was not until the dark years of 1881–5 were well over that constitutional socialism as distin-guished from revolutionary socialism began to grow.[6]

Whilst it will not be argued as some crude political paradigm of action and reaction that the Ship Canal project was a direct response to a changing working class political consciousness, it will be suggested that the new political climate, in which trades unions and working class represen-tatives felt more confident to make demands of employers and of the State, provides a key element in explaining both the form that the Ship Canal movement[7] took, and the fact that the Canal was finally built. For the Manchester Ship Canal was a qualitatively different project from the commu-nication infrastructure developed from the 1830s onwards by the railway companies through the orthodox capital markets.[8] It was always presented as more than just a profitable outlet for capital, as E. H. Pember's remarks, quoted at the start of this chapter, indicate. The Ship Canal, its proponents argued, would make existing industries more competitive by reducing transport costs, would attract new industries and new jobs, and would cut food costs. Supporters of the scheme were presented as local patriots. It was a populist programme with a producer–consumer ideology intended to transcend class interests and to create instead a community of interests. It was seen and presented as epitomising the Liberal principles of Free Trade and drew significantly on the inspiration and strategies of the Anti-Corn Law League in the 1840s – a feature which is discussed in Chapter 4.

The movement, launched by Daniel Adamson, a substan-tial engineering employer, was masterminded by leading

SOWING TARES.

(With a thousand apologies to Sir John E. Millais, Bart., R.A.)

*Punch* cartoon in February 1886, critical of the effect of the socialist agitation amongst the unemployed.   *MCL*

members of the region's industrial bourgeoisie, with the support of a handful of urban professionals. It mobilized vast numbers of the working-class in Manchester and the sur-rounding towns behind this single central issue, and enjoyed the active backing and participation of the representative structures and institutions of that class. Crowds of up to 150,000 attended demonstrations and processions in support, and up over million people were estimated to have come to Manchester to witness the formal opening by the monarch. This sustained grooming of public opinion must rank as one of the most effective local propaganda cam-paigns conducted in Victorian Britain, and brought with it a unique level of material and public cooperation between capital and labour.

One basis for this accord can be found in the cooperative tradition of the North West, home of the first cooperative retail venture, the Rochdale Pioneers, and of the Cooperative Wholesale Society, for these bodies provided financial and ideological backing for the Ship Canal. It was also significant that several of the main trade union officials involved in the movement were members of the TUC's Parliamentary Committee which by this stage was pursuing closer links

The SS *Pioneer*, owned by the Cooperative Wholesale Society, which was the first ship to unload a cargo in 1894. *CWS*

with the Liberal Party as a strategy to achieve legislative reforms. Since many of the key supporters of the Ship Canal were active Liberals, the development of an informal "Lib–Lab" alliance at the local level was a natural step. This question is explored in detail in Chapter 4.

Explanations must also be sought by looking at the changing experience of the workers within the predominant industries of the area. Textiles, by far the largest sector, showed a marked degree of technological advance linked to strong trade union organization and continuing craft control by skilled workers such as spinners, but its growth

rate from 1880 onwards exhibited a dramatic slowing down. In three out of the previous four decades there had been an increase in production of between 50% and 60%, whereas in the following four decades the average increase had been reduced to 10%.[9]

If the depression in trade in the late 1870s and early 1880s, which presaged an historic downturn in the U.K. industry, was a factor in inducing a supportive attitude amongst workers towards the Ship Canal project, it did not deter them from withdrawing their labour at the workplace. The cotton trade unions' strategy was to maximise the

1894 Certificate for the SS *Pioneer*, the first Home Trade ship to be registered in the Port of Manchester. *CWS*

benefits they could get from the existing technology by negotiating highly complicated lists which governed the piece-rates payable, and different sections were prepared throughout the whole of this period to take lengthy industrial action against wage reductions and unilateral revisions of the lists – the most important being the five-month long lock-out of 100,000 spinners in 1892/3, which was settled with the Brooklands Agreement.

The contrasts with engineering, the other main industry in the area, were considerable and are interesting because this much smaller, but vitally important, sector was reaching a level of mechanization and standardised production by the 1880s which had been familiar in textiles 30 years earlier. This enabled rapid development in both the tradi-

tional areas like machine tools and textile machinery, and in newer areas like gas engineering and electrical engineering. The effects of these changes in the work process, which are explored in Chapter 5, were felt acutely by engineering workers represented by an essentially craft union, the Amalgamated Society of Engineers (ASE), which viewed with concern the loss of craft status and control and the growing practice of using semi-skilled machine operators.[10] The bad industrial relations that developed in the industry because of these changes resulted in such disputes as a two-year strike starting in 1883 at Sunderland over the restriction of apprentices, and a strike at Bolton in 1886–7 over overtime and wages, involving "riotous destruction of property".[11] Despite this general situation, however, the ASE,

13

through its general secretary Robert Austin, was willing, with reservations, to join the cotton workers and other unions in committing its support to the employer-led initiative of the Ship Canal movement.

Why were such different groups of workers, as well as others like the print workers and carpenters, willing to put so much organizational effort into a scheme about which they must have had considerable doubts? The argument of this study is that to a large extent the high expectations generated amongst workers in the region, and the support given by the trades unions, legitimized the project and therefore made acceptable municipal backing and public funding; and that support was forthcoming not only because of the depressed state of trade and the loss of jobs which followed, but also because the initiation of the Ship Canal movement carried with it, along with other political and ideological objectives, a tacit promise by leading members of the regional industrial bourgeoisie that capital and resources would be committed to this infrastructure development and that the local industrial base would be expanded and diversified. The significance of this commitment can be seen in Hobsbawm's general observation that:

This sudden transformation of the leading and most dynamic industrial economy into the most sluggish and conservative, in the short space of thirty or forty years (1860–90/1900) is the crucial question of British economic history. After the 1890s we may ask why so little was done to restore the dynamism of the economy.[12]

The period under observation represents the key period when British capital in general turned away from domestic manufacturing to foreign investment. The export of capital grew at such a rate that U.K. total investment abroad is estimated to have jumped from £1,200 million in 1870 to £3,500–£4,000 million by 1914, reflecting the increase in annual new portfolio investment abroad which rose from £40 million to a peak of £200 million. As A. R. Hall notes:

Nothing comparable in terms of proportions of resources devoted to overseas investments had occurred before over any lengthy period. Nor has anything comparable occurred since then.[13]

There has been little local level research demonstrating this process of capital outflow and its impact on domestic industries, but what there is strongly confirms the debilitating effect on the local economy. In a study of the jute industry in Dundee from 1850–1921 Lenman and Donaldson have shown how the policy of overseas investment by leading companies through investment trusts and share purchases gravely hampered the diversification of an economy over-dependent on a single industry.[14] Similarly the work of the Benwell Community Development Project has examined how on Tyneside in this period the failure to reinvest by the engineering and armaments manufacturer W. G. Armstrong

substantially weakened its competitive position with Vickers.[15]

By the 1880s a crisis was affecting the British economy which was far more than just a cyclical downturn and which required determined investment policies aimed at re-equipment and diversification. The Ship Canal proposals represented just such a policy, but the high costs and anticipated competition from the Port of Liverpool and the existing railway companies suggested a lack of profitability and deterred all but a few from investing. Despite a prolonged three year Parliamentary campaign, which resulted in the passage of an enabling Act, the initial response from local investors was unenthusiastic. Nor was Rothschilds Bank any more successful when a London launch of the shares was tried the following year. The indifference of local and London capitalists was a bitter blow and induced a major crisis of authority for the industrial and political leadership, and particularly for those whose names had been associated with the scheme from the start.

This crisis coincided with the growing unrest over the question of unemployment which reached its peak in 1886. Public concern over this issue helped to persuade important figures to fall into line and sheath their doubts about the Canal project in order to support the favourable recommendations of a Consultative Committee. But it became clear that neither this nor the resignation of the Chairman Adamson in 1887 was going to be sufficient to raise the necessary capital, unless further action was taken. In order that the Parliamentary powers under the 1885 enabling Act should not lapse, the Company (under Section 38) had to be able to guarantee that the entire capital of £8 million had been issued and accepted by 6th August 1887, but by May the subscription list for shares had only reached £3 million. The question of financing the scheme was therefore resolved (temporarily) by the adoption of two extraordinary expedients. In the first place the contractor, Walker, was persuaded to accept £½ million of the contract price in shares. Secondly Parliamentary approval was sought and obtained for a new Act to split the £8 million capital required into preference and ordinary shares. This course of action was agreed upon by those who had already indicated a willingness to subscribe for £3 million worth of ordinary shares; and resulted in the £4 million of new preference shares, which were underwritten and assembled by London-based finance capital, having the first call on any interest paid out. In this way the August deadline was met, enabling construction of the Canal to commence in November. But the under-capitalisation of the project, which had been foreseen by many commentators at the start of the Ship Canal movement, was to re-surface publicly three years later when the Canal lay half-completed with the money spent up, and with no prospect of further finance being found by the Company on the open money market.

The promoters' promise of capital and commitment to the region lay dangerously exposed as tattered rhetoric. Popular capitalism, a major organizing theme in the early days of the movement had not only failed to win the support of working men but had left many small shareholders with worthless savings. Too much political capital had been sunk in the scheme to allow it to fail, and so began a process of siphoning £5 million of new funds into the Ship Canal from the capital markets via the medium of Manchester Corporation. The task, however, was fraught with difficulties not only because of this sudden and apparently inexplicable volte-face in the Ship Canal company's fortunes, but also because of a turning tide in the City Council which brought to the Town Hall new councillors with different attitudes and loyalties. Several of these younger councillors were no longer willing to accept the easy hegemony exercised by a small number of mostly Liberal senior members of the Council, and were highly critical of the directors of the Ship Canal Company. But support for five million pounds of Corporation loans for the bankrupt enterprise was forthcoming, and in Chapter 7 the proposition will be explored that this underwriting of private capital by the local state was envisaged from the very start, and that plans to implement such a policy were put in hand as early as 1887 – when construction was first commenced – by recruiting sympathisers onto key committees in the Corporation. The idea of creating a public trust rather than a private company had indeed been floated at an early stage by some trade union speakers and progressive Liberals, but had been resisted by a combination of Liberals and Tories who saw the Canal as a vehicle for encouraging popular capitalism and working-class shareholding.

The responses of a range of actors to the problems thrown up in Manchester and its surrounding towns by mass democracy and by declining markets provide us with a revealing case study of major issues of transformation which were affecting other cities and the country generally between 1880 and 1914. Despite the importance of the questions raised, there has been surprisingly little historical study of the period at local level. In part this has been because an earlier generation of writers has seen the process of industrialization up to the 1860s and 1870s, the quintessential Victorian period of growth and enterprise, as the prime focus for analysis and explanation. Asa Briggs, for instance, in his pioneering study, published in 1963, provides a stimulating overview of six Victorian cities,[16] but is content to despatch the last quarter century of Victorian Manchester with just a few glancing references to its Town Hall, its University and the Hallé orchestra. The Ship Canal does not even get a mention.

Writers on the political structures of nineteenth century cities have similarly tended to recognize the early 1880s as a self-imposed end-stop for their research. Fraser, for instance, in an interesting account of the processes and forms of Victorian urban politics up to the 1870s, concludes with his view that "though politics in the 1870s were but an augmented echo of those of the 1830s the half-century beyond 1880 witnessed a fundamental change in the political process".[17] A more recent study by Garrard[18] on municipal leadership and power in Rochdale, Bolton and Salford, stops at the same point, recognizing a fracture that was opening up from the 1880s onwards which could not easily be accommodated within a framework constructed for the earlier period.

Hanham's classic account of politics and party management,[19] written some 30 years ago, moves closer into our period, but is not centrally concerned with the social and political changes which were impelling the parties into the twentieth century. His book, however, contains much interesting material on the 1870s, and is particularly strong in its treatment of the workings of the Liberal party machine, including those in Manchester. In contrast to those already mentioned, Hennock's well-researched study of the personnel and role of local government in Birmingham and Leeds, does continue up to 1914, but its quite deliberate emphasis on councillors and the activities of the council leads away from a consideration of wider class and power relationships – a limitation the author was aware of in his comment that "in history the choice of a period determines the perspective, and a project that ends in 1914 does not provide a good perspective for a study of working-class presence on town councils".[20]

More attention, however, has been paid in recent years to work and class relationships in ways which relate more closely to the interrelated themes of this study. An important early contribution came in Pollard's account of the development of labour in Sheffield, with its deliberate focus on the experience of the common people; and an interesting account of the economy and politics of Cardiff in the period 1870–1914 is to be found in Daunton's *Coal Metropolis*.[21] Pollard's emphasis was on the development of trade unionism and the industrial structure of the city, but the theme of work and class relationships which these developments threw up has been taken a great deal further in the work of social historians such as Gareth Stedman Jones, Joyce and Smith.[22] Joyce's work in particular – based in the Lancashire textile towns though not addressing the question of the local State – has raised interesting issues about conflict and cooperation at the workplace which are relevant to questions to be explored in Chapters 4 and 5 concerning the nature and dynamics of relationships established between capital and organized labour during the Ship Canal Movement.

It is curious, however, that the experience of Manchester itself in the period 1880–1914 has not been subjected to this kind of more rigorous historical analysis.[23] This may be partly due to its image as Cottonopolis, as the prototypical industrial city in the 1840s and 1850s, which contemporaries conveyed to the world outside. This image still pervades partly because such a mass of material has been written about discrete aspects of Manchester life that a comprehensive view is difficult to achieve. Kidd and Roberts[24] have begun to address this vacuum with a series of essays examining different aspects of class relationships and cultural production; and Kidd's own essay on Outcast Manchester sheds interesting light on the way that the question of unemployment and poor relief was handled by the voluntary charities.

The value of this study of Manchester's Ship Canal project is that it brings a focus on themes of state and economy at the local level which are mostly ignored in the literature of urban growth and local government. The general assumption, for instance in Hennock's work, is that the operations of the local state are largely independent of the local economy and the class relationships of production. Fraser's study of seven cities stresses the essentially benign and voluntaristic nature of municipal government, and he argues that once its powers had been laid down in the nineteenth century, the decisive feature was that local councils adopted a positive social role and recognized a responsibility for the general welfare of the community and for environmental control.[25] His acknowledgement that in order to do this town councils had to acquire the "social authority" which flowed from the participation of leading citizens in the urban community is a tacit recognition of the wider power and class relationships, but it goes no further. His study tells us nothing about the economic activities of the bourgeoisie whose factories and mills were causing the rapid population expansion and creating the environmental and living conditions which needed controlling by local councils; nor does it explore their relationship to the local state, the extent to which their interests were represented there, their attitude to the extension by central government of municipal powers, or what they expected to get from direct participation as councillors.

The reality in a large commercial city in Victorian times was that while industrialists who controlled thousands of workers in their factories could exert substantial influence, their sway was not absolute because the simple class/power structure of a small industrial town with a dominant employer was absent. In Manchester for instance substantial fractures existed between manufacturing and mercantile capital and there were also opportunities for effective intervention by other interest groups. This was the context in which the local state functioned – a seat on the Council may or may not have been an advantage. Garrard[26] has shown in his study of three northern towns that large proprietors were nearly always the largest group on municipal councils – and from this we may assume they were most influential – but the corollary, that small numbers or absence meant limited influence, does not necessarily apply.

Quantification may be indicative but it is not in itself very illuminating. The nub of the argument here is not that municipal affairs were unimportant to the bourgeoisie, but that studies of local government have, by their narrow focus on the municipality and its powers, effectively excluded any analysis of the relationship between state and local economy. They have neither demonstrated the dynamics and inter-action involved, nor explored the ways in which influence was used to further economic as well as political and social interests. Typically they have placed emphasis on the conflicts, especially between petit bourgeois "economistic" interests and social reformers over expenditure and rate increases, and failed to explore important questions about the attitudes and responses of both employers and workers to the gains which accrued from a healthier environment and a more active public sector. For just as it was claimed that the repeal of the corn laws and free trade ensured cheap food for the working class, so the provision by the local state of libraries, parks and clean water could be shown as part of the social wage.

In the case of Manchester, a proper consideration of this whole question has been further impeded by over-reliance on Beatrice Webb's caricature of the local councillors on her visit to the City in 1899. Her description of the City Council as consisting of "merely hard-headed shopkeepers" has, until recently, been accepted without hesitation and has been taken to be applicable from the 1870s at least.[27] The evidence from the Ship Canal years shows both that this view was wrong and that the close involvement of Manchester Corporation in the financing and management of the Ship Canal represented a significant first step in the local State becoming involved in the process of economic planning – planning which unaided private capital was unable to coordinate effectively.

In relation to the central state, however, it has long been recognized that the Manchester and Lancashire cotton interests exercised throughout the nineteenth century a powerful influence both on major economic questions such as Free Trade and Protectionism, and on specific policy areas like the development of the Indian sub-continent – where successive British Governments were persuaded of the advisability of railway investment to open up markets, and of low tariffs for British goods.[28] Primarily, this pressure was channelled through parliamentary representatives and trade associations, but behind these moves were the same merchants and manufacturers who were also active in shaping the policies of the local councils in Manchester and the surrounding towns. Involvement in the local council and on the local hustings was an important way of building a popular base and influencing public opinion in favour of particular policies.

The linkages in this chain of power and influence are complicated, but the crucial point is that the local state played a vital intermediary role in transmitting and legitimating the views of dominant interests. The complexity in the Ship Canal's case was compounded by the existence of major divisions between sections of the big bourgeoisie over the proper method of financing the Scheme. Because of its size and controversial nature – which resulted in many of the negotiations and disagreements being made public – the operation of winning support needed to be highly systematic and overt. As we shall see in Chapter 3, the major economic interests behind the Scheme were the export oriented manufacturers, particularly in engineering and cotton; once it became clear that private capital might fail to raise sufficient funds, they became committed to arguing for the overturning of orthodox economic doctrines in favour of intervention (on their terms) by the local state. In the depression of the previous decade, they had seen exports and profits dwindling as countries like the United States, France and Germany erected high tariff walls to protect their own domestic industries. Implacably opposed to Protectionism, which was increasingly espoused by the Tory Party in its bid for working class support, manufacturing capitalists viewed the prospect of a new deep-water communication link under their control as economically advantageous, consistent with their Free Trade principles, and as a demonstration to the working class of their commitment to the region and to maintaining low food prices. By contrast merchant capital in the city – as represented by some of the largest export–import houses – was untroubled by the problems of fixed capital investments and large workforces, and from the start was either hostile or indifferent to the Scheme. A mass campaign, as described in Chapter 2, to override this opposition became imperative. It was necessary not only to gain municipal support for the Parliamentary campaign for the Ship Canal Bill, but also to create a state of public opinion which would welcome massive investment in the scheme by the local state in the event of subsequent undercapitalisation problems.

The manner in which the City Council in Manchester was penetrated by the Ship Canal supporters and its 'independent' structures utilised to forward the project and overcome powerful opposition from both within and outside the Town Hall is explored in Chapter 7. The standard books on the development of local government in Manchester are those by Redford and Simon,[29] but both suffer from the limitations already noted in studies of this type in that they make no attempt to link municipal events to the economy of the city. Both give short accounts of the development of the Ship Canal with Redford paying more attention to the detailed debates in the City Council, and both rely heavily on the two-volume history of the Ship Canal written by Bosdin Leech and published in 1907.[30] The researcher who comes fresh to the subject cannot help being surprised at the vast accumulation of material that was or has subsequently been written about the scheme. A bibliography[31] of publications and articles on the subject lists over 80 pages of items held in libraries and archives in the North West. The main thrust of this material has been directed to exploring the Canal's significance as a piece of engineering, and its contribution to the economic history of the region. Virtually no consideration has been given to the social and political dimensions that are inextricably linked with its initiation and development.

The explanation for this involves fundamental questions about "history" and historically-based research which are both political and methodological. For ultimately in seeking explanations for events and actions historians are attempting, whatever theoretical constructs are employed, to describe the intentions of actors. But as Reddy has observed: "No act of observation is neutral. No observer has ever recorded information merely for its own sake. Observers in

Bosdin Leech, historian of the Ship Canal and committed protagonist.

the act of observation are engaging in social action; their desire is to change as much as to see. Their success in either endeavour is always limited".[32]

The first difficulty the researcher faces, therefore, is a methodological one of interpretation, for as Reddy points out in his study of the development of a market culture in France, documents cannot be treated at face value. The researcher has to get behind them, and behind the words being used. The conceptual schema buried in a phrase or sentence may obscure rather than illuminate the truth. It is not enough to say that "the Ship Canal was built to reduce transport costs" – which every book written about the Canal claims – without testing the evidence to check that it will support the claim. Some facets of this problem of interpretation can be seen in the account written by Bosdin Leech, and the stance adopted to the book and to Leech's critics by Farnie who, as an economic historian, has written extensively and authoritatively about the Ship Canal.[33]

Leech's book is a storehouse of information, and an invaluable source for charting the course of the project, and as such it has provided a short-cut for subsequent writers wishing to avoid the bother of reading original material. The danger of this is that too often Leech has been taken at face value, whereas the reality is that he was a committed protagonist of the Ship Canal Movement, who was keen to write an "official" history which reflected his own views. Another of his shortcomings was that he was a plagiarist; he often copied sentences and sections from newspaper reports as though they were his own writing, and this has misled many who have subsequently written about the Ship Canal. His comments about the attitude towards the Ship Canal of C. P. Scott, editor of the *Manchester Guardian* – which were in reality words used by Scott about himself – are a classic example of this, and induced Farnie to write a withering but totally unjustifiable attack on Scott. For details of this example and of the pitfalls of relying on secondary material, see Appendix A.

An interpretative mode of enquiry must aim to strip away rather than augment the 'layering' of truth. To achieve this, emphasis will be placed in the study on analysing particular events and issues which generated conflict and controversy. These provide the set pieces where the researcher is most likely to find the clearest articulation of position and conceptual framework; where the protagonists are most willing to commit their views publicly or in written form. But at the end of this process speculation about motivation will remain, not least because actors are prone to conceal their intentions. Document shredding is just a modern form for the disposal of inconvenient evidence.

The question remains, however, as to why such a one-dimensional history of the Ship Canal has been maintained over the hundred years since its construction was begun.

Why has there been such a willingness to recite endlessly and repolish the same narrow conventional portrayal of the project? Why has no one thought it useful to look behind the simplistic account of a city determined to reduce its transport costs and wrest control from Liverpool and the railway companies in order to consider the political and social background, the internal contradictions, and the class interests represented in the scheme? Why has no-one asked about the losses as well as the gains? For, as Farnie has observed, the project "was an expensive luxury for an island power and for a region with a highly articulated structure of transport and communication."[34]

Farnie himself, it should be said, has never set out to explore the period of construction of the canal and strays only occasionally into the years before 1894. This is certainly not the case, however, with a more recent contribution to the Ship Canal literature by Owen, whose book is centrally about the construction and financing of the Canal and the associated campaigning and publicity. But despite this and his reference to the extensive material available, it is apparent that he has seldom strayed far from Leech, whose account is accepted without demur and without qualification. "There could have been no-one more suited to write such a history, for he was interested in it from the earliest days."[35] There is no reference to political events or to the role of the trade unions, and no analysis of the Corporation's role in the context of debates about municipal socialism, and the changing role of the State; and no consideration is given to the political and ideological significance of this nineteenth century version of popular capitalism.

Manchester Victoria University, from Oxford Road.   *JRULM*

The reason for these omissions is that Owen is writing within the cabined tradition of economic history, in which social and political factors are deemed extraneous to and largely independent of the workings of the economy – a view which has its parallels in the "old-fashioned town biographies" which Cannadine describes as still appearing in the urban history of the 1970s, "all with a strong antiquarian commitment to one place, but lacking any awareness of the larger process of urbanisation, ignoring many of the themes and subjects which urban historians now treat as serious and important".[36] The tradition which Owen is following can be traced quite clearly back to a base in which Manchester itself was a significant part; its origins can be located in the 1890s and early years of the twentieth century at the very period when the Ship Canal idea was being translated into reality and Leech's book was being published. For, as Harte has pointed out, the University of Manchester made the second university appointment specifically in economic history in 1905, and was the first to create a chair in the subject in 1910.[37]

At the suggestion of T. F. Tout, the conservative and highly influential Professor of History at the University, the post was offered to George Unwin[38] whose dislike of *The State* was, in Harte's words, "crucial to the way in which the subject was to develop in his hands."[39] A flavour of this attitude can be seen in this quote from his revealing introductory lecture in 1908 in Edinburgh:

If the interference of the State was one of the greatest factors on the negative side in determining the rate of economic progress, so the heroic persistence of individual genius was perhaps the greatest factor on the positive side.[40]

The influence of this conceptual framework can still be traced today. The absence of a political and structural dimension in much of the work of economic historians and industrial archaeologists like Owen can be attributed to the style adopted by Unwin and others like him in these early days. As Tawney observed in an obituary notice, Unwin held the view "that history is not past politics, but that politics are the squalid scaffolding of more serious matters."[41]

The accounts which have been written about the Ship Canal and its origins can be seen, therefore, at one level for what they are – histories which gloss over the inconvenient. At another level, this corpus of material provides a case study not only in class relationships, but also in the organization and production of knowledge; we recognize that economic history, like literature, is socially constructed, is itself located in history and has to be interpreted by reference to the dominant values and class interests of its period. It is not accidental that the targeting of the trade unions by the promoters and the crucial role played by organised labour in legitimating the Ship Canal movement have been "hidden from history". Such activity could not be embedded within an image of reality reflecting those dominant values and ideologies. In this process of construction the Ship Canal has been depoliticized and translated into a symbol not of cross-class cooperation and alliance but of individualism and civic endeavour.

## Notes

1. *The Manchester Monthly*, 20 December 1893, p. 1.
2. *Ship Canal Gazette*, 17 January 1883, p. 132.
3. W. H. Brindley (ed.), *The Soul of Manchester*, 1929, p. 220.
4. B. Rodgers in G. Gordon (ed.), *Regional Cities in the U.K 1890–1940*, 1986, p. 42.
5. For discussion of these issues at the national level, see B. Semmel, *Imperialism and Social Reform. 1895–1914*, 1960; and M. Langan and B. Schwarz (eds.), *Crises in the British State. 1880–1930*, 1985.
6. Beatrice Webb, *Diary March 1895*. Quoted in P. Fraser, *Joseph Chamberlain*, 1966, p. 153n.
7. The word "movement" is chosen deliberately, although most writers have described the scheme in terms of a commercial project. At the time, leading figures had no hesitation in describing the Scheme as a movement because a primary concern was to attract adherents, especially working men. A printed DIRECTOR'S NOTEBOOK for 1886, for instance, includes a six-page section entitled "Stages in the Development of the Manchester Ship Canal Movement", ref. Manchester Central Library, MSC 386.41 M29.
8. For details see G. R. Hawke and M. C. Reed, "Railway Capital in the United Kingdom in the Nineteenth Century", *Economic History Review*, XXII, No. 2, 1969. In contrast to the entirely commercial nature of the railway companies, the Ship Canal project was conceived as a movement, encompassing all classes in the community.
9. H. A. Turner, *Trade Union Growth, Structure and Policy. A Comparative Study of the Cotton Trade Unions*, 1962, pp. 40–41.
10. R. Penn, "Trade Union organization and skill in the cotton and engineering industries in Britain 1850–1960", *Social History*, Vol. 8, No. 1, 1983.
11. E. Wigham, *The Power to Manage: A History of the Engineering Employers' Association*, 1973, p. 18.
12. E. J. Hobsbawm, *Industry and Empire*, 1969, p. 178.
13. A. R. Hall (ed.), *The Export of Capital from Britain 1870–1914*, 1968, p. 1.
14. B. Lenman and K. Donaldson, "Partners' Income, Investment and Diversification in the Scottish Linen Area, 1850–1921", *Business History*, Vol. XIII, 1971.
15. Benwell Community Development Project, *The Making of a Ruling Class*, 1978.
16. A. Briggs, *Victorian Cities*, 1963.
17. D. Fraser, *Urban Politics in Victorian England*, 1976, p. 281. See also Fraser's other book, *Power and Authority in the Victorian City* (1979), which takes as its central focus the

impact of the municipal reforms of the 1830s, and has little to say about the 1880s onwards.

18. J. Garrard, *Leadership and Power in Victorian Industrial Towns 1830–80*, 1983.

19. H. J. Hanham, *Elections and Party Management. Politics in the Time of Disraeli and Gladstone*, 1959.

20. E. P. Hennock, *Fit and Proper Persons. Ideal and reality in nineteenth century urban government*, 1973, p. 54.

21. S. Pollard, *A History of Labour in Sheffield*, 1959; M. J. Daunton, *Coal Metropolis Cardiff 1870–1914*, 1977.

22. G. S. Jones, *Outcast London. A study of the relationship between classes*, 1971; P. Joyce, *Work, Society and Politics. The culture of the factory in late Victorian England*, 1980; D. Smith, *Conflict and Compromise: Class formation in English Society, 1830–1914*, 1982.

23. For an excellent account of an earlier period see V. A. C. Gattrell, "Incorporation and the Pursuit of Liberal Hegemony in Manchester 1790–1839", in D. Fraser (ed.), *Municipal Reform and the Industrial City*, 1982.

24. A. J. Kidd and K. W. Roberts, *City Class and Culture. Studies of cultural production and social policy in Victorian Manchester*, 1985. Terry Wyke's preliminary bibliography for Manchester (included in the book), with its listing of 1200 items, indicates the volume of material available.

25. D. Fraser, *op.cit.*, 1979, pp. 157–170.

26. J. Garrard, *op.cit.*, chapter 2.

27. See for instance S. D. Simon, *A Century of City Government*, 1938, p. 401. Alan Kidd, *op.cit.*, pp. 13–15 convincingly demonstrates for the period up to 1875 that the shopkeepers though present on the City Council, were not in a majority, and that big proprietors were a larger group.

28. P. Harnetty, *Imperialism and Free Trade: Lancashire and India in the mid nineteenth century*, 1972; A. Redford *et al.*, *Manchester Merchants and Foreign Trade*, Volume 1 (1934) and Volume 2 (1956).

29. A. Redford, *History of Local Government in Manchester*, Volume 2, pp. 353–376; S. D. Simon, *op.cit.*, pp. 384–391.

30. B. Leech, *History of the Manchester Ship Canal from its inception to its completion*, 1907, 2 volumes.

31. P. M. Hodson (ed.), *The Manchester Ship Canal: a guide to historical sources*, Lancashire Bibliography, 1985.

32. W. M. Reddy, *The Rise of Market Culture. The textile trade and French society 1750–1900*, 1984, p. 16.

33. D. Farnie, *The Manchester Ship Canal and the Rise of the Port of Manchester*, 1980; D. Farnie, "The Manchester Ship Canal 1894–1913", in W. H. Chaloner and B. M. Ratcliffe (eds.), *Trade and Transport Essays in economic history*, 1977.

34. D. Farnie, *op.cit.*, 1977, p. 191.

35. D. Owen, *The Manchester Ship Canal*, 1983, p. vii.

36. D. Cannadine (ed.), *Exploring the Urban Past. Essays in urban history by H. J. Dyos*, 1982, conclusion, p. 203.

37. N. B. Harte (ed.), *The Study of Economic History. Collected Inaugural Lectures 1893–1970*, 1971. The first appointment was made at the London School of Economics in 1904.

38. H. B. Charlton, *Portrait of a University. 1851–1951*, 1951, pp. 89–90.

39. N. B. Harte (ed.), *op.cit.*, p. xxvi.

40. C. Unwin in N. B. Harte, *ibid.*, p. 45.

41. R. H. Tawney, *Economic Journal*, XXXV, 1926, pp. 156–7.

Early cartoon, showing the Canal being pressed into use for advertising purposes. *MCL*

# 2

# THE DEVELOPMENT
# OF A MASS CAMPAIGN

From the vantage point of the late twentieth century, the Manchester Ship Canal can appear as little more than an historical curiosity, but a hundred years ago it was very different. Canal fever gripped the city and the surrounding towns and public enthusiasm for the project was expressed in popular form on an unprecedented scale. The scheme generated an enormous amount of contemporary literature in the form of pamphlets, articles, handbills and letters and yet paradoxically one of the most difficult and intriguing questions to answer is how the Canal ever came to be built at all. Put another way, why was a movement to build this massive project, which did not produce a dividend for its ordinary shareholders for its first twenty years, started in the 1880s and successfully completed in the 1890s when it had failed so completely to get taken up in the previous sixty years? What were the forces which impelled the movement forward, despite the lack of interest of many of the city's big mercantile bourgeoisie and the implacable opposition of the railway companies and the Liverpool shipping interests? The explanations given in previous accounts have been largely vague and unconvincing due to the failure to relate economic arguments to central political and social developments.[1]

The 1880s saw the beginnings of "mass democracy" (Stuart Hall's[2] description of the move towards universal adult suffrage) and the Liberal Party machine played a central role in promoting the Franchise Bill and subsequently in raising popular support for the third Reform Act when the Bill was opposed by the House of Lords in 1884. The splits that followed in 1885 over the Home Rule issue, which led to the breakaway of the Liberal Unionists, served both to spotlight the Party's inability to hold together the conflicting interests of its constituent parts, and to open the way for the emergence of the Labour Party as an independent working class party. In the 1870s and early 1880s however, the Liberal Party was seen by most trade unions and radicals as the best means for pursuing social and franchise reforms; and by important sections of the industrial bourgeoisie as a vehicle for incorporating the skilled artisans and for reconciling the interests of capital and labour.

The argument of this chapter is that the initial driving impetus for the Ship Canal movement came from precisely these diverging interests within the Liberal Party and that this helps to explain the form the campaign took and its essentially political trajectory. Formally the Party had no role in the campaign and no acknowledged links with the promoters, but the close identification of many (although not all) of the promoters with the Liberal Association in Manchester and other towns was not accidental. This hitherto unrecognised aspect helps to explain the mistrust with which the movement was viewed in some quarters, and throws light on some of divisions which developed in the Ship Canal movement during this period and over the contested 1883 bye-election between the Tory candidate Houldsworth and the disowned Liberal candidate Pankhurst.[3]

It will also help to explain why the prime feature of the campaign was the mobilization of mass support in a frenzy of activity and meetings that went far beyond that required for the normal floating of a private company. This phenomenon was entirely missing, for instance, during the creation in the earlier years of the century of an entire railway network where the attraction of high profits was sufficient to gain backers. In the case of the Ship Canal what was being sought first and foremost was a demonstration of popular and working class support for the scheme. That this might deter large scale capital from investing was a secondary issue because the wider aim of the project, as will be seen in Chapter 6, was to create a new form of popular participatory capitalism for rich and poor alike – which would mirror on the economic front the moves being made towards mass democracy and franchise reform.

### Creating a Propaganda Machine

Writing in December 1882, A. D. Provand, an opponent of the scheme, commented that: "A sort of mild terrorism prevails. I think much of the enthusiasm is unreal ... there prevails a tacit understanding that even should one be a doubter, he must say nothing against the Scheme, as that would be unpatriotic". His views were being expressed in a hard-hitting pamphlet[4] which complained of the methods used to gain support for the Canal; and together with other pamphlets, articles and letters of the period enable us to build up a remarkably accurate picture of the structure, financing and methods adopted by the campaign organisers.

The general idea of a Ship Canal had been talked about at least from the 1820s, but it did not receive serious attention in the second half of the century until George Hicks, a young

A futuristic drawing of 1795, envisaging "the future wonders of canal navigation". From J. Aikin, *The Country from thirty to forty Miles round Manchester.*

Scots insurance agent who had come to Manchester, wrote a letter to the *Manchester Guardian* on 11th October 1876 proposing improvements to the navigation of the River Irwell. Over the next three years Hicks and others, with the Chamber of Commerce's backing for the scheme, made attempts to elicit the active support and interest of Salford Council and of big capitalists in the city, but they were unsuccessful.

The breakthrough in opening up a public campaign on the issue came towards the end of 1881. A series of letters was then published in the local press following a speech by Sir William Harcourt that praised the activities of merchants in Glasgow in developing the city's commerce. The most

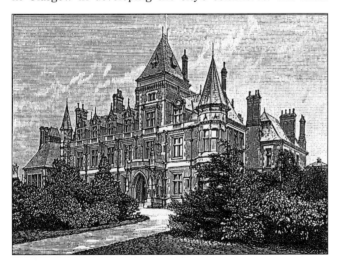

The Towers, home of Daniel Adamson, where the inaugural meeting of the Ship Canal campaign was held.
*Chetham's*

important contributor to this propaganda effort was James W. Harvey, writing under the pseudonym of "Mancuniensis", who was the head clerk in Hicks' office. The correspondence attracted the attention of Daniel Adamson, a successful businessman, engineer and inventor, to whom Hicks was introduced in November. Over the next twelve months the two men were in constant communication over the scheme, finally arranging an inaugural meeting for the Canal on 27th June 1882 at The Towers, Adamson's mansion in Didsbury. The Mayors of most of the surrounding towns and many of Lancashire's big industrial and commercial bourgeoisie were invited to this meeting.

Once a Provisional Committee had been formed, an early decision was made to employ a full-time organizer. Their choice was Joseph Lawrence who had been responsible for the successful promotion of the Hull and Barnsley Railway and Dock scheme a few years earlier. Hicks' letter to Adamson in August immediately after Lawrence's appointment shows that from the start the general method of moulding public opinion had been settled:

He will at once proceed to organize local Committees in every ward in Manchester and throughout the towns of Lancashire with a view to raising subscriptions and enlisting the sympathies of the people with the project. It will be an expensive process but I see no other way of rousing a great popular feeling to back us in Parliament and also to get the necessary £100,000 raised. [5]

Two points are worth noting here. Firstly there was the clear intention to develop a mass campaign; and secondly there was a tacit recognition that no groundswell of support for financing the project existed within the city's mercantile and capitalist class. By November this lack of support had become sufficiently well-known for the opening issue of the *Ship Canal Gazette*, a weekly one penny newspaper produced by the promoters and edited by Joshua Bury and Harvey,[6] to compare the slow build up of the fund with the Anti-Corn Law movement:

in 1844 a few Manchester merchants subscribed £60,000 to the Corn Law League Fund in less than two hours… Many of these illustrious names are still identified with the trade of the city, and are among the best known of the great firms of today. [7]

The reference to the League is interesting because significantly, as will be explored in a later chapter, much of the organisation and strategy of the Ship Canal promoters drew heavily on the experience of the League campaign 40 years earlier. The build-up of activity in the first year can be seen in the pages of the *Ship Canal Gazette*.

The first of the ward meetings took place in the Oxford Ward on 4th October and was addressed by the engineer Leader Williams and Bosdin Leech, a member of the Provisional Committee and a Liberal councillor in the city who was to play a central role in the movement.[8] Two days later a letter appeared in several of the local newspapers from Henry Heap, an active member of the Manchester Liberal Association's Council.[9] In the letter Heap referred to the Oxford Ward meeting and sought the names of gentlemen willing to help with furthering the campaign.

> We could all help by organizing effective ward and District organizations ... forming branch Committees to secure the passing of Resolutions, petitions etc.[10]

A week later the 17th October St. James Ward meeting was advertised in the papers, to be convened and chaired by Heap, and this was followed shortly by the St. Lukes Ward meeting where J. C. Fielden, another Liberal, was elected chairman.[11] By early November meetings had been held and committees formed covering all of the Manchester and Salford wards. On 3rd November the first conference was held between the central Provisional Committee and members of the Ward Committees from Manchester, Salford and the surrounding towns; and on 13th November a mass meeting of "the working classes of Manchester, Salford and the neighbourhood" was held at the Free Trade Hall. It was chaired by J. H. Slatter, General Secretary of the Typographical Association, who was supported on the platform by the general secretaries of six other major trade unions – Robert Austin (Engineers), Thomas Ashton and James Mawdsley (Spinners), George Kelley (Printers), James Murchie (Carpenters) and Peter Shorrocks (Tailors).[12]

In a similar way large public meetings were held in all the major towns around Manchester, and a mass of publicity in the shape of handbills, letters to the press, and pamphlets supporting the Ship Canal, flooded the area. Most of it was written by a handful of men who were supporters or paid employees of the Provisional Committee, and often it appeared under a pseudonym to give the impression of being an independent and unbiased publication. Joseph Lawrence for instance, the campaign organiser, wrote in 1882 the influential pamphlet, *The Manchester Ship Canal. Why It Is Wanted! and Why It Will Pay!* under the pen-name "Cottonopolis" and in early 1883 was the author of a lengthy tract in reply to Provand's adverse criticisms where he signed himself "A Supporter of the Canal". Like their Free Trade predecessors, whose propaganda work is graphically described in Norman McCord's "The Anti-Corn Law League 1838–1846", the promoters had been quick to realise the need for a central well-staffed propaganda machine to create an initial momentum for the scheme.

The rapid development and broadening of the campaign in the first six months was possible only because this had been established and because close personal links between the key activists already existed, in many cases established via common membership of the Manchester Liberal Association. The strength of the Ship Canal idea amongst Liberals was its multiple appeal; for the radicals it offered the chance of reform, of sweeping away the principles of non-

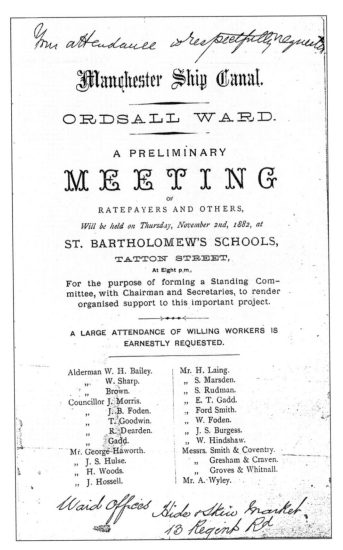

A handbill for one of the first ward meetings held in Salford at the start of the campaign.

interventionist *laissez-faire*, whilst for the trade union leadership it could bring new jobs for the unemployed, new industries and new ways of mobilizing the workers. To important sections of the industrial bourgeoisie who, despite challenge, still remained the dominant force in Manchester Liberalism, it offered the prospect of a cause that would help to promote Free Trade and stability, that was "above politics" and that could unite all classes in a common endeavour behind their leadership.

For this group the Ship Canal constituted at the local – and regional – level the single issue platform, which Gladstone as leader was constantly seeking nationally in order to unite the Party and the country with a common majority feeling behind a Liberal Government.[13] The Ship Canal idea was not presented as a Liberal platform but, on the contrary, as one requiring the support of "patriots" as non-political and as a uniting issue which deserved the support of both the great political parties. For Gladstone,

"Party is a legitimate and necessary, but essentially a secondary and subordinate instrument for promoting the public good", [14] and his supporters were prepared to accept this in the belief that in being seen to work for the public good above politics, the Party would gain.

We will return to explore this important feature of Liberal involvement later in the section [15] whilst noting here the often bizarre alliances thrown up across party and class divides. The Ship Canal movement was a coalition of interests that rode together uneasily and with hesitation. By the end of 1882 a more complete profile of the principal supporters and activists in the campaign was becoming clearer. Table 1 below gives information on the occupational position of 27 out of the 30 members of the Provisional Committee. [16] The largest single category of members is manufacturers with equal numbers of cotton and engineering companies represented. Merchants are included in the first general category with manufacturers, but the five involved, J. A. Beith, J. Boyd, C. P. Henderson, B. Leech and Marshall Stevens [17] are representative of the middle range to small scale companies supporting the Canal. The really big merchant houses, which were the base for some of Manchester's richest citizens were not generally supporters, as has already been indicated. The *Manchester City News*, committed to the scheme from the outset, was quick to hammer the point home: "The rich men of South and East Lancashire, with a few notable exceptions, have not rivalled the enthusiasm of the general public". [18]

**Table 1  Occupation of Provisional Committee Members**

| Classification | Sub-Total | Grand Total |
| --- | --- | --- |
| Large Manufacturers/Merchants | | |
| * Cotton | 5 | |
| * Engineering | 4 | |
| * Other Manufacturers | 5 | |
| * Merchants | 5 | 19 |
| Professionals | | |
| * Financial Services | 2 | |
| * Estate/Land Agents | 2 | |
| * Named Merchants | 2 | |
| * Others | 1 | 7 |
| Clerical/Unskilled Workers | 1 | 1 |
| Total Unknown Occupations | 3 | 3 |
| TOTALS | | 30 |

The technique adopted for drumming up support in the early stages involved holding almost nightly meetings in the principal areas and towns round Manchester, with speakers, drawn from a panel, attending sometimes as many as four or five meetings in a week. The names of these speakers (which are listed in the *Ship Canal Gazette* and in a subsequent article [19] on the campaign) give further evidence of where the active supporters were being drawn. Table 2 provides a breakdown, but excludes those speakers who were already on the Provisional Committee. The pattern shows a significant widening of support, with professionals, especially lawyers, becoming involved. An article [20] written by F. E. Cornwall, one of the campaign organizers recruited by Joseph Lawrence, suggests that some of the speakers, and especially three of the barristers, were brought in as friends of Lawrence and had little or no personal interest in the Ship Canal.

**Table 2  Occupation of Ship Canal Speakers**

| Classification | Sub-Total | Grand Total |
| --- | --- | --- |
| Large Manufacturers/Merchants | | |
| * Cotton | 3 | |
| * Brewers | 1 | |
| * Building Trades | 4 | |
| * Merchants | 3 | 11 |
| Professionals | | |
| * Middle Managers | 3 | |
| * Lawyers | 6 | |
| * Others | 2 | 11 |
| Trade Union Officials | 2 | 2 |
| Total Unknown Occupations | 1 | 1 |
| TOTALS | | 25 |

The friendship link may well be there, but the active support they gave indicates above all a canny ability on the organisers' part to seek out and select men with the orator's skills to move mass audiences. [21] A facility with words alone would never, however, have attracted and won over mass working class support for the scheme. Essential for this were men with a working class background and with organizational links with the trade union movement. Two of the speakers who fulfilled these conditions were trade union officials, W. Chappell, Secretary of the South Yorkshire Miners' Association, and Henry Slatter of the Typographical Association. A third was John Fielden, a cotton manufacturer who had "risen from the ranks" and had close links with the trade unions. Of the three Slatter's role was to be the most significant in the movement but all three demonstrate the drawing into the campaign of authentic voices representing working class and trade union support for a novel response to industrial decline.

With this range of speakers available, the organizers attempted where possible to select a name to match and attract the anticipated audience. The weakest area was amongst working class speakers, and suitable men like Slatter were continually pressed to do more. As Alfred Goodier, the campaign's chief outdoor organizer put it in a letter on Slatter's death:

Early drawing (published in 1883) of what the docks would look like.   *Chetham's*

Ever ready to influence the masses, his connection with the labour class was most valuable in enlisting their enthusiasm and support. It was to this class that we had to look to to start the boom ... It was never the wrong time to ask Mr. Slatter to put his shoulder to the wheel ... he was ever ready to appear on the platform of any public meeting .... He also attended many workmen's meetings in dinner-hour and addressed them.[22]

Beatrice Webb was clear of the ways in which campaigns had to be organised to be successful. "There is no such thing as spontaneous public opinion; it all has to be manufactured from a centre of conviction and energy radiating through persons";[23] and the sense of theatre, style, and presentation was evident from the start of the promoters' assault on the Lancashire public. For the initial series of meetings to establish committees in the out-of-town districts a carefully prepared set-piece would be enacted to maximise the sense of spontaneous support. As a "ward enthusiast" described it:

A local gentleman in the chair would frequently begin by saying that he really knew nothing about the Canal scheme, but he understood there were two gentlemen from Manchester present who would tell them all about it. It may be remarked at this point that those local chairmen, who previously knew nothing, were so well informed by the gentlemen from Manchester when the speaking was over, that they usually headed a subscription list on the spot.[24]

The success of this strategy can be judged from two confidential reports prepared in January by Lawrence for the Provisional Committee members and entitled, "Work Going on in Outlying Towns – Being a Record of Past Work and an Agenda of Future Work".[25] Borrowing directly from the organisational pattern developed by the Anti-Corn Law League, the campaign staff established Committees in eighteen different centres in Lancashire and Cheshire and in two other places – Halifax and Birmingham. In almost all

III. "That in the opinion of this Meeting it is the duty of all Municipal Corporations of towns which will be beneficially affected to render all the assistance that lies in their power towards carrying out the undertaking."

Copy of a resolution slip, circulated to sympathisers to ensure support at public meetings. *MCL*

cases a local secretary was appointed at £2 per week, offices acquired, and meetings organized with leading figures. At Stockport and Warrington vigorous canvassing took place, while at Blackburn about 700 people, nearly all working men attended a Town's meeting and passed unanimous resolutions in support.

Resolutions indeed came flooding in and often followed the exact wording of one of the three model resolutions which the Committee had printed for distribution.[26] At Ashton-under-Lyne, for instance, on 21st December all three were passed word for word, with J. C. Fielden and Bosdin Leech, "the gentleman from Manchester" typically seconding two of them. Indeed Leech's enthusiasm for the "planted" motion seems quite unashamed, for on another occasion after addressing a meeting of workmen at Sir Joseph Whitworth Limited at Openshaw he was quite happy to second a motion beginning: "We the employees of Sir Joseph Whitworth, heartily approve of the scheme for constructing a ship canal …"![27]

Meetings organized at workplaces with the support of sympathetic employers provided an easy way of reaching large captive audiences, but the public meetings in the wards and town meetings elsewhere were also attracting audiences of several hundred. The *Ship Canal Gazette* had been launched to build on this popular support and to embellish the campaigners' arguments, and by the end of the year was being sold at 86 newsagents in 59 towns and centres throughout Lancashire.[28] Circulation figures are unknown, and there were allegations that copies were often not sold or were given away, but the spread of distribution points suggests thorough and systematic organization. Its style was trenchant and knock-about, subjecting opponents like the Liverpool interests and the railway companies to regular attack. Lists of railway company directors were published on several occasions, with the suggestion that all opposition to the Canal scheme was merely a protection of vested railway interest; and the reports of meetings provide evidence of how the organizers dealt with anyone awkward enough to ask probing questions. A speaker at Longsight, for instance, who moved an amendment that the scheme should not be supported unless detailed estimates were produced, was "cleverly annihilated"[29] by the chairman, J. C. Fielden, and other objectors were threatened if they continued with publication of their names and addresses and "some account of their past history and present tactics".[30]

A great many of the leaflets and ephemera of the campaign have not survived but one short handbill entitled, *The Manchester Ship Canal. Reasons why it Should be Made*,[31] provides a flavour of the grounds on which the mass appeal was being made. Excessive dock and railway rates, the argument goes, are being:

> continually levied by these monopolies … with the object of protecting the interests of Railway kings, (with the result that) trade is handicapped, and wages kept low … The removal of these taxes would … effect the interest of the artisan and working classes more formidably than any other class of the community.

By 22nd December when the Ship Canal Bill was lodged, the campaign was well under way, but the first reverse in the Parliamentary struggle – which was, to continue for the next two and a half years – was not far away. In response to an objection from the Mersey Docks Board, the Bill was thrown out in January 1883 as in breach of Standing Orders. The grounds were that no plans of the Mersey Low Water Channel had been submitted. Once again the machine was whipped into action, this time to organize petitions to dispense with Standing Orders. Nearly 200,000 people signed the Manchester one, and a further 286 petitions were presented by Town Councils, Chambers of Commerce, Local Boards, Public Trusts and Trade Unions from all over the country – an amazing feat in just six weeks.[32]

The impact was considerable and when the Bill was represented the Standing Orders were dispensed with and the Bill allowed to proceed.[33] By 9th June, when the promoters' case had been heard before the House of Commons, 21 days of evidence had been submitted involving 67 witnesses – engineers, shipowners, manufacturers, representatives of a range of trades, three Members of Parliament and eight Corporation representatives from Manchester and elsewhere.[34] The evidence of the opposition – a coalition of shipping, railway and Liverpool Dock Board interests – was almost equally lengthy and stressed the potential damage to Liverpool, and the ability of the railway companies to cut their rates if the Ship Canal were ever to be built. The verdict of the House of Commons Committee was favourable, but the promoters' elation was shortlived for a month later the House of Lords rejected the Bill after only a few days sitting.

For the promoters the decision was a cruel blow, particularly as it had been made with no obviously clear reasons. Adamson, a key witness, had concluded his evidence before both Committees by saying that in Lancashire there had been nothing approaching the enthusiasm of the Ship Canal since the Anti-Corn Law agitation. He was so depressed at the outcome that he decided upon an

Drawing of Adamson in 1883. Of the hundreds of depictions of him, none were other than highly respectful – unlike the one overleaf of de Lesseps. *MCL*

immediate return to Manchester to consider the best course of action.[35] Surviving correspondence shows that on 11th August he fired off a series of letters to influential backers, asking their advice. The reply of Sir Joseph Heron,[36] Town Clerk of Manchester, is interesting because of the light it throws on the close personal support that Heron, in a key position in the Town Hall, was giving to the project and to Adamson. He points out that the subject of the Ship Canal is on the agenda of the forthcoming Parliamentary Sub-Committee of the Corporation which he hopes to attend, and ends with the careful comment, "Of course I consider that your letter is to *me* and *private* as is also my reply".[37]

Another reply came from James W. Southern, a prominent member of the Manchester Liberal Association and chairman of its General Purposes Committee. Though he had supported the original guarantee fund "too much from sympathy with my friend (Bosdin) Leech's enthusiasm, than by the calm verdict of my own judgment" and was most indignant at the Bill's rejection, Southern was not willing "to pledge myself as to my future course".[38] Though he was subsequently to become Deputy Chairman of the Ship Canal Company, the setback in the Lords had caused Southern and many others to have severe doubts about the wisdom of continuing.

Adamson and the Provisional Committee were not to be deterred however, and the autumn saw a renewed campaign to enlist support for a fresh application to Parliament. Mass meetings at the Free Trade Hall and in adjoining towns were again called, including one held on 19th November where Ferdinand de Lesseps, who had masterminded the financing and construction of the Suez Canal, was invited to speak in support. A programme of nightly meetings was also started in January 1884.[39] In the Committee stage before the House of Lords, doubts about the ability of the promoters to raise the necessary capital were allayed by Bosdin Leech's securing of the offers of £130,000 in five days[40]. The eventual approval of the Committee was met with enthusiasm, and a mass demonstration at Pomona Gardens on 24th June 1884 was organized by the Manchester and Salford Trades Council for some 50,000 people. Again, however, the promoters were to be disappointed for the Liverpool opposition had not died down and this time succeeded in persuading the Commons Committee to throw out the Bill on 1st August 1884.

## Liberal Influence in the Early Movement

The assertion of Liberal Party centrality to the Ship Canal movement during the first three years of the Parliamentary campaign is no mere statement about the overwhelming influence of Liberalism in Manchester. While the Party remained in a majority on the Council and on average received about 60% of the votes at Parliamentary elections between 1832 and 1859, the elections of 1868 and 1874 produced for the first time a majority of Tory voters in the city, and the defeat of Jacob Bright.[41] A. G. Symonds describes the decision made on the night of the result "to win back Manchester for the Liberal cause", and the systematic organization that went into regaining Bright's seat in 1876.[42] The result was certainly an improved and reorganized party machine by 1882, and a regaining of some ground for the Liberals, but it was by no means secure and depended upon an uneasy mix of politics and constituencies.

The bursting of the Ship Canal issue onto the political stage at this point was of enormous significance and, as outlined, was eagerly taken up by many Liberals. Ship Canal supporters vociferously trumpeted the all-party non-political nature of the movement, and historians have taken this for granted without looking further at the evidence. There certainly were Conservative supporters of the scheme and Liberal opponents, but a general pattern of Liberal support and Conservative suspicion can be discerned. An examination of the two principal groupings of Canal supporters provides the best starting point for assessing the significance of this. The two groups are the members of the Provisional Committee and of the Speakers' Panel. Information about political affiliation cannot be found for all the names, which may indicate at least three different things – that the individual was not a political activist, that he was an activist without the high public profile attaching to

Cartoon of Ferdinand de Lesseps, creator of the Suez Canal. *CFS*

councillors, MPs and party and trade union officials, or that he was simply representing a commercial, trade union or municipal interest.

Table 3 gives the political breakdown for the two groups. The figures may give a slight bias to the Liberals in one respect, because it has been possible to identify political membership in some cases through the minutes and lists of the Manchester Liberal Association and Liberal Union whilst comparable material is not available for the Manchester Conservative Association. However the bias is unlikely to be very significant since long lists of Tory supporters at the 1883 bye-election were printed in the newspapers.

**Table 3   Political Allegiance of Main Ship Canal Activists**

| Political Affiliation | Provisional Committee | Speakers' List |
| --- | --- | --- |
| Liberals | 15 | 11 |
| Conservatives | 6 | 4 |
| Unknown | 10 | 10 |
| Totals | 31 | 25 |

When it is remembered that the unknown figure includes men whose interest in the Ship Canal Scheme derived solely from the commercial advantage it would bring them, and who were not political activists, the list of 26 names of prominent or activist Liberals associated with the early campaign is highly significant. Especially notable is the inclusion of such key figures as Adamson and Richard Peacock,[43] the Chairman and Deputy Chairman respectively of the Provisional Committee, J. W. Southern, Chairman of the Manchester Liberal Association General Purposes Committee and J. A. Beith, Chairman of its Executive Committee, John Harwood and Bosdin Leech, who were to be the two main figures steering the Scheme through Manchester Corporation's Committee and council meetings, and Henry Slatter and John Fielden, the speakers who addressed more meetings than any others and played a central role in delivering trade union and working class support for the project.

In addition to holding these key positions in the campaign Liberals were also the dominating influence on the Manchester Ward Committees set up to arouse public support. Of the twelve chairmen (five of whom were also on the Provisional Committee or the Speakers' Panel) six were Liberal councillors, three were members of the Manchester Liberal Association Executive or Council, and only two were Conservative councillors (Henry Boddington and Hinchcliffe).[44] Compared with this Liberal phalanx, Conservative support was decidedly thin. Of the total ten known Tories on the Provisional Committee and Speakers' Panel, two were brewers (Boddington and James G. Groves[45]), two were lawyers (Tom Nash and N. C. Schou) and a fifth, James Croston, was a manager. The other two towns through which the Ship Canal would pass – Salford and Warrington – were Tory-controlled and added a further five representatives, all of whom were on the Provisional Committee. But apart from Richard Husband, Mayor of Salford from 1881 to 1883, their role in the movement was peripheral. They provided a semblance of all-party support, but in no way were the prime movers.

In these circumstances a dilemma confronted those Liberals in the movement, who were also key figures in the Party apparatus. If the Ship Canal was seen as a party issue, the Parliamentary campaign and indeed the whole project could be jeopardised fundamentally. The logic of this line of thinking was to argue the case on purely economic and commercial grounds. A parallel here can be drawn with the Anti-Corn Law League in the 1830s which, Fraser has suggested, may have actually had the effect of delaying the Corn Law repeal by making the question an overtly social and political issue.[46] On the other hand, the Ship Canal platform provided an ideal vehicle for regenerating the fortunes of the Party and creating a mass base amongst the trades unions and respectable working class. Depoliticizing the issue would be to waste a golden opportunity. In effect this dilemma was expressed in what can be described loosely as the two wings of the Liberal thrust – "the commercial industrial lobby" and "the radical trade union lobby". Moreover the position was further complicated by the case of Adamson himself, an individualist with little time for caucuses and party discipline, who came to wield enormous

George Hicks, a Scotsman whose early interest initiated the whole scheme. The history books hardly mention him.

influence as the movement mushroomed under his populist leadership. The tension between these different elements was always to be near the surface and ensured that the movement was always to have an essentially fragile base.

The evidence George Hicks gave of his initial soundings of people willing to attend the inaugural meeting shows a large majority of Liberals being invited and indicates at this early stage the danger of the issue becoming politicised.[47] The list may be partly a reflection of the close association between large-scale manufacturers and the Liberal Party, but is more likely to be a comment on Adamson's and Hicks' own contacts and political views. A letter[48] from Hicks to C. P. Scott, editor of the *Manchester Guardian*, shows that he was a Liberal supporter (although not an activist) and Adamson's Liberal attachments were well known. They were, however, both willing agents in introducing an important counter weight to this Liberal influence by appointing in August 1882 as campaign organizer, Joseph Lawrence who was to become Conservative MP for the Monmouth Boroughs from 1901 to 1906. According to his assistant F. E. Cornwall, several of the members of the Conservative Club where he was entertained to dinner on his arrival "regarded him as an indispensable man to the Scheme".[49]

Lawrence certainly had the experience through his involvement in the Hull Scheme, but it is likely that his political views were also an important factor. If this is so, then it may go some way to explaining the contradictory statement made about the origins of the ward and district committees formed in November 1882. While Cornwall insists that these were part of a grand scheme designed from the start by Lawrence to map out the whole areas into local centres for the rousing of interest and for the collection of subscriptions[50] "A Ward Enthusiast", in his article of the previous week,[51] is quite emphatic that the ward committees were formed following a meeting in early October of three Ship Canal enthusiasts whose objective was "to consider how to get at the masses, and establish an organisation *quite outside the work of the Central Provisional Committee*" (my emphasis). One of the three whose letter inviting help for the Scheme was published on 6th October was Henry Heap, an active Manchester Liberal, and it seems not improbable on the basis of these statements that his action was intended quite deliberately to maintain the propaganda and ward work as a significantly Liberal initiative. If so, it was remarkably effective, for as we have seen, nine out of the twelve chairmen were Liberals.

The political leanings of the campaign were evident on other fronts too, particularly as a number of the targets for attack in the *Ship Canal Gazette* and elsewhere were closely identified with the Conservative Party. One such example was the London and North Western Railway Company which was not only the largest and most powerful of the railway companies with assets of nearly £100 million, but along with Sir Richard Moon, its Chairman from 1861 to 1891, was well known to be associated with the Conservatives.[52] Another powerful figure to be alienated in this way was John William Maclure who was Chairman of the Manchester Conservative Association from 1868 to the early 1880s[53] and became MP for the Stretford Division of Lancashire in 1886. The dismissal of critics of the Canal Scheme as simply stooges for the vested interests of the railway companies was good radical copy, but would have incensed Maclure as he was a director of the Manchester, Sheffield and Lincolnshire Railway, and of the Bridgewater Navigation Company – a company which was condemned for allowing the channel to become silted up and virtually unusable as a consequence.[54] Lawrence was particularly aware of the dangers of this line of attack, and attempted to mitigate its damage. He wrote to the *Ship Canal Gazette*:

I have from the first, discountenanced the policy of unnecessarily attacking railway companies in connection with the Ship Canal movement, or of inflaming the public mind with sensational twaddle about the enormities and sins of railway interest,

and argued the case for the Canal as

a valuable auxiliary for the conveyance of cheap *unpaying* traffic, leaving the present lines … free for the accommo-

dation of the most valuable and best paying class of traffic – viz. passengers.[55]

Despite Lawrence's efforts the Conservatives' response in Manchester to the campaign generally was suspicious and non-committal. At a public meeting at the Moss Lane Conservative Club on 5th December 1882, with J. W. Maclure presiding, W. W. B. Hulton, in seconding a motion critical of the Government, referred to the Ship Canal Scheme and noted the way in which the two Liberal MPs, Robert Leake and William Agnew, "took great credit to themselves for the action they had taken in connection with the Scheme and, without damning the idea completely, noted that it had been around for forty years, and that the expenditure of £900,000 on new docks at Bristol had not stopped the city being supplanted as a port by Portishead and Avonmouth.[56] This attitude was scarcely surprising since the November Mass Meeting at the Free Trade Hall – considered by Adamson to be the turning point in public favour in support – had the trappings of a Liberal rally with long key note speeches by John Slagg and Jacob Bright, the city's two Liberal MPs.[57]

While the level of popular support for the Canal required the adoption of a careful stance and electoral calculation by the Manchester Tories a less circumspect response could be anticipated from the Party in Liverpool, where a mercantile community without an industrial working class had always ensured that the Conservatives maintained political control. Sir William Forwood, a member of an influential shipping and mercantile family, was a typical upholder of this tradition, and over the 58 years of his membership of the City Council was Mayor twice, President of the Chamber of Commerce for six years and a leading member of the Mersey Docks and Harbour Board. From this base he was to continue a sustained and powerful attack on the Ship Canal Scheme throughout the Parliamentary campaign. One of his first onslaughts came at the December meeting of the Liverpool Dock Board where he came quickly to the point in his reported speech:

If that Canal were judged solely by its merits it would quickly be relegated to the museum of exploded bubbles … but it appeared that an endeavour was being made to clothe the question with sentiment, and to make it a municipal and even a political question.[58]

It was clear in Liverpool to whom the campaign was being directed and the point would not have been missed by the speaker's elder brother, Arthur B. Forwood, who was Tory MP for the Ormskirk Division of Lancashire. Writing just two months later on the theme of "Democratic Toryism", he showed a clear grasp of the balancing act the Party needed to perform to maintain its influence in the new mass democracy environment:

My experience of the feelings of the working classes is that they are far from sympathising with the Radical

Shibboleth for abolishing class distinctions ... Whilst we in the abstract evince a sympathy with the labouring classes, we must not let our sentiments stop at this point, but let them take a concrete form. No selfish class legislation must mark our policy; we must pay as much regard to measures "conceived in the interests of the working classes" as we do to the wants of any other body of the community.[59]

For Conservatives in the North West "Democratic Toryism" had, in Patrick Joyce's words "More to do with the Toryism of the Democracy, than any democracy in Toryism".[60] Representation of the people meant exactly that; or, as Forwood expressed it: "they (the working classes) are alive to the necessity of Government being conducted by the better-educated people and those who have leisure to devote to the work".

It was a view no doubt supported by the manufacturing and commercial bourgeoisie who financed Manchester's Liberal Association; and whose perceptions were sharpened by the impact of Henry George's pamphlet "Progress and Poverty", and other socialist propaganda[61] which had started to spread since the founding in 1881 of the Democratic Federation.[62] There were, however, other elements in the city's Liberal Party which sought to achieve more radical change, and of these the Manchester Tory leaders like J. W. Maclure and William Henry Houldsworth were deeply suspicious.

Early signs of the emergence of this radical/trade union complex within the Manchester Liberal Association came in March 1879 when the Executive Committee, meeting to consider the report of the Hours of Polling Committee, passed a resolution on Joseph Chamberlain's Bill moved by Henry Slatter and seconded by J. C. Fielden. This gave support to the proposal that polling stations should not be closed until eight o'clock in the evening in order to accommodate the needs of working men. It was in flat contradiction to the evidence given by Sir Joseph Heron, the Town Clerk, to a Committee of the House of Commons where, speaking for the Corporation, he stated that there was no wish in Manchester to extend the polling hours and that "working men could vote now if they liked in the time occupied in smoking their pipes"![63]

While the resolution commanded general support, evidence of a significant split on the Executive came in 1882 when a list of 26 names was proposed for the 30 vacancies on the Executive. Two were successfully challenged, including Dr. Richard Pankhurst, a radical lawyer in the city with strong republican and Irish Nationalist sympathies. Nominations were, however, immediately requested for the six remaining vacancies, and Pankhurst was reinstated on a vote being taken, heading the list with 43 votes.[64] This indication of substantial division within the Association was a portent for a bizarre set of events which was to occur in the early autumn of 1883 following the death of Hugh Birley, the minority MP for Manchester.

Cartoon of Houldsworth in 1878, just before he became President of the Manchester Conservative Association.

*MCL*

### The Pankhurst Election: Wooing the Reluctant Tories

The Conservatives were less than enthusiastic about the Ship Canal Scheme, and none more so than W. H. Houldsworth, a wealthy cotton spinner who had been President of the Association since 1880. Their attitude of suspicion to the campaign and its strongly Liberal undertones was undoubtedly an important factor in dissuading many of the region's big capitalists from subscribing. The Liberal leadership was aware of this, and of the need to embrace Houldsworth if the claim of an all-party Ship Canal movement was to carry much weight. The death of Birley in early September provided the golden opportunity. If Houldsworth could be helped to win the seat, the price they might reasonably exact was a public commitment to the Ship Canal at a time when the movement was still reeling from the defeat of the Bill in the House of Lords Committee the previous month. This was not the first time that Liberals had tried to incorporate Houldsworth into their schemes, as indicated by a letter in 1882 from Thomas Ashton,[65] President of the Association, to C. P. Scott, who was also on the Executive Committee. Ashton, with Scott's support, was trying to establish a school for girls in the city, and writes:

31

I am afraid there is little chance of Houldsworth joining us. He gives very unwillingly of late to any educational work. I will see him when I can but I am sure no good would come of writing to him. I wish the Dean would join. Would Canon Tonge help us? As Birley's brother-in-law he would remove something of the radical complexion of the school.[66]

Delivery of the seat to the Tories was no easy task, but a recitation of the events of a four week period in September and October shows that this is precisely what happened. Birley died on a Sunday, and the announcement was made in the paper on the following day, 10th September. On the Tuesday, the *Manchester Guardian* reported that Houldsworth would be the Conservative candidate, but that the question of whether the seat would be contested by the Liberals would not be known until a meeting of the Liberal 900 had been held. On the Friday it was reported that Richard Pankhurst – who had severed his connection with the Liberal Party two months previously – would be standing as an independent Liberal, and on the Saturday some 70 members of the Liberal Association's Executive Committee expressed an opinion that they would not be putting up a candidate – a view that received the support of the full Council meeting of 600 members the following Monday, 17th September, when it was resolved that "It is undesirable under the present

Richard Pankhurst, the radical Liberal who stood against Houldsworth in the 1883 election. *Chetham's*

circumstances that any action should be taken by the Liberal Association to contest the vacant seat". Over the next two weeks there was a flurry of election meetings for the two candidates and after nominations closed on 1st October, a series of attempts were made by Pankhurst's supporters to gain the support of the Association's Council, but to no avail. When the result was finally announced Houldsworth, who had stood unsuccessfully in 1880, had received 18,185 votes, and Pankhurst only 6,216. This compared with 24,959 votes which the Liberal Slagg had received in 1880.

The coverage of the election campaign was considerable with the *Manchester Guardian* and *Manchester Courier* having, on most days, two to four columns devoted to meetings, letters and editorials; yet to the casual reader the attitude of the Liberal Association would have appeared an inexplicable mystery. Sir Wilfred Lawson, Liberal MP for Cockermouth, must have summed up the views of many when he told the East Cumberland Liberals that:

> it was the most extraordinary election that had taken place in his lifetime. They had an out-and-out Tory in the field against a Radical, and the Tory was supported by the Liberal Association and the Liberal press. He could not help thinking that if Mr. Gladstone saw a large majority for the old long-horned Tory, he would mutter under his breath 'save me from my friends'.[67]

Hanham interprets the episode in terms of the effectiveness of the consultation mechanisms and the tight control exercised by the Liberal leadership, and this is correct; but the reasons for not contesting the seat were not primarily those he suggests – lack of money and divisions over the Home Rule issue.[68]

There is a welter of correspondence, conflicting comment and articles on the issue, but the general drift of decisions is clear. Pankhurst's platform was based on a nine point radical programme that included abolition of the House of Lords, universal suffrage, free compulsory education, payment of MPs, disestablishment, abolition of the oath, nationalization of the land, and local self-government for Ireland.[69] He received enthusiastic support at packed meetings, had support from Michael Davitt, the Irish nationalist leader, and refused on principle to conduct his campaign by appointing paid canvassers, hiring expensive rooms, or taking voters to the poll in cabs. His candidature, according to Abel Heywood (Junior), his Campaign Committee Chairman, belonged "to the working class most particularly", and his nomination papers show him as receiving the support of a mixture of radicals and trade union leaders including Robert Austin (Engineers) and James Murchie (Carpenters), both Ship Canal supporters. The Conservative *Courier*'s assessment of him is probably a fairly accurate account of the views of both Tories and many of the Liberal leaders in Manchester:

> Dr. Pankhurst's address simply proves him to be the exponent of that ultra-Radicalism towards which the

Tory anti-Pankhurst election poster. Note the portrayal of the upstanding Liberal party gentleman advising against Pankhurst seeking election. Overleaf: a crude anti-Pankhurst poem. *MCL*

Liberal Party is tending, but of which the nondescript partisans who call themselves 'moderate' are so woefully ashamed.[70]

The Association's reasons for not fielding a candidate were confused and conflicting accounts were given. The *Manchester Guardian* had a very full reportage and several leading articles strongly opposing support for Pankhurst. Since Scott, its editor, was a leading member of the Liberal Executive, the *Guardian*'s comments on the first full Executive Meeting held on 17th September can be taken as the leadership's "official" reasons for not wishing to contest. These were the probable duration of the present Parliament, a feeling of respect for Birley, the difficulty of finding a candidate when the minority clause would be operating at a General Election, and the lack of questions of specific importance before the country at the time.[71] The evidence supporting three of these grounds looks somewhat thin. On the question of a candidate the *Yorkshire Post* of 11th September[72] did suggest that the Association was considering fighting the election with its own candidate and that several names were being mentioned, including those of Thomas Ashton and Sir U. Kay-Shuttleworth. However, it stated, the contest was only being considered because of Pankhurst's candidature as he might pose a threat to the Liberal candidates at a General Election if allowed to oppose Houldsworth single-handed. In other circumstances they would have been inclined to allow Houldsworth to succeed without a contest.

In any event by the 15th, at the General Purposes Committee, the line to be taken had become clear, with a majority of thirteen unfavourable to the Association contesting, three in favour, and three hesitating.[73] This majority view was formally adopted at the Executive Meeting, which followed immediately, in a resolution proposed by Councillor Gibson and seconded by Henry Heap. The speed with which this decision was made must raise doubts about the truth of Scott's argument in the *Manchester Guardian* about the non-availability of a candidate. Only five working days had elapsed between the announcement of Birley's death and the Executive's decision, even though nominations did not have to be in for another two weeks. A further sidelight on this issue is shed by a letter written to Daniel Adamson by a Liberal, James Whiting on 10th September, the day after Birley's death. In it Whiting proposed that Adamson himself should stand as the Liberal candidate, rather than the "republican" Pankhurst, against Houldsworth and the discredited Tory Party on the sole issue of the Ship Canal, in order to show conclusively that the working classes were firm supporters of the project. Significantly he suggested to Adamson that "you can avail yourself of your own canvassing staff to work the election on the Canal platform".[74] Whiting also referred to letters he had written the previous week "to the opposition papers" in which he had stated:

The working men of Lancashire owe the Chairman a deep debt of gratitude for so pluckily upholding their cause, and fortunately it is in their power to mark their sense of his exertions on their behalf by carrying Mr. Adamson into the House of Commons at the next election,[75]

and complained that he had taken this action because the *Manchester Guardian* had been refusing to print his letters. Although only circumstantial evidence, these comments add support to the theory that the Liberal leadership wanted

# THE CITY LANTERN

## AND FREE LANCE:

### A Weekly Journal of Wit, Humour, Satire, Politics, Art, Science, the Drama, Social Literature, &c.

VOL. IX.—No. 469.  FRIDAY, SEPTEMBER 21, 1883.  [PRICE ONE PENNY.

## DR. PANKHURST AND THE TORIES.

As the Doctor sat in his sanctum he pondered, and after reviewing matters, he was heard by the office boy to ejaculate *sotto voce* after the following: P.S.—The way in which the MS. came into our hands is peculiar. The Doctor's office boy and our "devil" are chums. Our d—l had borrowed from the Doctor's O.B. some chewing Cavendish, which was wrapped in said MS., and found by one of our men on the floor of the office. Now the secret's out!

> I'm a Radical rad,
> I am the "dad"
> Of all the Liberal crew.
> For what care I,
> Tho' they fight shy
> Of Irish Radical stew?
>
> I'd have them know
> That I can crow,
> And bark—and may be bite,
> Tho' certain to lose.
> I'll do as I choose,
> And "barney" with all my might!
>
> I've men at my back,
> Michael, 'Arry and Jack,
> Who'll never desert me or flinch;
> They're made of the stuff
> Called "dynamite puff,"
> And are not over nice at a pinch.
>
> What tho' I can't win!
> The Tories have "tin."
> And Houldsworth' the boy that'll spend.
> It's a good business "ad,"
> For a doctor who's sad,
> And anxious his name to defend.
>
> I'll stir up some work,
> By just turning "Turk,"
> And humbug the Tories all round.
> Sure from Ireland they'll send,
> For myself, as a friend,
> And make me M.P., I'll be bound!
>
> Then hurrah! hooroo!!
> I'm leal, I'm true,
> Tho' defeated, I'm not despised.
> By my own I'm known,
> And loved, ochone!
> By Ould Ireland dearly prized.
>
> Then come what may,
> My heart is gay,
> My spirits light and free;
> A hould I've got
> On Houldsworth's lot,
> An' I'll give them one! two!! three!!!
>
> While Liberals fear,
> And at me jeer,
> I'll fight tho' against great odds;
> Tho' the heavens may fall,
> And bury us all.
> Pankhurst defies the gods!

ARGUS.

## A RAINY DAY.

A RAINY day is a winter-luxury. A cold, wet, hazy, blowing night in December, gates swinging, trees crashing, storm howling—that is enjoyable—it is the weather to finish Christabel in. How full of heat, light, and comfort everything is within doors! The flickering fire beaten into a blaze, the bubbling urn, the rustled book, and all the scenery of a thoughtful fireside rise to the memory. Cowper describ...

neither a candidate nor a public discussion about possible candidates, because their objective was to give Houldsworth a clear run. This interpretation of events is given further weight by a letter written in "semi-code" to the *Manchester Guardian* by a Liberal Party activist signing himself, "One Who Worked for Bazley, Bright and Jones". The party's registration agent, B. L. Green, had alleged that Pankhurst's presence in the field had been the reason for not putting up a candidate, and the letter-writer, in rebutting this suggestion, had this to say:

> We know the Doctor's candidature had little or nothing to do with the decisions of the leaders of the Party not to contest the seat, that decision being virtually arrived at before Dr. Pankhurst entered the field; and what is more, it was personally decided by the most influential of the leaders before the Doctor signed his first address, or was even thought of in connection with this contest. *For good and sufficient reasons* (my emphasis) the leaders had long before made up their minds that it was not desirable to attempt to wrest this minority seat from the Tories and the difficulty was to bring the 900 to their way of thinking. Dr. Pankhurst coming to the front helped them out of this dilemma.[76]

To spell out the reasons would have only drawn attention to the one-party bias of the Ship Canal movement, which Scott and the other Liberal leaders were keen to avoid. But no such inhibitions affected the *Courier* which was only too happy to print a letter from John E. Redfern neatly summarising the professed and real reasons of the pro-Houldsworth lobby in the Liberal Party:

> Allow me as a Liberal to express an earnest wish that a contest for the seat … may be avoided by the unopposed return of Mr. Houldsworth. The Liberals of this city may well rest content with their proportion of the representation without attempting to snatch the temporary possession of the minority seat … for the occupancy

of which the party has no conspicuous aspirant ... There are at present no supreme issues at stake... Manchester can ill afford the direct and indirect loss inevitable upon a contested election. How much more conducive to the highest interests of Manchester and district if both parties on this occasion buried the political hatchet, and strenuously united in passing to a successful issue the great scheme for connecting Manchester with the Sea. Such a coalition would be worthy of the commercial sagacity of Manchester men, and would bear down the selfish opposition of vested interests and the contemptuous indifference of the House of Lords.[77]

In the contest which ensued between Houldsworth and Pankhurst it was highly unlikely that the Ship Canal would become a political issue, but it lay like a slumbering giant beneath the platforms ready to burst out if overlooked. It was the one local issue that Pankhurst specifically included in his election address,[78] and it hit Houldsworth at his first public meeting in Ardwick. At the end of a long speech on foreign and domestic policy, the Tory candidate was put on the spot. "Would you", asked an elector at the back of the hall, "assist the promoters of the Manchester Ship Canal to obtain the sanction of the legislature to such a Scheme?" Houldsworth's response was a model of prevarication:

I am a disinterested witness, I think, because I have not taken any active part in the promotion of this Scheme. It is a business scheme, ... and I do not as a rule mix myself up with any schemes that do not come into connection more or less with my own business, if I can possibly help it ... So far as I can see, there is nothing ... which should not receive the sanction of the Committee of the House of Commons.

But the questioner was not to be so simply brushed aside, and pursued his point: "I should like a more definite answer. I am a Conservative, and I wish to know if you are prepared personally to support the Bill". Houldsworth had been pursued into a corner and there was no relief. "Yes, I am", came his reply.[79]

It was the answer the Canal supporters had been seeking. The danger was that Pankhurst, as an independent and popular Liberal, might pick up enough votes to win and thus abort the plan to incorporate Houldsworth and the Conservative Party in the Ship Canal movement. Seen in this context the actions and Delphic utterances of the Liberal Association which punctuate the campaign take on a clarity and logic not at first apparent. The high moment in the *pas de deux* between the warring factions came at the special meeting of the Liberal Council on 3rd October when W. H. Burrow and Robert Austin, Pankhurst's supporters, put an innocuous-sounding motion: "that the free exercise of the franchise subject to no dictation or control but that of reason is the constitutional right of every elector in Manchester", only to have it amended by a large majority

supporting the addition of a clause stating that "the interests of Liberalism will be best served by this Association abstaining from any action whatever in the present contest".[80] A further motion stating that the Liberal electors of Manchester should be left free to exercise their individual judgment was then thrown out. Short of telling the electorate to vote Conservative, there was little more the Association could have done to support Houldsworth.

Pankhurst's radical political views did not win him the enthusiastic support of the big bourgeoisie elements in the Association, but it needs to be stressed that they did not put him "beyond the pale" of the Liberal Party for he stood as the Liberal candidate for Rotherhithe in 1885. He also received support from prominent Liberals including Hugh Mason MP for Ashton-under-Lyne, who sent a £100 donation for the campaign, and H. J. Roby who became MP for the Eccles Division of Lancashire in 1885. Here again, the Ship Canal question provides the key for both Mason and Roby were opposed to the making of the Canal on the lines suggested. Mason had written in August saying he was not prepared to encourage such a risky investment, and Roby was to head a Ratepayers' memorial in 1884 opposing an £18,000 contribution to the scheme by the City Council. Neither men were inhibited therefore from giving strong support to the candidate for whom Liberals would normally have voted.

Small drawing circulated for the election. *MCL*

The Pankhurst election was to mark an important stage in loosening the Liberal influence over the movement. The leadership's stance received the backing of the majority of trade union members of the Association – with only Murchie and Austin supporting Pankhurst – and this was reflected in the large number of abstentions. But the split was highly damaging to the Liberal Party, and was an important factor in the disastrous results of the 1885 general election when, under the Redistribution Act, six new seats were contested and five of the Liberal candidates (including the sitting MPs Jacob Bright and Slagg) were defeated. [81]

Houldsworth's conversion to the Ship Canal had been achieved at great cost to the Liberal Party, but it was still grudging and it was to be a further two years before he was to indicate a willingness to become a director. The first practical sign of a changed attitude came only three weeks after the election when he wrote a letter of support to be read out at a mass meeting at the Free Trade Hall, addressed by Jacob Bright and John Slagg. In the new mood of all-party collaboration, Slagg emphasised that an interest in the Ship Canal "… had no political significance at all … and that any of the citizens could associate with this great scheme … without political consideration of any degree whatever". [82] Houldsworth's letter contained some element of ambiguity, but was a distinct improvement:

I have much pleasure in stating I shall feel it my duty to support the passing of the Manchester Ship Canal Scheme … should the promoters bring in another bill. Of course I reserve to myself the right to consider from time to time any facts or arguments which may be brought against it. But at present I see no reason why the Scheme should not receive the sanction of Parliament. [83]

His ambivalent attitude was to reappear, however, when the Bill came before the House the following June. His terse six-line letter to the *Manchester Guardian* shows his anxiety that the Liberal press in the city was trying to use him:

Kindly correct one sentence in your report of my speech yesterday on the Manchester Ship Canal. I am not aware of saying 'I believe myself in the success of the Scheme', and I do not find these words in any reports except those of the Guardian and the Examiner and Times, which appear identical. [84]

It also created the distinct impression of vacillation if not dishonesty. Liberal Ship Canal supporters taunting him on the state of his memory and for "making a Sphinx of himself", were quick to point out that similar wording appeared in the *Liverpool Daily Post*, and that anyway he had written a warm letter of support only a week before to the Pomona Gardens mass demonstration of Trades Union and Industrial Classes hoping the Bill would pass the Commons. [85] Why would he want this, it was argued, if he did not believe in the success of the scheme "unless he wants to

play a gigantic *sell* on his constituents". The Liberals were outraged and demanded an unequivocal response. "If I were a Conservative", concluded James McMaster, one of the Ship Canal Ward Chairmen, "I should be wild to think how successfully he (Houldsworth) had put the razor to his political throat".

The episode coincided with the rejection by Conservative Peers of Gladstone's Franchise Bill and, with prompting from the National Liberal Federation, the Manchester Liberal Association organized an enormous demonstration meeting at Pomona Gardens at the end of the month. [86] Houldsworth's attitude on the Reform Bill is not known, but he must clearly have been worried about being outflanked by the Manchester Liberals on these two issues, one national and the other local. He could see the danger signs and, when the Ship Canal Bill was thrown out by the Commons Committee in early August, moved quickly to bring the Conservative Party into line. At the meeting of Ship Canal Subscribers later in the month, his conciliatory phrasing was to presage a new phase of collaboration:

In this large commercial community, there were many subjects they could meet together to discuss, and it was a pleasure when they could join in the furtherance of any scheme without regard to creeds or political party, and that was for the interest of the community in which they dwelt …[87]

The penetration of the movement by Tory elements was now beginning and was to be extended the following year when the receipt of the Royal Assent to the Ship Canal Bill provided the green light for the Board to start gathering in additional directors. The minutes of 25th August 1885 report that a small Tory delegation of Boddington, Marshall Stevens and Henry McNeil [88] had visited Houldsworth at his residence in Kilmarnock and that "after a very pleasant interview" he had consented to accept a directorship. He had also suggested a strengthening of the Board by bringing in Sir Joseph C. Lee – chairman of Tootal, Broadhurst and Lee who was shortly to become President of the Manchester and District Liberal Unionist Association after the split in the Liberal Party in 1886 – and Charles Moseley, a large telephonic equipment manufacturer and leading Tory. These proposals were immediately taken up by the Board who at the same meeting gave approval to the overtures McNiel was making to two of the great aristocrats of the region – Lord Derby and Lord Egerton.

Faced with the prospect, if the capital was raised, of a massive new investment in the region's infrastructure, the time had come for the big industrial bourgeoisie of the city to put aside political differences, and look to an alliance which would protect their common economic and class interests. Over the space of the next twelve months two General Elections were to take place bringing for the Liberals both defeat over Home Rule for Ireland, and a devastating split which led to the formation of the Liberal

Unionist Party. These events, of profound significance for the Liberal Party, in no way appear to have affected the new cross-party collaboration on the Board. More worrying to the directors and to the city's ruling classes was the agitation over the unemployed and the labour question which began to be voiced in the winter of 1885/1886 and coincided with riots and meetings taking place in many other cities – especially London.

The stabilisation and class issues involved in this question will be dealt with in later chapters, but before moving on we need to note a general point about the campaigning and politics of the Ship Canal movement, which have been described in this section. Substantial detail has been deliberately included to support an account which departs markedly from previously published ones. The reason for this departure is simple. A broad social and political framework of analysis has been adopted in order to wrest the subject matter from the hitherto unchallenged hold of very narrowly focused economic historians and industrial archaeologists. In doing this we have shown that far from being just an agitation about a new waterway, the Ship Canal movement was a significant political and ideological intervention which aimed amongst other things to win working class support for new forms of industrial ownership and State influence and for new channels of democratic representation.

## Notes

1. See for instance D. A. Farnie's chapter on the Manchester Ship Canal in W. H. Chaloner and B. M. Ratcliffe (eds.), *Trade and Transport, Essays in Economic History*, 1977, p. 191. Having perceptively drawn attention to the excessive reliance of commentators on the promoters' rhetoric of cost reduction, and pointed out the company's lack of profitability, Farnie goes on to wonder whether the project represented "a ritualised gesture of faith" in the relevance of the philosophy of free trade.

2. S. Hall, "The rise of the representative/interventionist state", in G. McLennan and D. Held (eds.), *State and Society in Contemporary Britain*, 1984, p. 15.

3. Richard Pankhurst was a lawyer and married to Emmeline. Their daughter Christabel was active in the women's suffrage movement.

4. A. D. Provand, *The Manchester Ship Canal Scheme. A Criticism*, 1883, MCL Reference 386.M79. Provand was a Manchester merchant and a Liberal who subsequently represented the Blackfriars Division of Glasgow as M.P. from 1886 to 1900.

5. Letter from Hicks to Adamson, Lancashire Record Office DDX/101/1

6. *Ship Canal Gazette*, 8 November 1882, p. 2. The Parliamentary Fund target had been raised to £100,000. The £60,000 figure was not reached until February 1883, and by 15 August 1883 (the last issue of the Gazette) it had only climbed to £66,242.

7. B. Leech, *op.cit.*, Vol. 1, p. 99. The first edition of the Gazette was issued on 8th November 1882, the last on 15 August 1883. Manchester Central Library Reference 386.M12. The last issue stated an intention to resume as a monthly publication. It was presumably Harvey's role as editor and early propagandist that secured him a position on the Provisional Committee despite his low status as an office clerk.

8. B. Leech, *ibid.*, Vol. 1, p. 94. Leech became chairman of the Oxford Ward Committee.

9. Heap was employed as manager of the Kinder Printing Company, a small textile business, leaving in June 1883 after an internal row over economies. The collapse of the company in the early 1890s created a small sensation. *Spy*, 23 April, 30 April 1892.

10. *Manchester Courier*, 6 October 1882.

11. Fielden, a salesman with the firm of Samuel Ogden (later described as a manager) was a radical Liberal who had been on the executive committee of the Manchester Liberal Association since 1879 at least. He was to provide a crucial link with the trade unions.

12. *Ship Canal Gazette*, Special Supplement, 18 November 1882. Slatter, Austin and Shorrocks were all Executive Committee members of the Manchester Liberal Association, and Murchie was on the Association's Council.

13. See D. A. Hamer, *Liberal Politics in the Age of Gladstone and Roseberry, A Study in Leadership and Power*, 1972, chapter 3, p. 57. It has an interesting discussion of the development of Gladstone's ideas in the 1870s and 1880s.

14. W. E. Gladstone, *The County Franchise and Mr. Lowe thereon*, 1877. Quoted in D. A. Hamer, *ibid.*, p. 65.

15. No published history of the Ship Canal pays any attention to this question. Leech in his two-volume history completely disregards the political dimension of the movement.

16. Of the remaining three for whom information has not been found, one was from Warrington, one from Dukinfield, and one from London.

17. Stevens was a young Garston shipping merchant, and became the first manager of the Ship Canal.

18. Quoted in the *Ship Canal Gazette*, 29 November 1882, p. 49.

19. "How we raised the Parliamentary Fund – by a Ward Enthusiast", *Ship Canal Gazette*, 22 November 1882, and 7 February 1883; *Manchester City News*, 6 January 1894.

20. "Ship Canal Pioneers; the Services of Mr. Lawrence and others", *Manchester City News*, 13 January 1894.

21. Two of these barristers, Alfred Sington and T. A. Hulme, were appointed in November 1882 as Secretaries to the

Conference between the Provisional Committee and the Ward Committees. Hulme was also the author of a pamphlet (under the pseudonym "A Manchester Barrister") entitled, *Some legal considerations in relation to the proposed Manchester Ship Canal; and the duty of municipal corporations to support the undertaking*, Manchester 1882.

22. *Manchester Evening News*, 10 July 1902.

23. Beatrice Webb 1903, quoted in the frontispiece of L. Brown, *The Board of Trade and the Free Trade Movement 1830–1842*, Oxford 1958.

24. *Manchester City News*, 6 January 1894, p. 3.

25. Reports dated 3 January 1883 and 18 January 1883, Reference Manchester Central Library 386 M.80 and M.85

26. Copies of the three model resolutions (in the form of slips to be circulated) can be found in the Manchester Central Library Reference 386 M 80. Model resolution No. 1 reads as follows:–
   "That it is essential in the interests of the increasing commerce and population of this District to adopt cheaper means than at present exist for the transport and handling of merchandise, materials etc. between Manchester and surrounding towns and the sea coasts and places beyond".

27. *Manchester Guardian*, 29 December 1882.

28. *Ship Canal Gazette*, 27 December 1882.

29. *Ship Canal Gazette*, 29 November, and 6 December 1882.

30. Quoted in A. D. Provand, *op.cit.*, p. 7.

31. Manchester Central Library Reference 386 M 18

32. *Ship Canal Gazette*, 7 March 1883. Of the 286 petitions, 37 came from local authorities, 31 from Chambers of Commerce, 95 from Local Boards, and 97 from Limited Companies in Lancashire and Yorkshire.

33. For full details of the Parliamentary evidence see B. Leech, *op.cit.*, Vol. 1, chapters 7, 8 and 9.

34. B. Leech, *ibid.*, pp. 145–6

35. B. Leech, *ibid.*, p. 130.

36. Heron had achieved a national reputation as the city's Town Clerk. Less well known are his Liberal connections. In 1879 he was shortlisted by the Executive Committee of the Manchester Liberal Association for the seat left vacant by Sir Thomas Bazley's resignation. See H. J. Hanham, *Elections and Party Management*, 1959, p. 129 (n).

37. Greater Manchester Council Record Office, papers of Daniel Adamson, letter from Sir Joseph Heron, 15 August 1883.

38. Letter from J. W. Southern, 11 August 1883, Lancashire Record Office DDX 101/2/8

39. B. Leech, *op.cit.*, pp. 137, 190.

40. B. Leech, *ibid.*, pp. 194–5.

41. See D. Fraser, *Urban Politics in Victorian England*, 1976.

42. A. G. Symonds, in W. H. Mills (ed.), *The Manchester Reform Club 1871–1921*, 1922, pp. 56–7.

43. Peacock was elected as Liberal MP for the Gorton Division of Lancashire in 1885 and retained the seat until his death in 1889.

44. See *The Ship Canal Gazette*, 14 March 1883 for the list of Chairmen and Secretaries. The political affiliation of the Medlock Street Chairman is unknown.

45. Groves subsequently became Chairman of the family owned Regent Road Brewery in Salford. He was MP for South Salford 1900–1906, and was Chairman of the South Salford Conservative Association.

46. D. Fraser, *Urban Politics in Victorian England*, 1976, p. 240.

47. *Manchester City News*, 6 January 1894.

48. Letter from G. Hicks, 6 January 1894, in C. P. Scott Archive, Manchester University Library (120/4).

49. *Manchester City News*, 13 January 1894.

50. *Manchester City News*, 13 January 1894.

51. *Manchester City News*, 6 January 1894.

52. H. J. Hannam, *op.cit.*, p. 87.

53. H. J. Hannam, *ibid.*, pp. 314–316.

54. Another outspoken critic of the Canal Scheme was Hugh Mason, Liberal MP for Ashton-under-Lyne, who wrote a critical letter to the Manchester Guardian on 6 August 1883, expressing his view that the project was a very risky investment, and that the first shareholders would lose their money. Mason was a director of the Midland Railway Company and of the Bridgewater Navigation Company. See *Ship Canal Gazette*, 15 August 1883.

55. *Ship Canal Gazette*, 17 January 1883, p. 135.

56. Volume of Ship Canal cuttings, Manchester Central Library, reference f386. M11.

57. *Ship Canal Gazette*, 18 November 1882.

58. Volume of Ship Canal Cuttings, *op.cit.*, 20 December 1882.

59. A. B. Forwood, in *Contemporary Review*, Vol. XLIII, February 1883, p. 299.

60. P. Joyce, *Work, Society and Politics*, 1982, p. 324.

61. See comments in E. de Laveleye, "The Progress of Socialism" in *Contemporary Review*, April 1883.

62. The Democratic Federation was renamed the Social Democratic Federation in 1884.

63. Letter to *Manchester Courier*, 22 October 1878. Reprinted in Pamphlet *Corporation Proceedings and Municipal Returns*, 1880. Manchester Central Library, reference 352.042 M14.

64. Manchester Liberal Association, Minutes of the Executive Committee, 27 February 1882.

65. Ashton was a cotton spinner of Hyde and Manchester, and left an estate of £526,000 when he died in 1898. He had been, according to an obituary in the Manchester Evening News "an intimate friend of Cobden and John Bright", and occupied a pre-eminent position in Manchester Liberal circles.

66. Letter from T. Ashton to C. P. Scott, 23 February 1882, John Rylands University Library, Manchester, C. P. Scott Archive Ref. 118/19.

67. *Manchester Guardian*, 5 October 1883.

68. H. J. Hanham, *op.cit.*, pp. 129–130.

69. *Manchester Courier*, 17 September 1883.

70. *Manchester Courier*, 18 September 1883. Pankhurst's daughter Sylvia states in her account that it was his radicalism that caused the Liberal Party to oppose him. She makes no attempt however to explain why the Party did not field its own candidate. See E. S. Pankhurst, *The Suffragette Movement*, 1931, pp. 60–65.

71. *Manchester Guardian*, 17 September 1883.

72. Extracts cited in *Manchester Courier*, 12 September 1883.

73. Manchester Liberal Association. Minutes of the General Purposes Committee, 15 September 1883.

74. Letter from J. Whiting to D. Adamson, Lancashire Record Office DDX 101/2/12.
75. See *Manchester Courier*, 6 September 1883, letter by WJ.
76. *Manchester Guardian*, 1 October 1883.
77. *Manchester Courier*, 12 September 1883.
78. *Manchester Guardian*, 17 September 1883.
79. The exchange is reported in full in both the *Manchester Guardian* and the *Manchester Courier*, 20 September 1883.
80. Manchester Liberal Association, Minutes of the Special Meeting of the Council, 3 October 1883.
81. This judgment about the damage done to the Party by the events of the Autumn of 1883 is supported by a letter written by Hicks twelve years later. Encouraging Liberals to support Pankhurst, who was standing as ILP candidate for Gorton, Hicks commented: "The desertion of Dr Pankhurst by his Party when he contested Manchester some years ago did incalculable harm to earnest Liberalism in this city", *Manchester Guardian*, 28 June 1895, p. 6.
82. *Manchester Guardian*, 1 November 1883.
83. Letter from Houldsworth, 22 October 1883, reported in the *Manchester Guardian*, 1 November 1883.
84. *Manchester Guardian*, 28 June 1884.
85. See letters from R. D. Rusden, Henry C. Pingstone and J. McMaster in *Manchester Guardian*, 1 July 1884.
86. W. H. Mills, The Manchester Reform Club, *op.cit.*, p. 26.
87. *Manchester Guardian*, 16 August 1884.
88. McNiel was a Manchester coal and metal merchant and member of the Conservative Association. He had been hired by the Board on August 8th 1885 to drum up support and capital from his mainly Tory contacts. He was to be an important go-between over the next two years.

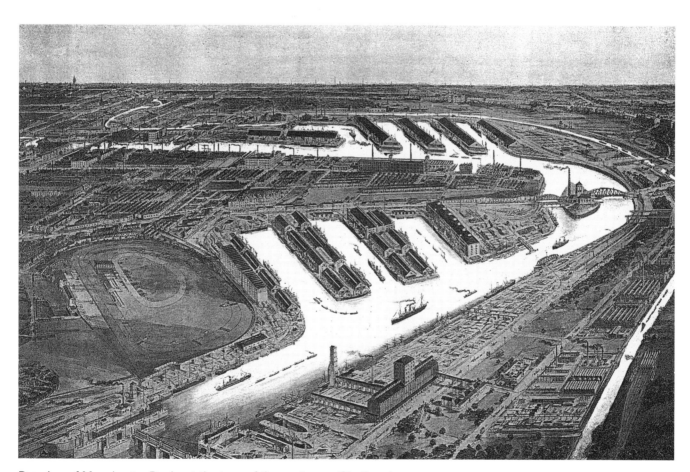

Drawing of Manchester Docks at the turn of the century.   *Chetham's*

# 3

# THE SHIP CANAL
# AND THE ECONOMY

There is almost a unanimity of opinion not only as to the desirability of having this Canal constructed, but as to its comparative necessity. It is regarded as one of those novel and necessary expedients that are calculated to meet the extraordinary necessities of the time ... The use of machinery has produced absolutely marvellous results ... and the banks have furnished every variety of facility ... the accountants have found the very best method of keeping the accounts, and it seems that everything that can be done to promote the course of industry in that locality has been exhausted with this particular exception.

Alderman Husband, Mayor of Salford, 1886.[1]

The Ship Canal Project was always more than a merely commercial scheme. Its wider political and ideological underpinning, though never entirely explicit, provided the momentum to carry the enterprise through a number of crises, any one of which could have dealt a terminal blow if normal commercial criteria had been applied. At the level of public debate, however, it was the economic arguments which received overwhelming attention. Three features received particular emphasis. Firstly it was argued that the high transport costs charged by Liverpool and the railways were crippling Manchester and the textile industry, and that a Canal would substantially undercut the charges. Secondly, it was claimed that this infrastructure development would be highly profitable and required widespread community support. The almost obsessional interest of some of the directors in promoting working class shareholding – which is explored in Chapter 6 – was the practical application of this belief. The third claim was that the construction of a large canal for ocean-going ships would, by bringing new industries to the region, help to expand and diversify the existing industrial base.

To judge the validity and purpose of these arguments, and the nature of the appeal being made to different classes and industrial sectors, it is necessary in this chapter to examine aspects of the economic and demographic structure of Manchester and the surrounding towns with particular reference to the two most significant industries, cotton and engineering. In doing this, it will be possible in part to address four important and related series of questions. What were the prevailing views about the local economy and its relationship to international markets, and about the appropriate economic policies that should be adopted by the State? To what extent did the views of capital and labour converge on questions of economic analysis and policy? What were the major sources of support for the scheme? And lastly, did the Ship Canal project represent a dynamic and original response to perceived problems of industrial decline, or simply a variation on a traditional pattern of response which can more properly be linked with long-held beliefs in the value of Free Trade and laissez faire State policies? The way these questions are answered is important because they relate to the issue and causes of Britain's long-term economic decline, the seeds of which in the view of many writers can be traced back to the 1870s and 1880s.[2]

For the economy as a whole there were, by the early 1880s, clear signs that Britain's commanding position in world trade was coming under sustained competitive pressure from newly emerging industrial countries. No longer could manufacturers rely upon the easy assumptions of an earlier period which Knowles graphically describes:

In the twenty-three years from 1859 to 1873 Great Britain was the forge of the world, the world's carrier, the world's ship-builder, the world's banker, the world's workshop, the world's clearing house, the world's entrepot. The trade of the world during this period pivoted on Great Britain. She was organized for a world economy when other countries such as Italy, Germany and the United States were only feeling their way to a national system.[3]

It is not easy to understand how people in Manchester and elsewhere perceived the changes occurring over the next twenty years, since reliable data is not always at hand. What has been called the era of the Great Depression from the mid-1870s to the mid-1890s affected other countries as well as Britain; and in any event is something of a misnomer, for world production continued to grow throughout the period. As Ashworth shows, the figures for quinquennial increases in the volume of world trade in the period 1881–1895 ranged from 2% to 10%.[4] Britain's economy remained firmly linked to foreign trade, and nowhere more comprehensively than Manchester, so that even by the onset of the First World War, she remained the largest exporter, as measured by value, of all industrial countries.

View of Manchester from the London Road Station (present-day Piccadilly). *Chetham's*

What was important, however, was that the rate of growth not only slowed down dramatically, but was also much lower than in other industrial countries. Britain's share of world trade dropped from 19.65% of the world total in 1876–80, to 18.22% in 1891–95 and 14.15% in 1911–13,[5] and the growth in her export of manufactured goods between 1899 and 1913 was to be only 47% compared with a growth rate of 100% in the United States, and of 120% in Germany. Most notable was Britain's failure to compete successfully in the markets of developed countries with, for instance, her exports to the United States from the 1870s to 1890s dropping in almost every category of manufactured goods. This compared with a growth of exports to the United States from industrial European countries of some 80% between 1874 and 1914.[6]

These general figures for the U.K. economy are paralleled by similar trends to be observed in the cotton manufacturing industry which, in 1881, in Lancashire and Cheshire employed a total of over 460,000 workers, or more than 20% of the entire workforce in the two counties. Since the textile industry was more geographically concentrated in Britain than in any other country, and the above figures represented 92% of all workers engaged in cotton manufacture in England and Wales, the fortunes of Manchester and Lancashire were inextricably bound up in the cotton trade.[7]

Some indication of the general problems facing the industry can be seen in Table 1 below, in the changing proportions of cotton deliveries in Britain compared with the Continent and the United States.

**Table 1    Percentage Deliveries of Cotton Bales**[8]

| Year | Britain | Continent | United States | Total |
|------|---------|-----------|---------------|-------|
| 1871–1875 | 47.2 | 32.9 | 19.9 | 100% |
| 1876–1880 | 42.3 | 34.6 | 23.1 | 100% |
| 1881–1883 | 39.9 | 35.9 | 24.2 | 100% |

Ellison, writing his account in 1886 at a time when trade was undoubtedly bad, argued that the depression had been caused by world over-production in 1882–3 in the three main producing areas. There was probably some truth in this but his figures also show that whereas Europe and the United States had, despite the depression, a steady annual increase in consumption of cotton bales for every year without exception between 1870 and 1883, Britain had experienced an actual decline in 1872, 1875, 1878 and 1879. Weaknesses can be seen too in particular markets. Sandberg for instance, shows that although there was growth in exports to countries in Africa, Latin America and China, British cotton cloth exports to Northern Europe declined by 33% in the period 1871–1887, and to the United States by 58%.[9] This latter point was highlighted by Sir Joseph Lee, the senior partner in Tootal, Broadhurst and Lee cotton spinners. In his evidence to the Royal Commission on the Depression of Trade and Industry he reported that in the period 1874–1886 his cotton-spinning firm's trade with America had slumped from a value of £700,000 or £800,000 to under £200,000.[10]

The difficulties experienced by the industry as a result of these adverse trade conditions were reflected in lay-offs, short-time and closures throughout Lancashire. J. C. Fielden, a key activist in the Ship Canal movement who enjoyed close relationships with the cotton unions, in his evidence before the House of Lords Committee in July 1883[11] claimed that losses in the Lancashire cotton trade in the period 1875–79 amounted to £24 million, and that in Todmorden alone 25 of the 29 firms that had existed in 1873 had become bankrupt or gone out of business by 1883. According to another cotton manufacturer who was himself forced to close, in 1878 there had been 169 failures of important firms concerned with the trade of the district representing liabilities of £32.5 million.[12] Samuel Ogden, another Ship Canal supporter, for whom Fielden worked as a manager, provided information for Manchester itself in his evidence to a House of Lords Committee in 1884. He was reported as being able to list engineering firms and mills which had closed down in the previous ten years in the New Cross Ward and Ancoats area which had employed 12,650 workers.[13]

The examples give support to the general argument that the cotton industry in particular was under substantial pressure but they need to be treated with some caution for a number of reasons. Firstly it is clear that the depression had a greater effect on smaller companies, and could be ridden out more easily by larger firms like Fielden Brothers of Todmorden, or John Rylands of Wigan and Manchester[14] – which enjoyed greater vertical integration, and had access to a wider range of markets – and by firms able to specialise. One large Manchester firm, William Holland & Son, initially involved only in fine cotton spinning, actually added a department for worsted spinning in 1878 and extended its Victoria Mills site at Miles Platting continuously through the 1880s to cover twelve acres of mill buildings by 1892.

It must also be recognized that the evidence being put forward by men like Fielden and Ogden was designed to promote the cause of the Ship Canal. A contemporary argument claimed there was evidence of a general trend of industries migrating to the coast because of the high carriage costs charged by the railway companies to inland manufacturers, and because of the preferential rates offered from coastal towns.[15]

The theme was picked up by several of the Ship Canal promoters including Adamson himself, who linked the closure of Manchester's Miles Platting steel works with the shift to West Cumberland of Wilson, Cammell, one of Sheffield's major steel works.[16] The move from Dronfield to Workington in 1881 was made much of at the time and resulted, it was claimed, in an annual saving of £60,000 in transport costs. But as Pollard points out, this was an entirely logical step for a firm of rail makers once the British railways had been re-equipped with steel rails and the main markets situated abroad.[17]

There could have been plenty of other reasons for firms closing down or relocating – for instance land costs, labour availability, and population movement – which were unrelated to transport costs. In the case of Manchester, although several companies – like William Holland, McConnel and Co., Rylands and Sons and Richard Haworth –

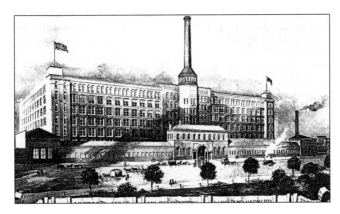

William Holland's Victoria Mills, which were expanding throughout the 1880s, when Manchester industry was alleged to be crippled by transport charges.  *MCL*

retained large mills in the city or in Salford, a dispersion of manufacturing to the outlying towns had been evident from the 1860s at least, with Thomas Houldsworth's first move to Reddish, near Stockport, in 1864 triggering off substantial new investment in that area.[18]

This process of dispersion from Manchester was given additional impetus in the 1870s by redevelopment programmes which saw the clearing of swathes of land to make way for warehousing, the new Town Hall and the Central Station. One consequence of these changes was that Manchester itself lost population in the period 1871–1881, dropping from 351,189 to 341,414 against a general trend of population gain in all other major industrial towns and cities.[19] It is difficult to use the Census figures with sophistication for comparative purposes because in many instances the methods of analysis and presentation differed in 1881 from those used in 1871. Nor should Manchester's figures be treated alone. They should properly include, as indicated in Table 2 opposite for 1871, the population not only of the adjoining city of Salford, but also of Chorlton, a residential area for both the professional and working classes, immediately to the south of Manchester city centre.

Strict comparisons between 1871 and 1881 are impossible because the Census summaries for 1881 do not include Chorlton and show occupations for all ages, not those for just 20 years and over. Total populations are given, however, and these reveal a truer picture for the conurbation, as Manchester's loss of population is more than compensated by a 41% increase of Salford's population from 124,801 in 1871 to 176,235 in 1881.

### Review of the Cotton and Engineering Sectors

These general Census figures showing a substantial population increase may not particularly support the view of Manchester as being in terminal crisis – which some of the Ship Canal supporters would have had people believe – but the more detailed occupational data for the cotton industry begin to give an indication of what was happening in the region. Using corrected figures for 1871, the compilers of the 1881 Census showed that over the ten-year period there had been an increase of 6.5% in the total numbers employed in England and Wales in cotton and flax manufacture, and a 10.4% increase in Lancashire and Cheshire (see Table 3).[20]

The cotton industry in Lancashire and Cheshire had increased at the expense of other parts of the country, but figures for the different towns show development in the North West was also uneven. Tables 4a and 4b give the Census data for 1871 and 1881 for cotton and flax manufacture, and the % increases in seven major towns for males and females. The 1871 figures are corrected.

In this crude form the data suffers from a major defect, in that while the 1881 figures include workers of all ages, the figures for 1871 are only for those aged 20 years or more. The 1871 Census does, however, have a general breakdown

**Table 2   All Adults aged 20 years or over, 1871 Census**

| Area | Total Adults | Class 1  (%) | Class 2  (%) | Class 3  (%) |
|------|-------------|--------------|--------------|--------------|
| Manchester | 140,419 | 3, 082 (2.2) | 13,164  (9.4) | 65,104 (46) |
| Salford | 70,327 | 2,387 (3.4) | 6,607  (9.4) | 29,606 (42) |
| Chorlton | 116,011 | 4,435 (3.8) | 12,965 (11.2) | 43,169 (37) |

Notes:   Class 1 – Professional Classes
Class 2 – Commercial Classes
Class 3 – Industrial Classes

**Table 3   Males and Females of all ages employed in Cotton and Flax Manufacture (with corrected figures for 1871)**

| Area | 1871 | 1881 | % Increase |
|------|------|------|-----------|
| England and Wales | 469,556 | 500,025 | 6.5 |
| Lancashire and Cheshire | 420,102 | 463,913 | 10.4 |

**Table 4a   Male Employment in Cotton and Flax Manufacture 1871 & 1881**

| Town | 1871 | 1881 | % Increase 1871–1881 |
|------|------|------|----------------------|
| Manchester and Salford | 9,976 | 11,595 | 16 |
| Oldham | 9,374 | 12,583 | 34 |
| Stockport | 3,720 | 4,427 | 19 |
| Bolton | 5,328 | 10,171 | 90 |
| Blackburn | 7,707 | 14,597 | 89 |
| Preston | 6,484 | 9,106 | 71 |

**Table 4b   Female Employment in Cotton and Flax Manufacture 1871 & 1881**

| Town | 1871 | 1881 | % Increase 1871–1881 |
|------|------|------|----------------------|
| Manchester and Salford | 17,978 | 23,861 | 32 |
| Oldham | 10,598 | 16,366 | 54 |
| Stockport | 5,872 | 7,901 | 34 |
| Bolton | 6,205 | 13,093 | 111 |
| Blackburn | 9,061 | 20,283 | 123 |
| Preston | 9,907 | 17,171 | 73 |

Note:   1871 Figures are only for those aged 20 years or more
1881 Figures are for all workers

**Table 5a    Male Employment in Cotton and Flax Manufacture 1881 & 1891**

| Town | 1881 | 1891 | % Increase 1881–1891 |
|---|---|---|---|
| Manchester | 6,945 | 9,144 | 32 |
| Salford | 4,650 | 5,779 | 24 |
| Stockport | 4,427 | 5,075 | 14 |
| Oldham | 12,583 | 13,164 | 5 |
| Bolton | 10,171 | 10,583 | 4 |
| Bury | 3,470 | 4,274 | 23 |
| Blackburn | 14,597 | 16,032 | 10 |
| Burnley | 7,913 | 12,495 | 58 |
| Preston | 9,106 | 9,852 | 8 |

**Table 5b    Female Employment in Cotton and Flax Manufacture 1881 & 1891**

| Town | 1881 | 1891 | % Increase 1881–1891 |
|---|---|---|---|
| Manchester | 13,633 | 16,955 | 24 |
| Salford | 10,228 | 10,274 | 1 |
| Stockport | 7,901 | 8,163 | 3 |
| Oldham | 16,366 | 17,499 | 7 |
| Bolton | 13,093 | 10,583 | 4 |
| Bury | 6,539 | 7,615 | 16 |
| Blackburn | 20,283 | 23,411 | 15 |
| Burnley | 9,956 | 15,305 | 54 |
| Preston | 17,171 | 18,646 | 9 |

for cotton manufacture employment between "young" workers (under 20 years old) and "old" workers (20 years old and upwards), which shows that for every 100 adult male workers there were 56.1 young male workers, and for every 100 adult female workers there were 71.3 young female workers. Extrapolating from these 1871 figures we would expect for 1881 that to have kept up the level of employment in this sector – and to take account of the inclusion of the young workers – it would have been necessary to show increases in the Census figures of at least 56.1% for male employment and 71.3% for female employment. Using this as an approximate benchmark it would appear that Manchester, Salford, Stockport and Oldham – all towns which solidly supported the Ship Canal movement – experienced actual losses in cotton employment between 1871 and 1881 while Bolton, which conspicuously failed to back the scheme, Blackburn and Preston, experienced substantial growth. The Census data therefore gives support to the view that Manchester and some of the other textile towns were witnessing some decline in Lancashire's traditional industry, but it was in the context of an overall growth and restructuring in the sector in which the

northern Lancashire towns were enjoying considerable expansion.[21] In the light of this, and the greater distance of these latter towns from Liverpool with its port and cotton market than Manchester and Salford, the argument that high transport costs were decimating local industries like cotton becomes insupportable.

In the following decade, employment in the cotton industry in Lancashire and Cheshire was to grow by 13% and, as Table 5 shows, none of the nine towns listed in the Census of both 1881 and 1891 experienced a decline. Again in these years before the Ship Canal was completed, there appears to be no evidence that transport costs were a critical element since there was above average growth notably in Burnley, and in male employment in Bury and Salford. Manchester's large figure for growth was due to boundary extensions in 1885 and 1890 and should not be taken to indicate any significant change.

In pursuing their arguments, however, Ship Canal enthusiasts were more concerned to win converts to the cause than bother overmuch with the Census or with substantiating the fine detail of their statements. This reservation must be applied with equal force to several of the claims made by Adamson himself, and by Bosdin Leech, the Canal's historian. Leech, for instance, in a handwritten note[22] of his evidence before a Parliamentary Committee in 1885, referred to a number of large iron and machine works, including those of Fairbairn and Co. and Adam Woodward, which had closed, he believed, because they could not compete with works situated in districts with more favourable transit charges. The first claim is a reference to the famous firm of William Fairbairn which closed in 1874 because of the serious depression and, because Fairbairn himself had withdrawn in 1853, the firm had lost its pioneering drive.[23] Transport charges appear to have been of no significance.

Not a great deal is known of the firm of Adam Woodward except that throughout the 1870s until the early 1880s Woodward himself is listed in the Ancoats directory as a cotton spinner, an engineer and as a manufacturer of sizing and drying machines. Although in 1884 he is only recorded as a cotton spinner, by 1888 – six years before the Canal was completed – the directory shows that far from being driven from the city, he is back in business as an engineer, machine maker and gas plant maker at the same Queen's Foundry.[24]

The Ship Canal promoters chose to present a picture of stagnation which was reducing Manchester to the position of a second rate city because this would help to substantiate their argument about the stifling effects of high railway charges and Liverpool dock dues and the consequent need for a Ship Canal. As Mancuniensis put it in a one penny pamphlet issued in 1882:

> there are widespread complaints of the decay, and in some cases, total extinction of important industries, these disastrous effects resulting entirely from the too great cost of carriage between the producing centres and the consuming markets abroad.[25]

It has been suggested that these explanations – which hitherto have been accepted uncritically – give a very partial picture of changes and restructuring taking place in the cotton industry, and the same applies to engineering. Though far smaller in terms of numbers employed, the sector produced a disproportionately high level of support for the Ship Canal.

Far from being in decline there is clear evidence that British engineering, which was powerfully represented in Manchester and its satellite towns, remained generally competitive into the 1890s, and in some branches was a world leader until 1914. Indeed two significant Manchester firms, Renold Chains and Henry Simon, were established at this time with the latter building its first roller flour milling works in 1879 and its first coke oven plant in 1881. Henry Simon Ltd was to become the foremost British firm in the field of flour-milling engineering.[26]

In at least four major areas of engineering – textile machinery, locomotives, machine tools and boiler-making – there existed in the Manchester area firms with substantial international reputations and significant shares in world markets. In textile machinery, the largest of all engineering branches, Britain maintained in Saul's words "a remarkable technological and commercial superiority right to 1914".[27] Of the total U.K. workforce of 40,000 in this sector, 75% were employed by six large companies in Lancashire. Dominating all was Platts of Oldham, the largest engineering company in the country with 8,000 to 9,000 employees in 1884, rising to about 12,000 in the 1890s. By the time it was reincorporated in 1898, its capital was over £3 million and for the period 1873–1902 it was able to maintain an average dividend of 18%.[28] There were also other substantial employers including Dobson and Barlow of Bolton with 2,000 workers in the mid-1870s, and Manchester firms such as Mather and Platt and Brooks and Doxey who employed 2,000 in 1892, John Hetherington & Sons,[29] and Curtis & Son, employing 1,400 in 1875. Several of these firms gave strong support to the Ship Canal. Matthew Curtis himself, a Tory alderman on Manchester City Council, had been first elected councillor as early as 1839. In 1886 – despite his ill-health and inability to carry out normal mayoral functions – he was persuaded to stand as the City's Lord Mayor to demonstrate cross-party support for the scheme which was in danger of foundering.[30] The most substantial support from the textile machinery sector came from the Platt family. Both Samuel R. Platt, Chairman of Platts, and his brother, James Platt, sat on the Ship Canal Board of Directors and in 1887 together had a shareholding of £46,000 in the Ship Canal – which at the time was second only to that of John Rylands, Manchester's wealthiest citizen.[31]

John Rylands, 1801–1888.

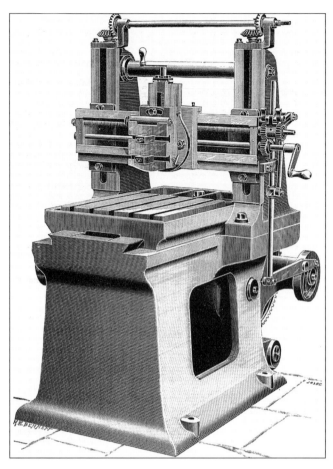

Planing machine made by Hulse & Co, a thriving Manchester firm in the 1880s. *JRULM*

Textile machinery manufacture was not, however, the only substantial engineering sector. Locomotive manufacturing was also a major branch, and in the early 1880s was represented in Manchester by Beyer Peacock and Sharp Stewart, respectively the second and fourth largest locomotive engine manufacturers in the country. In the period 1860–89 these two companies alone produced 4,922 locomotive engines, a third of all sales at home and abroad.[32] Together they held a commanding position over other British manufacturers in the European market, with Beyer Peacock alone supplying 25% of total British sales between 1860 and 1869 and 40% (of a reduced total) in the years 1890–1913. Richard Peacock, partner in the firm, was another keen advocate of the Ship Canal Scheme and Deputy Chairman of the Provisional Committee; like Leech he was quite prepared to make somewhat dubious claims to forward the argument about high transport costs. At one meeting in 1882 he was reported as saying: "I find it cheaper and better to send my goods through Glasgow, though I pay £30 an engine more by railway to get it to Glasgow than to Liverpool. I think that shows there must be something wrong in connection with Liverpool charges for rates and dues". Peacock and others failed, however, to respond

adequately to a searching critique from the pamphleteer Provand who pointed out that Peacock's argument failed to convince when the Liverpool charges on a 30-ton locomotive would not have amounted to more than £3.[33]

The support of Peacock and other engineering manufacturers was not of course illusory, but it had far more to do with how they saw their sector and markets developing than with simple calculations of existing transport costs via Liverpool. Figures of locomotive sales in the period 1860–1913 support this view for the dependence on overseas sales from the late 1870s is quite marked and represents a developing trend with fluctuations right up to 1913. Between the years 1881, when the Canal was first proposed in the press, and 1885, when Royal Assent was given to the Ship Canal Bill, overseas sales of locomotives for the nine major British firms more than doubled to 600, while home sales hovered around 200 per annum.[34]

Though textile machinery and locomotives were the largest sectors, there were also firms in other branches of engineering in Manchester which enjoyed substantial

Crossley Brothers' advertisement for their highly successful Otto engines.

reputations at home and abroad. In machine tools, though Whitworths were no longer a leading force, companies like Hulse, Muir and especially Cravens were of international importance. Of the nineteen principal machine-tool makers noted by Saul for the period 1840–1914 seven were located in Manchester.[35] The firm of B. & S. Massey had achieved a pre-eminence in forging steam hammers, with their exhibits at a Philadelphia exhibition in 1876 being described as "not only of a very high character, but far more extensive than anything of the kind exhibited even by the machine tool makers of the US". Similar reputations had been achieved in boiler-making with firms like Adamsons and Galloways in Manchester, together with Babcock & Wilcox in Glasgow, dominating world trade up to 1914.[36] Again this sector was powerfully represented in the Ship Canal movement with Daniel Adamson chairing first the Provisional Committee and then the Ship Canal Company until his resignation in 1887, and Charles J. Galloway joining the Board of Directors in 1887 with a shareholding of £28,500.

Manchester was strongest in the old established engineering sectors where there was a general tradition of producing high quality, craft-made products designed to fit the individual requirements of the customer, but it was not entirely unrepresented in the newer engineering industries in the 1880s. It is true that sewing machines – dominated by the huge Singer plant in Glasgow – and cycles never gained a substantial foothold in the North West, but Henry Simon had been quick to develop grain-milling in the area following the important Vienna exhibition in 1877. Another significant growth area was gas engines in which the Manchester firm of Crossley Brothers played a decisive role. The firm had obtained the world patent rights for a German Otto engine in 1866 and ten years later switched to an improved four-cycle design, which was highly efficient. Significantly too the company achieved higher productivity rates than the German firm of Deutz from whom they had acquired the patents.[37] The achievements of the Company may be judged from the fact that by the turn of the century, twenty years after the opening of their Openshaw works in 1881, there were 2,000 workers employed, and the two brothers, Francis William and William John, had become the wealthiest of engineering manufacturers in Manchester, both leaving estates of over half a million pounds. The latter was also a staunch supporter of the Ship Canal, subscribed £38,700 to the share capital and remained a director of the company until 1906.

### Responses to Depression and Competition

Whilst it is clear that the occupational data and the review of the cotton and engineering industries demonstrate significant changes in Manchester's economy in the period between 1871 and 1881 – the decade immediately preceding the start of the Ship Canal movement – it has become equally obvious that the view of Manchester as a second-rate town in terminal decline in the early 1880s is a gross distortion. The reality was much more complex. Decline and development were spread unevenly, and presented contemporaries with substantial problems of interpretation. A depression certainly affected the cotton trade in the late 1870s and 1880s but its impact was far from uniform. Many smaller firms appear to have closed down in the period 1878–80, and in the downturn of 1885–86 there were considerable numbers of unemployed cotton workers as indicated by evidence from the Spinners' Union and elsewhere.[38]

In these two years the average cotton spinning company made losses of £31 and £686. But the effects of this were not severe enough to promote any major restructuring of the industry by the larger companies, as witnessed in Germany during this period. It was not until the 1890s that this was to take place when a run of bad years between 1892 and 1896 hit the industry, with dividends averaging 1%–1.75%.[39] The result triggered off a series of amalgamations[40], mostly in the late-1890s, of which the following were the most important consequences:

| | |
|---|---|
| 1891 | The Winterbottom Book Cloth Co. |
| 1896 | J. & P. Coats |
| 1897 | English Sewing Cotton Co. |
| 1898 | Fine Cotton Spinners' and Doublers' Association[41] |
| | Bradford Dyers' Association |
| 1899 | Calico Printers' Association |
| 1900 | Bleachers' Association |
| | British Cotton and Wool Dyers' Association |

The pace was set in spinning and finishing by the Paisley-based firm of Coats, but before long substantial numbers of Lancashire and Cheshire firms were forming their own combines. Of the 42 companies involved in the Fine Cotton Spinners' and Doublers' Association, for instance, the vast majority were from Manchester, Bolton, Stockport and Ashton-under-Lyne, with only eight firms from outside the two counties. There are two main features to be emphasised here. Firstly the moves were defensive in nature, and involved little modernisation or innovation. Secondly, and to state a truism, they represented the response of the industry to conditions in the 1890s, rather than those in the 1880s. The point is important because it helps to start answering the question raised at the start of the chapter about prevailing perceptions of the economy; the strengths and weaknesses of particular sectors and appropriate intervention. A few voices declared the imminent collapse of Britain's industries. The tone was populist, as can be judged from the words of Randolph Churchill in Blackpool in January 1884, but it struck a discordant unpatriotic note in free trade Manchester:

> Your iron industry is dead, dead as mutton; your coal industries ... are languishing. Your silk industry is dead, assassinated by the foreigner. Your woollen industry is in articulo mortis, gasping, struggling. Your cotton industry is seriously sick.[42]

Unemployment had risen in some years, particularly in the years 1884–1886, and wages and profits were generally lower. About that there was little dispute but to suggest or imply that there was some intrinsic structural weakness in the industrial base was a very different matter. Contemporaries could point to real, though slower, growth and were far more likely in the 1880s to see explanations in terms of trade cycles. Thus J. C. Fielden, a political economist and Ship Canal enthusiast, was led to conclude:

> that at least once within every ten years the growth of the Cotton Trade has been checked by a period of deep depression and disturbance. Reasoning from this experience, we may conclusively make up our minds that the future will repeat the history of the past.[43]

The issue was one of degree, with disagreement centring on the extent of the depression. Amongst local MPs, the Liberals tended to minimize the problems arguing for an extension of Free Trade policies, while the Tories put the depressed trade at centre stage and edged towards Protectionism. John Slagg, Liberal MP for Manchester from 1880 to 1885 who gave public backing to the Ship Canal from the start, was keen to distance himself from the prophets of economic doom in his speech at the first "Great Town's Meeting" held in October 1882 to launch the scheme: "I do not think there is any substantial evidence to show that we are in a condition of deep or dangerous commercial depression";[44] he argued the case for the Canal solely on the grounds of reducing carriage costs. Slagg was a strong Free Trader and three years later declined an invitation to sit on the Royal Commission on the Depression of Trade and Industry, established by the Tory Government, because the Liberals saw it as an attempt to introduce Protectionism by stealth. The question of the health of the local economy was an issue at the General Election in November 1885, and Schwann, the Liberal candidate for North West Manchester, adopted a not dissimilar position from that of Slagg. "He did not himself entirely believe", stated the *Guardian* report, "that there was any very great depression at present".[45]

Schwann was questioning the seriousness of the depression but his Tory opponent, J. F. Hutton, a cotton merchant with considerable West Africa interests, was quick to score a political point the following week by quoting an employer who had reduced his workforce from 1000 hands to 150. However neither candidate suggested that there were any fundamental structural problems in the economy, and Hutton went on to explain "candidly" to his supporters at the meeting that he had not hitherto subscribed to the Ship Canal Scheme solely because his funds were "at present tied up in his business connections".[46] Hobsbawm has observed for this period, "to the lasting misfortune of Britain, the depression eventually passed before business and politics had been sufficiently frightened."[47]

The prevailing view in the cotton trade was that the general cause of the depression was a temporary world overproduction, which did not reflect on the competitiveness of the home industry. "As respects the open markets of the world", declared Ellison in 1886, "Lancashire is practically unassailable by either Continental or American competitors",[48] and this analysis was shared by many including John Slagg[49] and Sir Joseph Lee, cotton spinner, of Tootal Broadhurst and Lee. Attending a meeting in 1885 in support of Schwann's candidature, Lee claimed that English cottons were now driving German and Swiss cottons out of the market, and went on to state his general view that "the powers of production of many classes of goods had increased enormously, and the powers of distribution had not kept pace with this production."[50]

Lee's attitudes are interesting, not only because he had joined the Ship Canal's Board of Directors a month previously and was to play a prominent part as vice-chairman from 1887 to 1893, but also because he was regarded locally and by the Foreign Office as an expert on foreign trade issues, and in 1881–2 was appointed British Delegate to the Commission which negotiated the renewal of Cobden's 1860 Anglo-French Treaty of Commerce.[51] The implication behind Lee's remarks was that the competitiveness in terms of production of British goods, and particularly cotton, was not the issue. Improved communications and transport were the key,[52] to be achieved within the framework of Free Trade policies, and this view was widely shared. Daniel Adamson for instance, during a speech to his workers at Dukinfield after the rejection of the Ship Canal Bill, stated his conviction that the Ship Canal "would confer invaluable blessings not only upon this country but upon all places known to mankind by facilitating cheap transport from and to the seats of manufacture".[53]

This stress upon communications above all else was later taken a stage further by Adamson after he had resigned from the chairmanship of the Ship Canal Company. In a widely-reported presidential address to the Iron and Steel Institute he stated his views that, "scientific discoveries may be of advantage to ourselves, but they are equally available for our foreign competitors, and the supreme necessity for us is the discovery of cheaper modes of transit and especially of readier access to the sea".[54]

Adamson's and Lee's attitudes to this whole question of the efficiency and competitiveness of British industry were not atypical, and relate to the central issue of Britain's declining position in the world economy, which has been re-examined recently by Elbaum and Lazonick.[55] Their argument in relation to the cotton industry is that there existed inherent structural and organizational characteristics which encouraged firms in a vertically specialized industry to adopt conservative and more costly solutions to the problems of more competitive markets. An example of this was the failure of the industry to introduce the ring spindle in place of the self-acting mule, despite the fact that the former was readily available as it was being manufactured in large numbers by local firms such as Platts of Oldham, Howard and Bullough of Accrington, and Tweedale and Smalley of

Ring Spinning Frame, made by Platts of Oldham, who were major financial backers of the Ship Canal.    *JRULM*

View of the mule spinning frame, which Lancashire cottonmasters were reluctant to relinquish.    *JRULM*

Rochdale. For the individual firm there was some logic in retaining the mule because in an industry in which the spinning and weaving was geographically separated, the use of the ring spindle would have involved higher costs in the transfer of heavy wooden bobbins, rather than the paper tubes used with the mule,[56] and because the industry was moving in the direction of a cost-savings strategy by which the quality and quantity of cotton used would be reduced. Principally this was done by sizing – adding clay to the material – which resulted in the yarn becoming less resistant. Within these constraints the introduction of the ring spindle with its continuous motion would create additional problems and a greater likelihood of timewasting breakages.[57] The long-term impact, therefore of a series of decisions by individual companies, was that the industry largely failed to introduce the more efficient ring-spindle with its lower-cost high-throughput technology.[58] By 1913 they represented only 18.7% of all spindles in the U.K., compared with 86% in the United States and 54% in Germany.

A further reason Lazonick advances for the growing technological backwardness of the cotton spinning industry was the attitude of the cotton spinners themselves, the strongest and best organized trade union in the region, whose members and General Secretary, James Mawdsley, gave powerful backing to the Ship Canal Movement. Spinning continued to be organized throughout the nineteenth century on a hierarchical basis whereby the spinners (or minders) employed and generally supervised two assistants (or piecers) on a pair of mules on a subcontract basis. The spinners were the principal beneficiaries of a piece-rate system in the industry which provided them with wages of over 30 shillings per week, or more than double that of their assistants. They were reluctant, therefore, to see the introduction of any changes which would put an end to the division of labour involved in the minder–piecer relationship. They were opposed both to the practice of "joining" – whereby the minder's job and the piecer's job was combined to make a new job with equal pay and status – and to the introduction of the ring spindle which was seen as a way of undercutting the minder by the employment of cheaper female workers. As Lazonick observes:

By the late nineteenth century the minders recognized full well that their relatively high wages were based, not on special technical skills or mental abilities, but rather on the power of their unions to keep their wages up, which, in the context of the joining system at least, meant their power to keep the wages of piecers down.[59]

The conservatism of the male-dominated cotton spinning unions tended, therefore, to reinforce existing structural weaknesses to be found in the organization and management of the industry, and a related criticism may also be made of engineering manufacturers. Despite its growth in the period 1875–1914, the industry failed to develop the degree of standardization and interchangeability which

American engineers achieved. The technology employed was essentially that of repetitive work combining a mixture of machine tools and special purpose tools to produce a customer-specific product.[60] Concerning the dominant force in Lancashire engineering, the textile machinery manufacturers, Saul for instance draws this interesting conclusion:

However distinguished their role in world textile engineering generally, and despite the size of their output, their machining techniques were a mixture of the conventional – not to say old-fashioned – and the highly specialized. The industry did little after 1850 to advance engineering technology in general.[61]

The failure to introduce technical innovation is evident in many sectors apart from cotton and engineering,[62] but it did not mean that capital and labour were impervious to the need to reduce costs in order to remain competitive. In times of depression the policy of employers in the cotton industry, for instance, was to propose a general wage reduction, which the spinners' unions were willing to accept if they considered the conditions of trade were bad enough. Had wages remained at the same level even in times of depression the pressure on employers to innovate with new machinery and new production methods would have been much greater, but only rarely was the argument put forward that wages should be a fixed cost.[63] As it was, employers were content to achieve productivity growth – and thus remain competitive – by increasing the speed of *existing* machinery and by an intensification of the work rate of the minders – a policy the spinners were prepared to accept in order to protect their own position.[64]

There was therefore considerable agreement in the early 1880s in the cotton industry about the basic principles of political economy, and about the range of options available for improving trade. But if for different reasons Manchester's cotton employers and unions were unable or chose not to see modernisation and technological innovation as an imperative in their search for competitiveness, why did they and others turn so decisively to the idea of a Ship Canal with its focus on the need for cheap transport? It is true that the idea of a Canal to Manchester had a long pedigree, and there were some difficulties caused by Liverpool's failure to modernise and extend its docks, but the massive investment required for the scheme always made the claims for cost savings dubious even at the start of the movement and, as we have seen, in a region that was already well served by communications the census and other evidence give no support for the argument that Manchester's problems were caused by high transport costs.

Part of the explanation is that canal development and improvements to navigations were highly fashionable. Although none went ahead finally, schemes were considered in several parts of the country – for example Blackburn, Sheffield and the Midlands. The Suez and Panama Canals were the subject of much debate,[65] and there was considerable interest in the river improvement work which had been carried out on Tyneside[66] and Clydeside.[67] But more important were changing attitudes to economic policy making, and to Britain's traditional economic and foreign policies. An analysis of these externalities is required to reveal the thinking behind the Ship Canal rhetoric and propaganda. The opening up of new markets and the extension of existing ones within the framework of an imperial foreign policy became, in the 1880s, the central focus for Manchester's manufacturers at a time when the policy of Free Trade, so closely and for so long associated with the name of Manchester and Liberalism, came under sustained assault from those who argued that tariffs and Protectionist policies were essential to defend domestic industries decimated by the imposition of foreign tariffs.

## The Ideology and Politics of Free Trade

It is difficult now to understand the significance attached in nineteenth-century Britain to the idea of Free Trade, which Hobsbawm has described as the "quasi-religious symbol" of traditional orthodoxy.[68] In Manchester contesting the principles of Free Trade was regarded by many as heretical, and Salisbury's Tory government after the split of the Liberal Party in 1886 was careful to steer clear of any full endorsement of Protectionism or "Fair Trade" for fear of losing the support of the Liberal Unionists. The abandonment by Britain of Free Trade, in the view of its adherents, would encourage retaliatory action and put at risk the export-oriented strategy of a whole range of industries and should therefore be firmly resisted. A Ship Canal Scheme massively supported by popular acclaim, could offer a very public means of resistance. By providing a "free" waterway it could be viewed as a powerful and tangible symbol of Free Trade. With a Ship Canal, the monopoly powers of Liverpool and the railway barons could be destroyed, "free" communication with the whole world opened up, and cheap food made available for the people. These were the arguments of many of the Scheme's promoters and reflected the views of others such as archetypal free trader John Bright MP, who wrote from Rochdale in 1881, opposing Protectionist policies: "The true course for England is to open her ports as widely and completely as possible whatsoever may be the tariffs of other countries".[69]

This aspect of the Ship Canal's origins has received no attention, but is central for a proper understanding of the dynamics that lay behind the Scheme in the early 1880s. A clue to its importance is provided by Leech,[70] for he mentions that the series of letters supporting the Canal Scheme – which appeared in the local press in October 1881 and brought Daniel Adamson's involvement and the start of the movement – was triggered off by a speech on Clydeside by Sir William Harcourt, the Liberal Home Secretary. No details are given by Leech, but the *Times* report is revealing about the perceived linkage between the local economy and economic policy:

Nowhere, upon this side at least of the Atlantic, can there be found an example of a city of which the greatness and prosperity have advanced with such rapidity … There is one matter to which I may be allowed to refer without trenching upon those political questions which are excluded from this hall, though I believe not from another (laughter and prolonged cheering) … I mean the shipbuilding trade; and if there be those – I doubt whether there are any in Glasgow – who are now disposed to embrace an old friend under the new name of fair trade, I think they had better come to Glasgow to confirm themselves in the existing commercial system of this country. In spite of all the croaking … I find that in the year 1880 … the building under contract exceeded that of any year, was four times that of 1878, and ten times that of 1859 … that fact alone is sufficient to convince any reasonable man that the commercial system which has led to such results is not founded upon an unsound basis. And if I wanted confirmation of those great principles which have been an unutterable benefit to the population of this country, I should say "Come to Glasgow; and if you want a monument of free trade, why, look around you".[71]

The speech was highly topical because, as B. H. Brown has indicated, 1881 was the year in which the Tariff Reform Movement got under way in earnest. In mid-May W. F. Ecroyd, whose book "The Policy of Self-Help" was the key text for Fair Traders, was elected Tory MP for Preston with a big majority and on a Protectionist platform; and at the end of the month the National Fair Trade League was formed. Its manifesto was launched in August. After several earlier Parliamentary defeats the Fair Traders were now making substantial headway. By September they were able to convene a conference of protectionist working men in London under the auspices of a linked body, the National League, and created confusion and divisions the following day when several of the delegates attended the TUC's Annual Conference.[72]

The immediate attractiveness of the Fair Traders' arguments was obvious. If other countries were imposing taxes upon goods sent to them in order to protect their home industries, why should Britain not do likewise to protect British industries and the jobs of British workers? Even in Free Trade Lancashire, James Mawdsley in 1886 considered that between a third and a half of operatives in the cotton spinning trade would have no objection to a system of reciprocal duties as proposed by the Fair Traders,[73] and similar doubts about the value of Free Trade policies had been expressed in a letter to the *Guardian* two years earlier by Joseph Waddington, one of Manchester's early socialists and an organizer of the unemployed.[74]

What then was the rationale for Free Trade which ensured that it continued to receive strong support despite the appeal of the Fair Trade arguments? Classical *laissez-faire* Liberalism was premised on the belief that the development of the economy could best take place in a free market in which the

51

operations of capital and labour were as far as possible untrammelled by State interference. The imposition by the State of tariffs or protective duties, the argument went, artificially inflated prices, and encouraged inefficiency by removing domestic industries from the discipline of the market and by putting them in a quasi-monopolistic situation. The principle of free trade and open markets convinced people because of its beguiling neatness, and because it appeared to work successfully. But its effectiveness as an economic policy for Britain had much to do with the time and place of its introduction. The success of the Anti-Corn Law League in establishing the principle in the 1840s in fact represented a victory for the newly-emerging manufacturing interests based in the towns against the old landed agricultural interests. It was in the former's interests to have cheaper (imported) food for their workers, and since Britain's industries, and especially cotton, were at the forefront in terms of technical innovation and efficiency, the application of Free Trade policies internationally helped to open up new markets for penetration by British companies. By the 1880s, however, the competitiveness of British industries was far from assured and, in this new situation, Free Trade became less attractive particularly in those areas, like the Midlands, dependent on sectors that were primarily oriented to domestic markets.

In the export-oriented sectors of the economy, such as Lancashire's cotton and engineering industries, Free Trade principles continued to hold their currency, not least because the pure form of Free Trade *laissez-faire* economy without State interference – if it ever really existed in any complete form – became quickly adapted to accommodate the economic needs of manufacturing and merchant capital. This was reflected in the way that Government policies – particularly in relation to the development of the Empire – were shaped to benefit the interests of British industries.[75] As Hanretty has shown in relation to India,[76] the Government did far more than just facilitate trade. Under continual pressure from Lancashire cotton interests to open up the country the State became the sponsor and provider of a variety of costly schemes such as establishing a railway infrastructure[77] and developing river projects and, where unaided private capital was unwilling to invest, the State provided a guaranteed rate of interest on the investment regardless of profitability.

This was the reality of *laissez-faire* policy in an imperialist context and helps to explain both the attraction of Free Trade in Lancashire, and why an infrastructure development like the Ship Canal Project was seen as a working embodiment of an economic theory.[78] Imperial expansion – or the "New Imperialism", as it has been called – became a key linked theme in the 1880s for Manchester's Free Trade Ship Canal supporters because the protected markets, once established, would ensure outlets for British goods where foreign competition was weaker. The Ship Canal would provide the means for Manchester's manufacturing capital to lock into a new global trading network, which was already being shrunk to "village" scale by the development of telegraphic and telephonic communication. Richard Peacock, vice-chairman of the Ship Canal Provisional Committee, colourfully described the situation, as he saw it, at an election meeting:

> The most urgent necessity exists at this moment for rivetting still closer the bonds which bind the colonies to their mother country. Our future prosperity is bound up in the federation of the Empire, which as Lord Roseberry pointed out a few months ago at the Free Trade Hall, means power, commerce and happiness for ourselves and those who are bone of our bone and flesh of our flesh. It implies the girdling of the world with a broad belt of British population.[79]

The theme and change of emphasis was picked up by Roseberry himself on his visit to Manchester shortly after becoming Prime Minister. After a tour of the completed Ship Canal as the guest of Sir William Bailey[80] mayor of Salford, Roseberry was presented with an address at the Reform Club and responded:

> … I rejoice to see that you say in this address that my aim is the elevation of the people and the glory of the Empire … I remember the time – it is not far distant – when you in Manchester were supposed to be indifferent to the second of those aims. It was supposed you limited the good of the community to the expansion of trade … I hope … that the members of the Manchester Reform Club are as aware as the generation that is growing up is aware that the greatness of Empire is not merely a source of glory to us but of advantage in commercial and other respects.[81]

Nowhere was this more true than in the case of India, which by the mid-1880s was importing more than a quarter of the entire output of the British cotton industry. The application of Free Trade principles to imports to India was demanded by Lancashire deputations of employers and trade unions throughout the 1870s, and was finally achieved in

Cartoon showing merchants with bags of gold, coming to Manchester from all over the world.   *MCL*

1882 when all duties on cotton imports were abolished.[82] But there was no mutuality of interest between India and Britain on this issue, as Gokhale, a nationalist leader in Congress, observed:

> Well, this free trade policy that has been thrust on the country has killed all our industries … The result is that our people are growing poorer and poorer … the old industries we had are swept away under the competition of steam and machinery.[83]

Indeed, the cotton duties issue provides, in Moore's words "an outstanding example of the imperial power's determination to adhere to a policy of free trade in order to dispose of her surplus manufactured items to India".[84]

An economic policy of Free Trade therefore had its attractions in Manchester and Lancashire, particularly if it could be reshaped for application at home as well as abroad. A major difficulty however was that from mid-1881 onwards Free Trade was to become a political issue. Only two months after Ecroyd's election as MP for Preston, John Slagg, Manchester's Liberal MP, was declaring in a speech on Free Trade and tariffs that: "At the present time these (matters) have a special interest derived from the fact that they appear likely to form a political battle-ground for the Tory Party".[85]

Inevitably this fact was to colour attitudes to other issues, including the Ship Canal, for the promoters were keen to promote cross-party support for the scheme. "Under no circumstances must any political or party character be given to the movement. The best men of all parties should be enrolled in the movement,"[86] stated the instructions issued to the ward committees in 1882 in the early days of the campaign. The reality, however, as has been indicated in the last chapter, was that the main movers and promoters were predominantly Liberal. Just as they were inclined to embrace the Ship Canal idea because of its Free Trade associations and imagery so the Tories in the city, with their leanings towards Protectionism, viewed it with considerable suspicion.

By the autumn of 1885, when the Ship Canal Act had received Royal Assent and the Scheme had substantial public backing, Tories like the Manchester MP Houldsworth were prepared to give their support, but the election campaign in October displayed the bitter divisions which existed between the two parties and leading supporters of the Ship Canal over the best economic policy to be pursued for the country as a whole. Balfour in East Manchester, referring to the strong support the Tories were receiving in this working class constituency, was insistent that "the narrow dogmatism by which Mr Bright and others supported Free Trade twenty years ago cannot be accepted",[87] and Houldsworth ridiculed the Liberals for boycotting the Royal Commission on the Depression of Trade, stating that it would have been "an absurdity" if Fair Traders like W. F. Ecroyd had been excluded from it.[88] In Stockport meanwhile, where the Fair Trader J. L. Jennings was standing for the Tories, leading Ship Canal

supporters were out in force to support the Liberal candidates Hopwood and Joseph Leigh, himself a director of the Ship Canal. At a meeting where both Daniel Adamson and Sir Joseph Lee were on the platform Fair Trade was denounced as "a monstrous fallacy and a humbug" by Hopwood, and Leigh argued that Protection would do great injury to the town's trade;[89] and at one of Peacock's meetings in Gorton the chairman, after referring to "the quack remedies of the Fair Traders", chose to seek support for the candidate on the principal ground that he was a Free Trader.[90]

The Ship Canal was rarely linked directly with Free Trade – to do so would have risked losing support. But the views of many of its principal supporters demonstrate the centrality of the principle in their thinking, and on one occasion at least the connection was explicitly made by Daniel Adamson. Requested to attend a Ship Canal demonstration at Eccles in June 1885, Adamson found himself addressing a mostly working-class audience on the day it was announced that Gladstone was resigning and that a General Election would be held in November. The opportunity was not to be missed and Adamson unguardedly spoke his mind about the Ship Canal:

> … even in the large cities and shipping ports of the continent, the scheme was watched with absorbing interest. Why? … because the working classes and traders on the continent were beginning to realize the benefits of Free Trade, and the cheapness of transit from one country to another … and during the ensuing elections it would be the duty of the working classes to see that they returned men who would stand by the interests of the working classes, and use their influence to promote works of this kind, works which tended to stimulate and foster trade.[91]

The Free Trade leitmotif can be seen too in the imagery employed by the movement's organizers and supporters. Enormous loaves of bread, huge joints of beef, and large packets of tea and sugar were not infrequently used by Liberal campaigners to illustrate the benefits of Free Trade,[92] and a massive loaf made appearances – usually carried in procession – at many of the large Ship Canal demonstrations. At the Great Demonstration at Eccles held in 1885 during the wakes week to celebrate the passage of the Ship Canal Act, it was reported that "several people had placed effigies in elevated positions in front of their houses, dressed after the fashion of the navvies. One of these was seated near a table, on which were a big loaf of bread, a jug, and a glass containing ale."[93] The event was the occasion for a "Roasting of the Ox" in the street, and distribution of 400 portions with free bread for the lucky ticket holders.[94]

Sugar appeared in a more unusual form – it was sent in carefully wrapped parcels on the day of the Canal's opening by Salford's Liberal Mayor both to his Tory counterpart in Manchester, Anthony Marshall, and to Leader Williams, the

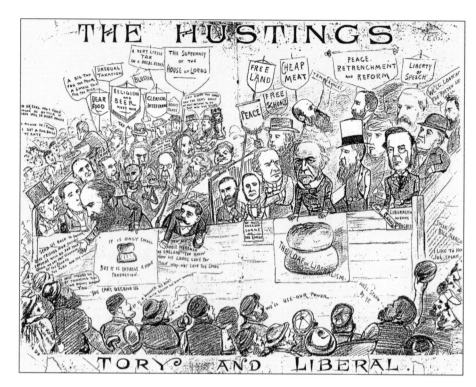

THE HUSTINGS

TORY AND LIBERAL.

Liberal poster used in the 1885 East Manchester election. Note Balfour leaning over the railings on the right and the large "Loaf of Liberalism" compared to the Tories' small one. *MCL*

Canal's engineer.[95] The ideas associated with Free Trade appeared in other media too. Cartoons and picture books were sold showing dark-skinned merchants sailing up the Canal to Manchester, and poems were written on a similar theme, celebrating mutual interests and the brotherhood of man:

> You'll see great ships from distant climes,
>   And men of every hue,
> Lay earth's vast bounties at your feet
>   And take your goods in lieu:
> Then trade will flourish all around,[96]

Drawing of members of the Bakers trade union with their Big Loaf at the Ship Canal demonstration in 1885.   *MCL*

went the lines of a poem written in 1882, and Edwin Waugh the dialect poet contributed the following at Leader Williams' request:

> The whole wide world is man's exchange,
> His market and his store…
> Let it float in free, from the open sea;
> Kind brotherhood shall win;
> And the good old town shall smile again
> When the ships come sailing in![97]

The close linking up of the Ship Canal with Free Trade did not go unnoticed by non-Liberals as can be seen in the opening verses of a song "The Ship Canal Navvy", which appeared in the Tory *Manchester Courier* of 6th January 1894, only days after the Canal's opening:

> I am a Ship Canal Navvy quite fresh from my job,
> which I've finished in style like an Eastern Nabob;
> And the flags of all nations you shortly will see
> Flying proudly as emblems of trade which is free.
> One-sided Free-trade does not seem a good thing
> And the time has arrived for good Balfour to bring
> A reform in our tariffs to set us quite square
> Upon a new basis that's equal and fair.

They help to explain why Balfour, first elected MP for East Manchester in 1885 and a senior figure in the Conservative Government, at no time gave any support to the Ship Canal movement. For its Free Trade imagery and arguments, reflected in the promoters' literature, and in particular in some of the handbills, would have caused him considerable

54

embarrassment in the Fair Trade atmosphere of his party. Few of these handbills have remained, but one published probably in 1882 or 1883 shows the lines clearly, referring to the railway and dock rates on goods conveyed through Liverpool as an "enormous tax" and "these protective duties". "The effect of the removal of these taxes" it continues, would be instantly seen in the "cheaper article", the "increased demand", the "development of trade." The conclusion is that a Canal is required so that "goods may be conveyed inward and outward without the imposition of artificial tariffs, which are … destructive of freedom of trade."[98]

The handbill is interesting for the way it has borrowed so freely from the Free Traders' critique of Protectionism, but it also illustrates one of the major arguments put forward in justification of the Ship Canal Scheme – that it was the exorbitant duties charged by the railways and by the Mersey Docks and Harbour Board which were crippling Manchester's trade.[99] There is no doubt that the perception of Liverpool as a parasitic partner in Lancashire's trade was a factor in the development of the Canal, and was made great play of at meetings and demonstrations, as is shown in the handbill for a meeting at Patricroft in 1885:[100]

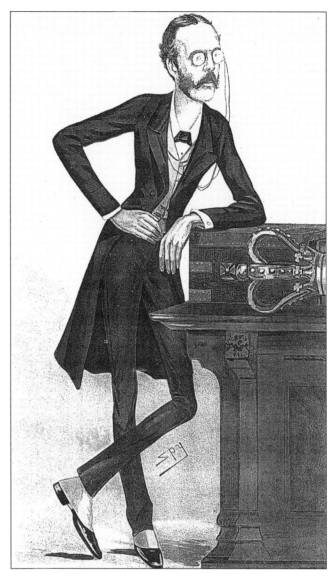

1887 Cartoon of Balfour, MP for East Manchester. He never provided any public support for the Ship Canal.   *MCL*

# SHIP CANAL

## PROSPERITY OR ADVERSITY ?

### WORKING MEN !

If you wish the former, shew the same by your presence at

### ✢ THE ✢ MEETING ✢

## On TUESDAY EVENING Next,

### JUNE 2, 1885,

# IN THE PUBLIC HALL,

### PATRICROFT.

If you intend being content with the latter, which means

### Mills Stopped, Short Time, Low Wages,

In consequence of the

### Liverpool "Toll-Bar !"

Remain Silent, while LIVERPOOL PEOPLE clamour for a continuance of their Monopoly.

Chair to be taken at Eight o'clock.

Be there in time, and support the Resolutions.

Printed at the Advertiser Office, Eccles.

This strategy conveniently brought the advantage of an implied mutuality of interest between Manchester's manufacturing capital and labour against a common enemy – the Liverpool monopolists and the "Railway Kings". However the evidence suggests that excessive transport costs were not a significant factor in explaining the depressed trade and the changes taking place in Manchester's economy – a point given force by the fact that mercantile capital in the city was on the whole unwilling to invest in the Ship Canal. In an interesting essay on "Intercity Development and Dependency", which supports this line of argument, Sharpless has explored the different relationships of ports to their hinterlands and suggests that Manchester and Liverpool, two major cities of a roughly similar size, can be viewed as examples of a "coupled nuclei'. In this less common model of development he argues "competing elite structures can form with distinctive cultural proclivities and political allegiances". Throughout the nineteenth century Manchester complained of its subservience to Liverpool, and was particularly resentful that out of the dock dues an annual payment of about £120,000 (called "Town Dues") was paid to Liverpool Corporation.[101] Yet Manchester's growth rate (taken with Salford's) was roughly the same as Liverpool's; and Sharpless concludes from an analysis of shifts in occupational structure in the two cities in the mid-nineteenth century that for this period at least the case for Manchester's subordination cannot be sustained.[102]

The opposition of Liverpool's mercantile and shipping interests to the Ship Canal agitation was part, therefore, of a longer-term animosity. In order to substantiate the argument about excessive transport charges this opposition was made much of by many of the Ship Canal campaigners, as was that of the railway companies – who were alleged to be behind any criticism of the Ship Canal. Undoubtedly railway rates in Britain were higher than in other countries because of the high capital burden built up over the previous half century. This meant, as the Secretary of the British Iron Trade Association noted in 1886, that in order to provide an acceptable dividend to shareholders British railway companies needed to seek an average income of £1,968 per mile, compared with an average of £608 in other European countries.[103] The resentment this fuelled among manufacturing and mining interests was a spur to both Liberal and

Tory Governments and resulted eventually in the Railway and Canal Traffic Act of 1888, which gave to the Board of Trade substantial powers to determine new rates and prohibit preferential rates.[104] But despite the high capital costs of the Canal and the great difficulties of raising the initial capital this alternative route to reducing railway rates – a small part only of total manufacturing costs – was never explored by the Ship Canal enthusiasts. In view of the incessant emphasis given to transport costs, it is only surprising that more doubting voices were not raised like that of the journal *Fairplay* (5th October 1888):

Have the millions already thrown away in this enterprise been judiciously expended in such a form? Could not the promoters have combined to fight the railways legally on the ground of their own "Acts" as interpreted by common sense?

This however was confusing rhetoric with reality. The key for understanding the economic imperatives behind the project does not lie in transport costs – a point endorsed by Joseph Lawrence, the Campaign organizer from the outset.[105]

It has already been indicated that the Scheme was seen by industrial capital in Manchester and elsewhere as providing a major boost to exports; but support for the Canal did not only come from this source. Manchester itself was already more a commercial than a manufacturing centre, and embraced a range of occupations related both to this activity,

UNLOADING COTTON FROM GALVESTON

Drawing of 1905 showing the unloading of cotton in Manchester Docks. *Chetham's*

56

Part of the large timber yards, which were successfully developed at the Docks.    *MSCC*

and to its growing role as a focus of distribution. A ship canal, as a major new investment, would substantially strengthen these regional functions, and as a result the project received important support from these sectors as well. The Cooperative Wholesale Society, involved in industries where processing and a break-in-bulk was required, was a good institutional example of this, and enthusiastically committed £10,000 to the Scheme. There was backing too from the timber trade,[106] from urban professionals like estate agents and lawyers[107] and from shopkeepers.[108]

We may conclude by saying that the enthusiasm with which the Ship Canal Scheme was adopted can be related to some extent to the reluctance on the part of employers and workers in Lancashire to adopt more modern technology at the point of production; and with its very public emphasis on distribution costs and Free Trade principles, the Canal may in some respects be regarded as a project more geared to outdated shibboleths than anticipating the economic needs of the future. The limitation of such a view, however, is that it overlooks both the massive investment entailed – which will be examined in Chapter 6 – and the fact that from the start there were supporters, who expressed the clear view

that the Scheme would be bringing new industries and new jobs to an area undergoing substantial structural change.[109] The vision they were offering was of a modern Manchester, in the vanguard of change and ready for the twentieth century. If private enterprise was unable or unwilling to find all of the costs they were quite prepared to argue for new forms of State intervention to achieve their objective. In this sense therefore we can answer to the question posed at the start of the chapter that the Ship Canal did on balance represent a novel and dynamic public response to problems associated with industrial change. Although both employers and workers may be criticised for their unwillingness *at the workplace* to tackle issues of restructuring and job demarcation, their enthusiasm for this collective vision for restructuring – as shall be seen in the concluding chapter – was to be entirely vindicated since the Canal and the adjoining Trafford Park industrial estate were to play a major role in encouraging diversification and bringing new jobs. This feature was of great importance and promoted a widespread belief, especially among the working classes, that the construction of the Canal would bring prosperity.[110] Their response and that of the trade unions to the promotion of the Ship Canal will be explored in the next chapter.

Early cartoon at the start of the campaign in November 1882.    *MCL*

## Notes

1.  Deputation to A. J. Mundella, President of the Board of Trade concerning the Manchester Ship Canal Bill to allow payment of interest on capital during construction, 2 February 1886, Manchester Central Library, Ref. F386 M8.

2.  See, for example, M. Wiener, *English Culture and the Decline of the Industrial Spirit*, 1981; B. Elbaum and W. Lazonick (eds.), *The Decline of the British Economy*, 1986.

3.  L. C. A. Knowles, *The Industrial and Commercial Revolutions in Great Britain during the Nineteenth Century*, 1921, p. 139.

4.  W. Ashworth, *An Economic History of England 1870–1939*, 1960, p. 118, Table VII.

5.  W. Ashworth. *ibid.*, p. 117.

6.  D. H. Aldcroft (ed.), *The Development of British Industry and Foreign Competition, 1875–1911*, 1968, pp. 17–19.

7.  Census of Population, 1881. See *Irish University Press Parliamentary Papers*, Vol. 20, explanatory introduction, p. 57. Of the total in the two counties, 432,146 workers were stated as being resident in Lancashire, and 28,485 in

Cheshire. This figure does not tally exactly with the number of 463,913 workers listed in the Census Tables for the North-West. There is no obvious explanation for this inconsistency. The latter figure has been used in the rest of the chapter.

8.  T. Ellison, *The Cotton Trade of Great Britain*, 1887, p. 100 (new edition 1968).

9.  L. G. Sandberg, *Lancashire in Decline*, 1974, pp. 145–6.

10. Royal Commission on Depression of Trade and Industry, 3rd Report. Evidence of J. C. Lee, 10 March 1886, Question 8244.

11. *Ship Canal Gazette*, 8 August 1883, p.175.

12. *Autobiography of a Manchester Cotton Manufacturer, or Thirty years' experience of Manchester*, by H.S.G., 1887, pp. 210–213.

13. A. W. Fletcher, "The Economic Results of the Ship Canal on Manchester and the Surrounding District", in *Transactions of Manchester Statistical Society*, 1896–7, p. 8. See also *Ship Canal Gazette*, 13 December 1882, where B. Gordon states that seventeen large works had closed in Ancoats in the previous five years.

14. John Rylands & Sons was a household name in Lancashire and became established as a limited liability company with a paid up capital of £1.5 million as early as 1874. By 1888 the company employed 12,000 workers and controlled seventeen mills and factories in Manchester and the surrounding towns. It had maintained a 5% dividend over the previous decade and in the 1890s had an average dividend of 10%, figures which were consistently much higher than the average in the industry.

15. W. H. G. Armytage, *A. J. Mundella 1825–1897. The Liberal Background to the Labour Movement*, 1951, p. 242. At the Social Science Congress in 1884 six major firms were reported to be leaving the Black Country and relocating in coastal areas for this reason.

16. *Ship Canal Gazette*, 18 November 1882, p.1. See also *Facts and Figures in favour of the Proposed Manchester Ship Canal*, by Mancuniensis, 1882 (revised edition), p. 8. Manchester Central Library, Ref. 386 M 18.

17. S. Pollard, *A History of Labour in Sheffield*, 1959, p.161.

18. W. Astle (ed.), *The History of Stockport*, 1922, p. 145. The following year Heywoods built their Hanover Mills, and in 1870 the Reddish Spinning Mills were erected by a consortium involving the Houldsworth family. Another substantial new cotton mill was opened by Houldsworths on their Reddish site in 1872.

19. Of all 47 Urban Sanitary Districts in England and Wales listed in the Census with populations over 50,000, only Bath showed a decline of population in this period and then only a drop from 52,000 to 51,800. Since the population of Bath had hovered around the 50,000 figure since 1821, it is scarcely comparable with an industrial centre like Manchester.

20. Census of Population 1881, *op.cit.*, explanatory introduction, p. 43. Because "retired" members of an occupational group had been included in that category in 1871, the 1881 Census compilers reduced the 1871 figure by 2% to obtain what they considered a more accurate comparison. Figures used here from the 1871 Census have all been corrected in this way.

21. In a speech in Manchester Town Hall in June 1885 on Conditions and Prospects of Trade, G. J. Goschen M.P. provided statistics for the cotton trade to show that even in the period of "depressed" trade between 1879 and 1883, the total number of cotton factories had increased from 2674 to 2841, and the numbers employed in the trade had increased from 483,000 to 513,000. See Bolton Operative Cotton Spinners Association, Annual Report 1885, p. 49. John Rylands University Library, Manchester. The growth of employment in North Lancashire in places like Blackburn was an expansion primarily in the weaving side of the industry which had experienced lower productivity growth in the previous 30 years than in spinning and needed, therefore, a corresponding increase in workers. The problem of high transport costs did not prevent expansion either here or in spinning areas in South Lancashire like Bolton and later Bury. For further discussion of these questions see M. Jewkes, "The Localization of the Cotton Industry", in *Economic History*, January 1930.

22. B. Leech, *Transcript of Evidence 1885*, Manchester Central Library, Ref. F386 M67.

23. *The Life of Sir William Fairbairn* (with an introduction by A. E. Musson), first published in 1877, pp. XX, 332. A comparable example from the North East was Hawks Crawshay of Gateshead, the oldest major engineering firm in the country, employing 1500 workers in 1863. The company went out of business in 1899 despite its easy access to the improved River Tyne through a failure to modernize and specialize. See S. B. Saul, "The Engineering Industry", p. 187, in D. H. Aldcroft (ed.), *op.cit.*

24. Another dubious example is given by Leech (Volume 1, p. 153) where he reports Adamson as having shown before a Parliamentary Committee in 1883 that companies like the well-known engineering firm of Sharp, Stewart & Co. and others "had been driven out of the city" to places where cheap rates of water carriage were available. In fact the firm moved from Manchester to Glasgow in 1887! Transport costs may have been one consideration, but more important was the fact that the lease of the premises in Manchester had expired, and a site had become available in Glasgow on the collapse of the Clyde Locomotive Works. See S. B. Saul, p. 197, in D. H. Aldcroft (ed.), *op.cit.*

25. Facts and Figures in favour of the proposed Manchester Ship Canal. *op.cit.*, p.6.

26. A. Simon, *The Simon Engineering Group*, 1953, p. 2; B. H. Tripp, *Renold Limited, 1956–67*, 1969.

27. S. B. Saul, *op.cit.*, p. 191. See also S. B. Saul, "The Market and the Development of the Mechanical Engineering Industries in Britain, 1860–1911", in *Economic History Review*, Vol. XX, 1, 1967. A substantial part of the detail on Manchester's engineering industry in this section is drawn from Saul's work.

28. D. A. Farnie, in *Dictionary of Business Biography*, Volume 4, 1985, p. 730.

29. *Manchester Today*, 1888, pp. 145–6. John Hetherington & Sons specialised in cotton spinning machinery and in machine tools. They were the first British company to manufacture a cotton-combing machine and by 1888 employed 1200 workers at their Vulcan Works. Curtis and Sons had the reputation for producing the finest self acting mule available, and were taken over by Hetherington in

1892. By 1895 the enlarged company was employing 3500 workers, with a further 1500 engaged on put out work.

30. *Manchester Guardian*, 9 November 1886, p. 5. This episode in the Canal's history is discussed in a later Chapter. Curtis died in 1887 during his year of office.

31. See List of Directors, Consultative Committee and Principal Shareholders (1887). Manchester Central Library Ref. F86 M85. Samuel Platt and his brother James each had a £10,000 shareholding and controlled a further £26,000 shareholding registered in the name of Platt Bros and Co. John Rylands had a shareholding of £50,000 and died in 1888 with an estate valued for probate at £ 2.575 million.

32. S. B. Saul, *op.cit.*, 1968, p. 200.

33. A. D. Provand, *The Manchester Ship Canal Scheme. A criticism*, 1883, p. 11. Provand was a Manchester merchant, and later became Liberal MP for Glasgow.

34. S. B. Saul, *op.cit.*, 1968, p. 198.

35. S. B. Saul, *op.cit.*, 1967, p. 121.

36. S. B. Saul, *op.cit.*, 1968, pp. 205–9.

37. S. B. Saul, *op.cit.*, 1965, p. 216.

38. See statement by James Mawdsley, General Secretary of the Operative Cotton Spinners to the Royal Commission on the Depression of Trade and Industry (2nd Report), 1886, Questions 5049–50. Mawdsley stated that 6% of his members were unemployed, a figure much higher than ten years previously. A fuller discussion of the impact of unemployment on the trades union is contained in the next chapter.

39. G. Sandberg, *op.cit.*, p. 105, Table 15. The norm for a company in these years was to make very small profits, and in the years 1892 and 1893 losses of £957 and £611. By contrast a large vertically integrated firm like John Rylands could achieve an average dividend of 10% in the same period.

40. See R. Robson, *op.cit.*, p. 155; and H. W. Macrosty, *The Trust Movement in British Industry*, 1907. The Winterbottom amalgamation in the specialist field of book cloth manufacture provided a pattern for later combines. Centred on Manchester it brought together nine separate companies including two in the South East, one in Germany and one in the United States for a total purchase price of £1.27 million. The Winterbottom family fared well from the arrangements with both the brothers William Dickson and George Harald amassing fortunes of over £1 million by the time they died, respectively in 1924 and 1934.

41. *The Fine Spinners' and Doublers' Association Ltd*, 1909, pp. 19–20. See also A. Plummer, *International Combines in Modern Industry*, 1938, pp. 60–61 for some discussion about non-interference agreements between Coats and English Sewing Cotton Co., a Manchester based combine of fourteen businesses.

42. Quoted in E. Williams, *British Historians and the West Indies*, 1966, p.155.

43. J. C. Fielden, *On the Employment of Surplus Labour, more especially during Periods of Commercial Depression*, 26 April 1882, paper read to Manchester Statistical Society. Fielden was according to one commentator, "the most powerfully intellectual force either as a debater or as a Parliamentary witness, throughout the three campaigns". *Umpire*, 2 October 1887.

44. *Ship Canal Gazette*, 18 November 1882, Special Supplement, p. 1. Slagg was chided by Leech for being "halfhearted" in his support because, under cross-examination before a Parliamentary Committee in 1883, he had indicated that he had not personally contributed to the preliminary fund, and was not sanguine of success (Leech, Vol. 1, p. 155).

45. *Manchester Guardian*, 7 November 1885, p. 5.

46. *Manchester Guardian*, 13 November 1885, p. 6.

47. E. J. Hobsbawn, *Industry and Empire*, 1968, p.239.

48. T. Ellison, *op.cit.*, p. 313. Ellison's arguments were based on statistics collated up to the end of 1884.

49. J. Slagg, "The Cotton Trade and Industry", in T. H. Ward (ed.), *The Reign of Queen Victoria*, 1887, p. 193. Slagg was seen as an authority on the cotton trade with India.

50. *Manchester Guardian*, 19 November 1885, p. 6.

51. *Manchester Faces and Places*, 1894. Lee was also a member of the Trade and Treaties Committee of the Board of Trade, and received a knighthood in 1882 for his work on the Anglo–French Treaty.

52. Lee appears to have been the main figure behind the organization of the Fourth International Congress on Inland Navigation held in Manchester in July 1890. His Visitors' Book reveals that he had written to many establishment figures including the Prince of Wales and A. J. Balfour inviting them to be Vice-Presidents of the Conference (see Manchester Central Library Archives Ref. M243).

53. *Manchester Evening News*, 9 August 1884, p. 2.

54. *Manchester Guardian*, 15 September 1887, p. 5. The speech was widely discussed because of its apparent shift towards Protectionism. The *Times*, 15 September, condemned it for its "denunciation of the Free Trade policy of this country".

55. B. Elbaum and W. Lazonick (eds.), *The Decline of the British Economy*, 1986.

56. But see G. R. Saxonhouse, and G. Wright, in *Economic History Review*, XXXVII (4), 1984, pp. 515–7, who question the extent to which wooden bobbins were a constraint by showing in the period 1890–1914 that Platt Bros, and Dobson and Barlow produced ring spinning machines with paper tubes, but only about 4% were sold to British firms.

57. W. Lazonick, in B. Elbaum and W. Lazonick, eds. *op.cit.* pp. 21–24; R. E. Tyson, *op.cit.*, pp. 121–122; W. Lazonick, in *Cambridge Journal of Economics*, 1979, 3, p. 231. In the weaving side of the industry there was a similar failure to adopt the automatic loom. By 1909 200,000 Northrop looms were in operation in the United States and only 8,000 in Britain.

58. R. Robson, *op.cit.*, p. 355. A detailed analysis by Saxonhouse and Wright, *op.cit.*, pp. 508–510 of the sales of the six major English firms manufacturing spindles shows that in the period 1878–1890 only 6% of spinning machines purchased by English firms were ring spindles.

59. W. Lazonick, *op.cit.*, 1979, p. 249.

60. Compare for instance the explanation of a United States locomotive manufacturer for his penetration of European markets. "Our success in coming into this field is very largely due to the making of 'standards'. We believe we know how to make a type of engine which will give the maximum efficiency … We develop our standard type and then we stick

to it … the American public has been taught that a builder of engines knows better how to design an engine than does the individual who only occasionally buys one". Quoted in F. A. Vanderlip, *The American "Commercial Invasion" of Europe*, 1902, p. 30 (new edition, 1976).

61. S. B. Saul, *op. cit.*, 1967, p. 114.

62. The construction work for the Manchester Ship Canal was regarded at the time as being highly innovative because of the extensive use made of Ruston and Proctor's "Steam Navvy" for speeding the process of excavation. For a description see J. Samuelson, *The Displacement of General Labourers by Machinery*, 1893, in M. Berg (ed.), *Technology and Toil in Nineteenth Century Britain*, 1979, p. 213. But as Raphael Samuel has pointed out (*History Workshop Journal* (3), 1977, p. 48), the steam navvy had been patented in America in 1841, and was extensively used there from an early date.

63. A. Bullen, in A. Fowler and T. Wyke (eds.), *The Barefoot Aristocrats*, 1981, p. 76.

64. See for instance evidence given by James Mawdsley to the Royal Commission on the Depression of Trade and Industry, *op. cit.*, 1886, Question 5077. Mawdsley considered that over the previous 20 years there had been a speed up of machinery by 12–15%, and an increase of 15% in the size of machinery managed by a team of spinner, piecer and creeler.

65. The Suez Canal had been completed in 1875, and on the strength of its success, its promoter, Ferdinand de Lesseps, had formed a Company to build the far more ambitious Panama Canal. Construction work began in 1881 but the company collapsed in 1889 with de Lesseps bankrupted and in disgrace.

66. See pamphlet *Visit of Members of the Provisional Committee and other Supporters to the Tees and Tyne*, October 1883, p. 11, Manchester Central Library. Ref f.386. M8. The Tyne Improvement Commission was formed in 1850 and was reported to have spent £5–£6 million on the improvement of a river less than a third of the length of the Ship Canal. This fact alone should have led to far more serious questioning of the original £5–£6 million estimate for the Ship Canal construction.

67. See J. Bird, *The Major Seaports of the United Kingdom*, 1963, pp. 76–97, for a chronology and account of the development of Clydeside. The canalized Clyde from Glasgow Bridge to Bowling was only 11 miles in length, where it became the Clyde Estuary; and as early as 1821 the Dumback Shoal, 13 miles below Glasgow Bridge, had been dredged to give a low-water depth of 17 feet. Again therefore comparisons with Manchester's situation were hard to justify.

68. E. J. Hobsbawm, *Industry and Empire, op. cit.*, p. 239.

69. Letter from John Bright, 2 September 1881 in H. J. Leech (ed.), *The Public letters of John Bright*, 1895, p. 56.

70. B. Leech, *op. cit.*, Volume 1, p. 74.

71. *Times*, 26 October 1881.

72. B. H. Brown, *The Tariff Reform Movement in Great Britain 1881–1895*, 1943, pp. 17–18, 32–36. The response of the TUC leaders to this episode is explored in the following chapter.

73. Evidence of J. Mawdsley to the Royal Commission (1886), *op. cit.*, (Questions 5160–5162). In answer to a further question, Mawdsley did not, however, think these same workers would support a duty on produce, because of the effect on food prices.

74. *Manchester Guardian*, 23 February 1884, p. 9. In the letter Waddington, a member of the SDF, was suggesting the need to find out just how extensive unemployment was, and wrote "I ask working men to investigate and say whether Free Trade has benefitted us". His own answer to the question was quite apparent.

75. For a discussion of the nature and significance of the British Government's foreign policy and the extent to which it was based upon the pursuit of British economic interests, see articles in a long-running debate in the *Economic History Review* started off by J. Gallagher and R. Robinson, "The Imperialism of Free Trade". *E.H.R.*, VI, (1953). Contributions have included D. C. M. Platt, *E.H.R.*, XXI, 2, (1968); W. M. Matthew, *E.H.R.*, XXI, 3, (1968), examining the case of Peru; A. G. Hopkins, *E.H.R.*, XXI, 3, (1966) examining the case of West Africa.

76. P. Hanretty, *Imperialism and Free Trade in Lancashire and India in the mid-nineteenth century*; D. C. M. Platt, *op. cit.*, 1968, p. 296 is forced to explain away the British State's interventionist policies in India as a special case.

77. See R. Sau, *Unequal Exchange. Imperialism and Under-development*, 1978, pp. 39–40. Sau points out that by 1881 India had 10,000 miles of railways and by the mid-1890s 20,000 miles, and comments "India, perhaps the poorest country in the world, was then in competition with the richest, in railway mileage". This policy of course not only opened up new markets, but also made possible a colonial commercialization of agriculture to meet Britain's raw material needs.

78. The experience of India had etched a powerful image on the minds of Manchester men. Significantly many people believed that one of the most influential men to join the Ship Canal movement was J. K. Bythell, who later became the first paid chairman of the Ship Canal Company. Bythell's appeal was as an East-India merchant who had been prominent in Bombay for 20 years. He had been instrumental in establishing there a Port Trust, with substantial merchant capital representation, which removed control of the harbour and docks from the hands of the Public Works Department, *Ship Canal News*, April 1890. He was, moreover, a strenuous advocate of railway extension in India. See J. K. Bythell, "Railways in India. Their Advantages and the Necessity for their Extension. A Defence of the Government of India's policy of Pledging the Credit of India for the Construction of Railways and other Public Works", in *The Journal of the Manchester Geographical Society*, 1887, pp. 27–41.

79. *Manchester Guardian*, 20 November 1885. Peacock, the Liberal candidate, was elected MP for the Gorton Division of Lancashire.

80. Bailey, an engineering manufacturer and Liberal was a staunch supporter of the Canal, and a director of the Canal Company. He held in 1887 £10,000 worth of shares in the Company, and in 1894 it was reported in different newspapers that he had a shareholding of £40,000 to £50,000.

81. *Manchester Guardian*, 4 May 1894, p. 8. Roseberry himself played a significant role in promoting the idea of the Empire. For a discussion of this, and the association of Liberal-Imperialism with Free Trade, see B. Semel, *Imperialism and Social Reform*, 1960, pp. 57–64.

82. J. Slagg, *op. cit.*, 1887, pp. 181–2. A first step had been taken in 1878 when duties were removed from a limited range of goods. There was strong opposition to this policy from Indian cotton interests.

83. Quoted in R. J. Moore, *Liberalism and Indian Politics. 1872–1922*, 1966, p. 70.

84. R. J. Moore, *ibid.*, p. 71.

85. J. Slagg, *Free Trade and Tariffs*, a speech on 20 July 1881, 15pp. (Tract issued by the National Reform Union).

86. From a list of 24 instructions included in an article published in Umpire, 18 September 1887.

87. *Manchester Courier*, 19 October 1885. Balfour decisively defeated the Liberal candidate as did four other Tory candidates in Manchester. Only one out of six Manchester seats was won by a Liberal in the 1885 election.

88. *Manchester Courier*, 20 October 1885. A year later at a meeting of the Manchester Chamber of Commerce, Houldsworth spoke strongly in favour of a Fair Trade motion, which was only narrowly lost. See *Guardian*, 2 November 1886.

89. *Manchester Guardian*, 20 October 1885. Joseph Leigh was a large cotton manufacturer in Stockport, employing 1500 workers. He was Daniel Adamson's son-in-law, and was later knighted for his part in the Ship Canal.

90. *Manchester Guardian*, 24 November 1885.

91. *Patricroft and Eccles Journal*, 12 June 1885, p. 8. See also comments by Alderman Walmsley about Protection and Free Trade, at the Great Meeting in the Free Trade Hall, October 1883. Manchester Central Library, Ref. f.386 M8, p. 29.

92. *Manchester Guardian*, 25 November 1885, p. 6, for details of such a display in one of the Liberal committee rooms to attract passers-by.

93. *Salford Reporter*, 31 August 1885. It was estimated that over 150,000 people were present at the Demonstration.

94. *Ship Canal Pamphlets*, Manchester Central Library, Ref. 386 M80.

95. Letter (in private collection) from Mrs. L. Williams to Sir William Bailey, 6 January 1894. "Please accept our best thanks for the loaf of sugar you have so kindly sent us, indeed quite an historical loaf as it came upon the first day our great waterway was opened".

96. Republished in *Ship Canal News*, 12 May 1888.

97. B. Leech, *op. cit.*, Volume 1, pp. 331–2. The words are from Waugh's poem. "When the ships come sailing in!"

98. *The Manchester Ship Canal. Reasons Why it Should be Made*. Manchester Central Library, Ref. 386 118/4.

99. This has been in previously published accounts the dominant explanation for the construction of the Canal, based upon contemporary claims. See, for instance, "What the Canal can save to Local Industries" (Chapter 4) in the pamphlet *Description of Project now before Parliament*, 1884, pp. 22–35. Manchester Central Library, Ref.386 M85. The pamphlet claimed that the Canal would save nearly £1 million in carriage costs per annum, and quotes at length the evidence given before the Parliamentary Committees by many manufacturers. Based upon very inaccurate estimates of construction costs, and over optimistic projections of traffic volumes, the claims were to prove wildly misleading. There was resentment too about the freight rates charged by the Liverpool shipowners, and it has been suggested that the construction of the Canal was intended to break their power (See F. E. Hyde, *op. cit.*, p. 134).

100. Manchester Central Library, Ref 386 M80.

101. See F. E. Hyde, *Liverpool and the Mersey. The Development of a Port 1700–1970*, 1971, p. 89. Manchester supported the formation of the Mersey Docks and Harbour Board in 1858, when the Town Dues were capitalised at a cost of £1.5 million, and discontinued.

102. J. B. Sharpless, "Intercity Development and Dependency. Liverpool and Manchester", in J. D. Wirth and R. L. Jones (eds.) *Manchester and Sao Paulo, Problems of Urban Growth*, 1978, pp. 131–155.

103. W. H. G. Armytage, *A. J. Mundella 1825–1897. The Liberal Background to the Labour Movement*, 1951, p. 258.

104. *Ibid.*, pp. 259–265.

105. See Note 55 in Chapter 2. Lawrence argued that there was room for both the railways and the Ship Canal, and expressed considerable sympathy with the former, and their need to maintain rates.

106. *Manchester a Timber Port*, by "Timber", 1883, 15 pp. The statement in the pamphlet that "it may be taken as an indisputable fact that few trades will be influenced more by the Ship Canal than will the Foreign Timber Trade", was to prove well-founded.

107. In a paper read to the Manchester Statistical Society in May 1885 Mr Fred Scott gave figures in an appendix showing that solicitors in the city had increased from 193 to 523 in the period 1874–1885 (M.S.S. Papers, 1885, p. 165).

108. See for instance *Eccles and Patricroft Journal*, 5 June 1885, where a speaker stated at a meeting of working men and other traders that "today the retail trade is almost at a standstill, and the shopkeepers are sorely tried".

109. See speech by J. C. Fielden at the Mass Meeting in the Free Trade Hall in November 1882 (*Ship Canal Gazette*, 18 November 1882), and comments at a similar meeting a year later by Jacob Bright MP and J. A. Beith (Great Meeting in the Free Trade Hall, October 1883. Manchester Central Library Reference f.386 M8).

110. See for instance letter (in private collection) from J. S. Aldhouse to his sister Hannah, 6 March 1887. Aldhouse, after complaining of the depressed state in Barrow where he was an insurance agent, wrote "If I decide to return to Manchester, do you think you and Emma could agree to start a business together. If the Ship Canal is started, there is sure to be some trade in Manchester soon".

# 4

# TRADE UNIONS, THE UNEMPLOYED AND THE SHIP CANAL

I propose as a working man – a stonemason – to give one day's wages to enable the Executive Committee with their able chairman, Mr Daniel Adamson, to carry out any new scheme … and appeal to all working men to make a similar effort … Unity is strength, and this is what our energetic Committee require at the present time.

Letter from William Moseley, *Manchester Guardian*, 8 August 1884.

"Selection confers status. Omission implicitly, if not intentionally, diminishes", has argued a contributor to the recent debate on the range and scope of history within the school curriculum.[1] Trade unions and the representative organizations of the working classes have not commonly been viewed as the stuff of mainstream history and have been largely ignored by historians as a result of this process of selective perception. Nowhere has this been more true than in the case of the Ship Canal movement. Leech, for instance, in his assessment of where credit for the Canal's construction lay, stated that "the middle classes" were "the people who were faithful to the end" and "were willing to make any sacrifice to achieve success"[2] – and in this way perhaps won for it the title of the "People's Canal"; but his references to the trade unions were few indeed, for he viewed them primarily as instigators of strikes and obstacles to progress. There are only three paragraphs in his 680 page history devoted to the major demonstrations organized by the Trades Council and no acknowledgement is given to the central role played by the trades unions in mobilising mass working class support for the scheme.

The present chapter is therefore concerned with redressing this balance by documenting from contemporary material the extent and nature of working class and trade union involvement in the Ship Canal movement. Making this visible, however, is only the start of a wider aim of exploring more general issues about class and politics, about notions of justice and equality, about relations between capital and labour, and about the changing language employed to delineate these issues for public debate. The Ship Canal project represented a major and unprecedented collaborative enterprise between industrial capital and the organized male-dominated trade union and labour movement in the region, and for this reason requires substantial reassessment.

Moreover, it occurred at a moment of social and political fracture which laid the foundations for a fundamental restructuring of British politics. The twelve years from the inception of the movement to the Canal's opening on January 1st 1894 encompassed a period which commenced with the founding of the Social Democratic Federation in 1881, saw the decisive split in the Liberal Party with the withdrawal of Joseph Chamberlain and the Liberal Unionists in 1886, and ended with the formation of the Independent Labour Party in 1893.[3]

Underlying this political fracture was an economic crisis which in the years of the "Great Depression" from the mid 1870s onwards was severely threatening the competitive position of Britain in world markets, and was to topple her conclusively from her position of 'Workshop of the world'. Taken together the economic and political crises facing Britain required new solutions and new institutions to be found from a variety of formulations and theories which were available and being canvassed. The argument being advanced was that the Ship Canal scheme was one such formula; it was both a response of a regional industrial bourgeoisie to particular economic problems, and a bid for political and moral leadership at the expense of the previously dominant finance and merchant capital interests of the region's two major centres, Liverpool and Manchester. It was, of course, only one response, and was inevitably limited by the single issue focus of the project, but it was carried out on such a scale that it can tell us much about the process of social transformation and reconstruction which, as Hall and Schwarz have pointed out, accompanies each moment of crisis.[4] It is important, too, for constructing a more robust analysis of how the trade union movement, and particularly the old craft unions, adapted to structural and technological change and the challenge of the New Unionism commonly associated with the Dock Strike of 1889.

The Ship Canal movement was the outcome of a campaign of agitation, highly populist in form and content, which provided a convenient vehicle for developing a cross-class ideology of cooperation and mutuality of interest. Since strong backing was sought and received from key trade union officials, many of whom were members of the TUC's Parliamentary Committee, the movement has to be assessed in terms of how far it was seen or intended by the two collaborating parties – manufacturing capital and skilled labour – as a model of industrial relations and popular capitalism which could have a wider national applicability. Its emphasis on place and local patriotism required a regional implementation, but by no means excluded its export to other areas.

Two dangers are apparent here for the unwary. No simple cooperative and consensual model between capital and labour should be assumed from the Ship Canal agitation alone; it needs instead to be interpreted in the light of industrial relations in the region throughout the 1880s and 1890s – and in particular employers' widespread efforts to achieve an intensification of labour. In cotton, for instance, the period was characterised by substantial industrial conflict with major strikes in the weaving and spinning sectors in the mid 1880s and in the early 1890s, and these need examination in some detail. By the late-1880s it was painfully apparent that as a model for a profit-sharing form of capitalism, the Ship Canal Scheme had been a failure.

The second danger concerns that of periodisation and is obvious in any attempt to draw generalisations from the events of a short number of years. Emphasis will be placed therefore not only upon change, but also upon historical continuity by drawing parallels with the 1870s and with the Anti-Corn Law League agitation in the 1840s.

However the immediate context is in itself most significant because the advent of mass democracy required politicians to woo working class voters, and subjected traditional structures and the class relationships which sustained them to close scrutiny. The Social Democratic Federation did not succeed in winning over any substantial numbers of the working class, but the writings of Henry George and the socialist ideas of Hyndman and the SDF, which challenged the fairness of existing wealth distribution and promoted the notion of an interventionist state, created a new and dynamic climate to which non-socialists – whether trades unionists or employers – were forced to react as much in Manchester or Salford as anywhere else. The effect could be seen both in the vocabulary of politics and in the language of the workplace. Involved here are both issues about conflict and cooperation between capital and labour which Patrick Joyce and Richard Price have debated recently,[5] and questions of division and fracture. As employers sought to introduce new practices and new technology, accommodation to the perceived political strength of the best organized could, for instance, bring gains to skilled workers at the expense of women and the unemployed; equally new alliances forged in a general realignment of the social formation could quickly bring to the surface tensions and conflicts of interest between industrial and mercantile capital.

In order to start exploring the issues raised here, the chapter will concentrate on the organization and nature of the trade union response to the Ship Canal issue principally in Manchester, Salford and Oldham; the dilemmas associated with alliances and some earlier experience; the manner in which a populist campaign was organized by the promoters to draw in working class support; and finally the impact that the agitation over unemployment, particularly in 1886, had on the general political climate and on the outcome of the Ship Canal campaign. These will be treated in four separate subsections of the chapter. Once the enabling legislation had been passed and the construction of the Canal was finally commenced in 1887, the engagement of active trade union support became less important and Chapter 6 shifts to addressing the changing experience of workers in the principal industries from which trade union support for the Ship Canal was derived.

## Trade Unions: Their Organisation and Respectability

With hindsight it is possible to see that the early 1880s saw the beginning of a period in which fundamental changes would affect the trade union movement. Not only was the "new trade unionism" of the late 1880s to bring in the unskilled and semi-skilled, but it was also to alter significantly the attitudes and expectations in the old craft unions. In July 1882, with the Ship Canal's Provisional Committee just formed, the picture would have been far less clear to the leading members of the Manchester and Salford Trades Council as they assessed the significance and prospects of the new proposal in the context of their current concerns. As active Liberal supporters, aware of the political parties' interest in the votes of working men, they would have read with some amusement about the new Liberty and Property Defence League[6] – formed by J. W. Maclure, a leading Manchester Tory, together with Lord Elcho,[7] Sir Edward Watkin and others – and the prominence given in its aims to the protection of "the rights of labour against undue interference by the State". With the annual TUC Conference due to be held in Manchester in September, they would probably have been more concerned about the series of articles and letters appearing weekly in the *Labour Standard* on the respective merits of Fair Trade and Free Trade policies, since this was the controversy that had erupted amidst confusion at the 1881 TUC Conference and led to the expulsion of six *soi-disant* trade delegates, espousing protectionist policies, whose expenses had in reality been paid by the "sugar interests"[8].

On the political front there was the sense of the growing power of respectable trade unionism, as indicated by this account of a procession and festival of 2,000 engineers in Manchester's Albert Square:

A bystander remarked that he had seen a hundred trade processions, but never before had he beheld so many well-dressed workmen …the union leaders, including Mr. Austen, bowed their silvery heads from an open carriage as … they were hailed by friendly voices. The owners of the silvery heads looked uncommonly like the members of Parliament, which the great body of Amalgamated Engineers ought to be able to make them.[9]

There were in short a number of indicators of how the trade unions might seek to further their economic and political interests, but support for a Ship Canal movement would not seem on first appearance to be of the highest priority. Nonetheless the driving force for the trade unions' involvement in the campaign came from a number of key officials, mostly based in Manchester, who were also active members of the Trades Council. Why was this support given so wholeheartedly? None of the officials actually attended the inaugural meeting held at Daniel Adamson's mansion in June,[10] and it is likely that the initial interest in the scheme was aroused by means of the Cooperative movement, for J. T. W. Mitchell, Chairman of the Cooperative Wholesale Society, did attend the meeting and had close links with three leading members of the Trades Council – Jim Mawdsley, General Secretary of the Amalgamation of Operative Cotton Spinners' Association, Henry Slatter, General Secretary of the Typographical Association, and James Murchie, General Secretary of the Amalgamated Society of Carpenters and Joiners. All three were well-known cooperators, and spoke out strongly in support of Cooperation and the importance of links with trade unionism when motions on the subject were put at the TUC annual conferences in 1884, 1885 and 1886; Slatter had read a substantial paper on industrial and distributive cooperation at the 1876 Congress.[11] In stressing the importance of the Cooperative movement here it should not be overlooked that both Daniel Adamson and W. H. Bailey, a large engineering employer in Salford and strong Ship Canal supporter, were also members of the Manchester and Salford Cooperative Equitable Society.[12] These links being created with the Cooperative Movement would undoubtedly have aroused suspicions among small traders and shopkeepers.

The response from the Trades Council was not immediate, but one of the first signs of support for the scheme from labour quarters came in an article "Manchester as a Port" in the Labour *Standard*, probably written by George Howell.[13] The tone was enthusiastic:

It is a grand idea, and in these days of great engineering achievements, we prefer seeing some engineering achievements executed at home, where there is little risk, and where the cost thereof will be disbursed among, and expended by the working classes of our own country ...[14]

September was the month of the TUC's fifteenth annual Conference, which returned to Manchester. Predictably the Fair Trade issue again figured prominently in the debates, with G. D. Kelley particularly condemning the scurrilous attacks made on Broadhurst and Howell by the Protectionists ejected from the 1881 Conference. In this context the eager support evinced by trade unions for the Ship Canal, with its strong Free Trade connotations, starts to take on added significance, and certainly for the Canal promoters the venue and timing of the TUC Conference could not have been more auspicious – as events quickly showed.

1883 cartoon in *The City Lantern*, showing the working man being cheated at the Coop. The magazine was fiercely hostile to the Cooperative Movement because of its threat to small traders. *MCL*

Once the Conference was over the task of raising support began in earnest. The first evidence of this appears in two resolutions sent to the Provisional Committee in early October by Kelley, writing firstly as General Secretary of the Lithographic Printers and secondly as Secretary of the Trades Council. Both congratulated the members of the Provisional Committee on the initiative, the first noting that it would "tend to find extra employment for the working classes of the surrounding District", and the second urging "the working classes of the country to assist their efforts in every possible manner".[15]

The *Manchester Courier* was quick to pick up the general message, and noted in a leading article: "So far as the working class community is concerned, the scheme is evidently looked upon as one which, if carried out, cannot fail to materially forward their special interests", adding that a special committee of representatives of trade societies was planning – in conjunction with the Reception Committee established for the recent TUC Conference – a mass meeting of representatives from Manchester and the surrounding towns.[16]

The 25-strong Reception Committee had been formed in March when 200 trade union delegates under the auspices of the Manchester and Salford Trades Council had met with Henry Broadhurst to plan the Conference. It was composed of representatives from the Trades Councils of Manchester, Oldham, Hyde and Stalybridge, and most of Lancashire's leading trade union officials – including Robert Austin, Conference President and later to become General Secretary of the Amalgamated Society of Engineers, together with Kelley, Mawdsley, Murchie and Slatter.[17] A more representative trade union group would have been hard to assemble, and the capacity of the committee to use the networks to mobilise support rapidly was impressive.

In a crowded Free Trade Hall on Monday evening, 13th November, a mass meeting of "the working classes of Manchester, Salford and the neighbourhood",[18] presided over by Henry Slatter, gave rousing support to a series of motions in support of the Ship Canal. These were moved and seconded by the four other members of the Reception Committee listed above, and by two other leading trade unionists, Thomas Ashton, Secretary of the Oldham Spinners, and Peter Shorrocks, General Secretary of the Amalgamated Tailors' and a veteran of the first TUC Conference held in Manchester in 1868.[19]

Ashton's reported remarks perhaps best summed up the mood of the meeting. "They, as operatives, knew what they had to sacrifice in consequence of the depression of the trade, and it was coming to this, that employers and employed must meet one another upon this question, and endeavour to find out what would be the best remedy". They were met with applause.

It was a powerfully confident performance from men who were used to commanding attention regionally and in national newspapers at the annual TUC Conferences. They also had experience of working together on other issues over a number of years. Most of them, for instance, were members of the Society of Trade Union officials, a body based in

Manchester and established in 1875, which held an "annual meeting" whenever a general secretary of a trade union was visiting Manchester – a useful forum for discussion of areas of common interest.[20] Most recently four of them, Austin, Kelley, Mawdsley and Murchie, had been orchestrating a campaign through letters in the local press to get School Board elections moved to a Saturday to facilitate working class voting, and to get Slatter elected.[21]

On the day after the meeting Kelley sent a circular to all the local MPs with copies of the resolutions, urging support and explaining that the demonstration, organized by a special committee of 45 members chosen from over 300 delegates, was "the most enthusiastic and unanimous meeting of the kind ever known".[22] Eight years later, after successfully seeking election as a Liberal councillor in the city, he gave his own retrospective assessment of the meeting in an interview:

> The attitude of the Trades Council at the inception of the Ship Canal movement should not be forgotten. That movement all along had our cordial support, and the late Daniel Adamson admitted that the meeting which the Trades Council got up for the promoters at the Free Trade Hall – when it was packed as it had never been packed before – was the turning point in public favour in support of the movement ... Our Council took an active part in its initiatory stages, and a great number of our members are shareholders today.[23]

The evidence in support of this general view can be further seen in the events of the next few months, for discussion and motions about the Ship Canal became a regular feature of trade union branch and district meetings. In Oldham the Spinners and the Trades Council cooperated with Samuel Andrew, Secretary to the Master Cotton Spinners' Association in organizing and arranging speakers for a town meeting involving the Mayor and Town Clerk;[24] while the Spinners' Amalgamation quarterly meeting strongly recommended "every branch of the Association to assist the movement by every legitimate means".[25] Other Trades Councils were also drawn in to support the scheme, not only in the surrounding towns like Oldham and Rochdale, but also as far afield as Birmingham.[26] The results of this activity could be seen in a flood of supporting resolutions, many of which were recorded in the promoters' weekly Ship Canal Gazette (see Table 1 overleaf).

This rapid growth of trade union support for the Ship Canal Scheme was not spontaneous, although both the Trades Council leadership and the promoters were happy to leave that impression; it was carefully constructed, using model resolutions and particular lines of argument, and was given an additional boost by the promoters' own campaign already described. Knowing this, Murchie, at the Free Trade Hall meeting, could in his seconding of a motion of support confidently refer to the view that trades union officials "should not use their positions for the purpose of giving expression to opinions on debatable points", and then joke

Market Place in 1878, with the cathedral in the background. The Trades Council held its meetings in the Falstaff Hotel (facing on the right).  *Chetham's*

**Table 1  Resolutions of Support from Trade Union Branches for the Ship Canal Scheme, November 1882 – January 1883**

| Name of Trade Union | No. of Branch Resolutions |
|---|---|
| Amalgamated Carpenters and Joiners | 16 |
| Amalgamated Society of Engineers | 16 |
| Steam Engine Makers | 16 |
| Weavers and Power Loom Weavers | 14 |
| Cotton Spinners and Minders | 6 |
| Miners' Association (N. Yorkshire and Cleveland) | 5 |
| Typographical Association | 4 |
| Operative House Painters | 4 |
| General Union of Carpenters and Joiners | 3 |
| Ironfounders' Society | 3 |
| Boilermakers' and Ironshipbuilders Society | 2 |
| Others | 8 |
| TOTAL | 97 |

that only canal boatmen could have a vested interest to protect because of their trade being injured by the construction of a Ship Canal.[27] But the truth was more complicated. Interests were being served as Abraham Buckley, President of the Oldham Trades Council made clear when he stated that he was "almost daily asked whether the canal scheme would benefit the working people or would it be mostly beneficial to the capitalists".[28] His view was that both would benefit, but the suspicion of collusion with the promoters could not be brushed aside so easily, particularly with the memory of the protectionist "delegates" to the 1881 TUC being thrown out for receiving payment from "the sugar interests". Kelley was the prime target as he was the front man for the Trades Council and responsible for writing to MPs. He was therefore seen to be making it a political issue. He had also reported to a public conference in early December that a resolution from the Trades Union Committee had been sent to Henry Broadhurst MP, and Secretary to the TUC Parliamentary Committee, urging his full support for the scheme both within and without Parliament.[29] A blistering attack on Kelley came the following month from an article in the *Manchester Examiner and Times* which denounced the dubious practices and the extravagant claims of the promoters and stated that "the services of a trade union official were secured to conduct the correspondence and every MP ... was pelted with demands to subscribe ... What is to follow the refusal of such demands, urged through such a suggestive channel, is easily understood".[30]

Kelley's letter of response followed a few days later – under the signature of "The Trades' Union Official Alluded to" – in which he asserted that "my services were rendered gratuitously, and not paid for, as your article would lead many to imply ... (nor) do I expect any remuneration". His statement may well have been true, but there is clear

evidence from the Board minutes that subsequently he did receive in 1885 a payment or "gratuity" of £10 from the Ship Canal Company after helping to organize another large demonstration after the Ship Canal Bill had received Royal Assent.[31] The equivalent of about six or seven weeks' wages for a skilled worker this sum was no trifle, and the not infrequent references made at Ship Canal meetings to "paid spouters" suggest that the independence of all the Canal supporters was not taken for granted.

The hint of undue influence and direction by the promoters contaminated the message of free cooperation between capital and labour, and was damaging to the interests of both parties. Moreover, there can be little doubt that there were plenty of dirty tricks and dubious practices employed to whip up support. According to an article in the *Umpire* about the promoters' campaign, probably written by Frank Cornwall, "The dogma which reigned was 'the End justifies the means', and certainly the axiom was followed in all its possibly obnoxious details. No use to disguise here the facts".[32] Opposition to these methods even came from the Chamber of Commerce – whose needs were supposed to be met by the Ship Canal – where complaints were made by William Fogg that the promoters had sought support from the lowest classes encouraging "resolutions from nightsoilmen and balletgirls".[33]

With the trade unions, therefore, particularly in Manchester, there was a need to move in public with circumspection, but this did not prevent James E. Platt, a provisional director of the Ship Canal Company and a director of Platt Bros in Oldham, writing privately to Adamson the day after the Ship Canal Bill had been passed by the House of Lords:

I have been thinking over our great victory. I think something ought to be done now the *iron* is red hot in people's minds, in the way of a series of demonstrations. I shall see S. Andrew tomorrow and arrange for one in Oldham at once.[34]

In the event nothing appears to have been organized in Oldham, but a major demonstration did take place a month later on 21st June at the Pomona Gardens, which, according to the *Manchester Guardian*,[35] the working men of Manchester and District were asked through placards posted on the walls "to attend in their thousands". According to the pamphleteer Samuel Ramsbottom, the notices on the hoardings were under the names of certain MPs and councillors and "27 secretaries and representatives of various trades".[36] The effectiveness of the planning was obvious, for an estimated 50,000 to 80,000 people proceeded from Albert Square down to Salford to hear the speeches and pledge their support. They were "mainly employed artizans and heads of families" according to the circular letter from Kelley printed afterwards.[37] The *Guardian* noted that "a few women were present". Although this "Demonstration of all the Trades Union and Industrial Classes" was organized under the auspices of the

George Kelley, Secretary of the Trades Council who played a key role in winning working class support for the scheme. *MCL*

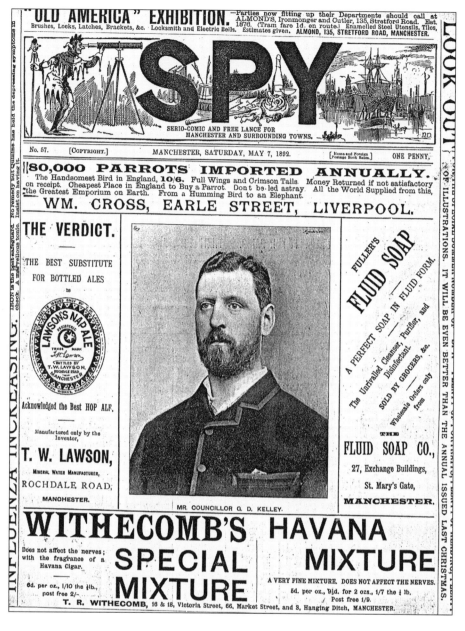

Trades Council with Kelley as Secretary to the Committee, and with Slatter and Shorrocks chairing respectively the main meeting and the overflow meeting in the Agricultural Hall, the element of cross class cooperation was made quite evident with the motion in favour of the scheme being put by Alderman J. Harwood from Manchester City Council and supported both by trade union and cooperative leaders and by Reuben Spencer, Managing Director of John Rylands and Sons.

Robert Austin supported this theme by urging his audience, and especially trades unionists, to take up shares in the scheme. Spencer's speech indicates that the idea for this mass "gathering of the industrial classes" had been proposed by "independent supporters" and via the ward committees some three months earlier, but had been felt then to be badly timed. Both Spencer and Slatter were at pains to stress that the organization of the demonstration was "in no way connected with the Provisional Committee", and that "not one penny of the expenses would be paid out of the funds subscribed for the Canal". A reasonable inference to be drawn, however, was that the costs of the demonstration were being paid, not by the trade unions, but by the wealthy manufacturing interests – represented by Spencer – which were backing the scheme.

What is clear from all this evidence is firstly the importance attached by the promoters to gaining a mass expression of working class support, and secondly the commitment given to the scheme by the local trade union movement and its leadership. There was in short a compact between manufacturing capital and the trade unions – set in motion

67

by the former – to seek ways together of finding a new solution to the problems associated with industrial restructuring and unemployment. There were arguments in favour of what was undoubtedly an imaginative and daring scheme, but equally there were risks for both sides in pursuing this course of action. Leech, in his account of this period, describes the sharp disagreements that existed amongst the members of the Provisional Committee with one section arguing for a change of policy "that would make friends, and draw rather than repel many of the influential people of the district whose help would be essential when capital had to be raised"; and notes the opposition to this of Adamson and Lawrence "who preferred the bolder policy of carrying the war into the opponents' camp, and taking the consequences, trusting to the public for support".[38]

For the trade unions and their leadership in particular the danger lay not so much in their association *per se* with the promoters – the Canal, if constructed, was bound to bring at the very least the short-term benefits of jobs – but in the prospect of the scheme's collapse or financial failure; they had done so much to encourage support for, and shareholdings in, the Ship Canal Company that their own standing and credit could be jeopardised with their membership.[39]

To explore the causes of this collaboration, and to explain its form, scale, and significance in terms of a changing class consciousness, it is necessary to look in greater detail at the organization of the trade unions, and the issues and concerns affecting them in the early and mid 1880s. At the start of the decade the trade union movement was facing an uncertain future. Unemployment for most skilled workers had hit a record level in 1879, with the Carpenters reporting 7% out of work, the Engineers 13%, and the Ironfounders and the Boilermakers 20%. Not all unions were affected to the same extent, but many of the smaller ones were forced out of existence. One indication of the impact of the years of depressed trade can be seen in the fortunes of the Trades Union Congress where, over the years 1874–1880, there was a substantial falling off of societies represented, and a consequent decline of members represented from over a million to under half a million.[40]

Estimates of the total numbers and density of trade union membership by industrial sector and geographical area are difficult to make because no official records were kept until the Board of Trade's Labour Department was set up in 1886 and produced its first – though far from complete – report the following year. The earliest estimate of the distribution

Navvies during the construction of the Canal.

A diver with support team in 1890 during the construction of the Canal.
*MSCC*

of trade unionists by county was undertaken by Sidney and Beatrice Webb for 1892, and although this is a decade later than the start of the Ship Canal movement, and therefore gives higher density figures, it provides a reasonably accurate picture of the comparative strength of trade unionism in the North West in the 1880s. The yardstick adopted by the Webbs – of trades unionists as a percentage of total population – shows Lancashire at 8.63%, compared to an average for England and Wales of 4.55%. Only the mining areas of Durham and Northumberland topped this figure with 11.2% but, in terms of numbers alone, Lancashire was head and shoulders above any other county with 331,500 ascertained trade unionists, or 25% of all trade unionists in England and Wales.

**Table 2   Trade Union Population in five highest unionised Counties, 1892**

| County | Number of Trade Unionists |
| --- | --- |
| Lancashire | 331,500 |
| London | 194,100 |
| Yorkshire | 180,000 |
| Durham | 114,800 |
| Northumberland | 56,800 |
| TOTAL ENGLAND AND WALES | 1,318,800 |

Source: S. and B. Webb, *The History of Trade Unionism*, Appendix 5, 1926 Edition

Lancashire and Manchester, as the principal city in the region, were at the centre of British trade unionism, and a substantial number of national unions were, for this reason, based in the city. They were a strategic target group for the promoters, and Table 3 indicates the total membership of the main trade unions which supported the Ship Canal movement and passed resolutions in favour.

Noticeably, only two of those listed, the Painters and the General Union of Carpenters & Joiners, experienced a drop in membership in the years 1871–1881. In the case of the latter it was because of a strike in 1877, which led to many members joining the Amalgamated Society. The others had grown in size, and successfully weathered the storm of the Depression. They were the best examples of the great centralized unions with sufficient resources and sector penetration to be able to mount effective resistance to employer domination; to be more than just friendly societies providing benefits for their members in accordance with strict rules of eligibility. In his first report as Labour Correspondent to the Board of Trade after resigning as General Secretary of the Engineers, John Burnett gave the Carpenters and Joiners (with 440 branches), the Engineers (with 432 branches) and the Steam Engine Makers (with 89 branches) as his first examples of what a strong union could achieve, and pointed out that all three were international in their scope with branches in the UK, USA, Canada, Australia, etc.[41]

These were the trade unions whose leaders in 1882 pledged their support for the Ship Canal, and worked tirelessly for the movement over the following years. Their positions gave them power and influence, but in seeking to explain why they threw their weight and the unions' resources into the campaign, account has to be taken of the pressures on them as leaders and accountable representatives – in their relationships not only with their members but also with the employers. The question of resources was indeed a key issue here because the widespread unemployment of 1879 had a

**Table 3  Membership of Eleven Trade Unions supporting the Ship Canal**

| Name of Union | Number of Members | | | General Secretary in 1882 |
|---|---|---|---|---|
| | 1871 | 1881 | 1890 | |
| Carpenters & Joiners | 9,764 | 18,765 | 30,693 | James Murchie |
| Engineers | 37,790 | 46,101 | 67,928 | John Burnett |
| Steam Engine Makers | 3,063 | 4,387 | 5,822 | James Swift |
| Weavers[1] | 13,000 | 37,539 | 46,102 | Thomas Birtwhistle |
| Amalg. Cotton Spinners | — | 11,719 | 18,145 | James Mawdsley |
| Typographical Assoc. | 2,687 | 5,362 | 9,016 | Henry Slatter |
| Carpenters & J. (G.U.) | 7,423 | 2,815 | 2,485 | Lindsay |
| Ironfounders | 10,019 | 11,201 | 14,821 | Edward Woods |
| Lithographic Printers | — | 951 | 2,235 | George Kelley |
| Tailors | 4,914 | 12,593 | 16,629 | Peter Shorrocks |
| Painters[2] | — | 2,505 | 3,047 | Thomas Sharples |

Notes
1.  The 1871 figure is the membership of the NE Lancashire Weavers, and this was replaced in 1884 by the larger Northern Counties Amalgamated Weavers. The figure in the 1881 column is actually the number of 1884.
2.  The figure for the Painters in Column 3 is for 1883, not 1881
    Source: Statistical Tables and Reports on Trade Unions

**Table 4  Financial Reserves of Eight Trade Unions supporting the Ship Canal**

| Name of Union | 1878 Reserve | 1879 Reserve | 1881 Reserve | Reserves per Member |
|---|---|---|---|---|
| Carpenters | 76,166 | 53,596 | 46,111 | £2.9.1 |
| Engineers | 251,675 | 141,116 | 145,957 | £3.3.3 |
| Steam Eng. Mkrs. | 13,939 | 8,761 | 8,771 | £2.0.0 |
| Cotton Spinners | 1,720 | 675 | 3,875 | £0.6.5 |
| Typographical Ass. | 4,216 | 4,295 | 6,982 | £1.6.0 |
| Lithographic Prtrs | — | 293 | 487 | £0.10.3 |
| Ironfounders | 38,895 | 1,909 | 9,945 | £0.17.9 |
| Painters | 15,909 | 13,809 | 16,483 | £1.6.2 |

Source: Statistical Tables and Reports on Trade Unions, 1887

devastating effect on the financial reserves of some unions (see Table 4). As Friendly Societies they were obliged to provide a number of benefits to their members in the event of sickness, accident, retirement, strikes, unemployment, etc, and to meet these obligations it was highly desirable to have substantial reserves and/or a large membership for levying income. Where these were lacking no union could afford precipitate industrial action for fear of sustaining a demoralising defeat.

At periods of high unemployment and when their organization was weak, there were therefore substantial reasons for full-time trade union officials and their executive committees, to seek ways of resolving conflicts with employers through negotiation, rather than through strike action, but this does not imply there was any necessary agreement about the underlying principles of political economy. Tactically it was better in certain situations to adopt consensual rather than confrontational approaches. This was not always popular with sections of the membership, and Davis notes that the Society of Trade Union officials, commonly called "the Peculiar People", which had been set up in Manchester had, as its chief object, "to protect an official who was unjustly dealt with by members of his society in consequence of using his influence to prevent strikes when a large minority was clamouring for extreme action".[42]

The ambivalent terrain occupied by trade union officials in this situation is well illustrated in the case of the spinners and two of their top officials, Thomas Ashton, Secretary of the Oldham Cotton Spinners, and James Mawdsley, Secretary of the Spinners' Amalgamation, who played a prominent role in trade union circles and with the Ship Canal. With the lowest reserves per member of the eight trade unions listed in Table 4, the spinners would have been in no position in 1882 to support any major strike action, but by 1885 with substantially stronger finances, under Ashton's and Mawdsley's leadership, they took on the Oldham employers in a three month strike when an attempt was made to impose a 10% wage cut. [43]

The letter books of Samuel Andrew, the Oldham employers' secretary, show the close working relationship he had both with Ashton – whom he met regularly in mill visits to sort out disputes, and with whom he had cooperated over the Ship Canal meetings in 1882 – and with Mawdsley. [44] Only a week before the mills closed on 24th July, Andrew was writing to Mawdsley disputing that it was a "lock-out", as the spinners described it; "I have no particular desire to have a paper war with you, but let things be known by their proper name … Let us call a strike a strike", and signing off "Yours with my usual kind regards". [45]

Mawdsley, however, had other worries, and under instructions from two Representative Meetings to accept no more than a 5% cut by way of compromise, he was busy marshalling his arguments and the union's resources for a prolonged struggle, in which he was to come under personal attack from employers in the town over his own role. In his letter to members he pointed out the enormous expenditure involved in keeping about 4,000 spinners supported, and the need for members to pay the weekly levy; then he issued a rallying call:

The men of Lancashire … have in the past proved themselves to be of sturdy metal. Almost every town has its record of strikes and lockouts, where the people without murmuring have withstood privations which, had they been undertaken in other causes would have, by historians, been termed heroic … The Oldham employers will on this occasion be taught a lesson they will not readily forget.[46]

Despite his later statement about the need to be able to "fight the employers to the bitterest of endings" but still "at its close, be able to shake hands with them knowing that neither side had forfeited that self-respect which constitutes the highest dignity of mankind", [47] Mawdsley, as the full-time official, was to be pilloried in an unsigned statement to the Manchester press suggesting that his encouragement of picketing was tantamount to "the revival of Broadheadism in Oldham".[48] Five months later he and other spinners' leaders were picked out for sweeping criticisms by James E. Platt, a Ship Canal director and one of Oldham's biggest employers, for misleading and unwise advice given to the workers on the question of accepting a further 5% of wage reduction. Platt's apparent ignorance that the advice given had, in fact, been to accept the 5% reduction caused no surprise, and brought only the resigned comment from the *Cotton Factory Times*

that defence should not be necessary for "the conduct of a class of men, who are, as a rule, wrongly condemned for the action of others".[49]

Concern about the union's finances was one strategic issue for trade union leaders in their initial collaboration with the Ship Canal promoters; another was the image of trade unionism with employers and the wider world. Self-respect and respectability were key notions in the lexicon of the old craft unions in the mid to late nineteenth century, and were commonly referred to and endorsed in discussion about the legitimacy and role of trade unionism. [50] When the miners in Wigan were seeking a new leader in 1881 it was said that "In the first place, he must appear respectable so that when sent to the masters, it will not be a disgrace for them to speak to him". [51] What were the reverberations and significance of these words, and what do they tell us about class relationships and class consciousness in Lancashire in this period?

Commenting adversely on a consumer boycott being organized by the Knights of Labour in America because a baker was selling bread to strike-breakers, the *Cotton Factory Times* referred in contrast to the situation here:

In England the trade unions are becoming respected, because on the whole they have proved themselves worthy of it. The moment they lose their dignity, and make themselves ridiculous, their influence will commence to wane.[52]

For leaders like Mawdsley the projection of trade union and artisan "respectability" was integrally linked with a wider project of achieving greater working class influence both at the workplace through extracting concessions from employers, and politically through the pursuit of "legitimate social reform". In doing this they had to face in two directions, not only towards the employers – many of whom feared the growth of trade unionism and the limitations it imposed upon the employers' control of the workplace, and of work practices – but also towards their existing and potential membership. Textiles and Lancashire had higher trade union membership than other sectors and areas, but even here it remained a minority involvement. By 1888 it has been estimated that between just 5% and 10% of the occupied population were in trade unions. [53] Not surprisingly Mawdsley used the first edition of the *Cotton Factory Times* – described by him as a "Workman's representative newspaper" – to appeal in class terms to that wide working class audience which the trade unions were attempting to draw into membership. The new organ would, he hoped,

be able to cultivate amongst the working men and women of the cotton manufacturing districts a still further appreciation of their influence and position, and of the most intelligent methods of consolidating their power; always, however, bearing in mind that the influence of factory workers and all other labouring classes is greatest

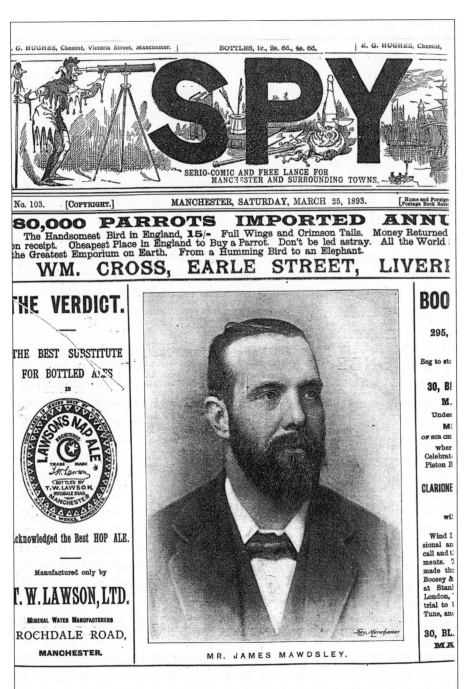

MR. JAMES MAWDSLEY.

James Mawdsley, Secretary of the cotton spinners' trade union and a supporter of the Canal. *MCL*

and can be used with most effect when trade is prosperous … it will consequently be no part of our policy to support hare-brained schemes which may prevent that steady flow of capital into our districts ….[54]

The appeal here, like that of the Ship Canal movement, is for responsible action, and is made to more than just a skilled artisan audience. It does not directly challenge capital or the rights of employers, but it does assert a common class position and interest. The influence of socialist ideas is evident,

as are the constraints. As Salman Rushdie has observed in another context about the early beginnings of Islam:

When an idea comes into the world, it's faced with two big tests: when you're weak, do you compromise; when you're strong, are you tolerant?[55]

Part of the compromise for the trade unions was to seek alliances with sympathetic employers and other progressive figures – certainly in the Ship Canal movement, but on other occasions as well – because paradoxically in this way the greater the influence and standing enjoyed by trade unionism viz-a-viz employers, the more likely it was that unions would be viewed as being able independently to represent the interests of workers; and the easier it would be to extend membership not only in the already organized craft areas, but in new areas too. In achieving and cementing an alliance with employers a concern for respectability and responsibility, which brought with it the power to negotiate on an equal footing, was considered critical.

Although the TUC from 1884 no longer felt it necessary to seek legitimation and respectability for their proceedings by inviting middle class sympathisers to give papers at their annual meetings – and indeed expressly rejected an overture from J. C. Fielden to address the Congress at Southport on the question of the Ship Canal[56] – at the local level the practice of involving local politicians and employers in particular events was not thought inappropriate. This was the case with Ship Canal demonstrations and meetings targetted especially at working men, where men like Leech, Boddington and Reuben Spencer moved motions of support.[57] Another example can be seen in a meeting of the Manchester District Committee of the ASE in 1886 when a public presentation of £100 was to be made to a member from the union's accident benefti fund. The meeting was actually presided over by the Dean of Manchester and addressed by three Liberal MPs, the Tory group leader on the Council and C. P. Scott, editor of the *Manchester Guardian* and unsuccessful Liberal Parliamentary candidate.[58]

The thinking behind this show meeting can be seen in an editorial article in the *Cotton Factory Times* which congratulates the Dean for his support and for not standing "aloof from those who form the backbone of England's greatness – and those are the intelligent portions of the artisan class – and constitute the trade union element of the country". On the basis of this endorsement of trade unions the article proceeds to argue that because trade unions are "necessary for the progress of the classes they represented", it followed that "those who refrain from doing their duty by keeping outside the pale of trades unionism are not true to themselves as workers, but are real enemies to the cause of freedom and progress".[59]

To imply a subordinated dependency role for the trade unions from this kind of event would, however, be simplistic. The meeting was partly intended as a platform for drumming up renewed artisan support for the Ship Canal after the failure of the first flotation, and both Jacob Bright and Scott spoke strongly in favour of the project. But equally it was designed to reinforce the status of the skilled worker and legitimate the trade union as an independent workers' organization by associating the ASE with the political establishment. It would help too to win over public opinion in support of the trade unions. The search for respectability here was far more than the simple aping of middle-class individualistic values – although even here it should be said that Kirk, in his study of Lancashire in the mid-Victorian

THE LATE MISS LYDIA BECKER.
(From a Photograph by Warwick Brookes.)

Lydia Becker, Secretary of the National Society for Women's Suffrage, who was constantly addressing meetings in Manchester in the 1880s on women's rights.
*Chetham's*

period, is at pains to emphasise "the indigenous nature of working class respectability".[60] As Gray has put it: "The claim to respectability must be set in the context of a strong sense of class pride. I would argue that it is properly interpreted as a claim to status recognition and citizenship on behalf of skilled workers as a corporate group."[61]

The notion of respectability was not all embracing. Some were included within its grasp and others excluded. The dividing line shifted as roles, perceptions and political expectations changed. The *Cotton Factory Times* refers to "The intelligent portions of the artisan class", and in the period of unemployment of the mid-1880s Mawdsley himself, in defending the Mayor from charges that he had not set up a Relief fund, asserted that the city's first citizen "would not knowingly allow any respectable citizen of Manchester to want for bread".[62] Respectability carried a moral value which could be cashed in by those within the pale.

The point here is that the alliance being created both within and without the Ship Canal movement in the 1880s, the language being developed to foster it, and the way in which the constituent elements of this alliance were assembled and reassembled over time raises subtle questions both about working class sectionalism and independence. Answers about this process of construction and change – though they

73

cannot be found from the snapshot of one year – begin to suggest themselves when the whole span of the Ship Canal years up to the mid 1890s is considered.

The respectability urged by the trade unions in the early 1880s, when the Ship Canal movement commenced, drew within its compass the skilled artisan, the honest worker and men. The unskilled, the unemployed, the "loafer" and women were not included. Patrick Joyce[63] has referred to the gender influence on the employment relation, and to the need to explore the extent to which male patriarchal values created shared perspectives of capital and labour. Equally we need to consider the significance and influence of the gender question in the context of the Ship Canal movement, for the 1880s saw the establishment of feminism as a major political force, with 1885 – the year in which the Ship Canal movement celebrated the royal assent to the legislation – being described by Jeffrey Weeks as "an annus mirabilis of sexual politics".[64] The position of women as well as the poverty of the unemployed and the plight of the unskilled were three major issues around which there was political and industrial agitation in the mid- to late-1880s, and all of them had a general impact on working class consciousness and political attitudes and on the layers of meaning associated with the concept of respectable society – a theme we will return to later.

**Constructing Alliances and Movements**

Just as the notion of respectability implied a series of attitudes about work, family, class and status, so also it had a political dimension which found expression in the phenomenon of the Liberal–Labour alliance of late nineteenth century politics. The principal vehicle for developing this "Lib–Lab" alliance was the TUC's Parliamentary Committee[65] and, as Table 5 shows, many of the key trade union officials supporting the Ship Canal movement were also members of this Committee.

**Table 5   Lancashire Membership of TUC Parliamentary Committee**

| Name of Trade Union Official | Years of Membership |
| --- | --- |
| Birtwhistle, Thomas | 1877–9, 1891 |
| Kelley, George D | 1871, 1883, 1887, 1890–1 |
| Mawdsley, James | 1882, 1884–89, 1891–96 |
| Murchie, James | 1883–86, 1888 |
| Shorrocks, Peter | 1873 |
| Slatter, Henry | 1877–89 |
| Swift, James | 1886, 1889 |

Source: B. C. Roberts, The TUC

Slatter, born in 1830, was the senior trade union official in Manchester supporting the Ship Canal, and had been – along with Thomas Birtwistle, Secretary of the Weavers'

Amalgamation – on the Parliamentary Committee since 1877. Widely respected as the General Secretary of the Typographical Association, Slatter played a pivotal role in the Ship Canal movement, chairing most of the large working class demonstrations in support of it, and addressing many others.[66] But it would be wrong to caricature him as representing a Committee simply composed of an 'old guard' locked into piecemeal slow reform through the Liberal Party, which was to be swept aside by the progressive new unionists of the late 1880s, like Keir Hardie, Mann and Burns, with their new socialist and collectivist vision. The new men being elected from Lancashire on to the Parliamentary Committee in the early 1880s – Mawdsley, Murchie and Kelley – were certainly representing the skilled labour aristocracy, but they were young men in their thirties, and saw their support for the Liberal Party as a way of best representing their members' interests, and of winning substantial gains for the working-classes. Nor was this an idle hope. At the 1885 Conference they were able to report that in Lancashire they had achieved an important advance by securing the appointment of four trade union leaders as JPs – Slatter in Manchester, Birtwistle in Accrington, John Fielding in Bolton, and W. Pickard in Wigan; and a couple of months later at the General Election, eleven Lib–Labs were elected as MPs, including six miners.

Some labour historians looking back to the early 1880s with the advantage of hindsight have too easily regarded this period as one of marking time before the watershed of New Unionism and the 1889 Dock Strike; they have seen the members of the TUC's Parliamentary Committee as the bearers of a tired and forgettable message. Thus Leventhal has generally described the 1880s as a period when the craft unions "adopted a fatalistic attitude to unemployment" and "the bankrupt union leadership held to the *status quo*".[67] Postgate specifically chose to belittle Murchie's contribution to the development of the Carpenters' union by affecting dismay that during his period of office most of the union's energies were spent in avoiding any struggles; he also dismissively referred to Murchie's activities in support of the Trades Union Congress.[68] Yet a proper analysis of the union's position would have taken account of the insecurity and defensiveness felt by joiners under the onslaught of mechanization.

Moreover a fair summary of Murchie's politics in relation to a changing working class consciousness would have emphasised his remarkably progressive views. In 1872 he was Secretary of the International Working Men's Association,[69] and in 1883 he was one of the few to give wholehearted support to the radical Pankhurst when he stood as Liberal Parliamentary candidate against Houldsworth.[70] Furthermore in 1885, when he was Chairman of the Parliamentary Committee, he spoke out forcibly at the Trade Union Congress in favour of working-class political representation.[71]

There can, however, be no doubt that the Ship Canal movement should be seen as part of a Lib–Lab alliance, and a proper assessment of the work carried out by members of the TUC's Parliamentary Committee should take account of this. This judgement runs counter to received opinion, primarily because the Ship Canal project has been thought of as *sui generis*, a towering but distinct phenomenon unrelated to a wider political environment. Thus Whitaker's detailed study of the Liberal Party notes that: "No moves have come to light towards setting up a "Lib–Lab" coalition in Manchester"[72] – a precise example of how something can be too big to be seen.

As has been indicated in Chapter 2, the early thrust for the Ship Canal came from powerful elements within the Liberal Party, and almost all of Manchester's leading trade union officials supporting the Ship Canal were closely involved with the Party, including James Mawdsley.[73] This point should be stressed because Roberts in particular, in his history of the Trades Union Congress, appears to assume that because of the tradition of working class Toryism in Lancashire, trade union officials were automatically Tory.[74] There were Conservative trade union officials, of whom one was certainly Birtwistle and another was Thomas Ashton, Secretary of the Lancashire Miners Federation, whose interest in the scheme was limited, and whose members appear to have given no support to the Ship Canal movement. As Table 1 indicates, only miners' branches in Cleveland and North Yorkshire, (where the staunch Liberal, Ben Pickard, Secretary of the South and West Yorkshire Miners, had more influence), passed resolutions in favour of the scheme – a point which further supports the argument about the Lib–Lab nature of the movement.[75]

The construction of the Ship Canal was the final fruit, the vindication of this alliance. For Lancashire's trade union leadership, which was vulnerable always to the charge of cosy incorporation and of achieving little of tangible benefit for their members, their support for the project provided positive advantages from the start. The high profile campaign gave them a platform where they could be seen to be playing an active and leading role. As the Trades Council Report noted in 1883, it was "an undertaking which during its construction will provide an immense amount of work for the industrial classes".[76] The sight of a few working class leaders installed on the Justices' Bench or in the House of Commons might not bring the working classes onto the streets excitedly waving flags, but bringing jobs for the unemployed by helping to promote a massive new injection of capital was a different matter.

The appeal of the scheme, offering the prospect of rejuvenating old industries and stimulating new ones, was widespread for a working class suffering from years of depressed trade, and even took opponents by surprise. Significantly too it won support from radical Liberals by anticipating several of the demands which were subsequently to be associated with the collective approach of the socialists and the independent labour movement. By this adroit response Lancashire's trade union leadership was able to steal a march on any potential opposition but, in doing so, they were helping to push the Liberal Party to a point where

HI KELLEY.

Dame Kelley: What does that spell?
Johnny Workman: Please, ma'am, Liberalism.
Dame Kelley: Read it Trade Unionism, or you'll taste birch!!

Cartoon of George Kelley. His support for the Lib-Lab alliance behind the Ship Canal Movement was seen as a threat by some to the cause of independent working class representation. He later became a Labour MP. *MCL*

the contradictions could no longer be effectively contained. As Edwin Guthrie, Chairman of the Manchester Liberal Union, put it in a letter written in the year of the Canal's opening:

> With respect to the Labour question generally the danger I most fear is that the Liberal Party may, by making concessions to, or standing out of the way of the irreconcilable section, alienate the infinitely more powerful body who are faithful to Liberalism.[77]

Examples of supporters for the Ship Canal scheme from the radical wing of the Liberal Party can be seen in the cases of John C. Fielden – a small cotton manufacturer and writer on political economy – and Richard Pankhurst and James Johnston. Pankhurst, who was given the honour of applying to the Quarter Sessions for a Final Certificate for the Canal on the day prior to its opening,[78] and Johnston, an electrical engineer and cooperator who played an important role in enlisting the support of the Cooperative movement, were clearly in Guthrie's "irreconcilable section"; and both were to move away from the Liberal Party in the 1890s and stand as Parliamentary candidates in Manchester for the Independent Labour Party at the 1895 Election.[79]

The political careers of Johnston and Pankhurst, growing out of the experience of the Lib–Lab alliance, and reflecting too the wider ferment of political ideas in the 1880s, are examples of a general process in which it became more difficult to separate the economic from the political. This distinction characterised radical Liberal debate in the mid-Victorian years,[80] and references were certainly still being made in the mid 1880s to the maintenance of this tradition. As Thomas Ashton put it at the annual Tea Party of the Stalybridge Spinners: "As trades unionists, they must steer clear of politics, and deal only with questions affecting labour". But the dam was already breached, and cross infection was inevitable, despite Mawdsley's advice at the same meeting that: "they should not pin their faith to one party, but act with that which would be best for them".[81] For the actions of the trade union leaders belied this open-handedness both through their support for the Lib–Labism of the TUC's Parliamentary Committee, and through their open espousal of Liberalism or the need for an independent working class movement. In the 1885 election campaign Jacob Bright, a consistently stalwart supporter of the Ship Canal from the outset, was strongly backed at public meetings by Austin and Murchie, and Slatter regularly appeared on platforms supporting Liberal candidates C. E. Schwann and Richard Peacock.[82] Murchie, moreover, as Chairman of the Parliamentary Committee, spoke openly of his active political involvement in Manchester at the 1885 TUC Congress and, indicating his disillusionment with relying upon "commerce" for political representation, argued that the working class would make little progress "unless they sought class representation, and called it such … "

Mawdsley himself, despite his advice to the Stalybridge Spinners earlier in the year, stood as the Liberal candidate on the incorporation of the Bradford ward into the city;[83] and the following year, at the TUC Congress on his return from an international trade union conference in Paris, he moved the adoption of a series of far-reaching proposals which had been agreed in Paris and required the intervention of the State on a major scale to improve workers' hours and conditions of employment.[84] In Robert's words "This was a jump from laissez-faire to collectivism with a vengeance".[85]

The direct influence of new socialist ideas is clearly evident here in Mawdsley's evolving position, but in the cooperative approaches being established at the very same time between capital and labour both through the Lib–Lab alliance and in the Ship Canal movement, we should note other important influences in which there was a strong element of historical continuity. Just as Reid[86] has argued that working class fragmentation and disunity is a normal part – and consequence – of the uneven development of capitalism, and does not negate the assertion of the essential commonality of working class experience and of an underlying conflict of interest between capital and labour, so

also it is important to identify those pressures – without attributing primacy to them – which push capital and labour to emphasise at certain periods and in certain circumstances alliance and common interest, rather than separation and conflict. The opening issue of the *Cotton Factory Times* expressed the tension neatly:

> The great gulf that has existed in the past between capital and labour has forbidden any very near approach between the officials of the masters and workpeople's associations. But we are delighted to find evidences of the development of a better understanding in the future between these two sections of the community. We hail with satisfaction the thought of cooperation. Why not?[87]

In Lancashire examples of this shared perception of mutuality can, in fact, be seen over a substantial period of the mid-Victorian years. We have already discussed in the last chapter the powerful influence that the belief in Free Trade had in coalescing the organizational strengths of both manufacturing capital and skilled labour behind the Ship Canal and in opposition to the Fair Traders. In the cotton industry, united by this common ideology, joint deputations to Government ministers composed of representatives from the Chamber of Commerce and the trade unions frequently argued a common case on Indian tariffs, or on the need to open up India with infrastructure and State-guaranteed investment.

Historical parallels for the Ship Canal alliance can also be discerned by looking at the structures and backgrounds of other movements in previous years where elements of a cross-class ideology were present or intended, and it is impossible to escape the conclusion that this experience was actively being drawn upon in the 1880s. The most recent case, some eleven years before the Ship Canal movement commenced, had concerned the sudden launching of the "New Social Alliance", the "New Social Movement" or the "New Departure" as it was variously called. The full details of this Alliance, which received a lot of press attention, are somewhat obscure, but the general background is illuminating. According to a report in the *Manchester Guardian*, when the story broke, an initiative had been taken early in 1871 by two or three Conservative peers. There was, at that time, considerable Radical and Republican agitation and criticism of the House of Lords, and it occurred to these Tory instigators that the workmen should be asked to commit their demands to paper, and that the early stages of creating a movement should be entrusted to J. Scott Russell, the builder of the Great Eastern who was considered to enjoy the confidence of the working classes. Discussions and negotiations took place with most of the leading trade unionists in London who were to form a "Council of Skilled Workmen", matched by a "Council of Legislation" formed of peers. The plans reached sufficient maturity for the announcement to be made in October of the completion of a new alliance "between an influential section of the Conservative peers and some of the leaders of the working men who are dissatisfied with the domestic legislation of the present Government".[88] Although the Alliance was to evaporate rapidly under a barrage of Radical and trade union criticism, what is intriguing from our point of view is the report in the next day's *Manchester Guardian*[89] that a Committee had been at work in the city as part of the Alliance and that it had already decided to arrange a public meeting at the Free Trade Hall to further the aim of achieving specific legal reforms. The names connected with the movement were those of the most prominent trades unionists and included W. H. Wood, Secretary of the Trades Council, J. D. Prior, General Secretary of the Amalgamated Society of Carpenters and Joiners (and predecessor to Murchie), and Richard Harnott, the well-respected General Secretary of the Stonemasons, together with Robert Austin, Henry Slatter and Peter Shorrocks. The last three were prominently associated with bringing the trade unions into the Ship Canal movement, and would have learnt the important lesson that an alliance so closely identified in the public eye with one political party ran the risk of being gunned down before it had got out onto the streets.

The other parallel case to which attention is inexorably drawn is the Anti-Corn Law League movement in the 1840s, not least because so many of the promoters specifically referred to it in the context of the Ship Canal movement. Daniel Adamson, always the great publicist, in his evidence before a House of Lords Committee in 1883, compared the enthusiasm for the Ship Canal with that felt for the League, because he knew that involvement or a personal link with the League was for many the brand-mark of the true Lancashire patriot. A clear example of this can be seen in the case of the Salford engineer, William H. Bailey, knighted for his work for the Ship Canal. Describing his boyhood (aged 6), seventy years earlier, he recalled somewhat improbably: "I often went with my father to Newall's Buildings committee meetings as a little boy during the agitation for the Repeal of the Corn Laws. I walked in procession with him, I think in 1844, when the taxes were taken off bread".[90] Bailey, too, knew the power of the League tradition and drew loud cheers from his audience at the Free Trade Hall in 1883 when he asked: "Am I ... a worthy son of the birthplace of freedom in trade, of a father whose proudest boast now in his old age is that he was one of the first members of the Anti-Corn Law League?"[91]

The League was seen as the inspiration for, and the source from which emerged, the twin principles of the Manchester School – Free Trade and *laissez-faire*. In the climate of depressed trade in the early 1880s – in which the Tariff Reform Movement and Protectionism were able to strike deep roots – looking back to the golden days of the League provided for Free Traders a beacon of hope and a blueprint for action. Indeed the point was made quite explicitly by Henry Ashworth of Bolton, a leading member and speaker for the League, in the introduction to the second (1881) edition of his book on Cobden and the League:

There seems a growing disposition to ignore the services rendered to this country ... by the League. Nor can I ... fail to see that the old fallacies of Protection still linger in our midst ... If by the publication of these Recollections I may help in my old age to refute these fallacies ... I shall feel myself amply rewarded.[92]

The twelve months of 1881 had brought out a rash of publications on Free Trade and the League, with John Morley, in his biography of Richard Cobden, referring similarly to its political timeliness, whilst cautioning that "it may disappoint those who expect to find in it a completely furnished armoury for the champions of Free Trade".[93]

The strategies of the League machine and detailed tactics of the campaign were laid out in these books, and the lessons to be learnt were clear for anyone seeking to fashion a contemporary movement, adapted to the issues and concerns of the 1880s. Paramount was the need to engage working class support. The series of sixteen articles on the Ship Canal which appeared in the *Umpire* in Autumn 1887 refer on a number of occasions to the seminal influence of the League; and include the statement that "Old Anti-Corn Law men saw a reproduction of some of their old organization tactics".[94] Another of these articles states that the suggestion to introduce one-shilling coupons as a way of encouraging working class shareholding came from the chemical manufacturer Peter Spence, who "used to dilate upon his earliest recollection of the pleasure and pride it gave him to possess an illuminated card attesting his small contributions to the Anti-Corn Law League".[95] An elaboration of this same point was carefully constructed by Bosdin Leech in an article in the *Ship Canal Gazette* in early 1883, where he referred critics of the shilling coupon scheme to the Anti-Corn Law movement "when the working man was asked to contribute even pence". Leech pointed out that the League newspaper had suggested that these contributions were proof of the strength and universality of the movement, and concluded that "Both movements were initiated with one object, namely to cheapen food and remove fetters from trade".[96]

Leech's statement is revealing, for as a councillor and Ship Canal auditor he was much more an active promoter and ideologue of the movement than the title bestowed on him of 'historian of the Ship Canal' would suggest or than he was prepared to admit. He was, however, only a small yarn agent and like Henry Heap, another Liberal and Ship Canal enthusiast, could be dismissed as "small fry"[97] by opponents of the scheme.

The position was different in the case of the representatives of large-scale industrial capital, who formed the other major bloc in the Ship Canal alliance, the reverse side of the coin from the trade union and working class interests. Evidence in support of the financial soundness of the project, which was submitted during the progress of the Bill, suggested frequently that the Ship Canal was backed by Lancashire's richest men. These assertions involved a substantial embroidery of the truth, a point half-acknowledged by

Daniel Adamson on being asked whether it was Lancashire's wealthiest citizens who were supporting the project. His ambiguous answer that "they claim to be" was greeted with laughter in the House of Lords. The largest fortunes in the county were, with the exception of John Rylands, those held by men involved with mercantile capital, and for the most part they did not give substantial support to the Ship Canal. Backing for the project came primarily from manufacturing capital, and it is useful at this stage to explore this aspect in some detail.

Collaboration with the trade unions on the scale of the Ship Canal movement brought distinct advantages, but was also problematic because it raised as many questions as it produced answers. In what circumstances and for how long was the consensual model implied in the movement appropriate? How did it relate to the strategies of employers' associations in the cotton industry; or to the work of the Iron Trade Employers' Association, based in Manchester, which a year after its formation had established a National Federation of Associated Employers of Labour in 1873 in order to counter the political activities of the TUC Parliamentary Committee?[98] How far was the approach of the Ship Canal promoters to be taken as a paradigm for a more general industrial relations strategy and management style which involved modernization and reinvestment based upon a commitment to regional growth shared by capital and labour alike? How far did the main participants have a shared perception of the economy, and how far were they occupying tactical positions in a transitional period in which allusions to notions of the community of the trade, to a community of interests were still made, but to which there was only a limited and conditional commitment?

For a start the alliance required manufacturing capital to deliver the funding. As the difficulties of achieving this became increasingly obvious, so the credibility of the big employers backing the scheme dropped, and criticism mounted. But there was a wider structural problem about the representativeness of the big bourgeoisie interests behind the project because of the inherent variety and heterogeneity of interests within manufacturing capital. Size, geographical location, relations with the workforce, investment levels, market position and penetration, the extent to which a company was export-oriented or had invested in new technology – these were all factors which inhibited a unified view despite a common concern for profitability, higher productivity and a tighter control over the workplace. Political and religious affiliations of the employers were also factors which ensured a far from uniform response. As we have seen, Lancashire's railway and coal companies, with strong Conservative affiliations, supported neither the project nor the underlying industrial relations strategy. But if they were reluctant, where did the main public backing come from? Careful analysis shows that support was sought and gained to give as wide a spread as possible using three main criteria – geographical location, industrial sector and political affiliation. Cotton and

engineering employers predominated with the main core coming from Manchester and Salford. The directors and key figures were household names in the city – Galloway, Crossley and Bailey representing engineering, Houldsworth, J. C. Lee and Rylands representing cotton. From the surrounding towns came two engineering interests – the Platt brothers (Oldham) and Adamson himself; and two cotton interests, Leigh (Stockport) and Jacob Bright (Rochdale). All apart from Houldsworth were Liberals. Significantly Bolton, the other major centre outside Manchester, with its predominantly Tory employers, was not represented, nor did its strongly Tory Council give any moral or financial backing for the scheme.[99]

Achieving a good cross-section of Tory employers was indeed the major difficulty. As we have seen in Chapter 2, Houldsworth – eager only not to be drawn into the net – was the main target for the promoters in 1883, and in the following year at the municipal elections, similar pressures were put on the Cheetham Ward Liberal Party not to put up their candidate against the Tory brewer, Henry Boddington, on the grounds that "he has been a most ardent worker for and supporter of the Ship Canal".[100] In Salford, Richard Husband, a Tory silk-hat manufacturer and Mayor of the city 1881–83, was persuaded to take a seat on the Board and a £2,000 shareholding – but apparently with reluctance. For in 1889, after he had resigned from the Board, Boddington wrote:

I have just taken over Alderman Husband's shares at par value, because we were morally bound to that mean gentleman to do so – this does not help the Company truly, but it lightens my pockets by so much.[101]

Warrington was the other main source of Tory support, and expediency required that it should be sought because of the route the Canal was to take through the town. Here again, however, a less than helpful public stance was adopted by Provisional Committee member Henry Bleckley, of the Pearson Knowles Iron and Coal company. Attending a railway shareholders' meeting, he was widely quoted as saying that the Provisional Committee had "to send the hat round to get civic support".[102] For the Warrington man who wrote in to one Manchester paper it was a quite inexplicable change of heart, and particularly so because the writer had been induced to invest in the Ship Canal because of Bleckley's strong speeches in favour.[103]

Bleckley's crime was far more heinous than Husband's because he was *publicly* undermining confidence in the project. The names and money of large-scale industrial capitalists, who were employing tens of thousands of workers in Lancashire, gave the movement its credibility and authority. If the Platts in Oldham, and John Rylands in Manchester were backing it, the argument went, then the project must be sound, and an appropriate investment vehicle for the savings of the ordinary working man. This was the agenda of the promoters – not only the construction of a Ship Canal, but along with it the creation of a regionally organized mass popular movement, a cross-class alliance that transcended the interests of capital and labour. This was a new form of popular capitalism that would draw in landowners, the middle class, the small shopkeepers and traders certainly, but was primarily aimed at the working class.

Since we have already suggested the powerful influence of the tradition of the Anti-Corn Law League on the Ship Canal promoters, what are the parallels to be found in looking at those attempts 40 years earlier to engage working class support for a movement? Ashworth's comment that "the working class, as a body, did not openly support the Protectionists; but for the most part, they held aloof from the League, and preferred to agitate for Chartism …"[104] supports Cobden's frank admission that the League "has eminently been a middle-class agitation".[105] Neither statement, however, should be allowed to conceal the lengths to which the League organizers went to seek cross-class backing, and the extent to which the League was successful in winning assent for its Free Trade ideology – which was to exercise such a tenacious influence on working class attitudes right into the twentieth century. As McCord's study shows,[106] the impetus for the League seeking a wider alliance resulted from the physical attacks made by the Chartists in early 1839, which made it virtually impossible for a while for the Free Traders to hold public meetings. Cobden's solution was to appoint a nineteen year-old Mancunian, Edward Watkin, who was given the task of forming a working class free traders' organization, or Operative Anti-Corn Law Organization, which was directly funded by the League. Within a short period it was holding regular meetings two evenings a week at a local tavern, and was able to attract 4,000 operatives to its first big rally in May. By 1841 Watkin and his association, with the aid of the Manchester Irish, had achieved control of the city after decisively routing the Chartists at a big rally held in Stevenson Square.[107] Watkin's account of events was published in 1891, and contains correspondence which reveals clearly the importance attached to achieving working class support. Writing to Watkin in early 1842, Cobden declares:

> The Council of the League have agreed to aid you in the expenses of a delegation to London, which I think is a very desirable step. As respects the necessity of organization and the importance of the working classes in carrying anything, I am completely with you,

and follows this up with a further letter a few days later:

> You'll see by the Times and Standard that there is a desperate effort made to make it appear the working class are not with us. This shows the importance they attach to their cooperation and it proves the importance of our bringing out the Trades if possible.[108]

No such explicit correspondence has survived from the Ship Canal agitation, but the replication of the methods and organization of the 1840s is plain, and can be seen in Joseph Lawrence's initial memorandum submitted in October 1882 to the Provisional Committee: "There are men who act as leaders of artisans' trades unions and others who should certainly be allotted a share in the proceedings. These men have a powerful effect in "developing" the views of members of Parliament and town councillors".[109] Furthermore, a direct link can be demonstrated with Watkin himself. A Liberal Member of Parliament for Hythe since 1874 (and before that for Stockport), Sir Edward Watkin, Baronet, had become influential in a number of railway companies, and was from the early 1870s chairman of the Manchester and Sheffield Railway. In this capacity he was employing in 1872 the 24 year-old, Joseph Lawrence, to issue the prospectus and raise the capital for the purchase of the Bridgewater Navigation. Ten years later Lawrence was to take up the post of manager for the Ship Canal Provisional Committee, and must surely have picked up from Watkin many of the organizational tactics employed. In both the campaigns, for instance, the first action of both young men on appointment was to map out the whole city and divide it into local centres, each with its own local association.[110]

Despite the similarities, however, the Ship Canal movement was distinctive, reflecting a different political and social environment. Though an explicitly socialist Democratic Federation provided in the 1880s an anti capitalist class-based critique, it developed no mass appeal like Chartism did in the 1840s. The opportunities for Lancashire's industrial bourgeoisie to project effectively a cross-class ideology of popular capitalism were objectively greater and were seized enthusiastically by the Ship Canal promoters; but they did so in a political context shaped by the crisis of the 1880s and an emerging labourist consciousness – which in turn was being stoked by the dissonant voices of socialism and respectable trade unionism.

**Promoting the Movement to the People**

To appreciate fully the undoubted impact of the Ship Canal movement we need to examine its underlying ideology. What were the particular ideas and imagery used to promote the Canal in the popular mind? How were these built up and related to Manchester and the textile-driven economy of Lancashire? How inclusive was the embrace of this cross-class alliance, and what was the role played by Daniel Adamson, whose name had become synonymous with the Ship Canal?

Although there were different and at times contradictory strands, a central theme of the promoters' case concerned the mutuality that flowed from common interest. Only days after the first mass working men's meeting organized by the Trades Council at the Free Trade Hall, Adamson and Boddington were addressing Adamson's workforce from a temporary platform rigged up in the pattern room. "Every tradesman, merchant, shopkeeper and working man" declared Boddington, "would be affected by it and would find it to his advantage and worthy of support"[111] – a theme picked up in his "Boddington's Map of the Proposed Manchester Ship Canal", published in early 1883, where it is pronounced that: "it is the duty, as it should be the pride, of every merchant, every tradesman, every shopkeeper, every working-man to forward this grand public enterprise ..."[112] Behind this lay the idea of a common citizenship, united through place – against which other non-belongers could be judged and found wanting – whether they came from Liverpool, from outside Lancashire, from London or from abroad. According to an 1882 pamphlet the Ship Canal should be supported because: "It is in the interest of every patriotic citizen to uphold the trading reputation of his city".[113] The theme was drummed out insistently and by none more than Adamson, whose handwritten notes for a big working-class demonstration in Eccles to celebrate the royal assent to the Bill, indicate his thinking:

Capital and its value if raised in
Lancashire and adjoining Counties

London and large capitalists
Should not be asked to find the money
for us – or they will get in dividends
the just fruits of our labour.

Let us keep the profit amongst us.[114]

A few weeks later at the Great Trades Procession he was to elaborate the same point more graphically:

They ought not to allow the directors to go out of this country – and as little as possible out of the district – to find the capital. The dividends ought to be distributed amongst the people of this district, and not sent to London for capitalists to gloat over.[115]

Contributing to the scheme became the touchstone for demonstrating a loyalty of place. As Jacob Bright put it: "The town of Manchester owed something to the patriotism of men who had given so much time and labour ..."[116]

Inevitably local patriotism and pride of place became linked at times with a wider xenophobia. Adamson was particularly adept at exploiting this when addressing big working class meetings, as the following press extract shows, where he talks of the problems of digging the canal:

If they were to bring over some thousands of men from India the work could be done in a day. – (Laughter) It might, however, cause some inconvenience to bring the men over, because there might be a difficulty in getting rid of them again – (Laughter). If they got an American "devil" it would do as much work as 50 men".[117]

His own gun-deck jingoism could be turned to advantage with other audiences too, as his remarks at an event to mark the success of the Cooperative movement indicate:

When they had got the Ship Canal, they would go in for an inland arsenal, so that if Woolwich should be lost, they could fall back on the skills of Lancashire workmen, and protect Liverpool in spite of her opposition.[118]

A steam navvy in use during the construction. It is surprising that more use was not made of mechanisation, given its more widespread application elsewhere. *MCL*

The message was that all classes of the community should contribute, whether employers, workers or cooperators, but the logic was that the greatest patriots were those who could contribute most. To them should be ascribed the leadership role in this cross-class alliance, and the adulation accorded to them, and in particular to Adamson, in the local press knew no bounds. The grand epithets flowed thickly about Lancashire's leading lights who planned the scheme and invested capital. For Hilton Greaves, an Oldham cotton spinner, it was "a glorious undertaking – a noble work putting altogether in the shade gifts of public parks and endowments";[119] while the *Newcastle Weekly Chronicle* declaimed of Adamson that "The faith he cherished in the future of Manchester rose into the sublime".[120]

Since the Canal was billed as anticipating high profits and a worthwhile investment for workers' shilling savings, a few voices were raised about the consistency of the arguments and the nature of patriotism, as in this letter from Henry Roby:

> Patriotic citizens who have the means may well subscribe to it, if it is likely to be only useful. It requires neither patriotism nor compulsion to make subscribers if it is likely to be profitable.[121]

But in the rush of the campaign, such views were brushed aside. The *Manchester Guardian*, in arguing against municipal contributions as State interference in the free market, was accused of being "lamentably short of local patriotism."[122] Doubters were branded as "croakers", opponents discredited as being men with dubious motives. Those who spoke their mind at public meetings were labelled "obstructive";[123] or were exposed, according to the pamphleteer Samuel Ramsbottom, on "a large placard headed 'Enemies of the Ship Canal'".[124]

Poster to celebrate the final passage of the Ship Canal Bill in 1885.   *MCL*

To the enemies were counterpoised the heroes, as in the triumphal arch at Eccles which told onlookers to observe the "conquering hero".[125] "Honour the Brave" enjoined a flyposter[126] published with bay laurel wreath to accompany the 1885 'victory' celebrations which marked the passage of the Bill. From it stare the stern proud faces of Adamson and Boddington, along with Marshall Stevens, the manager, Williams the engineer, and the two lawyers who had piloted the Bill through Parliament, Pember and Saxon. The imagery of a victorious leadership endowed with hope and noble purpose vanquishing all opposition was systematically developed, with Adamson promoted, in the period before he resigned in 1887, as a cult figurehead and popular hero. His bearded face appeared on commemorative handkerchiefs, jugs and plates and in the form of a grand firework display at Belle Vue;[127] his name was attached to ships and pubs, laced into ballads and rhyming verse, festooned across banners and posters ("Let every son of Adam help brave Adamson"[128]) or used to advertise the sale of goods and services. Even Leech who, as we have seen, had been very critical of Adamson in a private letter was assiduous two months later in following the public line at the 1883 "Great Meeting" in the Free Trade Hall, describing Adamson as "the life and soul of the enterprise", and concluding that "they were indebted to him for putting himself in the van … and as brave soldiers they ought to do what they could to help him, and in the end they would gain the victory".[129] The 'Official Song of the Ship Canal', published with words and music and a signed portrait of Adamson on the frontispiece, perhaps best sums up the popular representation the promoters wished to convey after the three year Parliamentary campaign:

> Too candid friends and open foes, your blatant croaking stay,
> While we for doughty Adamson wreathe coronal of bay;
> May Time ye scheming crew, to black Oblivion's deep,
> But green the fame of Adamson, let future ages keep!
> Now Stentors, shout for Ship Canal, cheer that stout hearted band,
> Who made the voice of Lancashire echo through the land;
> Not all may lead, but each can shew a glimmer of the fire
> That urged the fighting few to win the multitude's desire.[130]

Drawing in the "multitude" was the key objective of the promoters, and the populist campaign aimed specifically at Lancashire's working men was the vehicle for achieving this. With an estimated 100,000 people attending the 1885 Great Trades Meeting at Belle Vue, the promoters could not have hoped for better support. As a newspaper report concluded: "It was a beautiful moment for Mr Adamson when he stood up to speak to the vast multitude cheering itself hoarse at sight of him".[131] The trade unions had played a key role in this *mise-en-scène*, and fittingly it was Kelley, as Secretary of the Trades Council, who moved the first resolution of support. The report of the event lists the strength of the trades support, with the Engineers' 3,000 members making the most imposing show as they stretched out for a third of a mile.

The procession also demonstrated backing from another important source, the temperance movement, with 6,000 participating from six different Orders. Given the close association between Liberalism and temperance it was not surprising that from the start the promoters had always looked in this direction for support, but again this feature put further strains on the cross party nature of the movement. An election poster circulating locally at the time shows that while the Liberals paraded themselves as the party of cheap food (another commonly claimed benefit of the Ship Canal) and temperance, the Tories were represented as the party of dear food and beer.[132] The alum manufacturers, Peter and Frank Spence, who had founded the English Anti-Tobacco Society[133] were the principal temperance representatives on the Provisional Committee, and espousal of their cause was frequently linked with a successful outcome for the Ship Canal. For Mitchell, Chairman of the Cooperative Wholesale Society, the hope was that working men would be so keen to obtain one or two shares that they would save the money now spent on tobacco and drink so that it could be invested in the Ship Canal. Supporting this view at the same subscribers' meeting Adamson argued that: "If it did nothing else but encourage thrift and sobriety, the undertaking would be a blessing to Lancashire".[134]

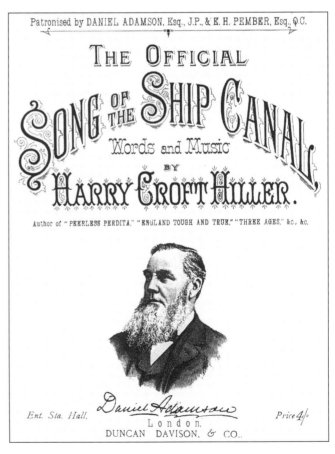

Cover for the official song of the Ship Canal, produced in 1885. *MSCC*

1885 Ship Canal demonstration, passing through Piccadilly in central Manchester. *MCL*

Moral reformism of this nature did not make friends universally but another method of popularising the project caused no such divisions in Lancashire, except perhaps amongst Blackpool's landladies. Inspired by the notion of the 'seaside' as a place of resort for health and pleasure, the campaign managers encouraged the representation of the Canal as bringing the sea to the city. Poems were written on "Manchester-on-Sea" where men could "dip in the briny" as the following 1884 extract indicates:

No longer from Oldham to Blackpool they run,
The shores of the Irwell show quite as much fun;
The waters rush in, bringing wealth with their flow,
What need then for pleasure to Blackpool to go?
A wonderful age, none could ever ask more,
The ocean is brought almost up to one's door.
From Stockport men often would wander afar,
Their craze for fresh places no distance could bar;
In search of soft ozone each year saw them roam,
All things of the past – they've now got it at home.
A truce to long journeys, to lodging-house fees,
We need them no longer, we've got the sea breeze.[135]

Ten years later in a sonnet commemorating the opening of the Canal, Mancunians were told the breeze had finally arrived:

The sounding city where her crossways roar,
Hears the great thunder of our island shore,
And mixed with breath from her ten thousand mills
She feels sea breezes on her brow today.[136]

Children too received a similar message. *Betty and Billy: A Child's Tale of the Ship Canal* told its readers that "The tide will bring you treasures",[137] while a one penny booklet with drawing and verse entitled "Manchester on the Sea" had a front cover (see page 20) with Manchester looking more like the sea front at Liverpool, and inside a drawing, 'Old Neptune Brings up the Tide' with the lines:

And the tide is rushing strong,
Wafting breezes fresh and cool,
As it waves from Liverpool,
Bringing with old Neptune's roar
Health and wealth to every door.[138]

By 1900, suggested a colourful poster, Manchester would have its own pier, with horse riding and bathing huts on the golden sands.[139] The seaside theme had intoxicated Manchester including one of its best known dialect writers, Ben Brierley, who pitched in with his *Dream of 1892*, describing how "Commodore Addy's gig, manned by a coastguardsman, shot eaut o'th 'harbour, for t'see if ther any smugglers hoidin their cargoes i'th 'caves o'Pomona".[140]

Only in Liverpool where the project was dubbed "The Canal Bubble" was disquiet expressed about the promoters' legerdemain in an article complaining that the people "have had called before their mind's eye delightful visions of … the green waters of the Irish sea washing up to the doorways of the warehouses and factories …".[141] It is hard to assess the precise impact of the maritime imagery on working class attitudes to the Ship Canal, but it cannot be questioned that it was an important factor in popularising the idea of the Canal, so that it was seen as more than just a "big ditch". The attraction of an estimated one million people to the Canal's official opening by Queen Victoria is evidence of this; and the *Illustrated London News*, which covered the event in an article entitled "The Romance of the Ship Canal", had no doubts about the fascination of the sea:

> Manchester-on-the-Sea – How strange it sounds! Yet it is hardly more than the truth … There is something peculiarly attractive in the idea of 'the briny' actually flowing under the very walls of the cotton mills.[142]

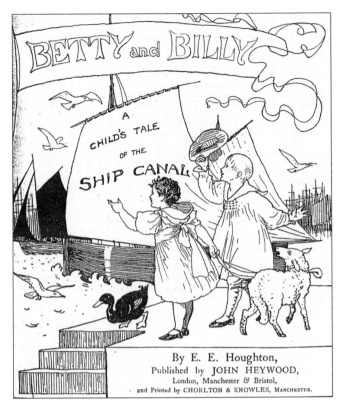

Cover for a child's story book with drawings.   *MCL*

Ballads and broadsheets, banners and bunting, pamphlets and posters, processions and pageantry – all of these were pressed into service to get the message across to a mass audience. The reasoned arguments could be put in the serious newspapers like the *Manchester Guardian* but, as was pointed out to C. P. Scott, "the majority of the electors belong to the working class, and working men do not read the "M.G.".[143]

It was for this reason, therefore, that so much attention was paid to holding meetings – public meetings, subscribers' meetings, works meetings, ward meetings, town meetings, mass meetings, and the huge set-piece rallies already described. In the days before the development of the mass media they provided the most direct way of winning support and, in the lengthy speeches at the meetings often reported verbatim in the local press, it is possible to see most clearly the ideological thrust of the movement, and the nuances of the different actors. The role of some of the trade union leadership, like Kelley and Slatter, was certainly important here in supporting the promoters' case. For the most part they stressed the bringing of new industries and new jobs, but they also gave strong backing to the proposal for working class shareholdings – as did another key figure, the radical Liberal John C. Fielden. Though a small cotton manufacturer, Fielden had close links with the trade union movement, and especially with the weavers, for whom he acted as adviser in arbitration cases.[144] Described by Leech as "a very gifted man who had risen from the ranks",[145]

and acknowledged by many as the "Cobden of the movement",[146] Fielden addressed hundreds of meetings in support of the Canal – probably more than any other single person – but the account he gives of his own experiences is of a man occupying uncomfortable terrain where the interests of the trade unions and manufacturing capital are not identical. Speaking at a testimonial meeting organized in his honour by the Northern Counties Weavers, he complained that he had been involved in "numberless discussions … amongst capitalists and employers with whom I associate. I have frequently gone through periods in which I have been looked upon almost as a leper". His unwitting explanation for why he might be held in this regard followed a little later:

> Some men tell me that Labour and Capital are identical … twins, inseparable and so on. Well, I think Capital is of enormous assistance to Labour, but I contend that Labour is the creator and therefore can never be the equal of the thing created.[147]

This was distinctly not the message of the manufacturing capital interests behind the Ship Canal, whose views were most commonly represented, until his resignation in 1887, by Daniel Adamson. A populist, who spoke with a strong 'Northern burr', Adamson was the epitome of the self-made man. In the five years in which he led the movement he sought systematically to develop an alliance between manufacturing

*Punch* cartoon in 1882.

MANCHESTER-SUR-MER. A SEA-DUCTIVE PROSPECT.

capital and the skilled working class. No promises were too much for him as can be seen in his claim that "he would not in future invest his money in works which were to compete against other works, but would invest it … in works, that would confer heard benefit upon all, and would injure none".[148] Under the banner of a producer ideology, the progressive sections of society were to be united against the backward elements of an old society, which included the aristocracy but was most especially composed of the mercantile non-producing classes.

Adamson presented himself as a man of the people, who "spoke on behalf of the people".[149] Referring at Eccles to his working class audience as "fellow working men", he claimed that he "always had been interested in the welfare of the working classes, because he was one himself".[150] It needed then only a slight shift of gear to argue that working men "without any very great trouble" would be able to find the remainder of the capital and claim "We did it, and it is our Canal".[151]

The very idea of a Ship Canal was a useful vehicle for developing this cooperative producer-driven model of popular capitalism. It focussed immediate attention away from the priorities and processes of production and responsibilities of

manufacturing capital, over which conflicts of interest could easily develop; and instead emphasised the issue of transport and stages of distribution, where a producer's consensus between masters and men against "the Railway Kings", "monopolies" and merchant interests could be more easily generated. The distinction was not sound logically or structurally – and was indeed one of the inherent and disabling contradictions in the movement – but it was a peg for Adamson to develop his theme.

Ironically this received its most clear exposition after his resignation, at a speech given as President of the Iron and Steel Institute, when there were no reporters present. According to the *Manchester Guardian*, Adamson was "simply pointing out that the interests of the merchant and manufacturer do not lie in parallel lines, and while he that does least gets the largest amount of profit, he that does most may be said practically to receive little or none."[152] But it was enough to bring howls of anger and a leading article in the *Times* condemning Adamson for a speech devoted to "a denunciation of the Free Trade policy of this country."[153]

In reality it appears to have been far less extreme than many of his speeches made earlier during his leadership of

85

the campaign. Though patently a capitalist himself – he had a £4,000 shareholding in the Ship Canal – he was keen to reject the support of finance capital ("London and large capitalists"), relentlessly attacked the Railway and Dock operators opposing the Canal and spoke scathingly about the mercantile interests traditionally associated with Lancashire's cotton industry. "The canal would help to destroy the living of the fat maggots – that had so long been subsisting upon the population connected with an old-established trade",[154] he told a subscribers' meeting in 1885. Nor was this just a chance remark, for a year earlier he had similarly lambasted not only "The parasites of Liverpool" but also the "men to be found in George Street who were bought over by bribery and corruption".[155]

Adamson was not, however, alone in developing this anti-mercantile capital line of argument, for his remarks were reflected at significant points, though not consistently, in actions and speeches of the Spinners' leader, James Mawdsley. Addressing the 1884 Pomona Gardens mass rally as President of the Trades Council, Mawdsley was beginning to map out the ground: "As a manufacturing and producing town, Manchester had been gradually getting lower and lower until it was now more in character like Liverpool and London, where material was stored and money dealt in, but there was not much employment for skilled labour".[156] A year later in his circular letter to members before the big Oldham strike,

"Warehouse-land" in Manchester, where Adamson and Mawdsley claimed the manufacturing profits were being pocketed. *Chetham's*

in which he sought the spinners' agreement to a levy, he extended the argument: "Is it worth our while to pay five percent of our wages to assist in averting the reductions proposed, or shall we allow it (and perhaps more) to be taken in the warehouse?"[157] The language here, it is true, is mild enough and the 'warehouse' reference somewhat opaque; but by 1892, during the bitter dispute with the cotton masters that led finally to the Brooklands agreement, Mawdsley's target in an article in the SDF's organ, *Justice*, is unmistakable:

… the last people to have their wages docked … should be the men and women who do the hardest and most unpleasant work … In Liverpool there are some thousands of men – brokers, bankers, merchants and others – who live in clover all the year round out of cotton … In Manchester, Oldham, Bolton … it is the same. These men swarm everywhere … Every one of these agents (as distinct from employers) from the first Liverpool broker downwards all make a handsome profit … They are perfectly useless … and yet they pocket at least £5,000,000 per annum … If expenses have to be reduced, it is these harpies that must be attacked and exterminated before the employers come to us.[158]

Nor was it words alone, as the case of the 1889 "cotton corner" reveals. As Beatrice Webb put it in her diary after a reference to the "brilliant victory" of the Dock Strike, which had just ended: "Meanwhile a new departure has been taken silently by north country Trades Unionists under the leadership of my friends, Mawdsley and Birtwistle". The initiative involved the unions agreeing with the employers' strategy of halting all production until the new cotton crop appeared on the market. In this way the masters would be able to "corner the cornerers" – the merchants who were artificially raising prices. Webb's concluding comment endorses the argument:

This is the first instance I can remember in which the Workers Association have made common cause with the masters against a common enemy.[159]

The paradox here, of course, for the big industrial bourgeoisie promoting the Canal, was that with this line of argument they ran the risk of cutting off their noses in spite of their faces. Identifying a mercantile class (which axiomatically included small merchants like Bosdin Leech and the influential J. A. Beith[160]) as a common enemy helped to achieve one objective – solidifying an alliance with the skilled working class – but simultaneously it jeopardised the main objective of building the Ship Canal because it alienated the very class which could provide the capital to finance the project.

The language of conflict was not, however, arrived at accidentally. The economic crisis of the 1880s, signalling a move from competitive to monopoly capitalism, was creating widespread job insecurity and manifest inequalities of wealth and living standards, for which explanations were sought across the political spectrum. Where the socialists and the Social Democratic Federation were positing a necessary antagonism between employers and employees, a division arose which instead united them as producers against the 'parasitic' and 'idle'[161] and offered the chance of a snugger fit with the Lib–Lab pact which the trade unions and employers were jointly pursuing. But what must be stressed is that the situation was one of fluid shifting alliances. Moreover, the meaning of concepts like socialism and liberalism was volatile. As Yeo has indicated: "Late-nineteenth century Liberalism was inclusive, spilling over beyond dominant meanings of liberalism with a small "l". The party and the ideology was being stretched by problematics constructed outside them, but which they had to try to digest, in the interests of their own continuity".[162] Liberal trade unionists in the Trades Council may have been quite explicit in their rejection of "socialism", with Mawdsley dismissing "the unworkable theories of Mr Hyndman of [sic] the communistic ideas which occasionally dribble over from the continent",[163] and others like Matthew Arrandale, Secretary of the United Machine Workers, and G. D. Kelley going out of their way in interviews to state that they were not socialists.[164] However, their language and explanations could at times move in quite different directions, reflecting the variety of meanings commonly ascribed to the word "socialism". At the Stalybridge Spinners Tea Party in 1885, Mawdsley argued that while "the upper classes" were far better off than they used to be, the working classes were not getting "a fair share of the increase of wealth".[165] A year later, he came back to the same issue but with a sharper tongue at a big rally in support of Martha Kilburn – "The Plucky Young Weaver of Rochdale", imprisoned for non-payment of a fine.

> The working people of England might not be very wealthy, they might not be able to ride in their carriages or to enjoy all the luxuries that wealth could bring within their reach, but when they got their pittance at the weekend they had at least the satisfaction of knowing that it had been honestly earned and had not been dragged out of the body and blood of their fellow creatures.[166]

The Martha Kilburn rally occurred at the height of the 1886 disturbances over unemployment, when demonstrations and riots were taking place both in the capital and many provincial centres, including Manchester. The impact of this agitation can be seen in the tone of Mawdsley's speech and on the alliances within the Ship Canal movement, and it is appropriate, therefore, to look more closely at the issue of the unemployed and how it was treated by the promoters and the trade unions throughout this period.

### The Threat of Destabilisation: Public Works and the Unemployed

The effects of the depression on their own members was a central concern for the trade unions in the early 1880s at the start of the Ship Canal campaign, but there was little incentive to extend this concern to the large mass of the unemployed.

Unskilled and usually employed on a casual or seasonal basis, they were far more likely to be regarded by skilled trade unionists as a reserve army of labour, which the employers would be keen to draw on to force down wages and for deskilling craft jobs. The presence of large numbers of urban poor dependent on relief and the workhouse was, however, always a threat to the political stability of Victorian cities, and had been a factor in Manchester at least from the harsh winter in 1878, when it was reckoned that 65,000 people were in receipt of relief. It was a situation that provided fertile ground for the Social Democratic Federation which decided to commence 1884 with the launch of a new organ, *Justice*, and with campaigning activities amongst the unemployed on a platform of municipal reforms and programmes of public work.[167] Lancashire was to be a major centre for propaganda activities and recruitment[168] but an immediate problem was that in important aspects the SDF had to tread a path already opened up by the Ship Canal promoters. Indeed Leech reports that on one occasion a local bank manager under the pseudonym of "Truth" wrote a letter to a local paper, declaring that it was the promoters who were the instigators of the agitation among the unemployed.[169]

Adamson, with his sensitive populist antennae, picked up the scent early. Participating in a delegation visiting the River Tyne, he linked the need for the Ship Canal with a growing threat: "It was fearful to contemplate the disaster which would happen to the community at large with the prospect of a huge, growing and unemployed population".[170]

Painting of William Morris, socialist and inspirer of the Arts and Crafts movement. His last visit to the city was in 1894, when he addressed 2000 people from a lorry beside the Ship Canal on the subject of "waste". *WCML*

The unemployed of London in March 1886, receiving handouts of food. *MCL*

The comment was to be echoed shortly afterwards in Joseph Chamberlain's assessment: "The cry of distress is as yet almost inarticulate, but it will not always remain so".[171]

An early start was made with the SDF agitation by arranging a speaking tour of provincial cities, including Liverpool by Henry George.[172] The veteran William Morris was sent to Manchester where he delivered a lecture on Socialism to an Ancoats audience including leading Liberals C. P. Scott, J. W. Southern and Councillor Rowley.[173] Five weeks later another member of the SDF national committee, J. Hunter Watts, was in the city, having been invited to a meeting of the local unemployed movement. Over this period the local press was full of reports of meetings of the unemployed organized by a committee chaired by Joseph Waddington and it included details of a mass meeting at Pomona of 2,000 unemployed where a resolution had been passed that "a petition should be presented to Parliament asking that precedence might be given to the Ship Canal Bill so as to give labour to the unemployed".[174]

Faced with this, Hunter Watts, who reported that he "had been sent down by a society in London ... to judge what movement it was that was afoot in Manchester", found the ground swept from under his feet, and had to fall back on

an appeal to local jingoism to discourage support for the Canal:

> If the Canal were to be proceeded with it would afford work for two or three years, but after that time they would be in a worse position than they were now, for the cutting of the canal would bring thousands of men into this district, who when the canal was concluded would be thrown out of labour and would lessen the chance of those who belonged to the neighbourhood of getting employment ... the rich class would gain all the advantage.[175]

A subsequent motion was adopted unanimously that:

> this meeting of the unemployed of Manchester and Salford desires it should be distinctly understood that this movement is neither communistic, socialistic, anarchistic or dynamitic in its object, but a simple appeal to wealthy philanthropists ...

This and a comment by Waddington at an earlier meeting that if a "Tory Government had been in power the working man would not now have been crying for bread",[176] reveal that at this stage the local movement of the unemployed was no SDF creature offering an alternative economic analysis, but that it looked for support to convention and established power structures.[177] In a search for respectability, they laid out sheets of paper at one meeting for the men to indicate names and occupations and thus substantiate the genuineness of their complaints, and demonstrate they were no mere "loafers".[178] The trade union leaders were unconvinced, however, and felt confident enough to treat the unemployed as marginal to their own project. Both Austin and Murchie preferred to align themselves with the Mayor, Alderman Goldschmidt, in emphasising how exaggerated were the claims of there being 40,000 unemployed, and Murchie was at pains to distinguish and distance his time-served members from the unemployed: "many call themselves joiners, who have no right to the name – men who during the great building society mania a few years ago found work in connection with the building of property, but who have no thorough knowledge of either joinering, bricklaying, plastering, masonry or anything else".[179]

The next two years were spent by the SDF locally in building up a membership and in holding lectures and open-air meetings. Lancashire was the principal centre for the federation outside London, with its Irish Catholic population in areas like Collyhurst and Ancoats providing an important base for recruitment.[180] Prominent members were H. M. Reade,[181] Joseph Waddington, Henry Harry, J. M. Hall, John Thompson, Alfred Settle, William Horrocks and George Smart, the last named successfully winning a seat in 1885 at the Salford School Board elections when he defeated Richard Husband, the Tory Mayor of the city and member of the Ship Canal Provisional Committee.

Although Thompson's comment that "from the start the Social Democrats assumed the leadership of unemployed organisation and agitation"[182] was not strictly accurate in the case of Manchester, it certainly held true by 8th February 1886 when the famous "Black Monday" riot took place in London in Trafalgar Square following the decision of the SDF to hold a demonstration in opposition to the one being organized by The Fair Trade League.[183]

The issue of the unemployed had been receiving substantial attention nationally and locally, with the Ship Canal supporters using this as an argument to justify the project.[184] Following the riot Adamson himself was once again quick off the mark with a letter to the *Times*, republished in handbill form, which argued that the Canal would mean "continuous employment of many thousands of labourers and artisans" and would do "so much to solve the great labour problem".[185]

This time, however, the SDF was not so easily wrong-footed, and organized two demonstrations on successive Sundays, 28th February and 7th March, described in the Watch Committee minutes as "ostensibly in the interests of the 'unemployed'"[186] – which were to be the start of a series of SDF events and activities running through to May. Rumours abounded about what was being planned, with the

"Bloody Sunday" 1886: Crowd breaking up at the unemployed demonstration in Trafalgar Square. *MCL*

*Courier* reporting that intelligence had been received that "during divine service in the morning the cavalry barracks in Hulme and the infantry barracks in Salford might be attacked by the mob".[187] Elaborate precautions were taken by the police with 477 members of the force being deployed on the streets or held in reserve[188] – action which was more than justifiable according to the *Courier* "with the grim spectre of London ruffianism, wreckage and pillage still fresh in their memory".

For the SDF, intent on propaganda, the danger lay in violent demonstrations provoking repressive action by the authorities. Indeed on 28th February, after the morning meeting organized and addressed by SDF speakers was over, a much larger demonstration of at least 15,000 people developed in the afternoon, spilling out of New Cross into Oldham Road, Great Ancoats Street and Oldham Street, leading to charges by the police and several arrests. By contrast, the following Sunday's demonstration of up to 7,000 people was a model of good order. The audience was "principally composed of respectably dressed working men" in which "the rough element formed a very insignificant portion". It was an ideal opportunity for Horrocks and others to develop their arguments on the unequal distribution of wealth between the "profit-monger" and the working classes, and explain that they were "neither Liberals nor Tories", and that by banding together under the SDF working men could "thus supplement the aid of the trade unions".[189] Even the Tory *Courier*, noting that "the speakers deprecated the interference of roughs", was prepared to listen:

It is for the good of all that whatever grievances Socialists have, or think they have, should be thoroughly ventilated … No-one who is at all read in the signs of the times can deny that the philosophical Socialist has a locus standi. It is undoubtedly true that wealth is gradually accumulating into the hands of the few. The larger capitalists are becoming more and more the masters of the situation.[190]

By mid-March for almost a week the Corporation was persuaded to provide daily work tickets for up to 1,500 unemployed and, significantly at a specially convened and well-attended meeting, the Trades Council agreed to press

## THE

# MANCHESTER SHIP CANAL

### AND

# INTEREST DURING CONSTRUCTION.

*Reprinted from* THE TIMES, *Saturday, Feb. 13th, 1886.*

#### TO THE EDITOR OF " THE TIMES."

Sir,—I have read with great satisfaction the speech of Lord Salisbury in reply to the deputation from the unemployed, and as one portion has special reference to a matter which deeply concerns the prosperity of this district, and with it the labour question, I trust you will allow me space for a few remarks upon a Bill which is now before Parliament. I refer to the Manchester Ship Canal Additional Powers Bill, asking for powers to pay interest during construction.

There may be a misconception placed upon your able leader were it not pointed out that the Regent's Canal Company, with the support of Lord Salisbury and Mr. Chamberlain, as President of the Board of Trade, obtained last session powers to pay interest, notwithstanding the strong vested interests which had to be contended against, and it is not unlikely that opposition to our Bill may come from those who consider their interests are affected, but who have already, during the construction of their own works, paid, and are now paying, interest themselves, although some leading railway directors have promised us their generous support.

In our case we cannot complete our new works or earn revenue from them for a period estimated at four years, during which time it will be necessary to outlay at least £8,000,000, and it is as monstrous to ask investors to lend their money without return for this period as it would be to ask for the materials and labour on credit.

All we want is that the works when completed by us should cost us the same price as though they had been constructed by a third party and handed over on completion to us at net cost, which of course would include interest.

No great undertaking in the world has been carried out successfully over a period of years without similar payments, nor is there in any country, excepting ours, a necessity to go to the Legislature to obtain the right, from which it may be assumed that it is only Englishmen who do not know their own business.

Our shareholders, already thousands in number, ask unanimously for the powers, which, if granted, will mean the continuous employment of many thousands of labourers and artisans, and new investors are ready to join us in our great national undertaking if Parliament acts upon the precedent of last year.

This is a question far above party, and I trust that all classes of politicians will unite to help us to proceed with a work which will do so much to solve the great labour problem and to assist the great industries of the country.

Yours faithfully,
DANIEL ADAMSON, Chairman of the Manchester
Ship Canal Company.
Manchester.

Letter from Adamson concerning the unemployed, which was circulated in the form of this handbill. *MCL*

for the extension of relief and to insist upon sending a delegation to the Mayors of Manchester and Salford, seeking the establishment of a relief fund similar to the one opened in London – which Goldschmidt, the Mayor in Manchester, was opposing.[191] Suddenly new alliances were being formed and divisions opening up.

Goldschmidt, a Liberal, when speaking as part of a Ship Canal delegation sent to see Mundella, President of the Board of Trade, had already created embarrassment by publicly disagreeing with Houldsworth, another member of the delegation, about the extent of unemployment:

"He was glad to say that there was not that distress in the Manchester District that Mr Houldsworth seemed to suppose".[192] Now social democrats and liberal trades unionists on the Trades Council were making common cause over the problems of the unemployed – an alliance which had the potential to distort the existing axis of the Ship Canal Movement.

The threat of destabilisation which these developments posed to an already fracturing ruling class also created other dilemmas for the authorities. Failure to respond to the evident suffering and even starving of 'decent artisans' would lose them the moral high ground, while a failure to deal firmly with the turmoil and violent clashes occurring on the streets of Manchester[193] would be seen as inability to maintain public control and as an encouragement to further disorder. For Chamberlain, President of the Local Government Board, writing privately at this very time to Beatrice Webb, the solution was clear – public work.

If men will starve rather than dig for two shillings a day, I cannot help them … It will remove one great danger, viz that public sentiment should go wholly over to the unemployed and render impossible that state sternness to which you and I equally attach importance. By offering reasonable work even at the lowest wage to the really industrious, we may secure the power of being very strict with the loafer and confirmed pauper.[194]

But even he – within days of writing this letter and issuing the "Chamberlain Circular" (15th March) authorising local authorities to set up public works schemes with the Poor Law Guardians[195] – was giving voice on 22nd March to widely felt worries at a private dinner party with Arthur Balfour, Albert Grey and Lord Rothschild:

I think the look-out is alarming. Any important relaxation of outdoor relief would produce most serious consequences. State Public Works are absurd. Yet if this distress goes on for three more years, we may find ourselves *en pleine revolution*; I may be wrong but that is my instinct.[196]

A further perspective on the extent of public alarm caused by the agitation over the unemployed at this time can be gained by a simple analysis of references to the "unemployed"[197] which appeared in the *Times Index* over the period of the Ship Canal campaign. As Table 6 shows, although not a new phenomenon, unemployment peaked as a political issue in the years 1886 and 1887, with the first quarter of 1886 in which the Manchester demonstrations occurred representing the zenith.

The response in Manchester to the agitation soon hardened, with the Watch Committee deciding on 18th March, after receiving a report from the Mayor, to have nothing more to do with the unemployed – or keeping men "playing at work" as one member put it[198] – and to leave responsibility to the Guardians. There was a clampdown, too,

**Table 6  References to "the unemployed" in the *Times Index* 1882–1889**

|       | Jan–March | April–June | July–Sept | Oct–Dec | Total |
|-------|-----------|------------|-----------|---------|-------|
| 1882  | 1         | —          | —         | —       | 1     |
| 1883  | —         | —          | —         | —       | —     |
| 1884  | —         | —          | —         | —       | —     |
| 1885  | 17        | 3          | —         | 8       | 28    |
| 1886  | 149       | 12         | 5         | 18      | 184   |
| 1887  | 22        | —          | —         | 102     | 124   |
| 1888  | 37        | 3          | 3         | 4       | 46    |
| 1889  | 13        | —          | —         | —       | 13    |

on public meetings with the result that when the SDF held a further protest meeting in May the Mayor came under sustained attack. Thomson denounced him to hisses from the audience because of his insistence throughout that there was no unusual distress, and was followed by Waddington who demanded, to prolonged cheering, that the Queen be petitioned to remove the Mayor and herself open a relief fund.[199]

The police were quick to act, halting the procession which followed in order to arrest Thomson and Waddington along with six others for begging and obstruction, for which they were subsequently fined. There was no protest which the radical Irish-born priest W. A. O'Conor, who had chaired the meeting, attributed to the strong anti-Irish feeling in Manchester.[200] The longer term impact was to reduce substantially the activities of the SDF in Manchester, which was never again to hold meetings on a similar scale in the city. Waddington himself announced his resignation as secretary of the committee,[201] and the following year the committee was informed by the Chief Constable that a procession of the unemployed would not be allowed to pass through the city.[202] When this decision was announced the following day at a meeting of the unemployed at Pomona it was accepted without objection, as was the condition imposed by the proprietor of the hall that they could continue to meet there provided that "speakers did not indulge in violent language against any person or class, and they did not encourage the Socialist element."[203]

Although the campaigning and political work of the SDF was curtailed in this way, the effect of their unemployed agitation on the turn of Ship Canal affairs was especially significant, for it not only brought changes in attitudes, but also helped to force through a major restructuring of the movement with consequent realignments. The support of the Mayor and Corporation were essential to the Ship Canal's success, and Mawdsley had moved quickly to hold that part of the alliance together by writing to the local press to condemn the "disparaging not to say impertinent remarks about the Mayor" which had been made at the meeting. But he also acknowledged Waddington's criticism – and in doing so restated the Trades Council's position – by agreeing that it might have been better if a relief fund had been organized.[204] More importantly, Mawdsley's attitude to the unemployed had begun to change as he showed at the International T.U.C. in 1886,[205] and at the T.U.C. annual

meeting when he addressed these words, as chairman of the Parliamentary Committee, to the delegates representing the country's skilled workers:

> We see hundreds of thousands of workmen unemployed throughout the country. We cannot ignore the fact that these men, women and children by scores and hundreds of thousands are starving. It does not do to shut our eyes to these facts, and to say that while the skilled trades of the country are doing well, we will leave others out of the question ... What we say is that every man should have his share of the produce of his labour and the workman should also have his hours of labour reduced.[206]

The clear distinction between the skilled worker and the unemployed was becoming blurred, as the former succumbed to job insecurity and the other consequences of a poorly performing economy, and looked for support from something wider than the community of the trade.[207]

The impact of the events of early 1886 was far from being confined solely to trades unionists. It was felt also by others alarmed at the break up of existing political structures – the seceding Liberal Unionists were to take 73 seats in the July General Election – and the inherent threat from the spread of socialist ideas. An important illustration of this can be seen in the case of C. P. Scott, influential editor of the *Manchester Guardian*, who agreed in June to contest North-East Manchester for the Liberals in the following month. Scott had been a supporter of the Ship Canal from its inception, but it was as an orthodox Liberal espousing Free Trade economic policies in which the State should play only a limited part. His views were reflected in an early editorial, advising against the Corporation's financial involvement on the prophetic grounds that:

> The construction of the proposed Canal is a highly speculative undertaking. No-one can tell how much it will cost, and no one can tell how much it will yield upon the outlay ... The risk is enormous, and the possibilities of loss are too real to be contemplated without great uneasiness on the part of anyone who has regard to the burden of local and municipal taxation ... If the Canal should prove a financial failure, the consequence would be a permanent addition to this burden.[208]

**A LITTLE HOLIDAY!**

*Fellow-Townsman (to Manufacturer).* "HULLO, JACKSCREW! YOUR WORKS CLOSED? HOW'S THAT? I UNDERSTOOD YOU WERE BUSY."

*Jackscrew (Brass-founder).* "SO WE ARE; BUT OUR 'ANDS TOOK 'EMSELVES OFF TO-DAY, TO JOIN THE PR'CESSION O' THE UNEMPLOYED!"

*Punch* cartoon of March 1886. The discussion shows a clear under-standing of the alliance that was being made between the employed and the unemployed. *MCL*

He had clearly, however, been affected by the unemployed agitation as he indicated at an eve of election open-air meeting – held at New Cross, the site of the February demonstration – which was called to provide him with the opportunity of countering Tory slurs that he was an opponent of the Ship Canal. Before an audience of four to five thousand, he stated that he personally had had several conferences with the leaders of the unemployed, and had tried to find them work, and finally when they were charged in May he had got a lawyer to defend them and went himself

92

to the Court to pay their fines on conviction. His principal reason "above all others", he explained, for being a friend of the Canal, was that "This city was at present suffering from want of employment", and he concluded unequivocally that "it was because of the deep interest which he took in the unemployed of this city that he was anxious that no time should be lost in getting the Ship Canal works fairly set on foot."[209]

Scott's identification of the political importance of the unemployed question provides the explanation both for his change of position from 1882, and for his involvement later in the year in the Consultative Committee, upon which also sat the two other public figures closely associated with the unemployed agitation – Alderman Goldschmidt, Mayor of the city, and James Mawdsley. The role of this Committee in seeking to resolve the tensions generated by the producer alliance within the movement, and by the unemployed movement without, are developed in Chapter 6.

Before moving on to look at particular industrial sectors, we can usefully summarise by saying that this chapter has demonstrated the centrality of the trade unions to the Ship Canal movement and explored why, in the early 1880s, in a period of economic and social turmoil, the offer of cooperation was seized upon so eagerly by the two parties to the alliance. Nor was this cooperation a flash in the pan for it had its parallels in the 1840s and in the 1870s. The bid by the promoters to win popular support was highly successful and demonstrated how a well-coordinated campaign could overwhelm the opposition of mercantile capital and other interests and create a new climate of opinion in favour of large-scale public intervention in Lancashire's economic infrastructure. The campaign's producer ideology however had its own contradictions, which were soon revealed when the voices of the unemployed were to be heard ringing out across the streets of Manchester. More than anything else

C.P. Scott, editor of the *Manchester Guardian*.

the issue of unemployment – as part of a wider economic restructuring – was to force a major realignment bringing together industrial and mercantile capital in support of the project, but it was at the expense of the producer alliance of manufacturers and workers which Adamson and others had been so assiduously cultivating.

## Notes

1. "Past masters" by J. Slater, former history HMI, *Guardian*, 25 April 1989.
2. B. Leech, *op.cit.*, Vol. 2, p. 17. Compare Brougham's remark: "By the people I mean the middle class, the wealth and intelligence of the country, the story of the British name"
3. For an analysis of the growth of socialism, which deliberately chooses to focus on exactly this same critical period, see S. Yeo, "A New Life: The Religion of Socialism in Britain, 1883–1896", in *History Workshop*, 4, 1977.
4. S. Hall and B. Schwarz, in M. Langan and B. Schwarz (eds.), *Crises in the British State*, 1985, p. 16.
5. *Social History*, VIII, 1983, and IX, 1984.
6. *Manchester Guardian*, 7 July 1882, p. 5(b). The title of the League had strong reverberations with the "Society for Preserving Liberty and Property against Republicans and Levellers" established with Government help ninety years earlier at the time of the French Revolution as an organisation to counter the growth of Radicalism. See G. D. H. Cole, *A Short History of the British Working Class Movement*, Volume 1, 1925, p. 47. At the TUC Congress in 1883 the suggestion of the League's Secretary that the delegates would be interested in the League's aims was met with laughter. W. J. Davis, *The British T.U.C.*, 1910, p. 98.
7. Lord Elcho had been responsible in 1867 for piloting a Bill through Parliament repealing some of the worst forms of discrimination against employees in the law of master and servant. In 1897 he became, as Lord Wemyss, the Chairman of the newly formed Free Labour Protection Association, designed to help employers break strikes. See H. A. Clegg and A. Fox, *A History of British Trade Unions since 1889*, 1964, pp. 171–3.

8. For details of this event see B. C. Roberts, *The Trades Union Congress. 1868–1921*, 1958, pp. 102–103.

9. *Manchester City News*, 12 August 1882, p. 5. Article "by an Old Trade Unionist".

10. *Gorton Reporter*, 12 August 1882, p. 8, 19 August, p. 8.

11. TUC Annual Reports. The role and links with the Cooperative movement are explored in chapter 6.

12. According to the evidence of the Salford solicitor, Clement Walmsley, Bailey had been approached as early as 1878 about taking on the chairmanship of a committee to press for an improved waterway from the sea to Manchester. Only later was Adamson approached. Walmsley was initially one of the solicitors for the Provisional Committee. See Summary of Evidence. Ref. Manchester Central Library f.386. M.67.

13. See F. M. Leventhal, *Respectable Radical; George Howell and Victorian Working Class Politics*, 1971, pp. 201–205. Howell at this time was acting as business agent for Ellis Lever, a Manchester coal agent, and was taking an active part in the running of Labour Standard before his election in 1885 as MP for Bethnal Green. He was one of the eleven 'Lib–Lab' members elected, and had been Secretary to the TUC and the Parliamentary Committee from 1871 to 1875, before this post was taken over by Henry Broadhurst.

14. *Labour Standard*, 15 July 1882.

15. Minutes of the Provisional Committee, 13 October 1882, Manchester Ship Canal Company Archive.

16. *Manchester Courier*, 28 October 1882.

17. *Labour Standard*, 1 April 1882.

18. See *Ship Canal Gazette*, 18 November 1882, for a full report of the meeting and speeches.

19. Shorrocks had been Secretary of the 1868 Conference, and was Secretary of the Trades Council 1877–1882.

20. See W. J. Davis, *The British Trades Union Congress. History and Recollections*, 1910, p. 89; and L. Bather, *History of Manchester and Salford Trades Council from 1880*, unpublished University of Manchester Thesis, 1956, p. 67.

21. *Manchester Examiner and Times*, 18 October, 20 October, and 30 October 1882.

22. *Manchester Examiner and Times*, 15 November, 1882.

23. *Manchester Faces and Places*, 10 March 1891. Kelley was the first representative of the labour interest to gain a seat on the City Council. He was unopposed by the Conservatives. The issue of working class shareholding is discussed in chapter 6.

24. *Oldham Evening Chronicle*, 7 December 1882; Oldham Trades Council Annual Report, 1883.

25. Amalgamated Association of Operative Cotton Spinners. Quarterly meeting, 17 December 1882.

26. *Labour Standard*, 10 February 1883.

27. The allusion here is to the keelmen of Newcastle-upon-Tyne, whose independence, self-sufficiency and ultimate displacement – as the river was deepened and docks were constructed – remains a part of popular Tyneside culture even today. By the 1880s they were almost extinct. See S. Middlebrook, *Newcastle upon Tyne. Its Growth and Achievement*, 1950, p. 248.

28. *Oldham Evening Chronicle*, 7 December 1882, p. 3.

29. *Ship Canal Gazette*, 6 December 1882, p. 62.

30. *Manchester Examiner and Times*, 26 January 1883. Kelley's letter in reply is to be found pasted into Leech's cuttings book.

31. Manchester Ship Canal Company Board Minutes, 1 December 1885. The original wording of the minute noted "That a gratuity of £10 be given to Mr Kelley in acknowledgement of services rendered". The phrase "in acknowledgement of services rendered" is ruled out with Daniel Adamson's initials and a date, December 8th 1885 added, suggesting the sensitivity of the issue in the Board's eyes. A subsequent application through the manager, Mr Marshall Stevens, for a payment of £10 to Mr Kelley was referred without comment to the Finance Committee (Board Minutes 26 February 1886).

32. *Umpire*, 4 October 1885, p. 5. Cornwall had been employed as one of the campaign staff. He resigned shortly before writing the article.

33. *Umpire*, 9 October 1887; B. Leech, *op.cit.*, Vol. 1, p. 121. Fogg, a cloth agent and Liberal, was a prominent member of the Chamber and of the Manchester Statistical Society.

34. Letter from James E. Platt to D. Adamson, 25 May 1884. Lancashire Record Office. Adamson Papers Ref. DDX/101/3. Samuel Andrew referred to was the same cotton employers' Secretary with whom the trades unions were cooperating in 1882.

35. *Manchester Guardian*, 23 June 1884.

36. S. Ramsbottom. Handbill "To the Working Classes. The Projected Manchester Ship Canal". MSC Archive No. 14.

37. Printed letter to Daniel Adamson from G. Kelley, Secretary to the Demonstration Committee. Manchester Ship Canal Company Archive; Provisional Committee Minutes B 10/1/1/2 – Greater Manchester Public Record Office.

38. B. Leech, *op.cit.*, Vol. 1, p. 138. Leech states that his decision in 1884 not to allow the continued use of his own name as a provisional director was because of the refusal to change direction. He put the same point more bluntly in a personal letter to Adamson: "I wish in the most respectful way to protest against the proceedings of yesterday. We want to make friends, and not enemies, and to my mind the personal attacks made will do us *incalculable* harm. Adamson's reply appears to be typical of his forthright and irascible style: "I am in receipt of your uncalled for letter of 28th – what I say or what I do not say will depend on my judgment and not on the dictation of any clique or individual party … " Letter from Leech to Adamson 28 August 1883, and reply from Adamson 31 August. Lancashire Record Office DDX 101/4/5.

39. So closely associated was the trade union movement with the Ship Canal that when a similar scheme was being contemplated to link Sheffield with the sea, a leading article in the local paper could comment: "This is a people's Question … Essentially it is a subject for the Trades Council and the Trades Unions. To working men the matter is of vital importance … " Sheffield Telegraph, 27 July 1888.

40. B. C. Roberts, *The Trades Union Congress. 1868–1921*, Appendix 2, 1958. See also S. and B. Webb, *The History of British Trade Unionism*, 1926, pp. 349–50.

41. *Statistical Tables and Report on Trade Unions*, 1887, p. 9. Board of Trade.

42. W. J. Davis, *The British Trade Union Congress. History and Recollections*, 1910, p. 89.

43. For a good account of this dispute see A. Fowler and T. Wyke (eds.), *The Barefoot Aristocrats*, 1987, pp. 87–90.

44. *Oldham Masters Letters Books*, John Rylands University Library of Manchester.
45. *Oldham Masters Letters Books*, 17 July 1885.
46. Circular letter "To Our Members" from Jas. Mawdsley, General Secretary A.A.O.C.S, 14 July 1885. Oldham Local Records Office. Ref. TU.1.
47. Quoted in A. Fowler and T. Wyke, *op.cit.*, p. 90.
48. *Oldham Chronicle*, 19 September 1885, p. 3. This is a reference to the confessions of Broadhead and other members of the grinders' trade clubs about the Sheffield outrages in 1867.
49. *Cotton Factory Times*, 19 February 1886, p. 1. The paper was first published in January 1885, and consistently reported sympathetically on trade union and labour issues. Trade union leaders like Mawdsley were able to insert articles on issues affecting the industry and the workers.
50. There has been substantial discussion about the significance of working class respectability. See for instance, G. Crossick, *An Artisan Elite in Victorian Society. Kentish Town. 1840–1880*, 1978; R. Q. Gray, *The Labour Aristocracy in Victorian Edinburgh,* 1976; E. J. Hobsbawm, "The Labour Aristocracy in Nineteenth Century Britain", in *Labouring Men*, 1964; F. M. Leventhal, *Respectable Radical: George Howell and Victorian Working Class Politics*, 1971; N. Kirk, *The Growth of Working Class Reformism in Mid Victorian England*, 1985; F. M. L. Thompson, *The Rise of Respectable Society: A Social History of Victorian Britain. 1830–1900*, 1988.
51. Quoted in R. Challinor, *The Lancashire and Cheshire Miners*, 1972, p. 179.
52. *Cotton Factory Times*, 5 March 1886, p. 1.
53. H. A. Clegg, A. Fox, and A. F. Thompson, *A History of British Trade Unions since 1889*, Volume 1, 1964, p. 1.
54. *Cotton Factory Times*, 16 January 1885, p. 1.
55. *Guardian*, 15 February 1989.
56. Manchester Ship Canal Company, Executive Committee Minutes, 25 August 1885.
57. For some examples of earlier employer involvement with trade unions in the 1870s see N. Kirk, *The Growth of Working Class Reformism in Mid-Victorian England*, pp. 291–1. This practice should be distinguished from employers' initiatives in organizing treats, visits and other benefits for their workers.
58. *Cotton Factory Times*, 19 November 1886, p. 4. Three Tory MPs were invited, but indicated their interest only by writing letters apologising for their absence.
59. *Ibid.*, p. 1.
60. N. Kirk, *op.cit.*, p. 220.
61. R. Q. Gray, *op.cit.*, p. 139.
62. *Manchester Courier*, 11 May 1886, "The Unemployed and the Mayor".
63. *Social History*, January 1984, p. 75.
64. J. Weeks, *Sex, Politics and Society. The regulation of sexuality since 1800*, 1981, p.87.
65. For the best account of the work of the Parliamentary Committee, see B. C. Roberts, *The Trades Union Congress (1868–1921)*, 1958.
66. For details of Slatter's role see letter in *Manchester Evening News*, 10 July 1902, from A. Goodier.
67. See G. Howell. *Trade Unionism New and Old*, 1973, Harvester

68. R. W. Postgate, *The Builders' History*, 1923, p. 335.
69. E. and R. Frow, *The International Working Men's Association and the Working Class Movement in Manchester*, 1979, pamphlet, p. 9.
70. *Manchester Guardian*, 1 October 1883. Robert Austin of ASE seconded Pankhurst's nomination, and Murchie was one of seven assenters to the nomination papers.
71. TUC Annual Report, 1885, p. 32.
72. P. Whitaker, *The Growth of Liberal Organization in Manchester from the Eighteen Sixties to 1903*, 1963, Ph.D. Manchester University, p. 209.
73. Mawdsley's political allegiances have caused confusion to labour historians who have relied excessively upon the Webbs' description of him as a Conservative. In their *History of Trade Unionism* (1926 edition, p.379) he is described as "cautious", and in Beatrice Webb's *Our Partnership*, published in 1948, the biographical index (p. 516) notes him as "one of the most conservative of Trade Unionists". He did, in fact, to everyone's surprise stand as a Tory Parliamentary candidate in 1899, shortly before his death, but in the early 1880s was a Liberal standing as a municipal candidate for the Party in 1885. He is recorded as being a Liberal Unionist in 1889 but the positions he adopted in the 1890s suggest a political view far more sympathetic to Socialism and the I.L.P. than has been acknowledged. This was recognized by Keir Hardie in an article in Labour Leader (29 December 1894). This confusion lies behind the errors in B. C. Roberts' account, who is forced to put forward ingenious explanations for why Mawdsley's progressive actions and statements were better interpreted as the wily manoeuvrings of a Tory. See B. C. Roberts, *op.cit.*, pp. 114, 147–148.
74. B. C. Roberts, *ibid.*, p. 107.
75. The issue of support of course turned on more than Ashton's personal political views. As Challinor points out, the Lancashire coalfields had more Tory pitmen than anywhere else and this made decisions about political activities by the union very contentious. It was also the case that after the seven week strike in 1881, with up to 50,000 miners not working, the coalowners, who were mostly Tory, adopted a far more conciliatory attitude, granting 10% wage increases in 1881 and 1882. The Lancashire coalowners did not support the Ship Canal project, and would have given no encouragement to the miners to support it.
76. *Manchester Guardian*, 22 December 1883, p.10.
77. Letter from Edwin Guthrie to C. P. Scott, 25 May 1894. John Rylands University Library of Manchester.
78. Manchester Ship Canal; Opening for Traffic, 1 January 1894. Speech of Dr. Pankhurst. Manchester Central Library, Ref. 386.M84.
79. See E. Sylvia Pankhurst, *The Suffragette Movement*, 1931, pp. 133–136, for an account of Pankhurst's campaign in Gorton. Johnston subsequently became the first Labour Councillor for St Georges Ward in 1898.
80. P. Joyce in *Social History*, IX, 2, 1984, p. 227.
81. *Gorton Reporter*, 21 February, 1885, p. 3.
82. *Manchester Guardian*, 19, 23, 24 November 1885.
83. *Manchester Evening Mail*, 1 November 1885.

84. TUC Annual Report 1886. Mawdsley had replaced Murchie as Chairman of the Parliamentary Committee. He was also sitting, as the only trade union representative, on the powerful Ship Canal Consultative Committee, established in the Autumn of 1886 after the failure to raise the necessary capital.

85. B. C. Roberts, *op.cit.*, p. 114.

86. A. Reid in *Social History*, Vol. 3, No. 3, 1978, pp. 358–361.

87. *Cotton Factory Times*, 16 January 1885, p. 1.

88. *Manchester Guardian*, 11 October 1871, p. 5. A fuller account of these events can be found in W. H. Fraser. *Trade Unions and Society*, 1974, pp. 160–164.

89. *Manchester Guardian*, 12 October 1871, p. 5.

90. *Interview in City News*, 16 November 1912.

91. Manchester Ship Canal, Great meeting in the Free Trade Hall, 31 October 1883.

92. H. Ashworth, *Recollections of Richard Cobden, MP, and the Anti–Corn Law League*, 1881, 2nd edition.

93. J. Morley, *Life of Richard Cobden*, 2 volumes, 1881, preface, p. vii. *The Life and Speeches of John Bright* was also published in 1881.

94. *Umpire*, 11 September 1887.

95. *Umpire*, 25 September 1887. Spence was a member of the Ship Canal Provisional Committee.

96. *Ship Canal Gazette*, 14 March 1883, p. 233.

97. This was the description applied to Heap by a correspondent, "T.R.H.", in the *Manchester Guardian*, 14 November 1884.

98. For some details of the Iron Trade Employers Association see E. Wigham. *The Power to Manage*, 1973, p. 14. The Opening Declaration of the National Federation of Associated Employers of Labour can be found in B. C. Roberts, *op.cit.* Appendix 1. The National Federation and the Ship Canal Provisional Committee both had the same initial address, 96 King Street, and the same Secretary, Henry Whitworth.

99. After the 1882 elections, the Conservatives held 49 seats in Bolton, to the Liberals 15. *Manchester Courier*, 2 November 1882, p. 8.

100. *Manchester Guardian*, 18 October 1884, p. 5 (Letter from Henry Heap). See also subsequent correspondence in the *Manchester Courier*, 31 October 1884, p. 8, and *Manchester Guardian*, 3 November 1884, p. 3. Strenuous efforts were also made to keep Boddington on the Board of Directors, despite his prolonged absence while suffering from nervous exhaustion, but his resignation was accepted in 1892.

101. Letter from Henry Boddington to Marshall Stevens, 24 December 1889. Manchester Ship Canal Archive No.63. Ship Canal shares were at this time trading at a substantial discount.

102. B. Leech, *op.cit.*, Vol. 1, p. 192.

103. *Manchester Examiner and Times*, 19 February 1884.

104. H. Ashworth, *op.cit.*, p. 24.

105. J. Morley, *Life of Richard Cobden*, Vol. 1, p. 249.

106. N. McCord, *The Anti Corn Law League 1838–1846*, 1958.

107. N. McCord, *ibid.*, pp. 97–102.

108. E. Watkin, *Alderman Cobden of Manchester*, 1891, pp. 87–88.

109. *Umpire*, 11 September 1887.

110. Compare, for instance, N. McCord, *op.cit.*, p. 98, with the account given of Lawrence's work by his assistant, Frank Cornwall, in two articles in *Umpire*, 4 September and 11 September 1887, and a further article in *City News*, 13 January 1894. The link between the two men is emphasised by Cornwall. Watkin was also a supporter of the Cooperative movement and was a speaker with Daniel Adamson and others at the 25th Anniversary of the Manchester and Salford Equitable Cooperative Society in 1884 (*Manchester Courier*, 10 November 1884).

111. *Gorton Reporter*, 18 November 1882, p. 5.

112. *Ship Canal Gazette*, 7 February 1883, p. 174.

113. *The Manchester Ship Canal. Reasons why it should be made.* Pamphlet 1882, Manchester Central Library.

114. Daniel Adamson Papers, Lancashire Public Record Office. Notes for Eccles Meeting, 31 August 1885, Ref.DDX 101/38.

115. *Manchester Guardian*, 5 October 1885.

116. *Ship Canal Gazette*, 7 February 1883, p. 173. The strong identification of leading employers with the city where their workforce resided was not unusual – e.g. Sir William Armstrong and Newcastle-upon-Tyne. See also D. Smith. *Conflict and Compromise. Class Formation in English Society 1830–1914*, p. 234, for discussion of the situation in Birmingham.

117. *Manchester Guardian*, 5 October 1885.

118. *Manchester Courier*, 10 November 1884, p. 6.

119. Letter from Hilton Greaves to Bosdin Leech, 1 December 1891, quoted in B. Leech, *op.cit.*, Volume 2, p. 107.

120. *Newcastle Weekly Chronicle*. 13 January 1894.

121. *Manchester Guardian*, 28 October 1884, p. 7. Roby, a classicist and former Professor of Jurisprudence, was a sewing cotton manufacturer and subsequently represented Eccles as Liberal MP 1890–95.

122. *Ship Canal Gazette*, 13 December 1882, p. 73.

123. *Ship Canal Gazette*, 8 November 1882, p. 3.

124. S. Ramsbottom, *The Manchester Ship Canal and its Supporters*, 7 September 1886, Manchester Central Library, Ref. 386 M80.

125. *Manchester Guardian*, 1 September 1885, p. 6.

126. Poster "Manchester Ship Canal. Honour the Brave", Manchester Central Library, Ref. f.386 M68 Box No. 1.

127. *Manchester Guardian*, 5 October 1885.

128. *Manchester Guardian*, *ibid.*, One banner bore a portrait of Adamson with the words, "The Hero of the Ship Canal". *Manchester Courier*, 5 October 1885.

129. Pamphlet, *Manchester Ship Canal. Great Meeting in the Free Trade Hall* (31 October 1883), Manchester Central Library Ref. f.386.M8.

130. Official Song of the Ship Canal, Manchester Ship Canal Company Archive No. 37 (Dated November 1885).

131. *Manchester Guardian*, 5 October 1885. The Cooperative News (10 October 1885, p. 939) gives a lower figure of 50,000 for those processing through the city prior to the Belle Vue meeting.

132. Electoral Poster, "The Hustings. Tory and Liberal" 1885, Manchester Central Library, Ref.ff324.942733 Ma1. For a discussion of this issue and the close association between drink, "the quickest way out of Manchester" and Toryism, see P. F. Clarke, *Lancashire and the New Liberalism*, 1971, pp. 34–36. Two important Tory supporters of the Ship Canal were the local brewers, Henry Boddington and J. G. Groves.

133. Full details of Peter Spence and his prominent position in the Manchester Temperance Union appear in his obituary notice in the *Ship Canal Gazette*, 11 July 1883, pp. 122–123.

134. *Manchester Guardian*, 22 August 1885.

135. "Manchester-on-Sea. An Idyll of the Future", 30 May 1884, Ref. Manchester Central Library, Ship Canal Cuttings f.386.M11.

136. *Manchester Faces and Places*, 1894, Vol. 5. p. 65. *A Sea Bridal* by H. D. Rawnsley.

137. Manchester Central Library, Ref. f.386.M31.

138. "Manchester on the Sea". Manchester Central Library. Ref. f.386.M12. The booklet was probably published in 1883.

139. Manchester Central Library, Ref. f.386.M68, Box No.1.

140. Ab-O'Th'-Yate and The Ship Canal: A Dream of 1892, Manchester Polytechnic Library, 1882. (Ref. LC 823.8 BRI). Curiously when the piece was republished in 1896 in Volume 3 of Sketches by Ben Brierley the title had been altered by the editor to "A Prophetic Dream of 1893", and the year of the original publication changed to 1884!

141. *Liverpool Chronicle*, 3 June 1885.

142. *Illustrated London News*, 26 May 1894.

143. Letter from A. Yates to C. P. Scott, 10 August 1912. Quoted in P. F. Clarke, *op.cit.*, p. 155.

144. Manchester Ship Canal. Enquiry before the House of Lords, 1885. Important commercial evidence given by John C. Fielden, p. 22. Manchester Central Library Ref. 386.M5. For an example of his role, see *Courier*, 5 September 1883, for a lengthy statement by Fielden to a mass meeting of striking weavers, where he reported on behalf of the union on the negotiations with the employers.

145. B. Leech, *op.cit.*, Vol. 2, p. 243.

146. *Umpire*, 2 October 1887.

147. *Cotton Factory Times*, 24 September 1886, p. 6. The *Umpire* article, *ibid.*, also describes how Fielden was alternately given fulsome praise and "the cold shoulder".

148. *Examiner and Times*, 27 June 1884.

149. *Examiner and Times*, 27 June 1884 (Town's meeting at Warrington).

150. *Patricroft and Eccles Journal*, 12 June 1885, p. 8.

151. *City News*, June 1887. Mr. Adamson's Scheme for Raising Capital.

152. *Manchester Guardian*, 15 September 1887, p. 6.

153. *Times*, 15 September 1887, p. 7.

154. *Manchester Guardian*, 22 August 1885.

155. Speech at Town's Meeting at Warrington. *Examiner and Times*, 27 June 1884. George Street was the area where many of Manchester's leading merchants had their offices and warehouses. Much of the promoters' invective was directed at "Liverpool" which was shorthand for the mercantile and shipping interests located there. Since Manchester's merchants had close working relationships with them, it was little surprise that they themselves felt directly threatened by the way the movement was being shaped. See also the *Umpire*, 7 June 1885, p. 6, for another reference by Adamson to the "parasites" of Liverpool.

156. *Manchester Examiner and Times*, 23 June 1884, p. 6.

157. Amalgamated Association of Operative Cotton Spinners. Letter from James Mawdsley. Oldham Local Studies Library.

Ref. TU.1. See also his complaint the following year about "the luxury of men who stood between the producer and the consumer and took the lion's share of the profit". *Oldham Standard*, 13 February 1886, p. 3.

158. *Justice*, 3 December 1892, p. 2.

159. *Diaries of Beatrice Webb*, Volume 13, 22 September 1889. pp. 1093–4. Webb Archive, London School of Economics.

160. Beith, a commission agent, was regarded as a key member of the Executive of the Manchester Liberal Association. The Provisional Committee minutes record his resignation from the Committee on 2 November 1882. At the Board meeting on 25 August 1885 his name was mentioned as a possible director, but the matter was left without action being taken.

161. For an interesting debate on the use of these terms in the first half of the nineteenth century, see P. Joyce, *Social History*, 1984, pp. 229–230.

162. S. Yeo, "Notes on Three Socialisms", p. 234, in C. Levy (ed.), *Socialism and the Intelligentsia. 1880–1914*, 1987. See also S. Collini, *Liberalism and Sociology*, 1979, chapter 1.

163. *Cotton Factory Times*, 16 January 1885, p. 1.

164. *Spy*, 19 March, 7 May 1892. Arrandale was President of the Trades Council from 1887, and a committee member of the Ship Canal Shareholders Association.

165. *Gorton Reporter*, 21 February 1885, p. 3.

166. *Rochdale Observer*, 20 March 1886, p. 6.

167. M. Beer, *A History of British Socialism*, Vol. 2, 1921, p. 248. Originally called the Democratic Federation, the name Social Democratic Federation was adopted in August 1884. The organization is throughout described here by its later name.

168. E. Morrison, *South Salford Branch of the SDF and the Spread of Socialism in Lancashire (1885–1894)*, 1978, Dissertation, Manchester Polytechnic.

169. B. Leech, *op.cit.*, Vol. 1, p. 193.

170. *Manchester Courier*, 26 October 1883, p. 8.

171. *Fortnightly Review*, No. 204, December 1883, Quoted in D. A. Hamer (ed.). *The Radical Programme [1885] by Joseph Chamberlain and Others*, 1971, p. xi.

172. Henry George's book, *Poverty and Progress*, had been published in 1879, and sold 400,000 copies. According to Beer "Four-fifths of the socialist leaders of Great Britain in the 'eighties had passed through the school of Henry George". M. Beer, *op.cit.*, p. 245.

173. *Justice*, 28 January 1884.

174. *Manchester Weekly Times*, 23 February 1884, p. 6, and *Manchester Guardian*, 19 February 1884, p. 8. The other three officers of the committee were Thomas Hamer, Francis Hursthouse and B. J. Cassidy.

175. *Manchester Guardian*, 12 March 1884, p. 7. In a report of the same speech *Justice* (22 March 1884) quotes Watts as saying: "the capitalist class would gain all the advantages".

176. *Manchester Examiner and Times*, 5 March 1884.

177. A letter to the *Manchester Guardian*, 23 February 1884, from the four office holders of the unemployed committee made their appeal for help to "ministers, Christians of all denominations and our fellow workmen".

178. *Manchester Examiner and Times*, 19 February 1884, p. 8.

179. *Manchester Weekly Times*, 1 March 1884, p. 6.

180. P. Thompson, *Socialists, Liberals and Labour. The Struggle*

*for London 1885–1914*, 1967, p. 114; E. Morrison, *op.cit.*, provides a good account of the SDF in this period.

181. See H. M. Reade, *Christ or Socialism – A Human Autobiography*, 1909, for an account of Reade's activities. He was secretary of the Salford SDF and in 1894 became secretary of the Manchester and Salford I.L.P.

182. P. Thompson, *op.cit.*

183. Accounts of this event can be found in D. Rubinstein, "The Sack of the West End 1886", in D. Rubinstein (ed.), *People for the People*, 1973; and in G. Stedman Jones, *Outcast London*, 1971, pp. 291–296.

184. See Letter to Salford Chronicle by J. G. Groves, 4 February 1886; and "Extract from the Times" February 6th, 1886 concerning a deputation of the unemployed to Lord Salisbury. Both of these were reprinted as handbills by the Ship Canal promoters. (Manchester Central Library. Ref. F 386. M8).

185. *Times*, 13 February 1886; Handbill, Manchester Central Library, Ref. 380. M80.

186. Watch Committee Minutes, 11 March 1886, p. 148. Manchester Central Library, Archive Department.

187. *Manchester Courier*, 1 March 1886, p. 8.

188. Watch Committee Minutes, *op.cit.*

189. *Manchester Courier*, 8 March 1886, p. 6.

190. *Manchester Courier*, *ibid.*, p. 5.

191. *Manchester Courier*, 17 March 1886.

192. *Manchester Guardian*, 24 February 1886. In the revised print of the Shorthand Writers' report, which was separately published by the promoters, his words have been changed to "There is no doubt that distress does exist in Manchester and in the district, as Mr. Houldsworth says." Manchester Central Library. Ref. F 386 M8.

193. *Manchester Courier*, 19 March 1886; *Times*, 19 March 1886, p. 5.

194. Letter from J. Chamberlain to B. Webb, 5 March 1886, *Beatrice Webb Collection*, Volume 8, p. 492, London School of Economics.

195. J. Harris, *Unemployment and Politics: A Study in English Social Policy 1886–1914*, 1972, p.75. This was the first significant occasion where the State intervened to propose procedures under the Poor Law.

196. B. E. C. Dugdale, *Arthur James Balfour*, Volume I, 1936, p. 98. Chamberlain's comments are those reported by Balfour (MP for Manchester East 1885–1906) in a letter to his uncle Lord Salisbury. At this point Chamberlain had already told Gladstone of his intention to resign from the Government over Home Rule for Ireland, a move which was to be the immediate trigger for the splitting off of the Liberal Unionists from the Liberal Party. Lord Rothschild played a central role in providing the capital for the Manchester Ship Canal.

197. The Pall Mall Gazette is credited by the Oxford English Dictionary (1926) with being the first to use the term "unemployed" in 1882. Harrison points out, however, that it was in frequent use by the republican Land and Labour League from at least 1869. R. Harrison, *Before the Socialists. Studies in Labour and Politics. 1861–1881*, 1965, p. 245.

198. *Manchester Courier*, 19 March 1886.

199. *Manchester Guardian*, 8 May 1886.

200. W. A. O'Conor, *History of the Irish People*, Volume 2, 1887, p. 178. The extent of Irish involvement in the unemployed movement appears to have been substantial. In the Courier article, 18 March 1886, describing the demonstration in Albert Square, it is noted that "many of the men wore sprigs of shamrock in their hats".

201. *Manchester Guardian*, 10 May 1886, p. 8.

202. Watch Committee Minutes, 20 January 1887.

203. *Manchester Courier*, 22 January 1887, p. 3.

204. *Manchester Courier*, 11 May 1886.

205. S. and B. Webb. *op.cit.*, p. 379.

206. TUC Annual Report, 1886, p. 10. Compare this with his refutation in 1885 of socialism as "a glowing picture, but I have not yet seen their proposals for dealing with the idle, the thriftless and the vicious". Industrial Remuneration Conference 1885. Report of Proceedings, p. 160.

207. Compare T. Wright, *Our New Masters*, 1873, p. 5. "Between the artisan and the unskilled a gulf is fixed". Quoted in A. Briggs (ed.), *Essays in Labour History*, 1960, p. 73.

208. *Manchester Guardian*, 30 November 1882.

209. *Manchester Guardian*, 2 July 1886.

# 5

# LABOUR, TECHNOLOGY AND WOMEN IN A DECADE OF CHANGE

While the previous chapter concentrated on the organization and structures of the trade unions supporting the Ship Canal and the interplay of a populist campaign with the issue of unemployment, the focus of this chapter shifts to addressing the changing experience of workers in the four principal industries – cotton, engineering, building and printing – from which trade union support for the Ship Canal was derived. These are treated in separate subsections of the chapter. The purpose of this is twofold. Firstly it helps us to understand how what was essentially a large building project could be converted, during a short period of economic and political crisis, into an engine for powering the construction of a mass popular movement. Secondly it enables us to explore how the events and political dynamics within the Ship Canal Movement reflected and impinged upon the wider industrial relations within Lancashire, with which they were intimately connected.

The producer alliance which the movement was helping to shape had an inherent instability because of its relatively narrow base of skilled craft workers. Its primary value as a model of popular capitalism – involving a closer and more cooperative relationship between employers and workers – resided in its being taken up at the factory and workplace level. The argument, to be developed by an examination of the main industrial sectors, is that this was not the case and that, as the 1880s proceeded, the industrial relations strategies developed by employers – in their search for higher productivity to counter foreign competition – became more confrontational, and more not less committed to notions of managerial prerogative. Moreover, the trade union movement itself changed radically in its composition and structure.

The *Manchester Evening Mail*, a Tory newspaper, could fairly claim after the great Ship Canal demonstration at Belle Vue in 1885 that, "Never perhaps has there been a movement of a local character in which the labouring classes especially have manifested such an amount of feeling".[1] However the facile conclusions that have sometimes been drawn from such statements by some historians do not stand up to close scrutiny – viz Grant's statement in a section about the trade unions and the Cooperative Wholesale Society that: "Workman, shopkeeper, merchant, millowner, factory owner and financier all were now being linked by a common bond – the desire to see the Canal built".[2]

There were certainly employers keen to emphasise the common interests of capitalists and craft workers as these comments by W. Mather, an engineering employer of Salford, show when he was invited to address the Boilermakers and Iron Shipbuilders Society's 50th jubilee celebrations in Manchester:

If only employers and employed were united and were determined to make the best things at the cheapest possible rate, then they might bid defiance to all competitors for the next fifty years (Applause). He would back the employers and workmen of England against the whole of the rest of the world ... if they stuck together (Renewed applause) ... it was only by masters and men working together amicably, mutually arranging any differences that might arise, that they could secure success for either party.[3]

But such expressions of hope should not be confused with an objective account of industrial relations in Lancashire. Collaboration – of which a symbolic example can be seen in the above invitation to Mather – went hand in hand with a widespread experience of conflict. The trades unions, forced into a defensive position in this period of depressed trade, responded by seeking a bargained relationship with the employers which would give them greater influence on the way that change was introduced. This context gives rise to a number of interesting questions. What were the particular factors that promoted collaboration rather than conflict at certain points in place and time? To what extent did the intensification of labour create a changing consciousness of the experience of work – and thus of the relationship between the employed and the employer? How far was the language used to describe this experience of work a reflection of attitudes to class and politics outside the world of work in the wider community, and how is this language best interpreted by us now?

Complete answers cannot be given to these questions, but an examination of Lancashire's major industries, and of engineering and cotton in particular, does start to shed revealing light on a very problematic area of historical research. In the discussion that follows reliance is placed on contemporary accounts of some twenty significant industrial disputes that took place in Lancashire in the Ship Canal years.

Particular attention is paid to Manchester and Oldham, the principal centres of the Ship Canal agitation. Although it may be objected that such a listing offers only a partial picture, it does provide a good starting point.[4] From the researcher's perspective, attitudes about class and work are difficult to unearth particularly where they are in flux. Where there is disagreement and conflict in the relationship between worker and master, or between one group of workers and another, there is often an incentive for one or both parties to remain silent. The researcher is dependent therefore on the written word – a dependency which gives a bias to the literate and the powerful – before he or she can begin to explore the nuances of language and the meandering meanings of words like "respectability", "class", and "worker", which are woven into late nineteenth century discourse. Strikes and industrial action are by contrast the one situation when the normal conventions are thrown off, when one party or both parties to a dispute about the organization or priorities of the workplace have decided on public action and demonstration, as opposed to private thought and negotiation. The differences in position, the relationships between the workers in the factory and the union leadership, the identity of key decision makers, and the role of negotiation in shaping the contract between capital and labour are all more clearly articulated here than elsewhere. A caveat has of course to be registered. The language employed, moulded for public use, and an important weapon in the bid for widening support, has to be contextualised against the different parties' aims and objectives.

To choose the terrain of industrial disputes is not to suggest that there are no other fruitful avenues to explore in opening up aspects of this debate about changing attitudes to work and class. In his broad-ranging study of class and social order in industrial England across the whole of the nineteenth century, Joyce demonstrates the rich veins of

popular culture to be mined by the historian, and argues that class – with its connotations of exclusion, conflict and economic relationships – is too restrictive a notion for embracing the entirety of experiences of "labouring people". The Ship Canal Movement, with its own powerfully effective populist ideology, its emphasis on the collaboration between employer and operative, and its resonance with the similar alliance of the Anti-Corn Law League is not inconsistent with Joyce's general argument. However, by juxtaposing it in this chapter with the changing industrial relations of the 1880s and 1890s we can see not only why it failed as a model, but also how its failure was reflected in the emergence of a more class-conscious trade union driven perspective among working people – which, in turn, was the product of powerful economic and social forces in this formative period of British history.

Concerned more with exploring the wider visions of the people rather than the impact of economic and industrial change, Joyce, through his examination of textiles, does acknowledge the role played by the trade unions in expanding the notion of class and creating a wider and national sense of working class solidarity, but he appears reluctant to recognize the significance of the 1880s, placing more emphasis on changes after the end of the century.[5]

Much of the problem of historical interpretation of course turns on what is chosen for evidence and how this is treated. Few, for instance, would dispute the assertion that a decade of government policies promoting privatisation and the market has changed attitudes in Britain today about collective provision and individual responsibility, but how would this be authoritatively demonstrated? An example of the interpretative difficulties which the historian faces can be seen in the weavers' dispute over a 5% wage reduction affecting North East Lancashire in 1884, which received national publicity through the efforts of Henry Slatter and others.[6] Originally accepted by the trade union leaders on the joint committee, the proposal for a reduction was thrown out by the workers in the Blackburn area and the dispute soon became acrimonious, with the employers putting pressure on the overlookers to bring in their relatives as blacklegs, and preventing collections at the mills. The employers were "interfering, as we can only term it in the mildest form, with the liberty of Englishmen. Therefore we would advise every working man to throw off that yoke and assert their independence ..." declared a statement by the Weavers' Association Committee but, with an eye for the morrow, they went on to express a hope that "the struggle ... will be amicably settled, so that the peaceable relations that ought to exist betwixt employers and employed whose interests are identical – may be maintained, without which no satisfaction or gain to either party can possibly arise".[7] The messages are mixed. The reference to "the liberty of Englishmen", with its populist connotations of a yeoman society, is counterpoised by the idea of the independence of working men. But does the "identity of interests" argument later in the statement suggest firmly

Herkomer's painting "Hard Times" portraying a navvy with his family exhausted by the search for work. It was purchased by the Corporation just a week after the Ship Canal Bill received the Royal Assent in August 1885. *CAG*

that the weavers of Lancashire had not a sense of class consciousness and of class interests, but instead a perception of the community of interests between workers and employers; a sense of the community of the trade?

The issue is a crucial one and is returned to on the very formal and public stage of the Royal Commission on Labour in 1891 when Thomas Birtwistle, Secretary of the North East Lancashire Weavers' Association – and himself a supporter of the Ship Canal movement – is giving evidence. Relations between employer and employed, and especially between the employers' committee and the operatives were, according to Birtwistle, "very satisfactory",[8] yet the questioning draws out a string of complaints on behalf of the 200,000 workers in the industry concerning rates of pay, wage deductions and fines, enforced overtime, accidents, steaming and driving; and leads revealingly for our purposes to this exchange a few minutes later between George Livesey, an employer representative on the Commission, and Birtwistle:

1382. Therefore there is not that community of interest which there would be if the two had an equal interest in the result of their labour? I should think not.
1383. Is there any possible means of obtaining such an identity of interest, do you think, in your trade? – I do not think so.
1384. No system of profit sharing or cooperation in the production of cotton goods would answer? I am afraid not.

This example demonstrates the subtlety of the conflict–cooperation continuum in the relationship between capital and labour, and the need for careful handling of written material. Both in the specific 1884 weavers' dispute and in the general period under study, the process has an inbuilt dynamic. Single-frame shots alone cannot do justice to the complexity of the subject, but as part of a sequence, built up from the episodic, they can help to construct a firmer picture of the change which was taking place.

In examining strikes we are primarily, though not exclusively, looking at the response of the craft unions and of skilled workers to forces, pushing them and pulling them, over which they had limited control. But these responses are also important evidence in a wider project, for the study of events at the factory and industry level in turn enables us to map the interrelationship between the politics of the workplace and the changing politics of the wider community. The latter embrace attitudes to work and respectability, the gender question, and the relationship between the skilled and the unskilled – all factors which we have identified as being of great importance in the political development of this period.

Howell has correctly argued in an essay on the origins of the Labour Party that in a sense "trade union activities were inherently protectionist".[9] Craft workers sought to maintain both stability in their relationships with other workers and their own high wage levels, but their activities were not exclusively defensive or concerned only with the prosecution of narrow short-term interests. Their support for the Ship Canal Movement, with its objective of bringing new industries and economic regeneration to Lancashire, is a testimony to this, but there are other examples too, where the trade unions were urging a long-term approach – for instance with the over-sizing of cotton goods. They declared the practice of adding a wash and substantial weight to the material to be "a source of great evil, as it was not only injurious to the interests of trade but detrimental to the health of the workpeople".[10] Another example can be seen in the pages of the *Cotton Factory Times*, first published in 1885, where articles and letters not infrequently appeared arguing the case for investment in new looms in the weaving industry as a more efficient way of increasing productivity, than the speeding up of production on existing looms.[11] Nor were these attitudes confined to weaving. Although the spinners unions were known to be anxious about the introduction of ring spinning because of the threat to their own position, this did not prevent Thomas Ashton, President of the Spinners' Amalgamated Society, telling the members at Stalybridge of the need for modernization: "He believed that old mills were destined to go to the wall. They could not compete with the modern mills, and unless they adopted ring spinning, they must go ... They must prepare by building mills on the most modern principles".[12]

The overall context was, however, one where the trade unions and their members were under assault from employers, seeking a general intensification of work and a greater control of workplace practices. The 1880s should be seen as a significant period in the transition from craft control to modern production and management, in which employers' strategies included the introduction of labour-saving technology, the increased division of labour and use of assistants and young apprentices, the threat of introducing female labour into traditionally male jobs, stricter supervision with changes in the supervisory role to be played by skilled workers, more use of payment by results and, above all, attempts to increase productivity by lowering wages.

Depressed trade and falling shares in world markets provided employers with opportunities for restructuring and increasing efficiency, which with hindsight they did not perhaps grasp eagerly enough. William Houldsworth, Tory MP for Manchester and reluctant supporter of the Ship Canal, summed up a common employers' view of the situation in remarks to the 1885 Industrial Remuneration Conference:

The instability and unsteadiness of trade are its best stimulant ... A sailor might as well expect stability and steadiness on the ocean ... as the man of business be he capitalist or workman expect regular trade and regular work, regular profits and regular wages.[13]

## Engineers and Metal Workers

The depression of the late 1870s and 1880s impacted unevenly upon different industries and sectors within industries, and the responses of employers and trade unions varied substantially.

In engineering, whilst there were certainly improvements in technology allowing faster, more reliable production, there were no major inventions in techniques which introduced fundamentally different forms of production or methods of working.

Undoubtedly, however, substantial efforts were made by employers to reduce their costs by means which did not require heavy capital investment in large-scale mechanization. [14] Essentially this involved increasing labour productivity by one of three methods. Firstly by reducing, through improved machinery and through the division of labour, the skill level – and consequently the payment made – for a given task; secondly by introducing greater control of the workplace and of the time spent on particular tasks; or thirdly by reducing the financial rewards received (via wage reductions or longer hours) for a given amount of work. While recognizing that this process was taking place, we should not exaggerate the extent of deskilling and erosion of craft control which was involved, as recent studies have pointed out. [15] The detailed evidence does not support the view that a homogeneous semi-skilled factory proletariat minding machines came to replace an earlier workforce characterised by its skill, manual dexterity, independence and control of the production process. This is a gross over-simplification both of the past and of the pace of events in the 1880s, but clearly in engineering there was a widespread belief not only that this process was taking place, but also that it was being pushed through much more rapidly than was the case.

The influential James Swift, General Secretary of the Steam Engine Makers, based in Manchester, provides a good example of this in his 1882 annual report, where he wrote:

Any member who will carry his thoughts back for even thirty years will remember that much was done in those days by manual labour that is now done by machinery; … the workman who thirty years' ago had to use mechanical skill with bodily force to manipulate a piece of metal to fit a vital part of an engine was continually improving his knowledge by using his own resources to manipulate such work. Now the machine does the greater part of this, and the workman meets with this kind of change so frequently that his workmanship is almost automatic, and governed by the machines which surround him. [16]

Four years later the period of transformation has been substantially foreshortened for in his 1886 report, Swift explaining that the depression of the last ten years had been caused by the "mania … to cheapen production", claimed that: "machines are adapted, wherever possible, to dispense with labour, and if not possible to dispense with humanity requiring a weekly wage, to let it be unskilled labour instead of a craftsman, as the large masses are more easy to deal with … than the skilled artisan who has a trade society to support him". [17]

Swift's overemphasis on the extent of the impact of new technology may well have been a consequence of being based in Manchester, for Lancashire was one of the principal engineering centres in the country where firms in the machine-tool industry, like Craven Brothers of Manchester, were pioneering the development of improved machinery. [18] In textile engineering Platts of Oldham were pivotal in the development of the ring frame – but not in its introduction in Lancashire. By the 1890s Luke and Spencer, a well-known firm in Manchester producing equipment for the finishing of metals, was informing James Samuelson that their customers had reported savings of 50% or more in labour time;[19] while John Whittaker, the Manchester full-time official of the Amalgamated Society of Engineers (ASE), stated that firms were producing locomotives in 50% less time than in the late-1870s. [20]

A final assessment of this general question is not easily made, but what is certain is that the kind of perception that was abroad – the perception of the dramatic impact of new technology – had a marked effect on the engineering unions in Manchester. It created a sense of job insecurity and had a powerful influence on workers' attitudes towards their employers, particularly when they were facing high rates of unemployment. [21] It helped to induce a cooperative attitude to employer initiatives like the Ship Canal, but a dispute at Galloways in Manchester, straddling the first early months of the Ship Canal Movement, demonstrates clearly the implicit tensions and provides details which support the general thrust of Swift's later comments.

According to the Boilermakers' report, the company, through the efforts of their "unscrupulous" foreman, was taking on unskilled non-union men and compelling the skilled boilermakers in the union to teach them how to do their jobs. Despite letters from the union written "in the most conciliatory terms", the company would not relent and a total of 70 men struck in May. [22] The dispute received no general publicity, and the note about it was inserted primarily because the union was seeking to make an additional halfpenny weekly levy for the benefit of non-union men who had come out in solidarity. Six months later the men were

Interior of Galloways boiler works.   *MCL*

102

List of names of blacks, who were brought into Galloways when the riveters went on strike.   *WCML*

still out, for the October monthly report simply carried, without further comment, a list of the names of 74 "blacks" – 56 riveters and 18 other trades now working at Galloways.

Although Charles Galloway was later in 1887 to become a member of the reconstructed Ship Canal Board of Directors with a £10,000 shareholding, in the early stages of the movement, with its emphasis on the manufacturer–worker alliance, his name is conspicuously absent from the list of 670 subscribers to the guarantee fund[23] – a pointed reminder that this important engineering firm was attracted neither to the collaborative model of the Ship Canal movement nor to its application to the industrial relations field, where the employers' prerogative to hire and fire was seen as paramount.

The clue for explaining the Galloway dispute is, in fact, to be found in the occupation of the majority of the "blacks" brought in by the company – riveting. Developments in riveting technology enabled the introduction of probably the single most important labour-saving device in this period. No details are given of why Galloways were taking on unskilled men and new riveters, but contemporary evidence in the "Notes from Lancashire" section of the trade journal *The Engineer* shows that only two months previously De Bergue and Company of Manchester had developed an improved mechanical and hydraulic rivetting machine.[24] The threat of this new piece of technology, or perhaps its introduction, is the clear backdrop to the dispute. Writing eleven years later, Samuelson describes the significance of the new machinery:

> Under the old system of hand-rivetting a certain amount of work occupied 3 men 6 days at 36s per week, and one boy 6 days at 8s per week: making a total cost in labour of £5.16.0. The same work can now be accomplished by machinery by one man working 2 days at 38s per week; helped by 3 labourers at 24s per week, and 2 boys at 8s (also for 2 days): making a total of £2.2.0. Saving on the work done: £3.14.0.[25]

The savings to be made by this kind of dilution were substantial, but even more widespread was the practice of employing boy labour and of increasing the number of apprentices – a practice which the unions were more or less forced to accept. John Whittaker, in his evidence to the Royal Commission on the situation in the Manchester District, thought that one apprentice to four journeymen was appropriate, but would settle for three. But in some departments he had to admit that the ratio was inverted with twelve apprentices to two workmen. Their best strategy with employers in containing the practice he reported had been "by waiting on them and drawing their attention to it".[26] Equally demoralising for the experienced craft worker was the practice of discouraging those who were over 40 years old from working. "As soon as a man gets a few grey hairs, or has to wear glasses" stated Whittaker, "he finds great difficulty in ever getting into the trade again" – a theme repeated in this poem from "Amal. Eng." in an 1890 edition of the *Gorton Reporter*:

> "What age are you?" the tradesman said,
> Outside the workshop door:
> The youngster blushed, and soft replied
> "Please sir, I'm twenty four".
> "Too young, too young" then said the boss,
> We've lots of lads to drive,
> Go somewhere else – call later on
> Come when you're twenty-five!"
>
> Then turning to another man,
> "What age have you put on?
> You seem to know a thing or two".
> "Yes sir, I'm forty-one".
> "Too old, too old", the taskman cries,
> For now we draw the line
> At one year less, so come again
> When you are twenty-nine!"[27]

103

The second area where the engineering workers were experiencing an employers' offensive was in the supervision of their time and of their work practices. Coincidentally a neat example of this can be seen in an article and picture of a new invention – Levy and Lane's patented "Workman's Time Recorder" – which appeared in *The Engineer* of 10th November 1882 in the week of the Great Workmen's Meeting at Manchester's Free Trade Hall, which formally signalled the commitment of Lancashire's trade unions to the Ship Canal Movement. "By a most simple process", the article reported, "an infallible and automatic record is made of the exact time each workman has arrived or left his factory, and which is absolutely proof against any deception or collusion between the operative and timekeeper."[28] Looking back a decade later over the previous 15–20 years, John Whittaker stressed the extent to which supervision had become more vigilant and gave instances of where "a workman has happened to look up from his work, broken his continuous employment to stretch himself, and the employer has discharged him immediately".[29]

The acquiescence of the engineering trade unions to aspects of this intensification of supervision was a product of their own weaknesses and vulnerability to the employers bringing in semi-skilled labour. However to the introduction

Workman's time recorder, 1882.   *JRULM*

Hydraulic riveting machine being used during the construction of the Ship Canal.   *TRAFF*

of piecework ASE was implacably hostile, having inserted in 1874 into its rule book a ban on its extension.[30] There was widespread opposition to payment by results amongst the engineering unions because the employer was able to reduce the piece-rate unilaterally if the wages of the worker paid at time rates were exceeded by a certain percentage. The policy, however, had inherent problems, not least because those who were paid at piece-rates received weekly wages at anything up to 50% more than those paid at time rates – which provided a substantial inducement not only to union members, but more importantly to non-union members.

The issue received an important airing in a strike at Ashburys Carriage Works in East Manchester in the three months immediately prior to the Ship Canal Bill receiving the Royal Assent. The dispute involved the smiths and smiths' strikers at the factory who came out when the company decided to impose a new piece work contract.[31] Although only 132 strikers were involved the Smiths' Society was able to rally substantial support from the local community and for some ten weeks the weekly *Gorton Reporter* carried full reports of developments. The proposal involved the payment of guaranteed day wages with the payment of a balance of the money after completion of the work. The strikers sought support for their cause by arguing in a document released to the public that the proposal "invested in the management the full power to confiscate whatever balance was made" and provided "no guarantee even for day wages".[32] Despite the weakness of this latter argument the men on strike had been able to organize on a mid-week May evening a highly effective demonstration round the streets of Gorton. Headed symbolically by a youth bearing a board with the words "Defence not Defiance" (the ASE motto), and accompanied by a brass band, the strikers, according to reports, "behaved most respectably" and were followed by "immense crowds of people".[33] Several other episodes are also recorded where crowds of up to 400 people – including substantial numbers of women and children – jostled the "knobsticks" who had been brought in to the factory, or hooted at the few smiths who had continued at work.

The heart of the dispute was the company's insistence, not on "confiscating" the balance of monies, but on its right to determine the division of these monies amongst the different workers – smiths, smiths' strikers, and assistants, and on its right to exclude absentees from a share in the piece work payments. Intent on pushing the agreement through, Ashburys were both able to find replacement labour and eager to see intimidation and assault cases brought in the police courts against strikers.[34] Since the wages of the smiths' strikers were only about 65% of the smiths' wages, the employers' strategy with its potential for increasing the former's wages at the expense of the smiths could have quickly split the workforce and emphasised their conflicting interests. But to judge from the widespread support received locally for the strikers the outcome seems, if anything, to have been a radicalising of the craftsmen as they deliberately sought backing from the young, the semi-skilled and the women of Gorton.

There is no record in the *Gorton Reporter* or elsewhere of the final settlement of the strike; indeed July brought reports of a wages dispute in Oldham which led rapidly to 25,000 workers walking out on strike and closing down the entire cotton production in the town.[35] The 1886 Wages Census covering engineering in Manchester reveals, however, that of 32 different occupational categories only smiths and smiths' strikers were recorded as receiving piece rate wages as well as time rate wages – 42 shillings for the former, and 32s 11d for the latter in the case of smiths – suggesting that Ashburys got their way.[36] The dispute demonstrated the extent of opposition amongst some craftworkers to the loss of control which accompanied piecework ("the vilest system"),

and the support they received from the public, but as in the similar and better known disputes in Erith in 1876 and in 1889, the employers were able to push the issue of piecework through. It is clear therefore that employer initiatives in Lancashire to increase output by the inducement of higher wages forced the engineering unions to accept piecework, with Manchester and Oldham at the forefront. As Arthur Coventry, partner in the Manchester tool-makers firm put it: "Piecework, as a rule, in the tool trade we find popular with the men, in fact, so much so, that it would be quite impossible for us to keep the best workmen unless we did work piecework. The tendency is for all the day-work shops to be denuded of their best men … (piecework) is quite a necessity of the trade, it is the custom of the trade.[37] This was less the case with engineering as a whole but, according to evidence submitted by John Whittaker to the Royal Commission on Labour, the Manchester District of ASE (the largest outside London) had 39% of its members doing piecework by 1891, while the comparable figure for Oldham was 31% (see Table 1). Of the big engineering centres only Birmingham was in the same league, while in London, Tyneside and Clydeside piecework was non-existent or marginal.

If the introduction of piecework was uneven, the practice of wagecutting when trade was depressed to reduce unit costs was a common experience whatever the area or sector. When the order books were thin, the trade unions found the practice difficult to resist, but compliance was based on the assumption that there would be restoration of the rate once trade picked up again.

In the Manchester District the Iron Trades' Employers Association (ITEA) had introduced a two-shilling wage cut in 1878, but only reluctantly in 1882 agreed restoration after ASE, following a representative meeting of its members at the various shops in Manchester and Salford, had intimated that they would take strike action if the advance was not agreed by the end of the week. Once it was conceded ASE was lavish in its praise of ITEA for acting "so honourably", expressed the hope that this would "further strengthen the good feeling which has existed for so long" in the trade, and immediately proceeded to agitate in other districts for the concession.[38] Though six months later ASE was – through the efforts of its full-time official Robert Austin – to throw its

**Table 1    ASE Membership and % doing piecework in 7 Engineering Centres**

| Area | Number of Members | No. doing Piecework | % doing Piecework |
|---|---|---|---|
| London | 8136 | 500 | 6 |
| Manchester | 5134 | 2000 | 39 |
| Newcastle on Tyne | 4042 | 0 | 0 |
| Glasgow | 2520 | 100 | 4 |
| Leeds | 2206 | 200 | 9 |
| Oldham | 1858 | 580 | 31 |
| Birmingham | 1754 | 700 | 39 |

Sources: Royal Commission on Labour. Group A. Parliamentary Papers 1893–4. Appendix XLVI
Evidence submitted by Amalgamated Society of Engineers, 1892

full weight behind the Ship Canal Movement, this did not prevent the employers taking the two shillings off again in early 1886 – ironically at a time when several of the big employers on the Ship Canal board of directors were mounting a campaign to encourage the working man to invest his savings in the Ship Canal shares. The lesson was not lost on the tinplate workers who, after lengthy deliberation, had responded by agreeing to invest £200 of their limited reserves.[39] Only a month later, at a special general meeting in December 1885, they recorded for themselves their reaction to the employers' latest move by resolving:

> That we as members of this Society cannot see our way at the present time to grant a reduction in our wages in the Case trade to our Employers as we consider the standard rate of wage is 35 shillings a week and we … consider that the masters have broken faith with us by asking the same.[40]

These, and other attacks on standards of living and working conditions led, without doubt, to a change in relationship between worker and employer and to a sense of a break with the past customs of the trade. The experience of new technology and new working practices touched every engineering worker and was a challenge to his sense of self-respect.

Record of resolutions of the Manchester Tin Plate workers in support of the Ship Canal Demonstration, 1885.

*GMPRO*

John Burns, himself an engineering worker, saw the situation as one where "the artisan of today is losing that individuality which was a feature in all workers some time ago".[41] Despite this John Whittaker was correctly telling the Openshaw Branch of ASE in 1891 that "strikes are not fashionable in Manchester in the engineering trade",[42] and for good reason. Given the ready supply of new labour available and the tendency to substitute semi-skilled machinists for skilled craftsmen, particularly in the machine shop, confrontational tactics had to be used sparingly.[43] A strategy of cooperation or "moderation" on the other hand secured wage levels consistently above the national average[44] and allowed ASE a greater influence in the way that changes were introduced.

A useful comparison with Tyneside engineering can be made here because, at the very time that Lancashire was celebrating the final success of the Ship Canal Bill, a big dispute hit the Elswick Works of Sir W. G. Armstrong involving 4,700 strikers, which for a month filled the columns of the national press. The complaint of the trade unions concerned the "oppressive and tyrannous conduct" of two of the managers, but the company saw the principle at stake – essentially of managerial prerogative – as more important than the dispute over the nine hours movement, and were prepared to have "the right arm of a great city suddenly paralysed."[45]

It is hard to believe that in the more collaborative style of industrial relations in Lancashire engineering, such a stand-off would have been allowed to develop by either side. This should not, however, be seen as implying a simply passive incorporated role for Manchester's engineering unions as was shown in 1891, when a joint committee representing ASE, the pattern makers, the boilermakers, the steam engine makers, the metal planers, the machine workers and the brass founders decided upon a strike against all firms in Manchester which had not agreed to comply with the unions' demand for a one-hour reduction in the working week to 53 hours. Soon after the action was taken many of Manchester's best known firms which had held out – like Galloways, Craven Bros and de Burghs – were signifying their adhesion to the demand, and within a short while all 200 of Manchester's engineering firms had fallen into line.[46]

The tactical question of timing is all important here, and a comparison of the "moderate" approach adopted by the engineering unions in Manchester with those in Bolton in this period is interesting. In the latter case with predominantly Tory employers, and without any Lib–Lab collaboration, the ASE District Committee had in 1887, in combination with the smaller engineering unions, decided to demand the restoration of the previous year's two shilling wage cut, which would have brought the Bolton rate closer to that prevailing in Manchester. When this was refused the unions responded by banning overtime and a collision course was inevitable. The ensuing strike involved some 1,300 men from four firms, and was accompanied by substantial violence, with the army being called in to break up serious rioting outside the works of Dobson and Barlow.[47]

Tin Plate workers and their Man in Armour at the 1885 demonstration. *Chetham's*

Although the five and a half months long strike gained sustained backing from the local community, the final result was a complete failure, for the strikers were forced to return to work at existing wage rates and accept a subsequent ruling by an umpire, Samuel Pope QC, that the status quo remain.

There was widespread moral and financial support provided for the strikers from other trade unionists in Lancashire, and in Manchester this was arranged by the Trades Council. Seven of their members were appointed – all of whom had represented their unions at the Great Ship Canal Demonstration at Belle Vue two years earlier – to liaise with the Manchester Joint Committee of Engineering unions about how the Trades Council's influence could best be deployed.[48] The wisdom of the strike was, however, likely to have been privately questioned by the Manchester trades unionists, as it was apparently by the ASE and Steam Makers Executives[49] – not least because in its poor timing and ultimately demoralising conclusion it bore a resemblance with a major strike of carpenters and joiners in Manchester a decade earlier.

## Carpenters and Print Workers

Since the two unions representing the carpenters and joiners put forward more resolutions of support for the Ship Canal than any other occupational group, it is useful at this stage to turn briefly to this sector of the building industry and the strike of 1877. For several years attempts had been made to increase hourly rates and reduce the length of the working week, and in November 1876 the unions settled for giving six months notice of a change in the local working rules requiring an advance of 1½ pence per hour and a reduction of 2½ hours per week. The employers would only concede a half penny extra, and on 1st May, following a mass meeting at the Free Trade Hall, 3,500 of Manchester's carpenters and joiners came out on strike.[50]

The existence of two unions representing carpenters and joiners, the General Union (GUCJ) and the Amalgamated Society (ASCT), did not help for unity of action, but despite this the strikers held out for 53 weeks, with the employers bringing in blacklegs and workers from abroad. The result, however, was a complete defeat for the men – a defeat which was still being talked about 60 years later by older members of the union,[51] and which had the effect of seriously undermining the status of carpenters and joiners and their ability to take independent action in defence of their position. James Murchie, as the elected secretary of the joint committee for the two unions, had the unenviable task of coordinating the strike, and not surprisingly seized the opportunity of committing the union five years later, when he had become General Secretary, to supporting the Ship Canal movement – an alliance which would help to build rather than destroy the union's prospects.

The carpenter's shop underwent substantial changes in this period as increasingly equipment for mortising, tenoning and shaping opened up work for which the semi-skilled could be substituted in place of craftsmen.[52] Again, as with engineering, impressions may have been somewhat exaggerated, as in this written evidence of 1885 to the Royal Commission on Trade and Industry produced by George Warner, Secretary of the Manchester Branch of the General Union of Carpenters and Joiners:

Emblem of the Carpenters and Joiners. *WCML*

With regard to the future, in my opinion, 10 joiners with the aid of machinery would supply the place of 200 or 300 joiners. Machinery is the ruin of the trade because it executes such a vast quantity of work in so little time.[53]

Combined with the importation of foreign manufactured joinery, and the employers' practice of taking on boys without proper regard to an apprenticeship system, mechanization put carpenters, of all the building industry trades, most severely onto the defensive and forced them to surrender areas like window-frames for large-scale standardised housing and to seek control by the craft of the non-uniform specialized work.[54] The fact that during the 1880s there was only one recorded strike by joiners in the Manchester area[55] is an indication not of willing acquiescence in the changes affecting the craft, but of the difficulties experienced in putting effective pressure on the employers in such a diverse and fragmented industry. For the ASCJ the 1880s was distinctly a period for consolidating the membership and a cooperative stance towards the alliance promoting the Ship Canal project – with its promise of substantial construction work – derived essentially from immediate self-interest.

As Manchester was the second largest printing centre in the country, the Ship Canal promoters were also able to draw upon the organizational strength of the printing unions, and most notably received the enthusiastic backing of the General Secretaries of the Typographical Association (TA) and the Lithographic Printers – Henry Slatter and George Kelley. Both these unions over the Ship Canal years were to show substantial growth, the Typographical Association increasing its members from 5,350 to 9,016 in the period 1880 to 1890, and the Lithographic Printers expanding from 833 to 2,235 in the same period. In both cases the Manchester Branch was the largest in the country, although the Lithographic Printers, with 317 members in 1890, was about a quarter of the size of the TA.[56]

The growth was partly the result of rapidly expanding demand for printed material, but it was also the result of the intensification of effort by the unions to recruit non-society print workers in order to blunt the employers' assault on the privileges they had won. As Zeitlin points out in an illuminating essay,[57] the composing room had become a major bottleneck in the production of printed material, whether newspapers, books or other publications. Relying upon the custom and usage of the trade, and upon a range of rules drawn up by the TA executive and chapels on rates of pay, apprentices, hours of work, etc, the society had been able to exert enormous influence on the working practices of the printing trade.

Without a working card it was virtually impossible to get a job at one of the recognized offices in the city, and a strict system was operated to ensure that vacancies were notified to the TA and filled according to a procedure controlled by the secretary of the local branch. When one local Stockport printer discharged a TA member for idleness at work he felt obliged to send a three-page memorandum of explanation to the local branch, complaining that the sacked man had "called me a slave driver and several other choice epitaphs [sic], and ended by telling me … that he would take good care I had no other man from Manchester, as he would make it hot at the rooms."[58]

The TA's influence was strongly challenged, however, in the 1880s by the employers, who developed two main strategies. The first involved the introduction of boy[59] or non-society labour, the second focussed upon the implementation of piecework methods of payment instead of the "stab" system,[60] or alternatively a mixture of piecework and stab. Two disputes which took place in the early Ship Canal years demonstrate the union's response to these strategies, and the different attitudes adopted by the local branch ("The Society") and the TA executive under Slatter's guidance.

The TA's formal position was that the number of apprentices in any one recognized office should not exceed three regardless of the number of journeymen,[61] but this was extremely difficult to enforce, particularly with the smaller printing shops, and the TA was forced to compromise in particular circumstances.[62] The dispute at Cuthbertson and Black first came up in late 1882, when the Society recommended to the Association that the office be closed because the firm would make no promise about reducing the number of apprentices it was employing. The TA executive initially advised a more conciliatory approach after the firm had intimated that it would conform to the rule when the apprentice in question completed his time after a further two years. Later, however, the Executive concurred when it became clear that the company intended to employ non-Society men from Scotland, was offering an inducement of extra wages to members to leave the society, and was "prepared to fight" if the TA took any action.[63]

In evidence to the Royal Commission on Labour, Slatter was forced to admit that it was "a very inelastic rule" which had been adopted, and which he would not like to defend,[64] but the TA executive in cases like the Cuthbertson and Black dispute was faced with a strong local branch with a militant membership wishing to impose the rule and walk out despite the consequences. The general result of the limitation, one employer noted, was "a large manufacture of journeymen in non-society offices".[65]

Among printworkers in Manchester strong feelings were therefore clearly held about the encroachment of the employers upon the customs of their trade, and it is evident from a second dispute following close on the heels of the first – and occurring during the period of the Ship Canal agitation – that again there were substantial differences of opinion. This time however the TA Executive and the local branch were both critical of the printworkers involved in the dispute, and for some time appeared to advocate a cooperative attitude towards the employer rather than outright confrontation. News of the dispute broke in May 1884 when about 40 of the members were given notice by Emmott and Co.[66] The dispute, however, had been simmering since the previous September when the Chapel unsuccessfully sought backing from the local branch for their demand that the newly appointed overseer should be called upon to join the Society.

A week later the father of the Chapel reported to a Special Committee meeting that a new form was to be issued the following week, but that all his members "who had seen it refused to fill it up".[67] It soon became apparent that Emmott was intent on introducing a piecework system but, since this was widely employed in London, the Committee decided that a cautious, non-confrontational line should be adopted. It was noted that the recording system proposed was "contrary to the usage of the trade", and agreed that every legitimate means should be employed to resist its introduction.

Four months later, with no further progress made, Emmott posted notice of their intention to introduce a partial piece system for the composing room which would result in the inside sections of several weekly and monthly trade journals being set on piece, while the advertisements would remain on "stab".[68] The notice signalled the start of a series of negotiating meetings at which the TA, worried at the low piece rates in operation, decided that they would insist that the piece price paid must be the higher one paid for weekly newspapers, despite the fact that several of the publications were monthlies. Increasingly frustrated by what it saw as the delaying tactics of the TA the company was nevertheless willing to make a number of concessions on the piece rates but would not accept that the payment system should be that for a weekly. They complained that "the Association shields itself behind the Society, and the Society is in like manner covered by the Association",[69] and finally gave notice of the intended lock-out on 2nd May.

Despite this it was reported to the branch that the employers had, on 9th May, talked "matters over with us for nearly three hours in a most reasonable and friendly spirit"[70] and had acquiesced in a number of further compromises. Keen to reach a settlement of the issue the Committee declined to see a deputation from the Chapel at Emmotts and passed a resolution accepting the employers' demand that the papers should be treated as magazines, but it was too late. Brinkmanship had led the firm to decide that it was easier to confront the TA and open a non-society shop instead; and when two years later the branch approached Emmotts seeking a meeting to discuss the question of reopening the office it was told brusquely that, since the company had no intention of increasing their staff of compositors, there was nothing to be gained from a meeting.[71]

The lessons of these two disputes would not have been lost on the TA executive and Slatter. In both cases adherence to a fixed position left the union outflanked by the employer without any base from which to bargain. They demonstrated the outrage felt by members at the employers' attempts to change the customs and rules of the trade, but it was the outrage of impotence which did not show the printworkers in the best light and would have gained them little wider support. Significantly no attempt was made to seek backing for the locked-out workers by publicising the dispute[72] – a reflection partly of the view that this was a "trade" matter, and not a wider community issue; and partly of the belief that it was for the Society to sort it out with the employers. Joining others in a craft issue of this nature ran counter to the notion of the printworkers themselves regulating the trade, and the willingness of Emmotts to discuss the issue at considerable lengths and over a long period suggests that in the mid-1880s this shared idea of a "community of trade" had not completely disappeared.

The sequel to the dispute provides some vindication of this view for in 1891 the Society was tipped off by a member in Altrincham that Emmott, despite – or perhaps because of – an impending libel action being brought by them against the Society's President and Secretary, was willing to open negotiations again. After a series of meetings the shop was reopened as a fair office in 1892 with the papers accepted as magazines, and with all 43 of Emmott's workers admitted into membership of the Society for half a guinea each.[73]

The printworkers were certainly under considerable pressure from the employers, but they regarded themselves as part of an elite. As Kelley put it in evidence to the Royal Commission on Labour on being asked if his members were educated and intelligent men: "… they are somewhat above the ordinary standard of workmen." While they were happy

Emblem of the Lithographic Printers.   *WCML*

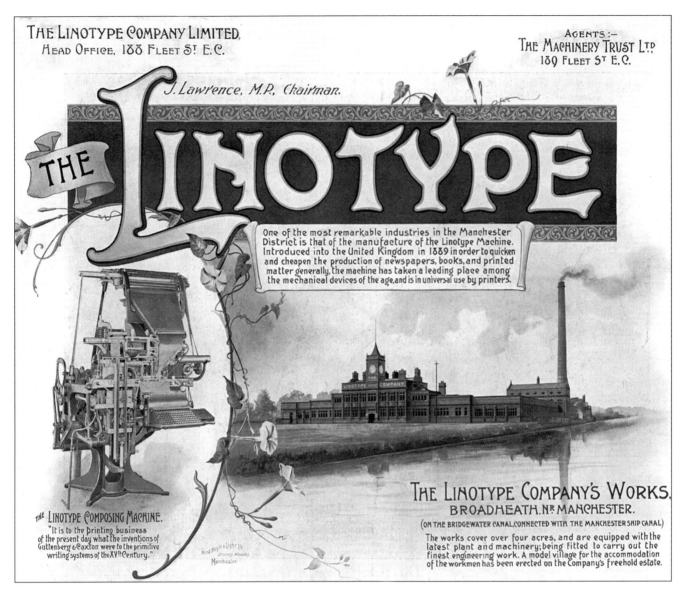

Advertisement for the Linotype Company which built a plant for the production of their revolutionary new printing technology in Broadheath near Manchester in the 1890s. *MCL*

to collaborate in an alliance with employers, as with the Ship Canal, the relatively self-contained world of printing did not require them to seek particularly close relationships with other trades;[74] and to the employment of women compositors, as Musson has shown, their position was effectively a hostile one since they viewed them as a cheap source of labour for the employers to substitute if given the chance.[75]

It would be quite wrong, however, to infer from the print-workers' attitude to other workers or from the two disputes described here, that the general position adopted was one of opposition to all change. In lithographic printing firms like Charlesworth and Company of Oldham were producing advanced machines able to increase speeds of production substantially,[76] but as Kelley indicated at a TA dinner, when speaking of the new machinery: "… though its introduction into lithography was at first looked upon with alarm, it was [sic] now felt that it was an immense advantage to the trade".[77] The union's attitude was to seek to gain advantage of the increases in productivity, and in 1891 by working with the kindred trades in the industry, it won a reduction in working hours from 55 to 52½ per week.[78]

In the case of the Typographical Association Musson puts forward a similar argument that the union's adaptability to change enabled them to adjust to a rapidly changing environment. The most testing period came in the

1890s with the introduction of the linotype composing machine, which had been invented in the United States in 1886, and was to revolutionise the printing trade. Although Slatter was publicly doubting in 1892 whether the new composing machines were really more cost effective that the hand compositor[79] the reality was that, following a TA delegate conference held in Manchester in February 1891 to determine a policy on the issue, the TA was involved in continuous negotiations over the wages and conditions for the introduction of the linotype.[80] In 1894 it had to face a major threat with the establishment by the Linotype Company of schools in London and Manchester offering free training courses on the machines of up to six weeks.[81] These were aimed at unemployed young men regardless of whether or not they were in the trade. The printworkers were well aware that their own positions could be fundamentally undermined and the responses to the new schools were conciliatory and did not lead to any strikes.

Slatter's role as General Secretary of the TA was central in setting a tone and mediating with the employers in this difficult period and, coincidentally, his support for the Ship Canal Movement in the early 1880s was likely to have stood the union well in their negotiations with the Linotype Company. For the Chairman was none other than Joseph Lawrence, the energetic campaign manager of the Ship Canal Provisional Committee, who had so adroitly drawn the trade unions into the Ship Canal alliance back in 1882 and who was substantially indebted to Slatter, as we have seen in Chapter 2.[82] The overall result was in the circumstances a good one for the printworkers, for the new composing machines remained in the hands of TA members, thus ensuring their continuing influence at a critical period.[83] Wholesale changes had, however, been driven through by the employers by the end of the 1890s and these seriously eroded earlier assumptions about a community of interests in the trade.

## Spinners and Weavers in the Cotton Industry

We have so far examined the experience of three groups of skilled workers – engineers, carpenters and printworkers. In turning now to the last group, the cotton workers, we are immediately faced with the problem of surveying an industry, with its spinning and weaving sections, far larger, more complex and more stratified than any of the others. While workers in the earlier three were commonly part of a relatively self-contained industry or firm, where the politics of the workplace did not naturally spill over into the local community, in the cotton industry, with mills employing hundreds or even thousands of workers, disputes regularly took on a public, even gladiatorial style, commanding substantial attention in local newspapers. Therefore, despite the size of the industry, the task of exploring changes in political consciousness, in attitudes to work, and in the relationships

between capital and labour, between different sections of the workforce, and between men and women, is made easier in several respects.

Lancashire's close association with textiles is evident in the 1881 Census returns which show that of the half million workers in cotton and flax in England and Wales 92% lived in the Northern Counties. Over the next decade the concentration in the North West became even greater, with numbers employed increasing by 13%. Of the total of 525,500 workers in 1891 58% were female, a far higher figure for women than any other major industrial sector, and exceeded only in "typical" women-dominated sectors like dressmaking, domestic service and teaching. The spread of women's employment across the cotton industry was uneven however, with the exclusion of women from spinning standing out like a beacon. The figures in Table 2 below give membership of the three largest trade unions and reflect the position clearly. They provide an essential backdrop to the discussion of changes affecting the industry in the Ship Canal years.

As with the other sectors discussed, a range of strategies was being adopted by the employers to improve productivity. This included both resistance to the unions' attempts to achieve standardisation of high piece payments or "lists" across the region, and implementation of lists paying lower rates. Two early examples of this, involving spinners, coincided with the start of the Ship Canal campaign. In the first, a five month strike by the Chorley spinners, which cost the Amalgamation over £3,000 in dispute and rations pay,[84] culminated in the union achieving a 5½% wage increase but having to accept a list based on Bolton rates, instead of payment indicator which had been demanded.[85] The second dispute involved seventeen minders at the Abbey Hey Lane Mills in Gorton, who tried to take on the might of the powerful John Rylands and Company by seeking a 5% increase on the Stockport list payments, which applied there, for the finer counts of spinning. Rylands' initial response was to close the mill down, throwing 1,200 out of work, and then reopen it placing the mules of the original seventeen in the charge of the old piecers or fresh minders. To rub salt into the wound, three of the new spinners were women brought in from the company's mills at Wigan.[86] The Amalgamation's report notes bleakly that the union had written seeking an interview but was completely ignored.[87]

In the weaving side – in which women workers predominated – disputes over wage rates and lists were a good deal more frequent. In Ashton a strike commenced in July 1883 closing the entire production of the town, when the employers sought to introduce the lower Blackburn list – applying essentially for plain goods – for the more complicated fancy work which was primarily done on jacquard looms. A main feature of the dispute was the strong support given by the women – support which would have been particularly striking for J. C. Fielden, who addressed more Ship Canal meetings than any other speaker, and who was a member of the trade union's negotiating team reporting back to some of the weavers' meetings. As the lengthy

**Table 2 Trade Union Membership in Three Cotton Trade Unions 1891**

|  | Male | Female | Total |
| --- | --- | --- | --- |
| Amalgamated Weavers | 24,700 | 40,300 | 65,000 |
| Cotton Spinners | 19,000 | — | 19,000 |
| Cardroom Workers | 6,500 | 18,500 | 25,000 |
| TOTALS | 50,200 | 58,800 | 109,000 |

Source: Evidence given to Royal Commission on Labour, 1891

reports in the *Courier* indicate, these were primarily mass meetings of *women* for "very few men were present". The negotiators to be sure were men, but the women were quite clear about what they wanted and about their negotiators' proposal that they should return to work pending a settlement. The report of the Hurst Weavers' meeting sums it up in dramatic script:

A WOMAN: I move that we have the list before we start. (Cheers)
ANOTHER WOMAN: We have done eight weeks, and we can do another four now. (Renewed cheers).[88]

The dispute, in fact, marked the start of a general offensive on the wages front, for a strike affecting the whole of North East Lancashire was announced in early 1884 over a proposed 5% wages cut, and others followed throughout the county.[89] There were also widespread complaints from the trades unions about employers' seeking an intensification of work by insisting upon higher output targets and by "driving" – the practice of using overseers to pressurise the shopfloor, and introduce closer monitoring of individual performance. Allied to this was the increasing insistence by managers on the exercise of employers' prerogatives – on their rights to fine, to hire whom they wished, to determine methods of manufacture, and generally to initiate changes in working practices. The introduction of new machinery was important here, bringing with it a special dowry – the potential for implementing new divisions of labour.

The process of effecting change and of introducing these new relationships was however fraught with difficulties. From the employers' perspective the risks of turning over settled ground could outweigh the advantages of any new system, and no better example can be seen than that of the spinners and the ring frame. The introduction of this new technology would have brought substantial economic advantage to the employers since they were faster – certainly for the lower counts – and could be worked by women at lower rates of pay. The cotton spinners saw the dangers as early as 1883, adopting a resolution at their March quarterly meeting that the "right hand of fellowship be extended to the workers on ring frames"[90] – who were mostly women – but they exaggerated the extent to which the ring frame was being introduced. There was plenty of discussion about the

issue and the advantages of ring spinning in the *Cotton Factory Times* and elsewhere,[91] but the employers were reluctant to proceed. When the influential Samuel Andrew, Secretary of the Oldham Master Cotton Spinners, argued the case for 1,600 new ring spindles – to be operated by the cardroom workers at a materially reduced cost – at one shareholders' meeting he was met with opposition and, though he had unanimous support from the directors, only just got agreement to the proposal at the following shareholders' meeting in a narrow 15–14 vote.[92]

The spinners' dominion within their sector was won not only at the expense of women, but also at the expense of their assistants, the piecers, whose rates of pay they could keep depressed whilst "brigading"[93] them into vassal piecers' organisations controlled by the spinners. There was no shortage of people commenting adversely on the spinners' favoured position,[94] nor was it necessarily employers alone who sought the introduction of the "joining" system – whereby the two men working on the mule, the spinner and the piecer, would divide the work and wages equally between them. The present position, wrote one Oldham correspondent, was "a crying evil", for which joining was a remedy "to prevent the despotism of one-sided trade unionism."[95] The piecer's attitude to the system was inherently ambivalent, because he could look forward to the same privileges if he could achieve a spinner's job though, as Tom Mann pointed

Mule spinning in Salford. *JRULM*

out in a brilliant cross-examination of James Mawdsley, only one in three piecers on average was ever able to become a spinner.[96] For the cottonmaster too there were advantages in the *status quo* because the spinner acted as his agent, controlling and overseeing the work of the piecers – a point reinforced in a 1889 County Court case, in which it was ruled that a piecer discharged without notice had no claim against the company, but only against the minder because "the operative spinner always engaged the piecer, whose servant he was".[97]

The issue of new technology, therefore, throws up conflicts of interest, as much between groups of workers as between workers and masters. Over time the particular patterns are likely to change. In the context of a male-dominated spinning sector – in which operatives and masters shared a common perspective that a woman's place was in the home – the exclusion of women (as well as the male piecers) from the benefits and higher wages gained by spinning trade unionism may have appeared defensible in the early 1880s, but as the decade progressed, and the position and rights of women became more clearly articulated, the spinners' attitude began to look more questionable. This is important for understanding changes in political consciousness and attitudes to work which were occurring in this seminal decade, but it also helps us to refocus on some of the questions thrown up by the Ship Canal alliance.

We have seen that the trade unions collaborated with the promoters in backing the Ship Canal for the sound reason that it would help substantially in reviving Lancashire's economy and providing new employment opportunities. In this respect they won substantial working-class support from a far wider section than simply their own membership. But in other respects their support for the alliance was problematic, and most notably in relation to its producer ideology – with its joining of masters and men against a merchant and middleman class – which Mawdsley as representative of the cotton spinners most commonly articulated. Perceiving threats to their jobs from technological change, engineers, cotton spinners, joiners and printworkers were keen to support the scheme. But the producer emphasis of the movement they were backing – given the record of hostility to women workers of some of the main unions involved – gave it a smeared tarnish of male exclusiveness. If the sound of class barriers being dismantled in a new democratic era was meant to be heard across Lancashire, for women the sight of gender shutters being erected in their place was probably a more likely impression of the Ship Canal alliance. Indeed the evidence from all the main public meetings and demonstrations in the early campaign years points to the unquestionable conclusion that the movement was almost a men only affair. The presence of women was sufficiently rare for it to be commented upon when it occurred[98] – in marked contrast for example to the situation in the 1883 Ashton Weavers' Strike already described.

As a model of industrial relations for wider application, the Ship Canal alliance had, therefore, a major flaw in its exclusion of women. The argument to be advanced here is that this flaw, coupled with the employers' assault across a wider front, was fatal for in the 1880s, and particularly from about 1885, women cotton workers became increasingly concerned with asserting their rights and with organizing to protect their interests. Underpaid and marginalised, they were far more likely to take to militant action against their employers than their male counterparts; and in the industrial relations turmoil of the late 1880s it was often they, rather than male trade unionists, who were playing the leading role in pressing for changes at the workplace.

Evidence of a change in the temperature of industrial relations in the cotton industry (and of the growing importance of the women's question) can, in fact, be seen very clearly in the crux years, 1885–1887, which coincide precisely with the middle critical period of the Ship Canal Movement – from the passing of the Bill to the start of construction. Most important were the employers' moves to depress wages across the sector, with strikes being triggered in 1885 in response in Rochdale, Chorley, Manchester and finally Oldham.[99] The Manchester strike occurred at the Brunswick Mills owned by Bannermans, a large integrated cotton company. It would have attracted little public attention had it not been for two cases in the police courts against minders charged with intimidation of some of the workers seeking to continue work there.[100] In the first case it was acknowledged that the defendants were drunk, and the severe sentence of one month's imprisonment with hard labour seems to have been imposed because the police alleged they had come as delegates from the Middleton Spinners branch to show support for the Manchester men. Taking place at the moment when the Ship Canal movement was winning the breakthrough for the final enactment of the Bill, the dispute is interesting for the light it sheds on the question of employers' changing attitudes.

No contemporary account is available, although a report to the Amalgamation acknowledges that the company had largely succeeded in its determination to bring in new hands.[101] A fascinating interpretation of the events is supplied by Mills in his biography of Charles Macara, who was managing director of Bannermans at the time.[102] Written in an adulatory style, and clearly based upon Macara's recollections, the account gives the introduction of new machinery and of a "temporary" lowering of wages as the reason for the dispute at the mill – described as "one of the fever spots of the trade … and the scene of eleven strikes in eight years". Deciding to test the resolve of the spinners Macara, "not perhaps without some slight enjoyment of the experience, took up the challenge", and brought in new minders and piecers from Oldham whom he billeted at night in the works as he was unable to ensure safe passage through the streets. When the striking minders and piecers sued for peace, they were refused employment on any terms.

Bannerman's action, taken in isolation from other employers, represented an overtly confrontational style of industrial relations in which the interests of the cotton masters were seen as being in conflict with those of the spinners, and in need of specific prosecution. No statements were made here about common interests and a community of trade, and no hint of a trade-off with the spinners. It was another straw in the wind for the "barefoot aristocrats" and for Macara it was a first step into industrial politics, from which he did not withdraw. In 1891 in the long Brooklands dispute involving the whole of the Lancashire cotton industry he was to play a prominent role and in 1894 he became President of the English Federation of Master Cotton Spinners Associations, a position he was to hold for many years. As with the Ashbury Carriage Works strike occurring in Manchester at the same time, where the employer was taking an equally confrontational line, the Brunswick Mills dispute disappeared completely from the public record in August as attention became focused on two much bigger spectacles – the celebrations to mark the passage of the Ship Canal Bill and the Oldham strike.

The dispute in Oldham was over the employers' decision to introduce a 10% wages cut and, as we have seen in the last chapter, involved all the cotton workers in the town and their leadership in a long thirteen-week conflict. It cost the union £30,000–£40,000 before a compromise of a 5% cut was reached. [103] In the context of the 1880s and changing workplace relationships, the Oldham strike marked an important watershed. It was an attack firstly on the pay and conditions of all the workers in Oldham's spinning industry – upon a whole working class community and not just on one group. While some of the spinners took care to distance themselves from the other workers and from the more militant demonstrations and picketing outside the mills this was not always the case, for the *Oldham Chronicle* reports that the minders were present "in no small numbers" at a big demonstration outside the King Street Mills in Oldham when there were clashes with the police and windows were smashed. [104] Generally the strike helped to show the common interests which the different groups of workers shared as against their employers, for the spinners could not have failed to notice that the non-society men and women were equally committed to supporting the strike, and that the employers made no distinction between them and other workers. Indeed, private correspondence from Samuel Andrew, Secretary of the Oldham Master Cotton Spinners, shows a distinct hostility to the spinners. As he puts it in a private letter to one of the millowners in mid-September: "… We may now quickly urge the members to get to work throwing the old minders overboard – and if necessary adopting the redistribution scheme". [105] His less private writings are likely to have had a tempering, perhaps even radicalising effect on Mawdsley, for the Spinners' leader had been able to extract from the Manchester papers the name of their anonymous correspondent who had libelled him in their columns, accusing him of "Broadheadism" and of

promoting "barbarous warfare". It was none other than Andrew himself, who was forced – doubtless as part of the settlement of the dispute – to write a public apology withdrawing all his allegations. [106]

Secondly, the strike led directly to the formation in 1886 of the Cardroom Amalgamation, a union of mostly female cardroom workers, involved in the carding and preparatory stages before the cotton could be spun. The course of events and handling of negotiations had highlighted for this low-paid group of workers the substantial disadvantage they suffered and in comparison with the spinners in the absence of a union through which they could organize effective collective action. Despite the charge of exclusiveness which is often levelled against the spinners their officials, particularly Mawdsley and Ashton, undoubtedly gave comfort and support to the cardroom workers in taking this move, advising on appropriate structures and procedures for the new union. [107] Moreover, in response to the accusation that trades unionists represented the selfish interests of "the aristocracy of labour", Mawdsley at the 1885 Industrial Remuneration Conference urged that the working classes generally needed only to follow their example and form themselves into trades unions; [108] this advice was echoed by many others in the skilled trades.

Thirdly, and through the development of the Cardroom Amalgamation, the dispute helped to bring a far larger number of women directly into trade union membership for by 1889 the union had 15,000 members. During the dispute itself newspaper reports show clearly the high participation rates of women – a feature already evident in the weaving side; and in a number of instances commentators noted their more militant stance. At one meeting attended by up to 500 people, the *Oldham Chronicle* reported that

> … the female element was conspicuous; and if anything they were more outspoken and demonstrative in their behaviour … In [sic] conversation with the men singly, there can by no question that, if left to themselves – and if all fear of intimidation were removed – unquestionably large numbers would go in on the masters' terms. [109]

## The Catalyst of Women Workers

The importance of this changing dynamic in industrial relations should not be underestimated. Now it was women who were challenging the certainties that had been taken for granted by men, whether masters or workers. Aware that the "community of trade" often excluded them, they brought with them the concerns of women workers which were not necessarily the same as their male counterparts.

A signal of the growing confidence of women to stand up for themselves and set an example came in September 1885 during the period of the Oldham strike with the case of Martha Ann Kilburn. A young weaver from Rochdale, she had been fined by her employer for turning in a faulty piece of cloth caused by a poor warp over which she had no control. Rather than accept the injustice of this arbitrary system, she refused on principle to pay and was fined five shillings by the Magistrates Court for alleged breach of contract. The case became a *cause célèbre* the following year when her stand led to her imprisonment in Strangeways Prison for seven days, and a detailed picture of events can be built up from reports and an interview in the local paper.[110]

Thrust unwillingly into the limelight, Kilburn comes over initially as the epitome of a respectable young woman. Aged 22, she lives with her parents, has a sweetheart, attends Sunday School regularly and during her stay in prison darns stockings at her own request and reads the Bible to a fellow inmate. When the policeman comes to arrest her she reports: "I was listening to a friend playing our piano at the time … and I asked him to wait … while I washed and put clean clothes on." Yet this picture of a God-fearing and demure young woman, quietly getting on with the preoccupations of her own life, fitting in to the conventions of a male-dominated world, is suddenly shattered the moment she walked out of the Magistrates Court with some friends defiantly declaring that "she would not pay a farthing". Far from submitting like a dutiful daughter to the authority of her parents, this was a woman who stated that, though asked many times, "I would not let either them or anybody else pay the money" with the result that by the time of her arrest, her parents "had become reconciled to it and were of the same opinion as me".

She was clear too about the vested interests lying behind the judgement against her: "If there had been a different bench of magistrates I should not have been fined, as the greater part were manufacturers". In a town where the union was weak, Martha Kilburn was solely responsible for taking on a notorious employer "Old Jack Pilling", and in the process was throwing off the conventional stereotypes of the meek submissive woman needing men to protect her whether at home or at work. The effect was immediate. At the rally a week later at Rochdale Circus, the editor of the *Cotton Factory Times* was able to draw laughter from his audience when he juxtaposed an image of feminine respectability with a young weaver's talk in rough dialect of crying, not over feelings or sweethearts, but over her warps at work. "Walking behind two very well dressed girls in the street", he had heard one saying:

Eh, man, they were two bad 'uns, them warps. Mon, I shrieked an' I shrieked an' I shrieked agen o'er 'em (laughter) and then they fined me half-a-crown o'er 'em". (Cries of "Shame").

Enormous interest had been aroused in this new phenomenon of a woman militant at the workplace, and cotton workers from all over Lancashire converged by train on Rochdale on the day of her release thronging the streets, and shouting "Let's yer her speak", and "Let's have a look at her". The rally was attended by 3,000 working men and women

Women cotton workers during the dinner break at Ancoats.

*Chetham's*

115

and heard a succession of weavers leaders praising Kilburn for her bravery which "should mark a new epoch in the life of the Lancashire weaver". For Mr Burrows from Padiham she was a "heroine" whose example should be copied by "every weaver and every other artizan and operative". Despite the "cowardliness" of the other weavers at Pillings Mills, the Oldham Weavers Secretary Buckley declared, "their battle had now been fought for them by a lady".

One illuminating twist in the story came in Buckley's revelation that the lack of effective organization amongst the weavers had resulted in Kilburn having to depend on the support of the spinners. Mawdsley therefore had pride of place in moving the motion of protest against the Magistrates, and he warmed to the occasion with a distinctly class-conscious analysis. Complaining that the employers were building churches and chapels out of the fines imposed on their workpeople, he went on:

> … the working men [sic] would now stand up in their majesty and no longer submit to being ruled by the finger and thumb and the dictation of the upper class … The manufacturers hung together tooth and nail; and the magistrates would not act against the interests of their own class".[111]

Support for women in the cotton industry was coming from other sources as well, and particularly from other women through collective organization. The creation of the cardroom workers union had provided the opportunity for women in the spinning sector to ensure that their interests were considered and, when in a dispute in Oldham in early 1886, the employers tried to reach an early settlement over a wages cut by offering to lower the female cardroom workers' wages, but maintain the male wages, the women themselves insisted that the vote on the question be taken only by the women and rejected the proposal with a large majority.[112] Over the first six years the cardroom workers in Oldham were involved in two substantial strikes in 1886 and 1889, the latter lasting eighteen weeks with over 700 of their members involved in an attempt to get a standardisation of piece rates.[113]

The 1886 strike at the Henshaw Street Spinning Company was very much more significant, however, in its specific introduction of a woman's perspective into Lancashire's industrial relations. The issue was the head carder's sexual harassment of young girls at the mill, and the company's refusal to reprimand or dismiss him, which led to the union withdrawing all its members in protest. The practice of male workers in positions of responsibility sexually assaulting or propositioning women whom they supervised was not uncommon according to evidence submitted by Miss May Abraham, an Assistant Commissioner for the Royal Commission on Labour,[114] but action to prevent it was not lightly undertaken, as the girl or woman complaining risked loss of both job and reputation. Sometimes there was sufficient evidence for a case to be brought before the

Magistrates Court, as happened in 1884 when the 44 year-old overseer at the Albion Mills in Pendlebury was charged with rape of a sixteen year-old.[115] However, it was not until the Henshaw Street strike that a trade union was prepared to challenge an employer over his implicit collusion with this shabby feature of nineteenth-century dominant male culture.

The case against the head carder, Robert Yates, had been put by George Silk, Cardroom Secretary to the employer, as early as June 1886, but despite his persistent record of molesting and assaults, and his boasting about his prowess to other people, the union was unable to persuade the employer to take any action against Yates. Nor was it successful in drawing in the Employers' Association on the grounds that it was "a personal question".[116] The eventual upshot was that the union's solicitor, Robert Ascroft, was brought in to take proceedings on behalf of the girls against Yates in the Police Courts,[117] and when these were successful Yates was dismissed. The striking carders were not reemployed.

An interesting account of the strike, drawing upon a detailed report by George Silk, has been written by Jan Lambertz,[118] who ascribes considerable influence to the parents of the young girls in pursuing the case against Yates, and suggests that Yates' behaviour "proved a challenge to patriarchal and brotherly prerogatives of female protection" – with the implication that this was more a matter of the assertion of traditional familial and moral principles. Undoubtedly the 1892 Nelson strike which she describes – fought on similar grounds by the better-established Weavers' Association – received more active and well-coordinated support, but this should not be allowed to detract from the achievement of the 68 female and male carders from a newly established trade union who struck at the mill. The union had decided to reimburse them with strike pay and a half, which amounted to twelve shillings a week for the women and fifteen shillings for the men. The total strike bill which the union had to meet was £2,033, which meant that the strikers were out of work for an average of ten to twelve months each. The Oldham carders had struck a first blow for women's rights at the workplace, and shown the important link between the "personal" and the "political"; and according to Miss Abraham the example, taken up in the later strike at Nelson, led to a marked improvement in the behaviour of overlookers and in the attitude of employers.

The dispute had, however, been a strong challenge to the absolute authority of the employer, as exercised by his representative and those who resisted faced blacklisting and hardship. Another form of resistance was action in the courts against the employer, and we get glimpses of the leading role being played here also by other women following in the footsteps of Martha Kilburn. The case of Jane Davies, a weaver of Newton Heath, is a good example. She took her employer, John Howarth, to the County Police Court to recover fourteen shillings wages deducted because she had been fined for being off sick for a day and a half. Evidence at the court hearing showed that Davies was introducing a new external issue into the workplace relationship between employer and worker for, as well as being ill, she had responsibility for making childcare arrangements. She had no-one to send to the mill to notify her employer of her illness because her husband had to leave at 5.30 am to find another woman to look after their children. Despite this, Davies was fined by Howarth under the company's Rule 3, which obliged all workers to give notice of any sickness or face a fine of three pence per loom; and under Rule 8 which allowed the employer to dock all wages in the event of Rule 3 being violated!

The company's position was put by their solicitor: "What they wanted was that the other hands should know they could not be allowed to stop away without leave" and, in a phrase reminiscent of Mawdsley's earlier strictures, the magistrate commented that "working people were exceeding keen in defending their own rights, and … they must be taught to respect the rights of their employers".[119] But the belt and braces approach of the company was too much for the Bench this time, which allowed the four shilling fine but ordered that the ten shilling deduction under Rule 8 be paid to the weaver.

Newton Heath was on the outskirts of Manchester with relatively small-scale weaving and a low level of unionisation, which made challenging an employer particularly dangerous for a woman like Jane Davies. The result of the court hearing was well-publicized in the local press and had an influence on the women weavers at the Britannia Mills who struck the following year against their employers, Etchells, on account of the low wages and excessive fines which the firm was imposing.[120] The seven week long strike is interesting because regular reports in the local press provide a great deal of detail about the style and attitudes of a previously non-unionised female workforce which sought to organize against a hostile employer, and the difficulties it encountered. At the outset 140 of the women joined the Oldham Weavers Association, with the result that they received substantial support from the Secretary Buckley, described by the company as "a paid agitator" and with whom it refused to deal. The women were incensed by the low wages, claiming to be 25% underpaid, but a feature of the dispute was their humour in the face of the employer's intransigence, and their refusal to discuss. To Buckley's question as to whether they should do more of the running came the answer: "No; we would not run after better fellows than him" (Laughter); and to his question whether a deputation should go, came the answer: "No, no … we will go in the summer when the cuckoo sings". (Laughter).[121]

The substantial coverage of the strike in the weekly *Gorton Reporter* was a reflection of local interest and, as the weeks went by, of growing support for the women, and antagonism towards the employer.[122] Without financial support however the women were unable to hold out and were additionally hindered by a seepage back to work of their colleagues, including some of the ringleaders. "This conduct", stated the *Gorton Reporter*, "has been most nauseous to the weavers … some very strong language has been at times used towards them, and threats held out".[123] By contrast Buckley came out with flying colours, looked upon by the women as a leader in whom they had confidence.[124]

It had been a salutary lesson for the strikers forced back to work without any gains and on the employer's terms. The need to belong to a trade union with the discipline, negotiating skills and, above all, financial resources had been made abundantly clear but the dispute was unusual in a number of respects. It was firstly a strike by unorganized workers, and by women at that, who were able to mount a concerted and disciplined action against their employer without outside assistance. This was a challenge to the conventional Victorian image of womanhood which saw women as passive objects and not as "ringleaders" setting "ablaze the discontent", as the *Gorton Reporter* described them. It provided moreover an example followed a few months later by the similarly unorganized weavers at the nearby Ten Acre Lane Mills, who took strike action when their employer sought a 25% wage reduction.[125]

Secondly, the coverage in the local paper was both lengthy and sympathetic, providing far more detailed information about the actions and disagreements of the strikers than was the case with many much larger strikes; and thirdly the reports which appeared were based upon an intimate knowledge of the flow of events and of the women's thinking. The journalist concerned clearly had the confidence of the strikers to allow him (her?) to attend private meetings and speak freely with the women. It is hard to believe that a properly functioning union would have permitted such open disclosure of its working because it would not have helped in its negotiations with the employer. It helps us, however, for this openness reveals far more accurately the state of mind and consciousness of the working women of Newton Heath than would be indicated by public statements carefully prepared for the press. It shows their recognition of the separate interests of employer and worker, and their strong sense of injustice but, most importantly, it reveals them as workers concerned with the issues of their working

About 60% of all weavers were women.   *JRULM*

117

environment – expressing anger, using humour and strong language, voicing disagreement and confusion and with their own ringleaders and backsliders.

A year later at the Albion Working Men's Club men like Abraham Park could still continue to applaud the magistrates for "putting down the bad language so common in our public streets ... that gave great offence to delicate ears", and talk about the need to preserve the purity and self-respect of the girls who went into the factory", [126] but for the working women and girls of Lancashire – who represented six out of every ten textile workers – the daily reality in the streets and in the factories far more closely approximated to the experience of the striking women at the Britannia Mills, than the idealised image conjured up by Park and many men like him. For skilled workers like the engineers and printers, the presence of women at the workplace was seen as a threat to their wage levels and therefore not welcome; and these attitudes were not confined to those sectors alone. When questioned on the issue William Mullin of the Cardroom Workers, and Thomas Birtwistle of the Weavers – both unions where women predominated – stated that if they had a choice, the vast bulk of working men in the cotton trade would also prefer to keep their wives at home if they could afford it. As F. M. L. Thompson notes however in this context: "Aspirations ... were not the same as achievements". [127]

From the mid-1880s onwards women, having always been in a majority in the cotton industry, became a majority of the *trade unionists* in the industry as well – a phenomenon which had inevitable knock-on effects on the standing and status of trade unionism, and on the associated notions of self-respect and respectability. The link which the skilled workers and their leaders were making between trade unionism and respectability in the early 1880s, as already discussed, was intended to give them greater credibility and strengthen their bargaining position with the employers, but it was a notion of respectable society in which women

were appendages to men, were "good wives and daughters" at home, kept separate from the world of work. The Britannia Mills dispute, the cases of Martha Kilburn and Jane Davies, and the Henshaw Street strike, were all symptomatic of the increasingly important role which women were playing in challenging the employers – and with the challenge came discredit for the narrow notion of respectability promoted by the old craft unions. The factory, as much as the home, came to be seen as the workplace for women in the textile districts, particularly from the mid-1880s because collective organization through the trade unions brought this to the attention of trade unionists and the public alike.

The changes in trade union culture being introduced in this way in Oldham and Manchester were not universally welcomed, and in one case at least brought a male backlash. At the Lostock Mills in Bolton, a closely knit and traditional spinning area, where the spinners had their largest member-ship, the employers T & J Heaton decided to open a new mill employing three of their women piecers as minders. For the Bolton spinners it was the thin end of the wedge and, after unsuccessfully trying to negotiate over the issue with the employers, 230 spinners came out on strike declining in future to train any female piecers. There followed over the next twelve weeks a succession of letters in the Bolton and Manchester press from J. T. Fielding, Secretary of the Spinners, putting the union's case that their objection to the women's employment was on the moral grounds that the postures which the women would have to assume in their work as spinners and their necessarily scanty attire were an offence to decency and an inducement to immorality. As one letter in support put it, the spinners were trying to put into operation an old maxim "Make it difficult for people to sin". [128] Fielding comes over throughout the correspondence as pompous and hypocritical, at one stage going so far as to argue that the dispute was not about wages "but on the much loftier ground ... of protecting other helpless girls and

VELVETEEN - CUTTING BY HAND

Women velveteen workers.
*Chetham's*

118

Inside the weaving shed. By the 1890s women cotton workers were gaining a more powerful voice.    *JRULM*

women from following an occupation which tends to degrade and demoralise them, and which may fitly be described as the worst and probably last of the evils of factory life". [129]

His patronising attitude to women shows elsewhere too. In one early letter he ridicules one of the employer's arguments by saying: "Surely their opposition must have a more substantial basis than that usually ascribed to the objection of a woman, of objecting because they do"; [130] and later in discussing the dispute, he permits himself a carefully barbed aside: "They have succeeded in obtaining the services of one or two women – I beg the sex pardon – females." Not surprisingly the employers had a field day, pouring ridicule on the union's arguments, pointing out that the female cardroom workers were no different, and berating Fielding for grossly insulting female piecers, "a class of women who are as decent and becoming in their behaviour as any other class of operatives". [131] Few others chose to attack the spinners' views openly, but one sardonic letter from "Dropstick" (surely a woman?) teasingly mocked them and Fielding for the company they were keeping: "How pleased the members of the Bolton Vigilante Association must be to

have found such powerful allies!"; and went on to indicate the inconsistencies between the spinners' position and other elements of respectable society, which they sought to copy: "Let us hope that ladies of the higher (?) classes who attend balls and dances will take the hint, and abandon the practice of exposing their fair skins to the gaze of members of the other sex. The resolution of the operative spinners has also this advantage that it will prevent the girls when grown up from being enticed by the prospect of good wages into such degrading occupations as that adopted by the women (may I use the term?) who are spinsters at the Lostock Mill." [132]

It was little wonder that in the early 1890s the Bolton socialists were to have one of their major successes when they helped to establish a separate Lancashire Piecers' Association in defiance of the stranglehold exercised by the spinners. [133] Away from Bolton, however, the progress being made by women continued to be marked. At the very time that the Lostock Mill dispute was running, the Ashton weavers, for instance, with their predominantly women members, embarked upon their longest strike of the period. Their purpose was to win a new list which would, as one woman grandly put it to cheers of approval, "regulate the weaving of fancy cloths all over the world". [134] Fully supported by the Northern Counties Amalgamation, and conducted with great discipline, the stoppage lasted eighteen weeks with 2,000 members withdrawn from work at a cost to the union of £17,000. [135]

The difficulties confronting women did not suddenly disappear of course with this upsurge of action – they still received lower wages, worked in poor conditions, faced problems not encountered by male workers, and had only a limited voice in the leadership of their unions – but a new climate had developed in which the issues facing women were high on the agenda; and it was a climate which had been brought about substantially by women acting on their own behalf. The point is worth making because some have seen the absence of female public voices in the cotton trade unions as evidence that the developments which brought women more directly into the unions and into union activity were primarily ones promoted by the male leadership. [136]

By the early 1890s the new spirit was clearly making its impact in Manchester as is evident in the case of George Kelley, prime mover in drawing the trade unions into the Ship Canal movement. As Secretary of the Trades Council, he was now turning his attention to a new initiative – arranging support for Lady Dilke of the Women's Trade Union League in her attempts to establish women trade unions in the city, which led in 1892 to the appointment of a woman organizer. As Richard Woosnam, a tinplate worker living in the Hulme area of Manchester put it: "… the urgent necessity for female organization is even of greater importance at present than the organization of male labour." [137]

Such a comment would have been unthinkable a decade earlier when the Ship Canal project was first being promoted, and indicates the extent of the change in consciousness that had occurred within the ranks of ordinary trade union members. By contrast the situation in 1882, following a period of deep depression, was one where, for a limited period, a consensus emerged between important sections of manufacturing capital and the trade unions that a massive injection of new capital into Lancashire's transport infrastructure was the single most important task in achieving economic regeneration. Though the two sides had different agenda, a shared belief in Free Trade policies – a hallmark initially of this Lib–Lab alliance – was an important ingredient, but ultimately also a factor contributing to the demise of the alliance since it alienated important Tory elements.

### Changing Attitudes, Changing Consciousness

In summarising the four sectors we have discussed, it is clear that the experience of overt confrontation between capital and labour was far from even. Despite the danger of *trompe d'oeil* which its size imparts, cotton was undoubtedly the most conflict-ridden of the four with substantial well-publicized disputes with deep-rooted community support taking place throughout the decade. But in the other three sectors disagreement over the terms of the work contract is also revealed as employers sought to raise profit and productivity levels. The detailed analysis of a number of disputes has enabled us to see the cleavage lines and flashpoints where the *status quo* had to be challenged or defended by one side or the other, but equally it has shown the search for accommodation between capital and labour, as each side recognized that only through bargained collaboration could they make headway.

In the Ship Canal movement this search for accommodation found a practical cross-class project, making links between workplaces, and between workplace and community to which thousands of Lancashire's working men were willing to give their backing; and which for a short time, with its producer ideology and its emphasis on popular capitalism, seemed to offer a way of linking the industrial and the political. The most important steer came from the engineering and printing sectors where the trade unions had achieved the bargaining power to enable them to exert some influence on the development of the worker/employer relationship. Undoubtedly, however, of the two, the much larger engineering sector was the more significant driving force, not least because the establishment of more collaborative industrial relations models within engineering was reflected in the strong commitment to the Ship Canal movement by large engineering employers – including Adamson himself – in Manchester, Salford, Oldham and Hyde.

In important respects, however, the Ship Canal alliance was ironically starting to break apart at the very moment, in 1885, that it was triumphantly celebrating the passage of the Bill. The agitation over the unemployed question, which peaked in the years 1885–86, put great strains on the trade unions as their members saw technological unemployment threatening all, regardless of individual skill level and status. This was a critical factor in explaining the positive attitude adopted by skilled workers to the development of New Unionism for the unskilled. [138] Furthermore, the conflicts between competing sections of the local bourgeoisie over the raising of finance for the scheme, and the general direction of the project, (described in the next chapter), were to culminate in 1887 in Adamson's resignation as chairman of the company. Although the political head of steam built up in support of the Ship Canal remained, the promoters never again resorted to the techniques of mass mobilisation which had characterised the five years of the Adamson era.

An equally powerful force in rupturing any longer term hopes of developing the alliance as a more general model of industrial relations was the employers' offensive, most apparent in the cotton industry but not exclusive to it, which reinforced the unequal nature of the partnership of the Ship Canal Movement and the inherent fragility of its producer ideology. A parallel example of the break up of a producer movement with an articulated political programme can be seen in Hamilton, Ontario, in the 1870s. [139] As Lancashire's trade union movement grew in size in the 1880s and became more representative of the wider working population, the skilled male trade unionists who had committed themselves to the earlier Ship Canal movement came to realize that their interests on the wider front were better served by joining an alliance with the women and less skilled workers of the new unions (who were not represented in the original Ship Canal movement) rather than with the employers who were threatening the customs of their trade and their standards of living. The point is reinforced at a general level by David Landes, who argues that the strategy of the English employer during this period was based upon the view that "his men and their children were destined to remain workers", and that the whole fabric of society would collapse if workers became rich and wanted a higher status.[140]

As ever Mawdsley was sensitive to these issues, putting into words what many cotton workers felt about the employers' attitudes. When the local secretary of the Stalybridge Spinners criticised public figures who complained that labourers bought "incongruous luxuries" and that "factory girls will spend fifteen or twenty guineas on sealskin jackets", Mawdsley responded by recalling a Preston master who rejected a wages claim from his hands with the statement:

You are getting too much already. I can see some of you walking out on Sundays and you are dressed as well as my wife and daughters.[141]

Clothing and dress were a conspicuous badge of status and respectability *par excellence* in Lancashire where workers in the cotton industry were able to make instant and fine distinctions between different types of material and their market value. Indeed, just as the technical terminology of textile manufacture has become "woven into the weft and warp" of the language generally,[142] so fabric comparisons were an integral part of everyday cotton town culture. The employers expected "cloth like a piece of writing paper", complained the Ashton Weavers Secretary to a mass meeting, and got a laugh when he said their looms by contrast "might have woven cloth to cover Egyptian mummies".[143] The refusal of Lancashire's employers to recognize as legitimate these respectable aspirations of their workers and families, a consequence of their own wish to maintain social distance, helped to create a solidarity amongst Lancashire's working class communities which transcended occupational groupings; and with this came a sense of exclusion and injustice. As Mawdsley commented to expressions of approval, about being dressed up on Sundays, "Why should they not be? Surely those who worked hard, had a right to dress up and go out when work was done".

Changing attitudes to notions about work, class, gender and respectability did not appear like some sudden metamorphosis, and similarly old habits died hard. As we have seen in the last chapter, the spinners were still prepared in 1889 to do a deal with the employers over the "cotton corner" – to the detriment of the cardroom workers who were on strike at the time[144] – and Mawdsley in the 1892 Brooklands dispute was still seeking to blame the merchants

and agents rather than the employers. Nevertheless a general pattern of changed perceptions and priorities does begin to emerge, which the disputes of unskilled workers in the late-1880s – commonly associated with the period of "New Unionism" – helps to reinforce.

Significantly, in an interesting reappraisal of New Unionism, Duffy[145] rejects the proposition that the 1889 London Dock Strike gave rise to a huge growth of trade union organization amongst the unskilled, and concludes that the period of New Unionism must be seen as starting at least from 1885. His survey of labourers and the unskilled makes no reference to developments in Lancashire, but the struggles of the women in the unskilled or low-skill sections of the cotton industry described here should properly be recognized as early exemplars of New Unionism predating, for instance, the London matchgirls strike in July 1888. In Lancashire by the early 1890s the image of women striking or demonstrating in support of their industrial or political rights, and often bringing a splash of laughter and humour in place of the more sober all male events[146] had become not that unusual and the public sympathy and support they received in the press was a contributory factor to the way that the 1889 Dock Strike was so favourably treated both by the press and by skilled workers generally. As one Manchester trade unionist put it in proposing collection boxes throughout the city to support the London dockers: "None of us should overlook the fact that the interests of the trades-unionists and the labourers are identical".[147]

There was not universal enthusiasm to the more militant style and policies of the newly organized unions, as is shown by the reported remarks of Entwistle, an engineering worker, at the opening of a new ASE branch in Openshaw who condemned "the methods advocated by some trade unionists and regretted the disruption of society that these methods produced".[148] This kind of view was undoubtedly reflected in some of the debates and resolutions in the TUC annual meetings during this period to which the Webbs and others have drawn attention,[149] but to the ordinary skilled workers the similarities between their position as trades unionists, and that of the semiskilled and unskilled general unions, soon came to be more important than the differences and perceived threats.

A good illustration of this came in a strike at Openshaw at the works of Messrs J Smith, stovegrate manufacturers, only a year after the new ASE branch had been opened. The National Union of Stove Grate Workers had been established the previous year in Rotherham by men who had been refused entry into the skilled craft unions because they were semi-skilled, and it quickly developed militant methods to establish its presence. When the secretary of the local branch, W. A. Shuker, was sacked a strike ensued which Smiths sought to break by bringing in twelve Glaswegians. The factory was already being picketed, but once it became clear that the company was making arrangements to take the Scotsmen to lodgings in Manchester, the strikers were able to summon up a crowd of up to 3,000 people drawn from the old skilled engineering workers and the newly emerging cotton trade unionists. Under a headline "Riotous Proceedings", the *Gorton Reporter* graphically describes the scene of a new kind of working class solidarity transcending sector, gender and inter-union demarcation:

> At 5.30 the crowd grew thicker, and amidst a steady downpour of rain, workmen from the Gorton Tank works and other establishments, with a large number of women and girls from neighbouring mills began to thickly line Ashton Old Road ... (near to Smiths) standing seven and eight deep on the pavement was a long dark line of workmen and lads fresh from work. Nearer the Tram Company stables, a number of women and girls had congregated". [150]

Nor were the old trade union leaders so slow to pick up the new mood of their members with Mawdsley using the opportunity of a national Church Congress in 1892 (at which he was an invited speaker) to put over his view of how the old established trade unions were adapting to new ideas about "socialistic" forms of organisation and more vigorous State regulation of labour:

> ... three years ago the new unionists came to the Congress fully believing that the skilled workers were their bitter foes whilst the skilled men looked on the labourers' unions with contempt. But it is impossible for those feelings to survive personal association, and it is not too much to say that another year or two will see the efface-ment of the line of demarcation between old and new and the unions of the whole country will be as homogeneous as the unions of skilled workers are today. [151]

Mawdsley's speech came exactly ten years after the Manchester Trades Council's first resolution of support for the Ship Canal and, like Woosnam's remarks about women discussed earlier, shows the extent of changes that had been taking place during the decade. It brings us back also to some of the questions raised at the start of the chapter. The growth of trade unionism amongst the unskilled and semi-skilled, the emergence of women and the general assault of employers ensured that the particular alliance of the Ship Canal Movement, though achieving its primary objective of the Canal, could not hold in the longer term; and that its producer ideology never struck deep roots either with employers or with the trade unions. It is for this reason that the Movement, as a political phenomenon, has largely been ignored by historians.

Other questions concerning the language of and about the workplace and its relationship to issues of class consciousness remain difficult to answer. The strikes we have explored, whilst demonstrating the conflicting interest of employers and workers, are for the most part accompanied by language which makes appeals to strikers and the general public, not by reference to shared class interests, but typically in terms of a benchmark of reasonable behaviour. Their letters are "conciliatory", and their claims "fair and just", their complaints are against "tyrannical" or "unscrupulous" managers, their wishes are conservative as they seek no changes from "the usage of the trade", and their search is for "peaceable relations" with the employers. Is this but a continuation of those "aspirations to a harmonious world of production encompassing master and man" which Joyce attributes to cotton workers in the period up to 1850? [152]

The vocabulary used often certainly appears to imply a symmetry of interests between capital and labour, which runs counter to our understanding of how political changes during the same period were bringing a general shift to the left, [153] and created the new Independent Labour Party (formed in 1893) with its emphasis on autonomous working class political action. Initial impressions have, however, to be tempered by looking at the wider context of industrial relations in Lancashire in which disputes were set. Across the board there is a sense of workers experiencing and protesting at the arbitrary power of employers. As Mawdsley put it at the Martha Kilburn rally "There were scores of honourable employers ... but there were also hundreds of them who fined their workpeople right and left". [154] Fines, discrimination on the grounds of age, sexual harass-ment by overseers, instant dismissals for petty offences, the introduction of piecework and the subdivision of labour, a refusal to take account of workers' domestic situations, and above all wage cuts, reflected the wider assertion of employers' prerogatives and the development of forms of management which are characterised by what Fox describes as a "low discretion, low trust syndrome"; [155] and which in turn had profound effects on workers' attitudes to their employers.

Where the language we have been exploring is being used as part of the public process of negotiating or renewing the relationship between employer and workers, it may well fail to reflect underlying attitudes and consciousness. It needs to be supplemented by other kinds of evidence, thrown up by demonstrations, interviews, court cases, Commissions, and finally the close reading of reports and minute books. While we have not been able to furnish final answers to the questions originally raised, the evidence presented in this chapter not only has given clear indications that working class consciousness, especially amongst women, was changing in this period of economic and political crisis, but also has provided detailed evidence of the process by which this change was taking place at the factory and community level.

# Notes

1. *Manchester Evening Mail*, 3 October 1885.
2. R. Grant, *The Great Canal. The Story of one of the greatest engineering feats of all time*, 1978, p. 40.
3. Boilermakers and Iron Shipbuilders Annual Report, September 1884, p.16.
4. See J. Haydu, *Between Craft and Class. Skilled Workers and Factory Politics in the United States and Britain. 1890–1922*, 1988, p. 24; and J. L. White, *The Limits of Trade Union Militancy. The Lancashire Textile Workers, 1910–1914*, 1978, for a similar reliance on strikes for studying factory politics.
5. P. Joyce, *Visions of the People*, 1991, chapter 5.
6. *Times*, 1 February 1884, p. 10. Following a meeting between trade union delegates from all over the country and Gladstone over the Extension of the Franchise Bill, Slatter successfully moved a resolution pledging support for the weavers' strike from delegates numbering over two hundred.
7. *Manchester Guardian*, 9 January 1884, p. 14. See also Royal Commission on Labour, 1886, Abstract No. 1. Strikes and Lock-Outs, p. 50.
8. Royal Commission on Labour, Report of Evidence, 10 July 1891, Question 1341.
9. D. Howell, "Was the Labour Party Inevitable?", in *North West Labour History. Labour's Turning Point in the North West*, 1984, p. 6
10. *Manchester Guardian*, 7 January 1882, p. 3. Over-sizing was a frequent subject in the *Cotton Factory Times*. See, for instance, *C.F.T.*, 27 March 1885, p. 7, where it is noted that cloth for the Indian and Chinese markets was so heavily sized that its cost was about half the normal price, weight for weight; and *C.F.T.*, 5 February 1886, p. 7, which notes the consistent opposition of trade unions leaders to oversizing, and describes the process and its harmful effects.
11. *Cotton Factory Times*, 5 March 1886.
12. *Gorton Reporter*, 21 February 1885, p. 3.
13. Industrial Remuneration Conference, 1885, Report of Proceedings and Papers, reprinted 1968 with an introduction by John Saville, p. 233.
14. J. B. Jefferys, *The Story of the Engineers*, 1946.
15. See, for instance, J. Zeitlin, "Engineers and Compositors: A Comparison" in R. Harrison and J. Zeitlin (eds.), *Divisions of Labour*, 1985. At a more general level a similar argument is put forward in A. Reid, *The Division of Labour and Politics in Britain 1880–1920*, in W. J. Mommsen and H. Husung (eds.), *The Development of Trade Unionism in Great Britain and Germany*, 1985.
16. Steam Engine Makers, Annual Report 1882, p. xiv.
17. *The Engineer*, 18 February 1887, p. 133.
18. *The Engineer*, 17 February 1882, p. 128. gives an account of some of their latest equipment.
19. J. Samuelson, *Labour-saving Machinery*, 1893, chapter III, p. 23.
20. Royal Commission on Labour. Evidence given on 14 June 1892. Question 22737.
21. The annual report of the Amalgamated Society of Engineers for 1883 shows, for instance, that in the period January to December monthly out of work returns increased from 1893 to 4090. *Manchester Guardian*, 17 April 1884, p. 7.
22. Boilermakers and Iron Ship Builders, monthly report, May 1882, p. 14.
23. Manchester Ship Canal. Subscriptions to the Parliamentary Fund, 4 January 1883, Manchester Central Library, Ref. f386/M67.
24. *The Engineer*, 24 February 1882, p. 145; 3 March 1882, p. 162.
25. J. Samuelson, *op.cit.*, chapter III. *The Engineer*, 27 January 1893, pp. 73–75 has a detailed account of the impact of improved rivetting equipment (again supplied by De Bergue) for the Liverpool Electrical Railway. It was named the "Allen's Patent Portable Pneumatic Riveter".
26. Royal Commission on Labour. Evidence of Mr. J. Whittaker, 14 June 1892, Questions 22761–64, 22 943.
27. *Gorton Reporter*, 16 August 1890, p. 8.
28. *The Engineer*, 10 November 1882, p. 358.
29. Royal Commission on Labour, Evidence of J. Whittaker, 14 June 1892, Question 22,937.
30. J. B. Jefferys, *op.cit.*, p. 100.
31. *Gorton Reporter*, 2 May 1885, p. 5.
32. *Ibid.*, 20 June 1885, p. 5.
33. *Ibid.*, 23 May 1885, p. 5.
34. In some cases these led to fines being imposed, but it is interesting to note that on those occasions when Richard Peacock, engineering employer, was sitting as a J.P. the defendants were discharged with a caution only and no fine. Peacock was Deputy-Chairman of the Ship Canal Provisional Committee, and at the time was being canvassed to become the Liberal Parliamentary candidate!
35. *Courier*, 15 July 1865, p. 7 provides an account of the police court case brought against three men charged with intimidation at Ashburys. This is the last reference found to the strike.
36. 1886 Rates of Wages. Engineering and Machinery Works. Parliamentary Papers 1893–4, LXXXIII. The absence of piece-rate wages should not be taken as evidence that piecework systems of payment were not affecting at least part of the wage packet of other engineering workers.
37. Royal Commission on Labour. Evidence of Mr. A. Coventry, 27 July 1892, Question 25661.
38. *The Engineer*, 3 February 1882, p. 90; 24 February 1882, p. 145.
39. Tin Plate Workers Society, Manchester Branch, Minutes 19 November 1885, Greater Manchester Public Record Office.
40. *Ibid.*, 21 December 1885. In a similar vein, James Swift of the Steam Engine Makers in his annual report for 1887 wrote of the 1886 cut, that "much bitter feeling had been engendered in consequence of this aggressive act".
41. *Justice*, 21 February 1885, p. 2.
42. *Gorton Reporter*, 14 March 1891, p. 8.
43. The growth of the Manchester-based United Machine Workers Association provides one illustration of this process, for the union expanded from a membership of 386 in 1882 to 2501 in 1890. For details of changes affecting the machine shop, see H. A. Clegg, *A History of British Trade Unions since 1889*, 1964, Volume 1, p. 138.

44. 1886 Rates of Wages, Engineering and Machinery Works, Parliamentary Papers 1893–4.
45. *Manchester Guardian*, 9 September, 10 September 1885, p. 5.
46. *Manchester Guardian*, 27 April 1891, p. 5; 28 April 1891, p. 12. United Machine Workers Association, Annual Report 1890.
47. A detailed account of the strike is provided by G. Holden in *Manchester Region History Review*, Vol. III, No. 2, 1989/90, pp. 15–20.
48. *Manchester Guardian*, 17 September 1887, p. 7.
49. According to G. Holden, *op. cit.*, the ASE executive did not provide strike money. The 1888 Steam Makers Annual Report also indicates a less than enthusiastic attitude at the start. But the General Secretaries of both these unions, R. Austin and J. Swift, wrote letters strongly supporting the strikers to the *Bolton Weekly Guardian* at the end of June.
50. Amalgamated Society of Woodworkers, *Our Society's History*, 1939, pp. 111–113.
51. Amalgamated Society of Woodworkers, *ibid.*, p. 111. The immediate aftermath of the strike was a decision by the Amalgamated Society to offer admission to members of the General Union on favourable terms. The policy led to mass defections from the General Union, which went into permanent decline – dropping in membership from 11,841 to 1,725 in the years 1877–1886 – while the Amalgamation went from strength to strength.
52. J. Samuelson, *op.cit.*, p. 11.
53. Royal Commission on Trade and Industry 1886, Volume 2, Part 2, Appendix, p. 64.
54. F. M. L. Thompson, *The Rise of Respectable Society*, 1988, p. 236.
55. *Cotton Factory Times*, 6 September 1889, p. 4. The strike was in Bury. It coincided with the London Dock Strike and the TUC Annual Conference, and as a result received little publicity.
56. The members of the Manchester Branch of the TA numbered 1681 in 1895. They were probably nearer to 1,400 in 1891.
57. J. Zeitlin, *op.cit.*, "Engineers and Compositors: A Comparison".
58. Memorandum from George Taylor to the Manchester Branch of the Typographical Association, 30 December 1882.
59. The Lithographic Printers faced similar problems. See T. Sproat (compiler), *The History and Progress of the Amalgamated Society of Lithographic Printers. 1880–1930*, 1930, p. 14, for an account of disputes in Nottingham in 1881 and 1882 over cheap boy labour.
60. "Stab", short for "establishment" involved the payment of a fixed rate of pay per week regardless of output.
61. A. E. Musson, *The Typographical Association. Origins and History*, 1954, pp. 178–183.
62. In the 1882–1885 Minute Book of the Manchester Branch of the TA is a handwritten draft of a note agreeing a maximum number of apprentices at five.
63. Typographical Association, Manchester Branch Minutes, 25 November 1882; 17 March 1883; 7 April 1883; 18 April 1883.
64. Royal Commission on Labour: Group C, Evidence of H. Slatter, 11 May 1892, Questions 22800–22808. Earlier in the same day George Kelley of the Lithographic Printers had given evidence that his union allowed one apprentice for every five adult workers (Question 22720).

65. Quoted in A. E. Musson, *op.cit.*, p. 179.
66. *The Typographical Circular*, June 1881, p. 4.
67. *Ibid.*, 29 September 1883.
68. *Ibid.*, 19 January 1884.
69. *Ibid.*, 15 March 1884. Letter of 7 March from Emmott and Company.
70. *Ibid.* 10 May 1884.
71. *Ibid.*, 20 February 1886.
72. Since Emmott & Co shared the same building as the *Manchester Guardian* Printing Works, this would not have been a difficult task.
73. Manchester Typographical Association Minutes, 2 January, 16 January 1892.
74. An indication of a change in this respect in the late 1880s came with the decision by the Society to affiliate to the Trades Council. By 1891 they were voting for 4 delegates to attend the meetings.
75. A. E. Musson, *op.cit.*, pp. 102-103. Formally they stated they had no objection to women compositors, provided they were paid the same rate as the men.
76. *Manchester Guardian*, 30 August 1887, p. 8.
77. *Typographical Circular*, April 1883.
78. *Manchester Guardian*, 30 April 1891, p. 5. Royal Commission on Labour. Group C. Evidence of G. D. Kelley Question 22,702.
79. Royal Commission on Labour, *ibid.*, Question 22,815.
80. A. E. Musson, *op.cit.*, pp. 192–194.
81. Full details of the advertisements of the Linotype Company and of the Typographical Association, which appeared in the newspapers on this question are to be found in *The Typographical Circular*, October– November 1894.
82. See letter from A. Goodier in Note 22, Chapter 2.
83. A. E. Musson, *op.cit.*, p. 199.
84. Amalgamated Association of Operative Cotton Spinners, Quarterly Reports 1882–1883.
85. *Manchester Guardian*, 7 July 1882, p. 4; *Labour Standard* 15 July 1882, p. 1.
86. *Gorton Reporter*, 12 August 1882, p. 8; 19 August 1882, p. 8.
87. Amalgamated Association of Operative Cotton Spinners, Quarterly Report for Quarter ending 31 July 1882, p. 16.
88. *Manchester Courier*, 5 September 1883.
89. *Manchester Guardian*, 9 January 1884, p. 4; E. Hopwood, *A History of the Lancashire Cotton Industry and the Amalgamated Weavers' Association*, 1969, p. 55.
90. Amalgamated Association of Operative Cotton Spinners, Quarterly Report, 18 March 1883. Quoted also in A. Fowler and T. Wyke (eds.), *The Barefoot Aristocrats*, 1987, p. 87.
91. See for instance *Cotton Factory Times*, 6 March 1885, p. 8, for report of a lecture in Rochdale; *Cotton Factory Times*, 1 May 1885, p. 7; and *Oldham Evening Chronicle*, 24 September 1885, p. 3.
92. *Cotton Factory Times*, 16 April 1886, p. 6; *Oldham Standard*, 17 July 1886, p. 6. The same page of the Oldham Standard reported that a similar scheme involving 31,000 ring spindles at the Sun Mill was met with hostility at the shareholders' meeting and "the subject was talked out".
93. S. and B. Webb. *The History of Trade Unionism*, 1920, p. 7. See also H. A. Turner, *Trade Union Growth, Structure and Policy*, 1962, pp. 141–3.

94. See for instance letter from "Piecers' Friend", in *Cotton Factory Times*, 30 October 1885, p. 7.
95. *Oldham Standard*, 9 February 1886, p. 3, letter from "MBD".
96. Royal Commission on Labour, Group C. Evidence of James Mawdsley, 26 June 1891, Questions 778–804.
97. *Cotton Factory Times*, 18 October 1889, p. 7.
98. Only at the 1885 "Victory" celebrations is there a reference to significant numbers of women being present. See *Manchester Evening Mail*, 5 October 1885.
99. *Manchester Guardian*, 12 June 1885, p. 4; 17 July 1886, p. 4. The Chorley dispute was the longest, lasting seven months.
100. *Manchester Guardian*, 30 July 1885, p. 7; *Manchester Courier*, 30 July 1881, p. 7; *Gorton Reporter*, 15 August 1885, p. 5.
101. Amalgamated Association of Operative Cotton Spinners (AAOCS) Report for the Quarter ending 31 July 1885, p. 6.
102. W. H. Mills, *Sir Charles W. Macara, Bart. A Study of Modern Lancashire*, 1919, pp. 67–70. Mills incorrectly puts the date of the strike as 1884.
103. Royal Commission on Labour: Group C. Evidence of James Mawdsley 26 June 1891. Question 737. For a good general account of the strike, see A. Fowler and T. Wyke (eds.), *The Barefoot Aristocrats*, 1987, pp. 88–90.
104. *Oldham Chronicle*, 19 September 1883, p. 3.
105. *Oldham Masters Letters Book*, letter from S. Andrews to Mr. Fletcher, 19 September 1885. John Rylands University Library of Manchester.
106. AAOCS. Report for the Quarter ending 31 October 1885, pp. 8–11. The original note from Andrew appeared in the *Manchester Examiner and Times*, 17 September 1885.
107. A. Bullen and A. Fowler, *A Centenary History of the Amalgamated Association of Card and Blowing Room Operatives*. 1986.
108. Industrial Remuneration Conference, 1885, The Report of Proceedings and Papers, reprinted 1968, p. l62.
109. *Oldham Chronicle*, 19 September 1885, p. 3.
110. *Rochdale Observer*, 13 March 1886, p. 5 and 20 March 1886, p. 6.
111. Quotations for the Kilburn case are all from the *Rochdale Observer*, where the reports of speeches are lengthy and seem to be verbatim. Another report of Mawdsley's speech appears in *Cotton Factory Times*, 19 March 1886, but editorial intrusion, or even rewriting by Mawdsley, is evident. Reference to an "upper class" has been omitted, and the criticism of the Bench has been diluted to "The sympathies of the Magistrates were with their own class". The filtering process here is a reminder both of the limitations of written material, and of the significance of the class based language, which Mawdsley was now beginning to use.
112. *Oldham Standard*, 30 January 1886, p. 3; 6 February 1886.
113. According to evidence submitted by George Silk, Secretary of the Union, the two strikes cost the union respectively £2033 and £3401 in strike pay. Evidence on Royal Commission on Labour: Group C, 26 June 1891, Question 522.
114. Royal Commission on Labour, Volume 34, 1893–4. Report on "Conditions of Work" in the Cotton Industry of Lancashire and Cheshire, dated 28 July 1892. Miss Abraham refers to the Oldham strike, and to a similar case in Nelson in 1892.
115. *Pendleton Times and Reporter*, 21 June 1884, p. 8.
116. Royal Commission on Labour: Group C. Evidence of George Silk, 26 June 1891, Question 539.
117. *Cotton Factory Times*, 28 January 1887, p. 4.
118. J. Lambertz, "Sexual Harassment in the Nineteenth Century English Cotton Industry", in *History Workshop Journal*, No. 19, 1985.
119. *Gorton Reporter*, 25 February 1888.
120. *Cotton Factory Times*, 13 December 1889.
121. *Gorton Reporter*, 11 January 1890, p. 6.
122. *Gorton Reporter*, 18 January 1890, p. 6.
123. *Gorton Reporter*, 4 February 1890. p. 4.
124. *Gorton Reporter*, 11 January 1890, p. 6.
125. *Gorton Reporter*, 7 June 1890, p. 6.
126. *Gorton Reporter*, 14 March 1891, p. 3.
127. F. M. L. Thompson, *The Rise of Respectable Society*, 1988, p. 197.
128. *Bolton Journal*, 1 January 1887, p. 7.
129. *Cotton Factory Times*, 3 December 1886, p. 7.
130. *Cotton Factory Times*, 19 November 1886.
131. *Manchester Guardian*, 13 January 1887, p. 8.
132. *Bolton Journal*, 18 December 1886, p. 7.
133. H. A. Turner, *op.cit.*, p. 141.
134. *Manchester Courier*, 4 January 1887, p. 8.
135. Royal Commission on Labour. Evidence of W. H. Wilkinson, 10 July 1891, Questions 1655–61. The dispute ran from December 1886 to April 1887.
136. P. Joyce, *op.cit.*, p. 125.
137. *Workmans Times*, 12 September 1890, p. 1; 19 December 1891, p. 1.
138. The cotton spinners in Rochdale, for instance, who supported Martha Kilburn in 1886 reported that 100 out of 350 spinners were out of work at the time – an unemployment rate of 28%. *Rochdale Observer*, 6 March 1886, p. 5.
139. B. D. Palmer, *A Culture in Conflict: Skilled Workers and Industrial Capitalism in Hamilton, Ontario, 1860–1914*, 1979, chapter 4.
140. D. S. Landes, *The Unbound Prometheus*, 1969, p. 320.
141. *Gorton Reporter*, 21 February 1885, p. 3.
142. See for instance colloquialisms like "classy", "cobbler", "backing off", "minder" or transformation for mainstream usage of words like "apron" "canvass", and "shuttle".
143. *Manchester Courier*, 5 September 1883.
144. H. A. Turner, *op.cit.*, p. 146.
145. A. E. P. Duffy, "New Unionism in Britain 1889–1890", in *Economic History Review*, Vol. 14, No. 2, 1961, p. 306.
146. See, for instance, *Oldham Chronicle*, 31 July 1893. – quoted in J. Liddington and J. Norris, *One Hand Tied Behind Us*, 1984, p. 94, for an account of women demonstrating in favour of the Eight Hours' Campaign.
147. *Manchester Guardian*, 4 September 1889, p. 6.
148. *Gorton Reporter*, 5 July 1890, p. 8. Entwistle was ASE delegate to the Trades Council, and a conservative in politics.
149. S. and B. Webb, *The History of Trade Unionism*, 1926, chapter VII; B. C. Roberts, *The Trades Union Congress*, 1958, chapters III and IV.
150. *Gorton Reporter*, 8 August 1891, p. 4.
151. *Times*, 5 October 1892, p. 5. The hand of a woman may even have been at work here! For Beatrice Webb writes that two

weeks before the Conference, Mawdsley "begs me for hints" about the speech, and that "a socialist discourse is promptly supplied him. It remains to be seen whether he accepts it". B. Webb, *Diaries*, 17 September 1892. Entry No.1270. London School of Economics Archive. Similar arguments to Mawdsley's were put by Thomas Burt in an article in *Nineteenth Century*, Dec. 1892, pp. 864–874 in response to an article by Joseph Chamberlain on "The Labour Question" – which had been especially critical of the old unions.

152. P. Joyce, *op.cit.*, p. 91.
153. For a further discussion of this, see E. J. Hobsbawm, "Artisan or Labour Aristocrat?" in *Economic History Review*, XXXVII, No. 3, 1984.
154. *Rochdale Observer*, 20 March 1886, p. 6.
155. A. Fox, *Beyond Contract: Work, Power and Trust Relations*, 1974, p.191.

# 6

# RAISING THE STANDARD FOR POPULAR CAPITALISM

Who are the monied classes and where are they? … They are the workpeople of Oldham … of every grade and every class … they are the people in Oldham and out of Oldham who have chosen to subscribe for shares. (Cheers). The truth is that there has been amongst us a silent revolution of which many men are still unconscious".

Jacob Bright, MP for Manchester 1883.[1]

In previous chapters we have shown the nature of the Ship Canal Movement as an alliance between manufacturing capital and the skilled trade unions, which under its initial Liberal leadership sought mass support for the scheme from Lancashire's working men. Enveloped in the early 1880s by a belief in the need for responsible action and respectability, trade union officials and their members were more than willing to give active backing to a pact with the employers which promised economic regeneration and the prospect of jobs and employment. But as the crisis of the 1880s developed, employers turned in the opposite direction – away from the collaborative model implied in the Ship Canal project towards a confrontational strategy, and in their turn the working men *and women* of Lancashire came more fully to recognise their separate and common interests as workers and the need to register and defend those interests through trade union organisation rather than via employer alliances. Though vestiges of the old producer ideology remained especially among the cotton unions, the architects of the new industrial relations in the 1890s brought different emphases to the fore and in the process wished to slough off the unsuccessful experiments of the previous decade.

One casualty of this change of emphasis has been our understanding of the Ship Canal movement itself; in particular it has not been appreciated that the movement represented a radical (though failed) approach to piloting a new form of popular capitalism. The Ship Canal originators were the nineteenth-century forerunners of those Conservative politicians from the 1970s onwards who have used privatisation programmes as the means of extending individual share ownership in contemporary Britain – and thereby dismantling the public and collective forms of ownership which have developed in the twentieth century.

This aspect of the movement has been entirely overlooked in the literature covering the political and social history of the late nineteenth century, but the inspiration for this vision of democratic capitalism is firmly rooted in the traditions of mid-Victorian England. Ideas of individualism had a strong hold not only in the political discourse of the period through the likes of Herbert Spencer, but also in the non-conformist religious traditions of a northern working class. It was these wellsprings into which the Liberal promoters of the movement were seeking to tap – with community and hence society being defined here by individual participation via the contribution of money. Subscription lists for projects were not uncommon in Lancashire as evidence was sought of widespread backing. Public memorials to well-known figures and Manchester's first Open Space for the public, Queen's Park (1843) – though this was primarily through donations from the wealthy – were promoted in this way, and working class support for the Anti-Corn Law League was encouraged by inviting one shilling and even penny contributions.

The Ship Canal project marked a new departure because its vast scale gave it the potential to be a demonstration project for something far bigger than monuments and local parks. If the working men of Lancashire could be encouraged to sink their savings in Ship Canal shares, here was a transferable working model which portrayed men and masters, not locked in conflict but putting their shoulders together in common endeavour. The scale of the project was its great strength. Larger than any other civil engineering scheme previously undertaken in the country, Lancashire's 36 mile long "Big Ditch" from Manchester to the Mersey estuary required for its construction the removal of 53 million cubic yards of material, the deployment of 97 steam excavators, 173 locomotives and 6,300 wagons on 228 miles of railway lines, and the labour of an army of 16,000 navvies. Suddenly at one daring stroke provincial Manchester was being catapulted onto an international stage, its scheme like those of its two epoch-making rivals at Suez and Panama, reflecting clearly the dominant ideas of imperialism and foreign trade which characterised the period. With a project of this size, Manchester could be sold as a world city and as the economic centre of the country with a huge industrial population in its hinterland.

The immense size of the project was however also its fatal flaw, because the true costs of such an enormous investment in the region's infrastructure meant that recourse to large

Panorama of the Canal entrance at Eastham during construction.

scale capital was inevitable, unless a revolution was brought about in working class spending and investment patterns. It was a task that turned out to be quite beyond the promoters' reach. Wedged in a cleft stick by the contradictions of their position they had simultaneously to "talk the project up" and "talk the project down". In order to impress its value upon the watching world and Parliament they had to use every device to stress its stature, economic potential and absolute necessity; but in order not to scare off investors with its vast scale they had to minimise the likely costs. The present chapter is concerned with explaining how this complex issue of the financing of the project was dealt with in the first five years up to the cutting of the first sod in 1887, and how the contradictions involved in the promoters' case were finally resolved through a restructuring of the Ship Canal Board and the calling in of large-scale London-based finance capital. In the following chapter the issue of the subsequent funding of the Canal in 1891 is taken up through an examination of the role played by Manchester City Council in providing a further £5 million of debentures.

## Costing the Project

Most historians who have written about the Canal have acknowledged that the construction costs far exceeded the original estimates, but like Leech have claimed or implied that this was because of forces outside the company's control.

This was not, however, a universally held view and the conclusion of the Yale Review in 1894 that "never in the history of a great engineering undertaking in England, were the estimates more deplorably at fault"[2] suggests that a reassessment of this question is highly appropriate. By the time the Canal was opened in 1894 to universal acclaim so much money, both private and public, had been staked in its construction that there were few in Manchester who would have wished to dwell publicly over past errors. The charge of serious miscalculation and misleading the public is, however, strongly indicated by the earlier evidence which confirms that leading figures were prepared to go to any lengths of deception to achieve their objective.

There is no doubt that minimising the costs of the Canal in order to win Parliamentary approval for the Bill was in the short term interests of the promoters and this was done in three different ways. Firstly, the estimated costs were fixed at a low level – which was not difficult since the assumptions for the calculations were not disclosed – and more bizarrely at other times were treated as though they were of no significance. Secondly, items which were necessary for the proper functioning of the Canal and the Docks were simply omitted from the calculations; and thirdly other financial devices were adopted which would throw some of the costs on to other shoulders. Details of the estimates at different stages are given by Leech, who shows that the initial figure of £4.5 million in 1882 had risen to £9.8 million in 1885, was recalculated by the company at £12.65 million in January 1891, and then revised upwards by the company by £2.5 million 18 months later.[3] The final cost of the Canal by mid-1894 was £15.4 million.

Conventionally criticism of the inadequate estimating has been countered by arguing that increased costs were caused by flooding damage in 1890 and additional works required by Acts of Parliament, but the chronology shows that the extra £2.75 million required after the 1891 estimate simply cannot be explained away in this manner. Leech does admit that the statements and predictions which he personally made in speeches in the early 1880s were incorrect, but his explanations are very much *ex post facto* concerned with justifying his own and the other promoters' actions.[4]

The evidence, particularly from the period of the Parliamentary agitation 1882–85, shows that there was on the part of many of the Ship Canal supporters both a wilful disregard for proper estimating, and a cavalier attitude displayed towards the question of costs. Leech himself provides one of the earlier examples,[5] as in a speech to the City Council in September 1882, in "talking up" the merits of deep water navigation systems he inadvertently explains that the River Tyne Commissioners had spent £6½ million simply in improving and providing dock accommodation for a section of an *existing* river, where the principal city, Newcastle, was only 11 miles from the sea compared with Manchester's 35 miles. This and other evidence led many to question the accuracy of the initial estimates, including the originator of the scheme, George Hicks, who stated in an

Fascine workers, brought from Holland to produce a strong lining for the Canal's banks.    *TRAFF*

interview in early 1894 that he had initially suggested that £14 million was a possible cost.[6] The *Manchester Guardian* prophetically put a figure of £15 million as the highest it was likely to be,[7] and argued that there was a total lack of "the most elementary information necessary for gauging the probable cost". For this action the paper was to be condemned for many years by many of the promoters with Adamson ridiculing the notion of £15 million and backing the estimates of the engineer Leader Williams with the remark that "he had the greatest faith in them, seeing that they were founded on exact matters of fact, and as near the truth as the human mind could arrive at".[8] It was more a question of the blind leading the blind, or as one Liverpool writer put it, "Mr Adamson, not an expert in canalisation, employs an engineer, who … probably never constructed navigation works of one-tenth the magnitude of those proposed".[9]

Most damning in the early months was a trenchant and closely argued pamphlet produced by Manchester merchant Andrew Provand which Cornwall, Joseph Lawrence's assistant, described as "a bid for the 'upper ten' the leading merchants and traders, to unite to stamp out the movement".[10] Provand chided the promoters on the inconsistencies of their arguments and noted that supporters like the Vice Chairman

A tipping crane used during the construction.

of the Provisional Committee, Richard Peacock, appeared to think cost was irrelevant when he had said at a mass meeting: "They had been told the canal would cost 5 or 6 million; suppose it were to cost twice that, it would be the cheapest bargain Lancashire ever made".[11] This populist line of argument was adopted too by J. C. Fielden who is reported as saying at another meeting: "Talk of twenty millions. Why, that was nothing! The Canal would be cheap at fifty millions!!"[12]

Crucially, Provand's critique dwelt also on the second method of cost minimisation employed by the promoters – failure to make provision for the docking and warehouse accommodation which would be necessary to handle the volume of traffic being estimated. Despite the fact that Liverpool Docks had £2 million worth of warehouses and plant, the Ship Canal promoters argued that there was no need for them to make allowance for this in Manchester because it would be supplied by private capital – or because according to Leech there was ample and suitable warehousing already in existence.[13] It was an obvious weakness which Marshall Stevens, the Ship Canal manager, was trying to meet as early as 1887 by encouraging the Manchester merchant Samuel Ogden to build a produce warehouse on property he owned in the city centre.[14]

The general outcome, however, was a marked lack of success in bringing in more private capital – an outcome Provand had anticipated. In 1895 therefore the Ship Canal Company had to enter into a "sweetheart" arrangement with a separately registered Manchester Ship Canal Warehousing Company – owned by some of the Ship Canal's largest shareholders – under which warehouses were built on land leased from the Manchester Ship Canal Company and then leased back to the Ship Canal at 5½% of cost on a full repairing lease.[15]

The embarrassment which the undercapitalisation caused the company can be seen too over the issue of equipping the Docks. In February 1890 the Board had to write to shareholders asking agreement to their seeking a further £600,000 capital under a new Bill in order to construct railways and install appliances for the quays, on the grounds that the

Overturned trucks after the floods at Flixton in 1890.

The Canal produced employment for thousands of navvies, who came from all over the country. *MSCC*

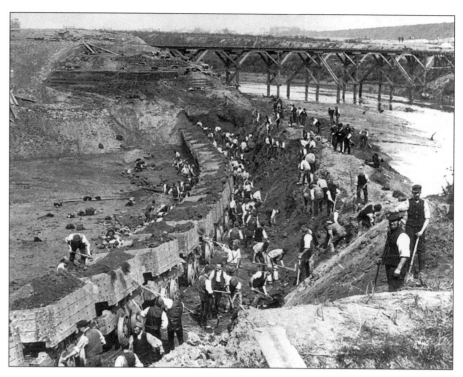

works were "not originally contemplated by the Company ... who ... considered that ... private firms would provide such works".[16] Despite this the chairman of the Board had still to write to his successor, J. K. Bythell only six weeks before the opening of the Canal:

I do not like to take responsibility of not pressing the equipment of the Docks, considering we got a special Act of Parliament for that purpose, and we might be justly found fault with if the Docks are opened without sufficient appliances".[17]

Moreover, the issue was brought more prominently to public attention by the Manchester City Council engineer, G. H. Hill the following year when he reported that even when the Ship Canal Company came to seek further Corporation loans in 1892 the "estimate did not contemplate or provide for many important works or for equipment which might, in the future, be necessary and to which attention up to the time had never been directed".[18]

The third method of cost reduction was the most bizarre of all and involved the Ship Canal Company switching contractors when the first set of contractors, Lucas and Aird – appointed on 19th July 1886 – indicated that they were not willing to accept £500,000 in paid-up Ship Canal shares as part payment for the work. As a result a new contractor, Thomas Walker was appointed in 1887, who not only agreed to accept the £500,000 in shares in lieu of cash, but also agreed to cover out of his own fees the underwriters' fees of 3½% which the promoters had refused to pay.[19] It may have appeared at the time to have been a smart move since the Board was desperately seeking to meet a deadline set in

the enabling Act for raising the capital, and could count the £500,000 as paid up capital, but in the longer term it represented a major error and involved a falsification of the true financial position. Choosing a 59 year-old contractor with Bright's disease was in itself questionable – his death two years later brought the issue of the contract and its exact terms into stark relief and was only resolved a year later when a deal was struck with Walker's executors to terminate the contract. Under the arrangement £250,000 of claims by the executors for disputed matters and work done were set off against £250,000 of shares which Walker had been obliged to take.[20] Although the executors claimed that the other £250,000 of shares had been purchased by Walker, which would have made him the largest shareholder, the reality is that most of this worthless block of shares (to the nominal value of £240,000) is still in trust today, held jointly by the chairman of the Ship Canal Company and the leader of Manchester Council.

If the ways adopted to float the company and deflect sceptics look odd to us now, they were no less strange to many people in the 1880s. Andrew Provand was particularly critical,[21] and even George Hicks writing privately to C. P. Scott at the opening of the Canal was of the opinion that:

The populace led by Adamson and Lawrence took up the attitude – "unless entirely with us, then wholly against us" – and so prudent friends and bitter enemies alike were yelled at and abused".[22]

Such comments demonstrate that this was no ordinary company flotation and that in Provand's words, the "apparently voluntary uprising of the people against the tyranny of

Thomas Walker, contractor for the Canal.

Railways, Docks and Cotton Brokers was as much promoted as the Canal itself".[23] The promoters of the 'uprising' were of course keen to see a Canal built, but they were equally concerned with the construction of a cross-class movement to be led by new men. In this context the method of financing the scheme was every bit as important as the Canal itself.

## The Search for Working-Class Shareholders

The chosen method of encouraging mass working class shareholding was evident from the very start and can be seen clearly in the attitudes of Adamson and Peacock, who had been elected to the Chairmanship and Vice-Chairmanship of the Provisional Committee. From an interview Hicks gave in 1894 to the *City News* we know that Adamson wished personally to take only a £500 shareholding in order to encourage the widest possible share ownership[24] and Peacock too made his views clear when he chaired the meeting in September 1882 to decide which scheme for the Canal should be chosen:

> No few individuals should be expected to subscribe and form a company for mere gain; it should be taken up by the public; and if it is not … I for one should say drop the scheme; … individually I will have nothing to do with the scheme unless I see the public coming forward in a hearty manner … I trust that you gentlemen here today will look at the matter from that point of view … I feel that I cannot say too much as to … the national importance of the scheme".[25]

Adamson and Peacock, both active Liberal Party supporters, had differences in perspective but they shared common views on the public nature of the movement they were helping to establish. Before starting to look at how these

Contractor's payslip

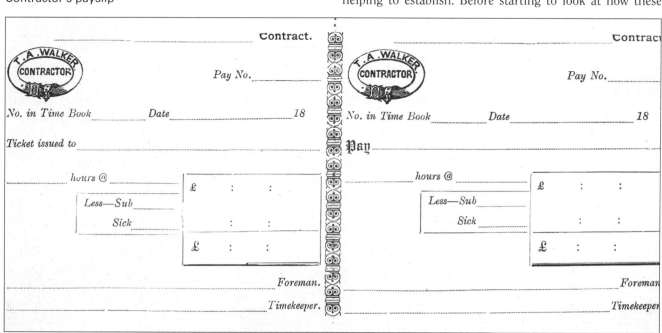

general views were developed as the movement gathered pace it is useful to explore the models which they, and others involved in the scheme, were seeking to copy. There were some, particularly on the trade union side, who were looking to the formation of a public trust, but Hicks' statement to the *City News* indicates that Adamson had no sympathy with this, and proposals of this nature were headed off. Adamson was a member of the Manchester and Salford Cooperative Society and saw the Cooperative Wholesale Society and the local Cooperative Societies as fertile recruitment grounds for the movement. They were limited, however, for the most part to consumer cooperation, where the dividends were secured by purchase of goods not shares. It is at this point that our attention is inevitably drawn to Oldham and to the development of the limited liability spinning companies in the 1860s and 1870s, to which Jacob Bright is referring in the opening quotation of this chapter.

Bright argued that a social revolution had occurred in Oldham which had transformed the town into a share-owning democracy in which the working classes could fully participate, and the theme was taken up by others. When large capitalists were unwilling to support the Ship Canal scheme, Leech responded:

Fortunately wealth does not all lie in a few hands; the mass of the people are heart and soul in the scheme. It is this class who have found their millions in Oldham …"[26]

While a few months later Mawdsley urged the spinners and weavers of Stalybridge that they: "were as good as those of Oldham … Instead of taking their savings elsewhere – to invest in mills in other towns or put in the savings bank, let them invest the money in mills in their own town".[27]

Oldham was the exemplar, the base from which to develop this working model of popular capitalism. But we need to ask two questions. How firmly rooted were the foundation stones, and what is the evidence that working class share ownership in Oldham was widespread? Clapham identified the importance of the Oldham Limiteds in developing in the 1870s the extended use of *loans* which came mainly from the "working classes in the immediate vicinity", but states that only a small part of the share capital, perhaps 5%, was owned by cotton operatives.[28] This view was based on the evidence submitted by men like Mawdsley to the Royal Commission on Depression of Trade in 1885, and Birtwistle and Mullin of the Cardroom Workers to the Royal Commission on Labour in 1891.[29]

Despite this Farnie, in his study of the English Cotton Industry, while acknowledging that the depression of 1877–79 discouraged working men from further investing in shares, claims boldly that in 1872 75% of the Limiteds' capital was raised from the working classes, that this share had dropped to about 50% by 1875, and that local investors increased from 8.3% of the population to 20% between 1873 and 1875.[30] His evidence for this precise record of the "golden age of the working class limiteds", as he puts it,

Three of the working men directors at the Sun Mill, Oldham.  *Oldham*

133

is however extremely thin and is based upon off-the-cuff estimates appearing in the *Cooperative News*,[31] and letters quoted in the paper from William Nuttall, a keen cooperator and company promoter. Thus Nuttall is relied upon for the 1875 figure, when stating that it is difficult to:

form a very accurate estimate of the proportion of capital supplied by the working class, and the proportion supplied by the non-working class (if there be any such in Oldham). Still I think there can be no question but that the working classes supply one-half of the capital of all these companies".[32]

When it is realised that a man like the brewer Henry Boddington, with a £27,000 shareholding in the Ship Canal, could appeal for support at a shareholders meeting as a "worker",[33] it is obvious that Nuttall's throwaway statements should not be treated as reliable sources.

Analysis of share registers is the only effective way of examining this issue further, and two such studies are available. The first, by Tyson, looks at the case of the Sun Mill Company and does conclude that about 75% of the shareholders were manual wage earners. Sun Mill, the proto-type for the Limiteds, was however atypical for, as the author points out, the promoters were nearly all skilled men and cooperators.[34] We would expect them to have recruited working-class shareholders, and in fact also find that the Oldham Cooperative Societies had 784 shares in the company. The other study, by Roland Smith, is of the 1877 share register of the Moorfield Company and four smaller companies in Oldham and has the very different finding that "references to shareholding by cotton workers were exceptional".[35] Smith is quick to emphasise that it would be unwise to draw general conclusions from his limited study, but in the light of the general acceptance of evidence of men like Mawdsley and Birtwistle to the Royal Commissions in the 1880s

and 1890s – that there were very few cotton operative shareholders – it is impossible to accept that the structure of share ownership in Oldham changed so radically in a decade, as Farnie has implied.

Contemporary observers of the cotton industry like Bright, Leech and Adamson wanted to believe that cotton workers in large numbers had become investors in the companies, and so were easy victims of the kind of unsubstantiated reporting from the *Preston Guardian* which trumpeted that:

Hundreds of cases could be instanced in Oldham of working men, in receipt of from £1 to £1.10s a week, who have their hundreds of pounds invested in these companies".[36]

In the context of the Ship Canal Movement, the significance is that so many of the Ship Canal promoters had this strong utopian belief in the myth of the Oldham working class shareholder and were determined that their project would be the vehicle for universalising him. The importance of this aspect cannot be overstated because it explains so much of the populist nature of the movement. Working class shareholding was an integral centre piece of the entire scheme, being actively canvassed from the outset. At an early conference between the Provisional Committee and the Ward Committees, Leech himself proposed a motion encouraging shilling contributions from working men and expressed the hope that they would soon have a further scheme for collecting sums "perhaps as low as a penny".[37] Two days later it was Adamson's turn when he arranged to address his work people in the pattern room on the scheme and the shilling coupon system; having offered to guarantee payment himself if they set up a committee to bring in subscriptions, he was able the next week to announce that they had promised £430.[38]

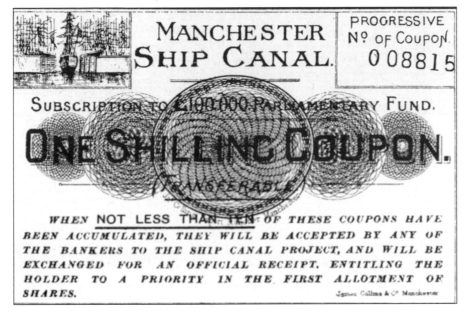

One shilling coupon, promoted to bring in working-class supporters.

The bandwagon was rolling. At the big working men's rally on 13th November, Murchie suggested that they could support the scheme by holding a Ship Canal Saturday,[39] and by the beginning of December a detailed scheme was published. It explained that the coupons would be transferable for shares and suggested that the ward committees should arrange meetings in every workshop in their area.[40] A meeting of the Provisional Committee Executive delegated to Leech and the campaign organiser Lawrence the decision as to whether as many as 20,000 of the explanatory memoranda should be printed.[41]

The *Manchester Guardian* gave support, describing the ingenious plan as "calculated to help forward the movement amongst the working classes to a great degree", but other papers were sceptical, doubting the chances of the Canal paying a dividend, and arguing the need "to warn the working man against it, as a mode of investment he ought in all prudence to avoid".[42] Over the next two years a few small successes are recorded amongst the workshops of Manchester and Salford, with the employees of the Eagle Foundry, the Crown Chair Works (£37), Tootal, Broadhurst and Lee, and John Rylands & Co. (£188) all agreeing to contribute (often via employer loans);[43] and so impressed was one Warrington working man after hearing one of Adamson's more populist speeches that he wrote to the Chairman personally: "I will contribute my mite … I shall endeavour to become a shareholder and either sink or swim with the Manchester Ship Canal".[44]

No flood of working class financial support was forthcoming however in the early Parliamentary phase, and the promoters were not helped by the activities of Samuel Ramsbottom, an eccentric auctioneer and broker living in Collyhurst. Having been an investor in the Lancashire Cotton Spinning Company – promoted in 1874 to work a mill in Royton near Oldham, which then went into liquidation – Ramsbottom regarded himself as one of the victims of unscrupulous company promoters, and commenced in 1883 a one-man campaign against what he described as the "Adamsonian Delusion" and "the South Lancashire Bubble". Tracts and broadsheets flowed from his printer, John Heywood in Deansgate; and when notices appeared on the hoardings announcing the mass meeting in June 1884 to support the scheme, Ramsbottom produced his own leaflet entitled:

TO THE WORKING CLASSES – The Projected Manchester Ship Canal – WHAT IS IT? A MYTH! A PHANTASY!

and warned "Be not ensnared, beguiled or cajoled into investing money".[45]

The emphasis given to gaining working class support for the Canal was also having other adverse effects; in particular the promoters had difficulty in raising mercantile capital and support. Large industrialists like John Rylands, Henry Boddington and the Platts in Oldham were willing to make substantial contributions, but Manchester's wealthy merchants were alarmed by the political alliance between manufacturers and workmen, which the movement was seeking to build up, and saw little incentive to invest their capital. In his evidence before the House of Lords Parliamentary Committee in 1884, Leech claimed that the commercial men in the city were almost unanimously in favour,[46] but when he came to write his account of events twenty years later he acknowledged that many of the "leading townsmen were either hostile or lukewarm in the cause"[47] – a point made more forcefully in a profile of Marshall Stevens written in 1894:

Should the inner history of those dark days come to be written, it may be found that it was not the avowed enemies – the railway companies and the Docks Board – which most retarded progress, but leading Manchester men who held aloof and looked askance at the movement".[48]

## TO THE WORKING CLASSES.

### The Projected Manchester Ship Canal.

#### WHAT IS IT? A MYTH! A PHANTASY!

Gymano Turonomy first conceived the idea many years ago, but it was not till the days of Daniel Adamson that anything was attempted by way of putting Gymano's conceptions into practical shape.

When Daniel and his band re-opened this question, I looked favourably on the scheme, but in consequence of the treatment I received in the Ship Canal Office, I was led to reflect upon the project. Meditation on the subject produced quite a revulsion in my opinions on the Canal Scheme. It is exceedingly mysterious to me, that I should have been led to pursue the course of action I have towards the Ship Canal. I had no desire to be thus at variance with the popular will; and I never could have held such an attitude towards the scheme if Mr. H. Whitworth, unfortunately, had not been Secretary to the project. I say unfortunately, but perhaps I am wrong, for I believe there is such a thing as Providence. I have no desire to delude myself, but when I take all the circumstances into consideration connected with my conflict in this matter, I can come to no other conclusion than that Providence has determined or appointed that I should oppose this—as the chairman of the London and North Western Railway terms a "Wild Project"— and for this reason, very extraordinary means have, and are still being resorted to by the promoters to influence the Working Classes to take up shares in the scheme. I feel that my mission is to this, my own class of the community, and my message to you is, be not ensnared, beguiled, entrapped, or cajoled into investing money in the Manchester Ship Canal Scheme. Let me solemnly impress upon you this fact, so sure as you part with your money to support this project, as sure will it be lost. I have no objection to Mr. John Rylands and other men of wealth investing their £50,000 or £100,000 in the scheme. I say if they have faith in the scheme, they are the men to find the money to execute the work.

#### Beware! Beware!! Beware!!!

On Saturday next, according to a Leviathan Bill now on the hoardings of the city, an attempt is to be made to excite in you admiration of the scheme, which will ultimately lead you to take up shares therein. I notice after the names of certain M.P.'s, follow an Alderman, then Town Councillors, then 27 names of Secretaries and Representatives of various Trades. BUT BE YOU NOT BEWITCHED BY THEIR INFLUENCE.

I know there are those who will say, "Take no notice of Ramsbottom, he is mad." My reply is, that it is much easier to make such a statement than to prove it. But mad or not, I am honest and sincere in my opposition to the Ship Canal Scheme.

Is it not a fact, that in the past, many schemes have been set before the public which were to be grand schemes for making money and benefiting the whole community? By the plausible tales of the promoters of such schemes, as in this Ship Canal Project, they have got hold of large sums of money, and often thousands of the working classes have been great losers, when it has turned out that the projects were failures, and in a many instances the promoters have secured themselves from loss, and for ought that they cared their dupes might go to Tangitoria or Mungacaroimea.

Therefore, though curiosity or the desire to mingle in a great crowd may tempt you to the Meeting on the 21st, don't pledge yourselves to support a scheme that is sure to result DISASTROUS IN MANY WAYS.

Yours respectfully,

Manchester, June 18th, 1884.                    SAMUEL RAMSBOTTOM.

Handbill circulated by Samuel Ramsbottom in 1884.

*MSCC*

135

The tensions generated within the movement over the raising of capital were substantially disguised during the period of the Parliamentary agitation, but by the summer of 1885 friction between Adamson and Joseph Lawrence, the man recognised by insiders as the strategist and brains behind the campaign,[49] had reached such a pitch that Lawrence decided upon resignation. Leech is entirely silent over the issue, but the Provisional Committee minutes record a disagreement over whether he should be based in London or Manchester, a rejection of unspecified proposals from Lawrence, and a lengthy discussion over his resignation letter, which was in the end simply accepted, but only after Fielden and Boddington had failed by 12–3 votes to get a motion passed acknowledging his valuable services.[50] Whatever Lawrence's proposals were, his actions clearly caused great acrimony, but in the interests of the movement a veil of silence was drawn over the event. Lawrence's personal assistant, Cornwall, who resigned at the same time, felt no such compunction however and, when the *City News* offered him a platform to describe the Ship Canal pioneers, he explained that the real reason for Lawrence's resignation was Adamson's reckless claims that he could raise £30 million in Lancashire, or if necessary in Paris since "Monsieur de Lesseps had told him so", and his insistence that no commission be paid to the brokers.[51]

At this stage Adamson, the charismatic cult hero of the movement, was a far too powerful figure to be effectively challenged by Lawrence who was henceforth quietly erased from the historical record; but as we shall see eighteen months later, when the first Rothschild's share offer had failed, it was to be Adamson himself whose future with the Company was to be called into question. In August 1885 however, once the Bill had finally received the Royal Assent, Adamson, the victorious leader of a new popular movement, took the offensive once again. If working men were unconvinced up to now, then all that was needed was to talk up the advantages. Addressing an enthusiastic meeting of subscribers he claimed that the Canal had a strong prospect of generating nine million tons of traffic, and that it would be difficult "to keep the dividend under 20%".[52] Lawrence, now freed of an employee's responsibilities, responded on the same day with a letter scathingly critical of the methods being used to gain public support for the Ship Canal and obviously directed at Adamson:

> Speeches are at best often inconsecutive and uninstructive ... When some consist entirely of personal adulation, or in some instances hold out prospects of 20% dividends, they become in the former case nauseating, and in the latter illusory".[53]

Manchester and Lancashire however were besotted with Adamson, filling the streets with banners as he passed – "Long life my Uncle Daniel", as one read at the Eccles demonstration;[54] and wherever he went Adamson hammered home the same messages – the prospects of great wealth, and the need to exclude from this producers' cornucopia an

indeterminate group of non-producers. "Many people were now squealing like young pigs to suck the Ship Canal dry", he told a Warrington audience, "but they had not their interests at heart. It was the interest of those before him to make the Canal and get their money with the least possible expenditure for commission, and with as few middlemen as possible".[55]

His style was messianic, brooking no opposition. At the Free Trade Hall just two days after the great Belle Vue demonstration, he declared:

> I have lived by estimates, and I have prospered by estimating their true value ... But I have never calculated a single contract out ... where there was such a prospect of such undeniable dividends and such profits ... To him who has little, I say risk that little; to him that has much I say risk considerable of that much ... It is the certainty of results; it is the positive language of truth that I have tried to use".[56]

Adamson was not alone in singing this song. Fielden told an audience at Patricroft that the "movement was essentially a bread and butter question – a working class question", and advocated shareholdings as "a sound and lucrative investment",[57] while Marshall Stevens, the new manager, stated that they were keen to receive share applications,

Joseph Lawrence, the strategist behind the campaign.
*MCL*

136

The directors of the Cooperative Wholesale Society on board the SS *Pioneer* on the day of the Canal's opening. *CWS*

"especially from the working classes".[58] The idea was developed in the pages of the press with one correspondent arguing that if the system of share subscription could:

> be fully explained to the million house or cottage holders interested in the Canal, the question of money is at an end, and the Canal the property of the working classes, without troubling Lord Rothschild or Sir Cunliffe Brooks for a penny. That this can be done is a certainty".[59]

The only problem was of collection, and another correspondent suggested this could be dealt with via the weekly visit of the rent collector.[60]

The issue of effective marketing of the scheme to the working classes was taken up by the promoters with enthusiasm, for at their meeting in mid-August the Provisional Committee requested Stevens to consult with Kelley from the Trades Council and other trade union leaders, in order to obtain their assistance in the preparation of a manifesto to be issued to their branches; and in a parallel development three of the members were deputed to arrange a meeting with the Chairman of the local Cooperatives Societies as soon as possible.[61] At the CWS Finance Committee held on the same day it was reported that Adamson had already had an interview with the Committee about the Ship Canal Project.[62]

The Cooperative Movement had been targeted early on by the promoters, and particularly by Adamson, because its ideology of consumer cooperation was seen as akin to the producer cooperation of the Ship Canal movement. If the Sun Mill cooperative could provide a model for the development of the Oldham Limiteds, then the Coops could do likewise for popular capitalism. The previous year at the 25th anniversary of the Manchester and Salford Cooperative Society, twelve thousand of their members had witnessed the close links being established between the two movements when their President, H. C. Pingstone, and Secretary James Johnston – both keen Ship Canal supporters – shared a platform with the Dean of Manchester and Adamson.[63] Cheered as ever when rising to speak, Adamson had stressed the promoters' wish to have the support of cooperators,[64] but it was left to the other main speaker, Sir Edward Watkin, the former Anti-Corn Law League organiser in the 1840's, to make explicit the ideological function of Cooperation as he saw it:

> He looked upon Cooperative Societies as the golden bridge which spanned the interests of competition with the interests of cooperation. It was the resource which where there were conflicts between capital and labour, came in so usefully and so well, to show men that they had mutual interests provided they had mutual trusts".

Adamson's early persistence had paid off, for within only a short period of the Bill receiving the Royal Assent, Alderman Bailey, supported by other Ship Canal promoters, was chairing a meeting with representatives from eleven Cooperative Societies, which recommended the promoters to apply to all the local Societies; and by mid-September the CWS had decided itself to take a £10,000 shareholding.[65]

While support of this nature was coming from the Cooperative leadership and via resolutions encouraging shareholding at the big public meetings and demonstrations, there were however many other voices adopting a more sceptical or hostile line, particularly following the Belle Vue and Free Trade Hall meetings in early October.

Samuel Ramsbottom was quickly off the mark with a letter to Adamson scoffing at his claims of 16% or 20% returns and his attempts to 'dazzle' people with prospects of the *Big Divi*. When it was returned to him unanswered, he published it as a pamphlet, *The Rejected Letter*.[66] There was criticism too from a trades unionist C. M'Donald of Hulme who complained about canvassers coming round to workshops and houses and about the Trades Council's "manifesto" urging working class tradesmen to take up shares: "I cannot understand why the working-man should be pressed so much in this matter".[67] Most worrying for the promoters was a perceptive article in the *Cotton Factory Times* by the respected dialect poet Ben Brierley who acknowledged that the Belle Vue demonstration was a "good display by working men", but recognised that it was more about developing a personality cult than raising money:

> Very Flattering, no doubt, are such demonstrations for the heroes of the hour. But cheering and holiday-making, if not backed up by capital will never bring a cargo of cotton to Cornbrook".[68]

Despite these adverse critics, the idea of promoting working class shareholding through weekly shilling

**MR. BEN BRIERLEY.**
*Lancashire Author and Poet.*
*(From a Photograph.)*

Ben Brierley, one of Lancashire's most widely-read dialect poets.   *Chetham's*

contributions continued to be promoted energetically as Stevens reported in November to the Ship Canal Board. He had had meetings with "gentlemen interested" in the proposal, and the board expressed their entire approval. By early 1886 it became clear that the "gentlemen" were J. C. Fielden and some trade union officials, who had formed a new Cooperative Shares Distribution Company (CSD) specifically to promote share ownership in the Canal by working men. In February details of their scheme were submitted to the Board, which agreed to allot any shares which the CSD applied for within the next three months.[69] The prospectus, issued on 15th February – at the height of the demonstrations over unemployment – has a roll-call of mostly trade union officials as directors of the company, and complex rules for the allocation of and payment for Ship Canal shares. So draconian were the clauses about forfeiture in the event of individuals not regularly maintaining payment of their weekly shilling contributions that Leech, in a pencilled note on his copy of the prospectus, wrote "It will seem an attempt to benefit by the improvidence of the working classes", and concluded, "Undesirable any one prominently connected with the Ship Canal should be prominent".[70] It could have done nothing to increase the attractiveness of the scheme – indeed it added the cost of a small management fee if the Ship Canal Company was not permitted to pay interest out of capital during the construction period – and within four months it was proved a complete failure. When no applications were received a resolution moved by Adamson was passed by the Board terminating the agreement with the CSD.[71]

No doubt the resolution was moved reluctantly but by this time the Board was primarily concerned that the necessary capital for the entire project was simply not going to be forthcoming. In February an additional Bill had been put forward by the Company to secure the right to pay interest out of capital during the period of construction (and before the Canal was producing any income). Hitherto Adamson had argued that this was completely unnecessary to attract investors, but in a letter to the *Times* his tune had changed. Now it was "monstrous" to ask investors to lend money without any return for four years,[72] and he claimed thousands of Ship Canal shareholders were demanding these powers.

The *Liverpool Daily Post* presented a more accurate picture explaining that the powers were needed to carry through the scheme "by borrowing the remainder of the capital from the famous millionaires".[73] The reference was to Rothschilds, and for Adamson particularly the change of tack was most unwelcome, for it meant relying upon the London capitalists whom he had for so long castigated.[74] The Bill was presented as a general measure to ensure that the capital was raised but in reality it was quite specifically targeted. As Lord Rothschild himself admitted before a House of Lords committee, the Bill was not aimed at the small investor but "is a bait which you hold forth to large capitalists … it is the large capitalist who advances £40,000 or £50,000 who wants to make sure of his money".[75]

Despite the creation of these new powers to pay interest, the floating of the share issue in July 1886 by Rothschilds was still a complete failure, with only £100,000 being subscribed in four days. It marked a nadir in the fortunes of the promoters but quickly led to a regrouping over the question of financing the scheme. Whilst Adamson saw the Rothschilds failure as a vindication of his views that the Lancashire working man should be relied upon for the capital, others – soon to be ascendant – saw a restructuring of the company as a normally financed business operation, without its populist baggage, as the greatest need.

The method adopted to initiate this transformation was to establish a Consultative Committee ostensibly to examine afresh the feasibility and financing of the Canal and produce a report. The suggestion to do this had come from Rothschilds, as can be seen from private notes of Marshall Stevens on 27th July, "No definite promise from R. Seek Manchr. report and come again … Their present temper is to get out".[76] On the following day the Board appointed the Consultative Committee with Adamson, Lee and Houldsworth representing the Board, and others were to be selected by them. By the end of August however a decision had been made to create a Committee "entirely independent of the Board",[77] and steps were taken to assemble a powerful group of Manchester men as members. Its construction was carefully organised to embrace new talent and any potential opposition. Notably it included a number of wealthy Manchester merchants who had been lukewarm about the scheme. Among these was J. K. Bythell who later became the first full-time chairman of the company. Additional members included Lord Egerton, a representative of great landed capital and leading Conservative, the Mayor of Manchester and James Mawdsley – who had both been closely involved in responding to the unemployed agitation six months earlier – and finally representatives of the three leading Manchester papers, Scott, Sowler (*Courier*) and Ireland (*Examiner and Times*).

The Committee was to meet on a number of occasions finally reporting in December, but in the meantime the campaign to entice Lancashire's working men to become shareholders was relaunched. The start came with unsigned letters placed in the local press from for instance, a "working man shareholder" – "What I propose is to start a Ship Canal Club, for workmen only, at 1s. per week per share" – and from "A Working Man's Wife" describing a shareholders' meeting, "I was pleased to see so many of the working classes; would there had been more".[78] A few days later a big push came from the Board itself with Adamson taking the lead by inviting Digby Seymour, a London QC to outline to his own workmen a plan for floating another independent company with directors "risen from the ranks" for buying Ship Canal shares. Details of the scheme, including Seymour's claim that "38 or 40% as a *bona fide* dividend" was not unrealistic, were well publicised, and the following day Adamson was able to issue a press release that the men at his Hyde Works had agreed to work two hours extra per week and allow the extra wages earned to be deducted and invested on their behalf in Ship Canal shares. This would raise up to £3,000 per annum and the statement concluded, "If the employees of 1,000 other firms of equal magnitude could be found to follow this example, hardly any subscriptions would be wanted".[79]

A couple of days later, Sir Joseph C. Lee, banker and deputy chairman weighed in with his own "Plan to enable Working men to become Shareholders" via the issue of one shilling vouchers with double counterfoils, and was followed shortly afterwards by another director, William Bailey, with a third alternative plan,[80] whereby one shilling adhesive stamps – sold weekly by the Ship Canal Company's collecting agents – would be posted into a registration book and after about four years exchanged for a £10 Ship Canal share. Holding up the Cooperative Societies as an example of the organisational form in which "that difficult social problem the fusion of capital and labour first found a happy solution", Bailey was convinced that "workmen's shares' were the mechanism to enable the working class "to become partners in the enterprise".

For a brief period the Manchester papers were full of articles and letters on the respective merits of the schemes, but for Leech, angry that "in Manchester our leading citizens as a rule won't trouble themselves to inquire into the merits and capabilities of the canal", the issue was a wider one of leadership in a period of political and industrial change. Giving his full support to the schemes for drawing in the working classes and to the Ship Canal promoters who found themselves "banded between the classes and the masses", he declared:

We shall have to take copy from the industrious bees, who when their queen gets drowsy, make a fresh one. So we must get fresh leaders to the front whom rich and poor alike will respect and follow.[81]

A new leadership was indeed to emerge, but not on the back of mass shareholding in the Ship Canal movement. The Tory *Manchester Courier* had been full during this period of letters criticising existing free trade policies. The tone can be seen in one from Edwin Burgis: "For years (working people) have been gulled with the talk about the *big loaf*" which was picked up by "M.E.W.", a cotton worker supporting import controls, who concluded that because the wealthy were not subscribing for shares, "we can club together for objects much more beneficial than the Ship Canal".[82] If the Tories were to seize the initiative from the Liberals on the economic front and give the Ship Canal their stamp, they had to act fast to arrest the mass shareholding bandwagon and find an alternative. Characteristically it was Houldsworth who made the first move, stressing the importance of the newly formed Consultative Committee and declaring, "Proposals for enabling persons of small means to take shares are most interesting … but it is not business. We want to know what the larger capitalists, the merchants, manufacturers … think of the project".

His views were quickly picked up by another prominent Tory, Ellis Lever:

> The practical and sensible business letter of Mr Houldsworth, MP hits the nail on the head, and will commend itself to many who, like myself, have no faith in the proposal to raise the sum of £5,000,000 by the weekly shillings of working men.[83]

Equally significant was a derisive letter from a radical trade unionist and tinplate worker Richard Woosnam, pointing out that most skilled workers were on short time: "Many suppose that the Working Classes are only waiting while one of the different schemes is decided upon, and after this the money will flow in without further trouble ... The very idea is absurd."[84]

The combination of this new Tory-radical alliance and the low take-up of the shares was finally sufficient to kill off the active promotion of working class shareholdings, and little more was heard on the subject as attention became focused on the work of the Consultative Committee. It is impossible to provide any full assessment of the actual number of shares taken in the Company by manual workers, but all the evidence suggests that there were few. The number of shareholders, totalling some 39,000, was certainly very large but the bulk of them were, according to Leech, from "the middle-classes", from shopkeepers, traders, clerks and others from white-collar occupations in an expanding service sector.[85] The only specific evidence about the impact of the one-shilling contribution scheme is to be found in a report about an early outing on the Ship Canal by a Trade Council delegation, where it was reported that the officers had themselves formed such a Share Association and "something like 90 shares were taken". The same report states that two-thirds of the 200 delegates were themselves shareholders; this is an indication of the level of support given by trades council members personally, but cannot be taken as evidence of anything more than that.[86]

**Restructuring and New Directions**

For the Ship Canal Company the crucial arena in late-1886 was the series of meetings of the 23-man Consultative Committee or "Citizens Committee" which had been charged with the responsibility of producing an "independent" report on the financial health of the project. Although nominally chaired by the mayor, the driving force behind the group was Charles Moseley, the Deputy Chairman and a leading Tory manufacturer, and the evidence and reports – upon which the Committee's judgements were made – were mainly submitted by the Ship Canal Manager, Marshall Stevens, himself a Tory supporter.[87] Another figure known to have played an influential role was C. P. Scott who wrote part of the report.[88]

A new alliance was now being forged in the quiet of the committee room, in which former sceptics – anxious about the political instabilities created by the unemployment riots and by the break up of the Liberal Party – chose to rally behind a new leadership and give their decisive support to the scheme. The obstacle however, was Adamson himself – the populist who had won mass support for linking Manchester to the sea, but who was now a major deterrent when it came to persuading large-scale Lancashire and London capital to provide the finance. The chosen solution was to pin a stinging last clause to the Consultative Committee's short (and favourable) report, issued in early December, on the Ship Canal's prospects, "In our judgement it is necessary before the issue of any further prospectus, to reconstitute and greatly to strengthen the Board of Directors".[89]

The Mayor Alderman Goldschmidt had anticipated Adamson's hostility, insisting that Saxon, the Ship Canal solicitor, should not let the chairman have an advance copy of the report,[90] and for the next two months Adamson proceeded to protest and fight against the proposals to restructure the Board. Resignations and withdrawals were rife; according to notes handwritten by Adamson, he himself resigned for a period on 17th December together with his son-in-law Joseph Leigh, James Platt and Boddington. According to Leech, Bright and Lee also resigned for a few days, but Houldsworth would not withdraw his resignation until formal agreement to restructure had been reached.[91]

Houldsworth, together with Sir Joseph Lee, who had recently deserted to the Liberal Unionists, were the two key players and were implacably opposed to Adamson's populist style. A letter written to Adamson in late January by Henry McNeil, who was acting as intermediary with Houldsworth, seemed to suggest the possibility of a "friendly settlement of the crisis"[92] but this was to prove illusory. A week later the directors' report was issued to the shareholders, with Adamson's name conspicuously absent. Their recommendation was for a substantial restructuring through inviting five new directors to join the Board, including three of Lancashire's most prominent Tories – Lord Egerton of Tatton, Charles Moseley and W. H. Houldsworth.[93] Although there were still five Liberal members on the Board, their influence was now counterbalanced by the four Tories and four Liberal Unionists, from whose ranks were drawn the chairman and deputy chairman.

Completely outmanoeuvred Adamson absented himself from Board meetings throughout this period, and had no alternative but to resign as Chairman at the shareholders' meeting in early February when the Directors' report was adopted. As the brewer Henry Boddington put it, "The question before them was whether they would submit to the domination of one man".[94] The cult figure head, the man who had led the movement for five years, had been toppled, and his place was taken by Lord Egerton, a move that was to presage the introduction of a hard-headed approach to the raising of the capital in the London money markets. In Adamson's mind the particular *bête noir* seems to have been Sir Joseph Lee whose patrician style and hostile attitude to the trade unions had been made abundantly clear in his evidence to the Royal Commission on the Depression of Trade the previous year.[95]

For the new Board of Directors the imperative was to raise the capital before the time limit imposed by Parliament expired in August. With a new Tory–Liberal alliance – unencumbered by radical and populist Liberal rhetoric – now firmly established, a two-fold strategy was adopted. The first objective was to raise substantial capital in Lancashire, not so much from the clerks and working men of the Adamson years with their weekly shillings – although their support was still sought – but from the big merchants and manufacturers with the capital to invest thousands of pounds in a single down payment. By mid-May, through dint of hard canvassing and much arm-twisting, a subscription list of £3 million had been achieved. Popular backing remained strong despite Adamson's departure but this was, in Leech's words,

> in marked contrast to the tardy support given by many leading merchants and capitalists of the district, who either held aloof entirely, or contributed the smallest sum that decency would allow.[96]

Substantiation of this statement can be provided in the case of Lancashire's very wealthiest men by an analysis of the county's "Top Forty" wealth holders dying with estates worth over £500,000 who were at least 23 years old at the time. This select group of forty men provides a striking confirmation of Leech's complaint. The two Lists are based upon material provided by W. D. Rubinstein[97] and an analysis of shareholders listings. List I shows that only seven had shareholdings of £1,000 or more, with a further seven having shareholdings of under £1,000; List II provides details of the remaining 26 (65%) who had no shareholdings at all. The listings are partly a reflection of the hostility which the promoters had provoked through their crusade for a producer alliance between manufacturers and workers but they also mirror divisions within the local bourgeoisie

between on the one hand those merchants and manufacturers whose business and horizons were international in scope, and on the other those identified with the Ship Canal Movement who looked to protect their interests by investment at home and stimulation of the local economy.

This fracture, recognised in the writing of Katherine Chorley – who bemoaned the flight of urban wealth from Manchester – and more recently investigated by Simon Gunn, lay at the heart of the problems associated with the financing of the project.[98] It substantially weakened the position of the Ship Canal Board in negotiating for additional London-based finance capital and did nothing to inspire external confidence for the scheme as is evident from surviving correspondence. Immediately after the toppling of Adamson, Whitworth, the Company Secretary, had written to Rothschilds informing them that the Board of Directors had been "reformed upon the lines suggested by Lord Rothschild in July last",[99] and for the next two months the deputy chairman Sir Joseph Lee was involved in protracted discussions which had run into the sand by the end of April. As Lord Rothschild put it in a private letter to Lee:

> Your latest proposals have met with no better reception … it is useless to further continue the negotiations … I have used my personal influence in the matter and still without overcoming their objections.[100]

Rothschild was acting for a large consortium of merchant banks who doubted the profitability of the Canal, and for a while the whole project threatened to disintegrate. The solution to the impasse was finally to offer them priority payment – by splitting the capital into ordinary and preference shares by a special Act of Parliament – and by issuing the whole of the £4 million preference stock to the merchant banks with a 1½% commission.[101] The effect was to make even less likely the payment of any dividend to some 35,000 holders of ordinary shares, but even so the commitment of the banks remained finely balanced up to the last moment. The enabling Act received the Royal Assent on 12th July,

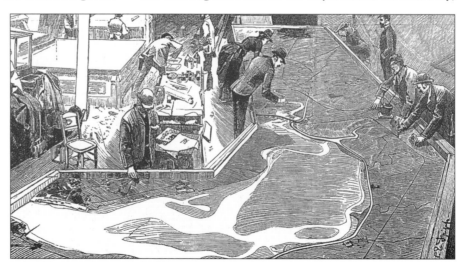

Model of the Ship Canal, prepared for the Royal Jubilee Exhibition in 1887 to encourage wider shareholding. *Chetham's*

## List 1  Ship Canal Shareholdings of Wealthiest Lancashire Men

| Name | Dates | Occupation | Estate Value | Shares |
|---|---|---|---|---|
| AGNEW William | 1858–1918 | Art Dealer | £600,000 | £5,000 |
| CRAVEN Thomas | 1850–1933 | Engineer | £795,000 | £1,000 |
| BROOKS Sir W CUNLIFFE | 1819–1900 | Banker | £1,250,000 | £10,000 |
| GROVES William | 1847–1927 | Brewer | £532,000 | £1,000 |
| HAWORTH Abraham | 1830–1902 | Yarn Agent | £632,000 | £20,000 |
| HOLT Sir Edward | 1849–1928 | Brewer | £1,000,000 | £3,000 |
| RYLANDS John | 1801–1888 | Cotton Mfr. | £2,575,000 | £50,000 |
| | | | | |
| CAWLEY Frederick | 1850–1937 | Bleacher | £901,000 | >£1,000 |
| CHEETHAM John F | 1835–1916 | Cotton Spinner | £566,000 | >£1,000 |
| DAVIES John H | 1864–1927 | Brewer | £513,000 | >£1,000 |
| HULTON Edward | 1838–1904 | Newspaper Owner | £559,000 | >£1,000 |
| KENYON Thomas | 1843–1916 | Bleacher | £975,000 | >£1,000 |
| PAULDEN William | 1838–1918 | Drapery Merchant | £551,000 | >£1,000 |
| WILLIAMS James | 1853–1925 | Mail Order Propr. | £635,000 | >£1,000 |

## List 2  Wealthiest Lancashire Men Without Ship Canal Shareholdings

| Name | Dates | Occupation | Estate Value |
|---|---|---|---|
| BARBOUR George | 1841–1919 | Cotton Exporter | £1,311,000 |
| BEHRENS Edward | 1836–1905 | Cotton Merchant | >£500,000 |
| BEHRENS Frank | 1839–1902 | Cotton Merchant | £541,000 |
| CHRISTIE-MILLER Wakefield | 1835–1898 | Hat Manufacturer | £1,014,000 |
| BROWN Andrew | 1852–1927 | Foreign Merchant | £515,000 |
| BULLOUGH Thomas | 1858–1915 | Machinery Mfr | £790,000 |
| BUNTING John | 1839–1923 | Cotton Spinner | £743,000 |
| BURTON Frederick | 1828–1913 | Merchant | £773,000 |
| DEMPSTER Robert | 1851–1925 | Gas Engine Mfr | £519,000 |
| EVANS Joseph | 1817–1889 | Colliery Proprietor | £680,000 |
| FIELDEN John Ashton | 1859–1942 | Cotton Spinner | £1,147,000 |
| FIELDEN Samuel | 1814–1889 | Cotton Spinner | £1,170,000 |
| FINNIE Robert | 1827–1905 | S.America Merchant | £893,000 |
| JAMES John Arthur | 1853–1917 | Cotton Merchant | £500,000 |
| JOHNSON Arthur R | 1854–1941 | Barrister | £733,000 |
| KNOWLES John | 1828–1894 | Colliery Owner | £577,000 |
| LAW Alfred | 1824–1913 | Flannel Manufacturer | £584,000 |
| LEES Charles E | 1840–1894 | Cotton Spinner | £914,000 |
| LEES Eli | 1814–1892 | Cotton Spinner | £857,000 |
| PORT John | 1829–1903 | Sale and Bed Manufacturer | £519,000 |
| PRESTWICH John E | 1848–1932 | Cotton Spinner | £762,000 |
| RUTHERFORD Sir John | 1854–1932 | Brewer | >£500,000 |
| WINTERBOTTOM Gerald H | 1861–1934 | Book Cloth Manufacturer | £1,012,000 |
| WINTERBOTTOM William D | 1858–1924 | Book Cloth Manufacturer | £1,064,000 |
| WRIGHT Edward A | 1808–1891 | Cotton Spinner | £676,000 |
| YATES Peter | 1854–1944 | Wine Merchant | £1,248,000 |

Scene at the Royal Exchange with many of Lancashire's wealthiest citizens pictured. The Ship Canal supporters are prominent in the centre.

but on the following day correspondence between Rothschilds, Barings, Hambro and Cohen and Sons shows that anti-German feelings in Paris on the eve of the Bastille day celebrations – which had been discussed in the *North German Gazette* and were reported in the morning edition of the *Times* – were leading to last minute nerves. As Louis Cohen wrote to Hambro:

Do you not think that Barings and Rothschilds ought to weigh it well before committing themselves to the issue of the Ship Canal – matters have taken distinctly a worse turn since Monday … Our continental advisers are also distinctly fidgety.

Fortunately for the Ship Canal promoters, Rothschild, who moved in the highest circles and [102] had been discussing with Chamberlain and Balfour the previous year's rioting by the unemployed in London and Manchester, remained unworried and committed, "I attach very little importance in the North German Gazette at the same time you will know Friday morning if there has been any disturbance in Paris …[103]

Two days later the prospectus was jointly issued by Barings and Rothschilds, and with the shares underwritten the project could proceed since the August deadline for raising the capital had been met. Just four merchant banks – Rothschilds, Barings, Morgan and Hambro – had emerged as by far the largest investors holding between them

Group of navvies with their employing gaffer in the centre.
*MSCC*

£1½ million preference shares.[104] There was an interesting parallel here with the Suez Canal for it had been Rothschilds Bank which twelve years earlier had raised at very short notice exactly the same figure of £4 million for the British Government to enable Disraeli to buy up the Khedive's shareholding in the scheme.[105] The decision in the case of the Ship Canal marked unequivocally the strong assertion of the importance of London and finance capital in the direction of funds for industry and infrastructure in the regions, and ensured Rothschilds involvement in the subsequent financing and development in the 1890s of the adjoining Trafford Park, the world's first large scale industrial estate.

The commencement of the Ship Canal was assured – with the first sod being cut by the chairman in November – but the achievement had been won at the expense of Adamson's shattered dream. Just as the standard bearer for popular capitalism had been deposed in the February board restructuring, so his model for incorporating working men through the ownership of small shareholdings finally imploded with the last minute rescue by the London banks. Henceforth when the discussion moved to the involvement of the working man it would not be about soliciting his penny contributions, but about whether the company could afford another halfpenny on his wage rates.

Manchester would still make its mark with the final completion of the Canal in 1894, but the failure of the bid for a new form of popular capitalism was absolute. Lancashire's big manufacturing capitalists, the heavyweights behind Adamson and the scheme, had attempted a regional solution to the crisis of the early 1880s, but found they were powerless either to deal with the economic and political consequences of the depression or to influence working class attitudes to savings and capital ownership. Popular capitalism via the device of mass shareholding was not to be the "golden bridge" for spanning the gulf between capitalist owners and toiling workers, nor the medium for dissipating the sense of alienation felt by these workers at the growing loss of control experienced at the workplace. In the context of these changes and the employers' generally more confrontational strategies, the ideology of the Ship Canal movement – though not its practical objective – became irrelevant. It gave way to new patterns of industrial relations where employers and workers created formal structures which allowed recognition to their separate and distinct interests.

## Notes

1. Speech at Great Meeting in the Free Trade Hall, 31 October 1883. Manchester Ship Canal pamphlet, Manchester Central Library, Ref f386.M8.
2. *Yale Review*, November 1894, Quoted in G. S. Messinger, *Manchester in the Victorian Age*, 1985, p. 168.
3. B. Leech, *op. cit.*, Vol. 1, p 85; Vol. 2, p.129.
4. B. Leech, *ibid.* Vol. 1. pp. 107, 114.
5. B. Leech. *ibid.*, Vol. 1, p. 86; *Manchester City News*, 16 September 1882.
6. *Manchester City News*, Ship Canal Supplement, 6 January 1894.
7. *Manchester Guardian*, 30 November 1882.
8. *Ship Canal Gazette*, 18 December 1882, p. 74.
9. *Manchester Guardian*, 15 August 1885.
10. *Manchester City News*, 13 January 1894, "Ship Canal Pioneers".
11. A. D. Provand, *The Manchester Ship Canal Scheme. A Criticism*, p. 13.
12. *The Umpire*, 2 October 1887, Article No. IX. See also comments by Fielden in *Ship Canal Gazette*, 8 August 1883, p. 175.
13. Reply of Mr Pember Q.C. on behalf of the Promoters of the Bill, 20 May 1884. Pamphlet, chapter XIV; handwritten copy of evidence of B. Leech to House of Lords Committee 1885, Manchester Central Library, Ref. F386. M67.
14. Letter from Marshall Stevens to Samuel Ogden, 24 August 1887. Manchester Ship Canal Company Archive No. 47.
15. D. Farnie, *The Manchester Ship Canal and the Rise of the Port of Manchester*, 1980, p. 48. The effect of the arrangement was of course to siphon off income which otherwise could have been used to pay off the mounting arrears on the City Council debentures, or to pay a dividend to the ordinary shareholders.
16. Circular letter, 13 February 1890, "Manchester Ship Canal (Various Powers) Bill".
17. Letter book of Lord Egerton of Tatton, 14 November 1893, Chester Record Office, Ref. DET 3229/81.
18. Manchester City Council Proceedings, 6 June 1894, report by Mr G. H. Hill, p. 540.
19. *Manchester Guardian*, 1 September 1886 and 29 August 1887; B. Leech, *op. cit.*, Vol. 2, pp. 12–13.
20. B. Leech, *op. cit.*, Vol 2, pp. 45, 75.
21. A. D. Provand, *op cit.*, p. 5.
22. Letter from George Hicks to C. P. Scott, 6 January 1894, John Rylands University Library of Manchester.
23. A. D. Provand, *op cit.*, p. 6.
24. *Manchester City News*, 6 January 1894.
25. Manchester Ship Canal, Report of Proceedings at a Meeting of the Provisional Committee, 26 September 1882, Manchester Central Library. Ref. F386. M67.
26. *Manchester Guardian*, 14 November 1884.
27. *Gorton Reporter*, 21 February 1885, p. 3.
28. J. H. Clapham, *An Economic History of Modern Britain. 1850–1886*, 1932, pp. 141–2.

29. Royal Commission on Depression of Trade and Industry, 1886, Question 5042. Royal Commission on Labour 1891, Questions 294–9, 1431–41.

30. D. A. Farnie, *The English Cotton Industry and the World Market 1815–1896*, 1979, pp. 250–252. Farnie's book is based upon his M.A. Thesis of the same title written 26 years earlier. The sweeping generalisations about working class shareholding in Oldham, which appear in J. P. Lewis, *Building Cycles and Britain's Growth*, 1965, pp. 125–6, all derive from Farnie's thesis.

31. *Cooperative News*, 21 March, 8 August 1874.

32. *Ibid.*, 7 April 1877.

33. *Manchester Guardian*, 2 February 1887.

34. R. E. Tyson, *The Sun Mill Co. Ltd. A Study in Democratic Investment*, 1962, M.A. Thesis University of Manchester, pp. 74, 222–4.

35. R. Smith, "An Oldham Limited Company 1875–1896" in *Business History*, Volume IV, 1961, pp. 40–42.

36. *Cooperative News*, 8 August 1874. The article is reproduced from the Preston Guardian.

37. *Ship Canal Gazette*, 15 November 1882.

38. *Gorton Reporter*, 18 November 1882, p. 5; 25 November 1882, p. 5.

39. *Ship Canal Gazette*, 18 November 1882, p. 7.

40. *Ship Canal Gazette*, 6 December 1882.

41. Provisional Committee, Minutes, December 1882.

42. *Manchester Examiner and Times*, 22 November 1882; *Gorton Reporter*, 25 November 1882, p. 5.

43. *Ship Canal Gazette*, 20 December 1882, 3 January 1883; *Manchester Guardian*, 7 April 1883; Provisional Committee Minutes, 17 October 1884.

44. Undated letter from John Crossley to Daniel Adamson, Lancashire Record Office. Ref DDX 101/3.

45. Handbill of Samuel Ramsbottom, 18 June 1884, Manchester.

46. Reply of Mr Pember. Q.C. 20 May 1884, printed pamphlet, Manchester Central Library, Ref. 386. M79.

47. B. Leech, *op. cit.*, Vol. 2, p. 16.

48. *Manchester Faces and Places*, 1894. *Biography of Marshall Stevens*, p. 72.

49. See for instance *City News*, 6 January 1894, for article by a "Ward Enthusiast" and *City News*, 13 January 1894, for a letter from a "Ward Secretary".

50. Minutes of the Provisional Committee, 3,5,9 June 1885, Greater Manchester Public Record Office.

51. *City News*, 13 January 1894, Cornwall's explanation of events showed that Adamson had simply invented the story about the de Lesseps conversation.

52. *Manchester Guardian*, 22 August 1885.

53. *Manchester Guardian*, 25 August 1885.

54. *Manchester Guardian*, 1 September 1885.

55. *Gorton Reporter*, 29 August 1885, p. 2.

56. *Manchester Evening Mail*, 6 October 1885.

57. *Salford Reporter*, 5 September 1885.

58. *City News*, 24 September 1885. Ironically on the same day that Stevens' remarks appeared, the Oldham press reported that the last minder shareholder in the Sun Mill had died. *Oldham Evening Chronicle*, 24 September 1885, p. 3.

59. *Manchester Guardian*, 12 August 1885. Brooks was a local banker.

60. *Manchester Guardian*, 26 August 1885.

61. Provisional Committee Minutes, 18 August 1885.

62. CWS Finance Committee Minutes, 18 August 1885, p. 410.

63. *Manchester Guardian*, 10 November 1884, p. 4.

64. Six weeks later the CWS Finance Committee minutes (23/12/1884) report that the Ship Canal Company had written enquiring about the possibility of shares being taken up by individual cooperators.

65. *Manchester Guardian*, 31 August 1885, Provisional Committee Minutes, 28 August 1885. CWS Finance Committee, 15 September 1885, p. 439. The £10,000 shareholding was on top of the £3,500 contributed by 27 of the local Societies to the Parliamentary fund.

66. *The Rejected Letter. The Manchester Ship Canal and the Working Man as a shareholder thereof*, 15 October 1885, Manchester Central Library, Ref. M386. M80. See also letter from 'Citizen' along similar lines in *Manchester Guardian*, 18 October 1885.

67. *Manchester City News*, 31 October 1885.

68. *Cotton Factory Times*, 9 October 1885, p. 4.

69. M.S.C. Board Minutes, 24 November 1885; 5, 9,12 February 1886.

70. Cooperative Shares Distribution Company Prospectus, Manchester Central Library Ref F386. M67. Of the 15 directors, eleven were Trade Union Officials, e.g. Thomas Ashton (Oldham Spinners), James Ashton (Beamers and Twisters), Thomas Ashton (Miners), W. Bancroft, Birtwistle, Fielding, Hallam, Kelley, Mawdsley, Murchie and Slatter. J. T. W. Mitchell and W. Bates of the CWS were also directors.

71. MSC Board Minutes, 7 May, 22 June 1886.

72. *Times*, 13 February 1886. The letter was reprinted as a handbill (see illustration on p. 90).

73. *Liverpool Daily Post*, 15 January 1886.

74. Significantly a delegation of 15 MP's together with representatives from Manchester, Salford, Oldham and the Company which went to see Mundella as President of the Board of Trade to press the case, did not include Adamson. See Pamphlet "Deputation to A. J. Mundella, 23 February 1886", Manchester Central Library. Ref. F386. M8.

75. *Manchester Guardian*, 2 June 1886.

76. Directors' Notebook of Marshall Stevens 1886–87, M.S.C. Company Archive No. 51. See also B. Leech, *op.cit.*, Vol. 1, p. 326.

77. *Manchester Guardian*, 1 September 1886, Half–yearly meeting of Shareholders.

78. *Manchester Guardian*, *Manchester Courier*, 2 September 1886, p. 7.

79. *Courier*, 13, 14 September 1886; *City News*, 18 September 1886; *Cooperative News*, 18 September 1886, p. 944.

80. Lancashire Record Office, Beaumont Papers (Ref. DDBe); *Courier*, 14 September 1886; *Manchester Guardian*, 21 September 1886.

81. *Manchester Examiner and Times*, 23 September 1886.

82. *Manchester Courier*, 2, 4 September 1886, p. 7.

83. *Manchester Guardian*, 2, 4 October 1886.

84. *Ibid.*, 11 October 1886.

85. G. Anderson, *Victorian Clerks*, 1976.

86. *Manchester City News*, 7 April 1894.

87. Stevens subsequently became Tory MP for Eccles 1918–22.

88. *Manchester Guardian*, 2 October, 1891, p. 6(3).

89. Report of the Committee formed to consider the Project of the Manchester Ship Canal 1886. Manchester Central Library Ref.386 M80.

90. Letter from W. Saxon to D. Adamson, 8 December 1886, Lancashire Record Office DDX 101/38. From handwritten notes of Adamson in this same collection of papers, it would appear that he knew on December 2nd about the proposal to insert the clause.

91. B. Leech, *op. cit.*, Vol. 2, pp. 3–5.

92. Letter from H. McNeil to D. Adamson, 21 January 1887, Lancashire Record Office DDX 101/6/3.

93. *Manchester Guardian*, 29 January 1887.

94. *Bolton Journal*, 5 February 1887. Adamson did not formally resign as a director until later. He died three years later before completion of the Canal.

95. Royal Commission on Depression of Trade and Industry 3rd Report. Evidence of Sir J. C. Lee, 10 March 1886, Questions 8054–8066.

96. B. Leech, *op.cit.*, Vol. 2, p. 7.

97. I am grateful to W. D. Rubinstein for providing me with detailed information about wealth holders. This was collected for his study, 'Men of Property' 1981 Croom Helm. It should be noted that the figures, based upon probate returns, do not take account of landed wealth.

98. K. Chorley, *Manchester Made Them*, 1951; S. Gunn, *Manchester Middle Class, 1850–1880*, 1993, Ph.D. Thesis, University of Manchester.

99. Letter dated 15 February 1887, The Rothschild Archive (London), Ref. RAL/X1/122/28A.

100. Copy letter dated 29 April 1887, The Rothschild Archive (London), General Letter Copy Books.

101. B. Leech, *op.cit.*, Vol. 2, pp. 8–10.

102. Chapter 4, Note 196.

103. Letters from Louis Cohen to Hambro, and Lord Rothschild to Lord Revelstoke, 13 July 1887, Baring Brothers and Co. Archive, Reference HC3.135

104. The four largest preference stock holders were Rothschilds (£453,000), Barings (£427,000), Morgan and Co. (£410,000) and Hambro (£254,000). The fifth highest holder with £205,000 was Alexander Henderson of the stockbrokers, Greenwood and Company who had with Sir Joseph Lee acted as intermediary with the banks.

105. Lord Kinross, *Between Two Seas: The Creation of the Suez Canal*, 1968, pp. 268–271.

# 7

# LAUNCHING THE MUNICIPAL LIFEBOAT

The cutting of the Canal's first sod was carried out by Lord Egerton in the late Autumn of 1887 in a quiet corner of a Lancashire field. The event lacked the ceremony and triumphalism which had characterised so much of what had preceded, but it marked nevertheless the culmination of five years' struggle to turn the idea of a passageway to Manchester for ocean-going ships into a politically viable project; and no doubt there were many who thought that all that remained was to bring in the engineers and the navvies to complete the task. Within two years however the main contractor, Thomas Walker, was dead. For a year the project limped along under the direction of his executors, but in November 1890 with the Canal only half built, the Directors were forced to make a settlement with them writing off half the capital which Walker was to have put into the project. The deal and their taking over the management of the construction works was kept secret for ten weeks but by early 1891 the City Council was being requested to provide a three million pounds loan needed for the completion of the Canal; and two years later the Royal Assent was given to a Bill allowing Manchester Corporation – rather than Salford or Oldham which had applied for Parliamentary Bills as well – to lend a further two million pounds. In all a total of £5 million of new monies were to be channelled by a public body into propping up a private company.

This was a major *volte face* in the fortunes and financing of the project and was to have a marked impact on the city for many years – and on the ratepayers who had to pay the bill.[1] Manchester was certainly the wealthiest of the Lancashire towns, raising in 1882 £278,000 in annual rates – compared with £61,000 for Salford, the next largest town[2] – but a £5 million loan still represented an enormous commitment. The city's total debt in 1891 stood at £7,682,000 – up £1.2 million on the early 1880s – but it effectively doubled the figure to £15,087,000 over the next five years using most of the increase to accommodate the problems of the Ship Canal.[3]

These dramatic events raise important questions about the role of the local State in the late nineteenth century and its relationship to the interests which lay behind the Ship Canal Movement. In this last major chapter of the study we will investigate precisely how the City Council came to take on such an unprecedented role, but in order to explore this effectively we need to place the enquiry within a theoretical framework. We have argued that manufacturing capital was the dominant force in the Movement. In seeking to achieve its objectives, it was faced with the opposition of mercantile capital, an important fraction of the bourgeoisie in Lancashire – with close links with Liverpool shipping interests – which had only limited fixed capital in the region. Mercantile capital was therefore more internationalist in perspective and, initially at any rate, uncommitted to the scale of local investment required for the project. In resolving this conflict we will follow Poulantzas in arguing that the State plays the role of political unifier of the power bloc, forming the "contradictory locus of condensation for the balance of forces that divides even the dominant class itself".[4] Although within this framework the State overwhelmingly serves the interests of the hegemonic fraction, Poulantzas allows for the relative autonomy of State institutions from ostensible class interests. Through an empirical examination of the events leading up to the decision to launch the *Lifeboat* operation we will be able to explore the extent to which it exercised this relative autonomy by responding to and compromising with other elements which had a political voice in the Council.

An interventionist role for the local State was not an entirely new phenomenon in the nineteenth century but what is certain is that the development and extension of this role in the areas of social investment and social consumption[5] accelerated rapidly from the beginning of the twentieth century. In order to understand how Manchester's experience fitted into and influenced this pattern we will ask what precedents there were for public financial interventions of this scale and nature, what discussion took place in the city during the 1880s and 1890s about such a shift in policy, and what this tells us about changing perceptions of the appropriate roles to be played by the State and private enterprise. In addition we will explore the mechanisms set up by the promoters and the interests they represented to ensure that key committees in Manchester and elsewhere had been infiltrated in advance. Finally we will investigate the extent to which changes of political control in the local council and the increasing politicisation of the party machines in the Town Hall influenced the course of events and the role played by the local State.

The issues are complex not least because the Ship Canal alliance was exactly that – it embraced people and interest groups with different and often conflicting positions.

Some of the big industrial bourgeoisie who were the principal promoters – Adamson certainly because of his wish to promote the idea of popular capitalism, but also others like Sir J. C. Lee and Sir William Houldsworth who joined the Board of Directors in 1885 – were keen to promote the public nature of the scheme, but opposed the idea of it being a public trust. Others, such as Deputy Chairman Richard Peacock, appear from the start to have favoured a public commission of trustees[6] and this was certainly the position adopted by many of the radical Liberals in the early days of the movement and by socialists in the 1890s when the proposals for local authorities making loans were being discussed.

In the event Adamson and those wishing to have a private company got their way but they needed to secure their position in the event of finance running out. As we have seen in the previous chapter, estimating and providing for the costs of the undertaking was carried out in a very unprofessional and bizarre fashion. Undercapitalisation hung like a spectre over the "Big Ditch" even in 1887 creating from the start a highly vulnerable foundation for which contingency planning was required to ensure that, if needed, the Canal could be baled out by public funds. In this chapter it will be argued that none of the £5 million of public monies which were put up by the Council would have been forthcoming had there not been canvassing and organising for such an eventuality from the very inception of the scheme in 1882; and that in the event of these monies being required, the key issue in determining suitable structures would be whether control of the company would remain with the existing shareholders or pass to the City Council as the price of mounting the rescue operation.

Although the name of Manchester is often considered synonymous with the doctrines of *laissez faire* and minimal State involvement, a tradition of intervention had in fact been evident from as early as 1817 when a public meeting had authorised an increase in the Police Rate in order to finance the setting up of municipal gas works.[7] As Thomas Hopkins, a prominent Lancashire industrialist, declared in 1834 "it is highly desirable that the inhabitants of a large town like Manchester should have the ownership of works

Manchester's Town Hall, completed in 1877 at a cost of £1 million.   *MCL*

148

like the gas works … what security would there be for its (the gas) being good if the works went into the hands of a joint stock company?".[8]

More recently the role of the local State had been brought into greater prominence by two significant events in 1877. The first involved the opening of Manchester's "civic palace" which was celebrated by a large Trades' procession to Albert Square like the Ship Canal demonstration at Belle Vue eight years later. The decision to replace the building had been made in 1867 in a report which stated that the Council was committed to "a Town Hall which shall be in every respect worthy of the great and important city in which it is to be placed, and which shall be equal if not superior to any similar building in this country".[9] As for cost it was assumed that "the Council is prepared to expend any sum which may be reasonably required". This was fortunate as no one had anticipated that expenditure on the project would ultimately rise to £1 million! In the words of the Mayor Abel Heywood at the formal opening, Waterhouse's building was "a monument of the greatness of the Manchester Corporation. It must not be weighed in the balance with some of those smaller buildings which appeared from time to time in connection with municipal corporations".[10]

The second event was the decision of the Corporation to proceed with plans to construct a water supply pipeline of 96 miles length from Thirlmere in the Lake District to Manchester. Opposed by local landowners and commenced in 1886, the supply was formally turned on in the city in October 1894 after the Corporation had invested some £4 to £5 million in the project. As Sir John Harwood, implicitly describing an emerging new role for the local State, put it at the opening ceremony: "The preservation of the general health is the first consideration of an enlightened community. Health secured, there is no limit to the enterprises in which the sons and daughters of Manchester may engage".[11] Nor was it physical health alone that the Corporation was concerned about, for it had already embarked, through the work of its libraries and art galleries, upon a programme of public education aimed at enlightening and inspiring the masses.

Examples like the gas and water undertakings and the higher profile adopted by local councils like Manchester and Birmingham were drawn upon by men like J. F. B. Firth – who formed the London Municipal Reform League in 1881 – and Sidney Webb who wrote the Fabian pamphlet, *Facts for Londoners*, published in 1889. They argued for extensive municipal programmes as the only way to alleviate the

Ford Madox Brown's painting "Work" which was purchased by Manchester Corporation in 1885.   *CAG*

problems of housing and squalid conditions facing so many who were living in the capital. In the 1880s however in Manchester – as was the case with other cities – there was no driving force from within the Council seeking to push the local State into the area of housing provision through the expenditure of substantial monies on improvement schemes. Although the 1875 Artisans' and Labourers' Dwellings Act gave powers to demolish poor housing areas and rebuild on the site, the only slum clearance to have taken place was in the central areas as a result of commercial pressures. Opposition to municipal housing was fierce and sustained on the grounds that this was the proper province of private enterprise – despite the plea from the Medical Officer of Health in 1884 that "if helping the poor in this way – doing for them what they cannot do for themselves – be socialism or communism, the more we have of it the better".[12] It was left to individual reformers to press the case, with G. H. Pownall pointing out in a paper to the Manchester Statistical Society that in a city with the worst mortality rates of the country, 50,000 lives could have been saved if the Council had spent the £6–£7 million which the Health Committee had reckoned in 1878 was needed to rid Manchester of its slums.[13]

Despite the experience with housing therefore, there is clear evidence that the city fathers in the early 1880s were already seeing Manchester as the flagship for municipal enterprise on a new scale. There were precedents for a new and expanding role for the local State but it was the scale of

The Ship Canal Digger, a bronze by the Irish sculptor John Cassidy. *CAG*

the eventual contribution which might have to be made by the City Council to the Ship Canal which was most worrying; and it was this issue of scale that debate focused on from the outset. While supporters of the scheme took the view that the Corporation should seek Parliamentary powers to contribute to the cost of the undertaking in order to have some right of control, others like Alderman King, initially a forceful opponent, argued that their liability could increase to £3 million or more as "once they had put their finger to the movement they must carry on with it."[14] In one local paper it was pointed out that it was safer to estimate a cost of two or three times as much as the initial estimate of £5 million and that "control will be in the hands of those who hold the larger half of the stock".[15] The *Manchester Guardian* was more forthright, counselling against the Council's involvement in "a highly speculative undertaking" and pointing out shrewdly that:

It is not the amount of the contemplated investment ... but its risk which induces its advocates to desire the Corporation to undertake the work.[16]

The way round the objections was to propose in the first instance merely that powers be sought to contribute financially to the scheme and that the Canal be set up as a trust for the benefit of the public in general – a formula which won overwhelming support in the vote, with only three senior aldermen, Grundy, Heywood and King, opposing.[17] The matter did not surface again until 1884 when a contribution of £10,000 was being proposed from the Corporation. Again the *Manchester Guardian* endorsed the opposition put up by Alderman Grundy and was joined by pamphleteer Samuel Ramsbottom, who issued a colourful broadsheet with the title *The Adamsonian Delusion, and its influence on the Manchester City Council*.[18]

This time the effect was more telling as a group of merchants in the city organised a ratepayers' memorial on the "Ship Canal Rate" opposing the city's involvement. This was supported by 128 signatories and sent to the Secretary of State for the Home Department.[19] Although it failed in its attempt to get the two penny rate stopped, it caused great consternation amongst the Ship Canal supporters and signalled the hostility of some of the city's most powerful mercantile interests. Major firms like Barbour Brothers, A & S Henry, Reiss Brothers, William Graham & Co, Thomas Hoyle, and J. Y. Wilkinson who were included on the list saw no great material advantage to be gained for themselves. They had moreover suffered the insults and opprobrium meted out to them by Adamson, as he sought to build up an alliance between manufacturers and workers at their expense, and they were determined on resistance.[20]

In the long term this was highly damaging to the financial standing of the Canal – indeed was perhaps the major reason why the Corporation had ultimately to rescue the project – but in the short term these mercantile interests were overwhelmed by the propaganda power of the promoters and their ability both to win popular support (as we have seen in Chapter 2) and achieve major political leverage on key decision-making bodies throughout the region. Despite the massive scale of the project, public opinion in Manchester and Lancashire was being groomed to create a groundswell where financial support for the project could be provided by the local State whatever its cost. Before exploring the impact of this campaigning and propaganda it is necessary to look at some of the methods used by the Promoters to win backing for the scheme within the key local authorities potentially affected by the building of the Canal.

While Manchester was always the most important authority, there was a recognition from the start that the support of others should be actively sought. At the 1882 inaugural meeting the mayors of seven towns – Salford, Warrington, Rochdale, Stockport, Ashton, Stalybridge and Macclesfield – were reported as being present.[21] The first two – both Tory controlled – were initially of the greatest importance since the Canal would pass across their boundaries. As we have seen, this presented some difficulties to the predominantly Liberal alliance promoting the Canal, but was dealt with by bringing on to the Provisional Committee the Mayor of Salford and three members of the Warrington Council. Six months later the Mayor of Manchester, supported by fellow aldermen, the Town Clerk, the Engineer Leader Williams and the ubiquitous Bosdin Leech (himself a Manchester councillor), was entertaining the Mayors and representatives of some twelve local corporations at a conference about the project, where the Mayors of Salford and Oldham were also prominent speakers.[22]

As the first citizen in every town the Mayor was the key representative to be used as a public figurehead. He had also the advantage to the promoters of being seen as politically neutral. Clear encouragement was given to these men to organise public meetings to describe the merits of the scheme and generally create a favourable climate for the project – a practice that was widely adopted at an early stage as is evident from reports of meetings taking place all over Lancashire.[23] In Stockport the promoters were able to secure a strong position through initially appointing to the Provisional Committee the Mayor James Leigh and, subsequently to the Board of Directors, Daniel Adamson's son-in-law, Joseph Leigh, who was Mayor of the town in 1884 and 1886–1888.

Infiltration of the Council chamber was also evident in Oldham in the case of the Platt brothers. Both James E. Platt and his older brother S. R. Platt were early directors of the Ship Canal and large shareholders, with both of them successfully seeking election to the Council in October 1882,[24] and S. R. Platt holding the office of Mayor from 1887 to 1889. As the largest employer in the town, with a workforce of over 10,000, the Platts wielded great influence on and off the Council. Their decision to seek election at this point was of great significance and was to provide the means whereby the Canal Company was later able to play off the Councils against each other over the terms of public financial support.

Packing of the council chamber was most evident, however, in the case of Manchester. The ward committees established to drum up support for the campaign, described in Chapter 2, were also instrumental in ensuring that a very large majority of those seeking election for the Council were standing specifically on a Ship Canal platform or were pledged to support the scheme;[25] and by 1884 the same appeared to be the case with Salford, to judge from correspondence appearing in the local press.[26] A further important step was taken the following year after the final passage of the enabling Act, when the Salford Alderman William H. Bailey was appointed to the Board of Directors. A Liberal member of the Council since the mid-1870s and a large employer, Bailey played a significant role in steering Ship Canal items through the Tory controlled chamber and himself was Mayor of the City in the year of the Canal's opening. The one large Council which the promoters failed to bring effectively into line was the Tory stronghold of Bolton where the Liberal hue of the Ship Canal alliance would have only helped to increase the town's long-held suspicion of Manchester initiatives. As the local paper put it when the Council decided to defer consideration of the matter *sine die*, "a conclusion unfavourable to the project, or at least one of absolute indifference to it, has been arrived at".[27]

The attitude of Bolton's Tories was not seriously damaging but the position adopted by the Tory Party in Manchester and the view they took of the Lib–Lab alliance between manufacturers and workers was a very different matter, and of considerable importance when it came to the decisions to be adopted by the City Council on Ship Canal affairs. At the level of municipal elections up to and including the early 1880s there were understandings between the local Tory and Liberal parties as to who should contest a seat, with compromises and "swaps" agreed so that one or the other party could take a seat unopposed,[28] but the context was one where the Liberals had a decisive majority. An ex-member of the Council may well have been able to claim without too much exaggeration in 1878 that once elected to the council the new member would be surprised by "the total absence of political feeling".[29] As the 1880s developed, however, the splits in the Liberal Party and pressure for other forms of working class representation created fiercer competition, which was reflected in a decline in the number of Liberal councillors and in the reports of the Liberal Union where members were reminded of "the great importance of doing the utmost not only to retain the seats now held by Liberals, but to secure others wherever practicable".[30]

For the alliance which was pushing the Ship Canal scheme this posed worrying problems. From 1885 it is true that the Tory MP Houldsworth had agreed to join the Ship Canal Board of Directors, and that from 1887 with Adamson's departure he was joined by another Tory, Lord Egerton, but the driving forces behind the scheme remained Liberals and seceding Liberal Unionists. The Tories were mainly reluctant supporters, with Houldsworth and Egerton taking on positions as figureheads on a board that still retained nine Liberals and Liberal Unionists to four Tories in July 1887.[31]

View of W. H. Bailey's works in Salford.

## Political Composition of Manchester City Council

An indication of the changing political composition of the City Council and the difficulties this could create when large scale financial support from the Corporation would be required in 1891 can be seen from Table 1 which details membership of the important Finance Committee over the Ship Canal years. The years 1889–90 and 1890–91 show the switch of control between the Tory and Liberal parties.

Information on the political make-up of Manchester City Council was not publicly available in a comprehensive form and has had to be pieced together from many different sources. Table 1 reflects the clear domination of the Council by the Liberals in the early years and the start of their problems once the Liberal Unionists seceded in 1886. Although they were still the largest group, with an absolute majority up to November 1889, the balance shifted following the municipal elections in that month to make the Tories

the largest single party in 1889–90, giving them 36 representatives compared with 31 Liberals and 7 Liberal Unionists. The elections the following November were therefore of enormous interest to both parties because seven new wards to the east of the city were to be incorporated, increasing the total number of wards to 25 and bringing in 21 new councillors and seven new aldermen. The results moreover were to be of the greatest importance to the Ship Canal Company because over this same period the Deputy Chairman, Sir Joseph Lee, was drawing to a close negotiations with the contractor's executors which would, after settling outstanding claims, leave the Company with virtually no capital to complete the works. The overall composition of the Council and the membership of the key committees which would have to consider any requests for financial support were critical factors in their calculations. This explains the secrecy of their actions over the deal with Walker's executors – finally made on 24th November – as the events were to reveal.

In an election in which both parties made considerable play of being "the friends of the working classes",[32] the initial results brought the Liberals an additional sixteen seats to the Tories' six (including 14 of the 21 in the new wards), which they were able to capitalise on the following week at the aldermanic elections in the council chamber, by voting in six new Liberal aldermen and only one Tory. The vote, according to the *Manchester Courier*, was "a purely political one" and in the resulting bye-elections which were all contested, the Tories by contrast had substantial successes winning four seats to the Liberal Party's one. The explanation for the ratepayers' voting according to the *Courier* was that over the question of the aldermanic positions, "the Liberal members of the Council had allowed their political prejudices to get the better of their judgement".[33] The state of the parties over this period up until March 1891 is summarised in Table 2 below with a full listing of councillors and aldermen and their political allegiances as at the end of 1890 provided in Appendix B.

### Table 1   Manchester Finance Committee by Party, 1882–1894

| Year | Number on Committee | Liberals | Liberal/ Unionists | Tory | Chairman (& Party) |
|------|---------------------|----------|--------------------|------|--------------------|
| 1882–83 | 12 | 9 | — | 3 | Thompson (L) |
| 1883–84 | 14 | 10 | — | 5 | " |
| 1884–85 | 16 | 11 | — | 5 | " |
| 1885–86 | 19 | 14 | — | 5 | " |
| 1886–87 | 14 | 7 | 2 | 5 | King (LU) |
| 1887–88 | 13 | 7 | 2 | 4 | " |
| 1888–89 | 14 | 8 | 2 | 4 | " |
| 1889–90 | 12 | 4 | 3 | 5 | " |
| 1890–91 | 18 | 9 | 2 | 7 | " |
| 1891–92 | 18 | 10 | 2 | 6 | " |
| 1892–93 | 19 | 9 | 3 | 7 | " |
| 1893–94 | 18 | 8 | 3 | 7 | " |

Sources: Municipal Handbook and Election Reports

Despite the foul play claims of the Tory councillors, the Liberals had been able to reverse their decline and become once more the largest party on the council.[34] The price they paid however was that the smooth understandings which they had with the Tories might not hold so readily in the future. They were moreover heavily dependent on the Liberal Unionists. The voting patterns on the Council rarely followed precise party lines, but over issues like temperance and the financing of the Ship Canal – though not support for the Canal which was by now cross party – there is no doubt that party was an important factor.

By Christmas it had become clear what the strength of the parties was to be in the coming year but in understanding how the issue of financing the Ship Canal was to be dealt with we need to understand some of the non-party factors as well. The original moves to commence the project had been taken some eight years earlier and in that time the composition of the Council had changed dramatically. By the end of 1890 out of a total of 104 councillors only 38 had been elected in the years preceding the final passage of the Ship Canal Act in 1885; the remainder were new men who were coming to the Council chamber with new ideas and new loyalties. They did not share the same experience of working together over many years, as is evident by looking at the case of the powerful Finance Committee in Table 1. Whereas in 1882 the median length of service on the Council of the members was nineteen, by 1891 this figure was seven. Moreover in the new political climate, where calls were being made for more public accountability and for independent working class representation, the new men were willing to consider alliances based upon different political judgements from those of an earlier generation. Liberal control of the Council would not automatically therefore deliver to the Ship Canal Board of Directors exactly what they wanted.

In terms of influencing decisions at the Town Hall, the two key members of the Council for the Directors were Sir John Harwood and Bosdin Leech – both Liberals but very different men in their attitudes to the Company. Harwood was a long established alderman with a reputation for powerful speaking, independence and strong views,

having been first elected as a councillor in 1866. At the Town Hall he was, according to a local biographer, "respected and feared in pretty equal proportions".[35] A Methodist and compulsive worker he occupied the mayoral or ex-mayoral chair in the Council for eight years in succession in the 1880s and had been persuaded to join the Provisional Committee in August 1883 after the first Ship Canal Bill had been thrown out. He had also spoken out the previous year in favour of the Canal being run by a public trust rather than a private company. As a jobbing painter and plasterer from a poor family, who had made good by developing his own painting business, his background was totally different from the big manufacturing bourgeoisie who were the original directors on the Ship Canal Board.

Leech, a small yarn merchant, was by contrast a backroom man, at home with detail and machinations, and with a reputation for boring and stumbling speeches. Above all Leech was the man who put the Ship Canal on the Town Hall agenda – raising the matter first of all in September 1882 – and who kept it there over twelve long years; and for this he was rewarded. From 1885 to 1892 he was the shareholders' auditor, receiving an annual salary of £400;[36] in 1892 he was appointed a Corporation Director on the Board – where he remained until his death twenty years later – and in 1894 after the Official Opening he received a knighthood. As "an eager and militant partisan in the long struggle"[37] he played his most decisive role in the years 1890–1893 and for this reason his sanitised account of this period, drawn principally from his collection of newspaper cuttings, has to be treated with caution.[38]

## Seeking Loans from the Local State

Private approaches were made by Sir Joseph Lee on behalf of the Company to both Harwood and Leech in the December 1890–January 1891 period about the possibility of loans, but their thinking was very different as they surveyed the chances of support from within the new council. Leech was an instigator of the Liberal-inspired Ship Canal Movement

**Table 2    Manchester Council. State of the Parties, 1890–91**

| Date | Liberal | Tory | Lib/U | Total |
|---|---|---|---|---|
| 30 Oct 1890 | 23C + 8A = 31 | 28C + 7A = 35 | 4C + 4A = 8 | 74 |
| 2 Nov 1890 | 39C + 8A = 47 | 34C + 7A = 41 | 4C + 4A = 8 | 96 |
| 9 Nov 1890 ‡ | 34C + 14A = 48 | 34C + 8A = 42 | 4C + 4A = 8 | 98 |
| 13 Dec 1890 † | 35C + 14A = 49 | 39C + 8A = 47 | 4C + 4A = 8 | 104 |
| 13 Feb 1891 * | 36C + 14A = 50 | 38C + 8A = 46 | 4C + 4A = 8 | 104 |

Notes:
C = Number of Councillors
A = Number of Aldermen
‡ = Position following Aldermanic elections
† = Position following Bye-elections on 29 November and 12 December
* = Position after uncontested election of G. D. Kelley (Trades Council Secretary)

Group of Manchester councillors and others at the commencement of the Thirlmere works in 1886. Harwood is in the centre, seated, with Bosdin Leech standing immediately behind him. *JRULM*

and heavily committed to Adamson's idea of developing popular capitalism through encouraging working men to make shilling contributions to the scheme. For him the maintenance of the Canal Company as a private shareholders' concern was central to his vision of the project; and naturally he looked for support for this particular line of thinking from those other council members from the early days of the agitation who had also acted as chairmen of the

Official Opening Programme in 1894. Though Salford was excluded from the financing of the canal, the Council ensured that it benefited from a Royal visit at the opening.

ward committees promoting the scheme and the shilling coupons. By 1891 just four of them remained – Walton Smith (Liberal), Mark (now turned Liberal Unionist), and the two Tories Boddington and Hinchcliffe.

Harwood on the other hand was no "eighties" newcomer to the Council like Leech. His pedigree was as a longstanding municipal reformer, clear-sighted and efficient. It seemed only natural that he should assume the chairmanship of the important Waterworks Committee during the eight years' construction period preceding the 1894 opening of the Thirlmere project in the Lake District. Manchester's 'Joseph Chamberlain', he was committed first and foremost to the Corporation – to expanding its role and defending its interests and those of the ratepayers.

Both Leech's and Harwood's views could be accommodated within the shifting kaleidoscope of Liberal ideology, but increasingly it was the latter's which were seen to be more in line with the spirit of a new age which wanted more State intervention and greater public accountability. Over the next three years, as the Ship Canal Company looked more and more to public financing to salvage the project, the arguments were to rage around these pole positions, with a group of younger articulate councillors identifying themselves strongly with the more "forward" views expounded by Harwood. Drawn from both parties they included the Tories, Andrews, Williams and Richards (all elected in 1885) and the two Liberals Gunson and Rhodes.

By early February 1891 – when the question of a loan from the Corporation was first raised publicly – the initial interparty arrangements had been put in place by the ruling Liberal group. Significantly the Liberal Unionist Mark, one of the early Ship Canal pioneers – who had chaired the sensitive Amalgamation Committee which brought in the influx of Liberal councillors – had been retained as Mayor. Equally important in holding the support of the eight Liberal Unionist members was the retention of the other senior Liberal Unionist King as chairman of the Finance Committee. A further interesting development was the unopposed election to the Council (see Table 2) of G. D. Kelley, the Secretary of the Trades Council, who had been principally responsible for organising and delivering working class and trade union support for the Ship Canal Movement. Kelley came in as a Liberal in place of the retiring Tory councillor Schou – a move that could only have been taken with the furtherance of the Ship Canal loan in mind and with the active support of the Tory group.[39]

In opening up the discussion about public financing for the Canal, the strategy chosen was to start with a small sum. The first figure mentioned by Lee was £700,000[40] and over the next three months this was increased in stages to £1 million, £1.7 million and finally by the time it came to the full council meeting in March the amount of the loan to be sought had risen to £3 million. In the initial February debate where £1.7 million was being sought, the only dissenting voices came from two Liberal Unionists King and Clay on the grounds that Salford and Oldham authorities should be brought in to support the guarantee, but by March the decision to proceed was agreed without dissent. Even Leech felt it necessary to note with surprise that Alderman King, who had so strongly argued against public finance for the project in 1882, should speak in favour of the loan at the borough funds meeting.[41]

The *Lifeboat* operation – with all its enormous implications for the city – had been launched with great speed and with surprisingly little resistance, overturning years of orthodox economic doctrine, which had been fought over at great length in the previous ten years. It won universal cross-party backing in the Council precisely because the ground had been carefully prepared in advance, and because the project had mass support. Its failure at this point would have dangerously undermined Lancashire's industrial and political leadership. But once this far-reaching commitment had been made a new dynamic was quick to

emerge as sections of the City's councillors sought more influence over the way that their ratepayers' money was to be spent. The first evidence of this attitude was to appear only weeks after the decision was made, when Salford Council indicated that it would be willing to consider making a £1 million loan to be promoted in a Bill the following year. Their terms – indicated in a private letter from the Town Clerk Samuel Brown, but not made public – were that they should be able to insert a clause to this effect in Manchester's Bill, limiting Manchester's power to the raising of £2 million and giving Salford the right to proportionate representation on the Ship Canal Board. "If Manchester is sincere", wrote Brown to the city's Tory MP, Lees Knowles, "she cannot object to what we want",[42] but he had failed to note the unease that many of the Manchester councillors now felt over the role being played by the shareholders' directors and the lack of any control by the Corporation. Since Salford's proposal would only dilute their influence, the offer was rejected and the Town Clerk was advised to seek a separate Bill.

This initial show of consensus in Manchester about the loan to the Company and the exclusion of a neighbouring authority was unable however to disguise important differences which did not take long to emerge. As soon as the Bill came before the House of Commons, two Liberal MPs, Philip Stanhope from Burnley and Sir Joseph Pease, in an apparently unprompted move, proposed that the Company be converted into a public trust before any municipal aid be allowed. Sir William Houldsworth, a director of the Company, was quick to head this off in the Committee by arguing that the House should not discourage private enterprise and persuading the proposers to withdraw the amendment. But the episode had touched on a raw nerve in the city and was soon followed by a demand from the Corporation that

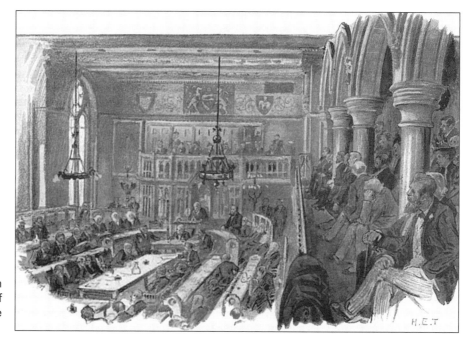

The strangers' gallery in the Town Hall, packed to hear the details of financial mismanagement of the project. *Chetham's*

155

there should be five council representatives on an enlarged Board of fifteen Directors – which the Company agreed.[43] The representation proposed by the Special Committee reflected the state of the parties with three Liberals (Harwood, Southern and Walton Smith), together with Mark (Liberal Unionist) and Chesters Thompson (Tory), but the full Council insisted on its own choice to substitute the Tory Boddington for the Liberal Smith.

There the matter would most probably have rested but scarcely eight weeks after the shareholders were called together in August to approve the loan arrangements, rumours started to sweep Manchester that a further £2 million would have to be found for the Canal to be finished. The satirical magazine *Spy* was the first to break the news publicly in late October[44] and over the ensuing months the full scale of incompetence, mismanagement and cover up by the directors or their staff became apparent. Nor was the

Cartoon of Sir James Harwood, closely involved in overseeing the Ship Canal works on behalf of the Corporation. Note the temperance pledge. *MCL*

matter improved when the Deputy Chairman Sir Joseph Lee wrote a letter to the press on 13th November in response to the rumours stating that "the resources of the company are ample to complete all the authorised works, and leave a substantial surplus".[45] With this on public record the two Liberal members on the Board of Directors, Harwood and Southern, were particularly incensed to be informed in the same month that the new estimate was £863,000 up on the February figure of £3 million and decided to produce their own minority report – with which, according to Leech, Mark and Chesters Thompson were in sympathy although they declined to be signatories.[46]

This was the context for the two all-day December meetings of the full Council which provided the stage for the mounting of a dramatic *exposé* to an eager public of the failures and omissions of the Ship Canal directors and their staff. With the strangers' gallery crowded out from half-past ten in the morning to five in the evening, there were few who were not critical of the way that affairs had developed but there were crucial differences in emphasis as to who was to blame. Setting the pattern for the Company apologists, Leech – now the Mayor – argued from the chair that the problems arose from the difficulties of taking over the contract from Walker and his executors, but he supported the argument for greater Corporation control of expenditure.[47]

In this general line he was followed by Mark, Walton Smith and a number of the older Liberal aldermen, but no such loyalty was felt by Chesters Thompson, the Tory leader and a director on the Board. He reminded the Council of the wild claims made about huge dividends, complained that not a penny had been spent on 50 hydraulic cranes which had been put in the original estimates and charged the engineer Leader Williams with the responsibility of omitting from his estimates an extra 3.5 million cubic yards of excavation. With his fellow Tory Andrews, he was quick to protest too when Liberal members tried to replace Boddington on the Board of Directors on the grounds of his continued ill health; and he made it plain that there was little love lost between him and the Board, complaining that "they, the representatives of the people, were in January last treated as nonentities outside the pale of the Board, by the Ship Canal directors."[48]

At the resumed meeting the following week it was clear that dissatisfaction about the disastrous course of events had led to substantial canvassing of opinion amongst the younger councillors with the result that a radical cross-party amendment was moved by the Liberal Gunson. Praising the example of Sir Joseph Pease for seeking in the House the previous summer the imposition of a public trust, he argued, with the support of the Tory Richards, that while accepting the report of the Special Committee the Corporation's Ship Canal Committee should be instructed to take immediate steps to increase the number of Corporation Directors on the Board to eight out of fifteen, obtaining Parliamentary powers for this if necessary.[49]

In a lengthy and at times acrimonious debate, it was left to the 'truthteller' Harwood to spell out the full extent of the muddle, extravagance and incompetence which the Corporation directors found when they went to apply their "experience and knowledge gained in fifty years" on the Council to the Ship Canal. The management he declared "had degenerated into a state of utter incapacity … [in which] they found themselves powerless". As for the arrangements with the contractor, he was even more scathing: "Practically there never was a contract for the Canal that was worth calling a contract. The contract with Mr Walker had no more binding obligation on Mr Walker than the piece of paper in his hand".[50] It was a dominating performance, received with prolonged applause, which won Harwood backing across the Council, particularly amongst the Tories, who saw his speech as an only slightly veiled attack on the Liberals on the Board.

When the vote was taken Gunson's amendment had been lost by the narrow margin of 41–39. But if the old Liberal campaigners for popular capitalism thought they had won the day, the analysis of the voting shows why the issue was not going to go away. Profiling by party shows a split right down the middle of both main parties, with exactly 21 Liberals and 17 Tories both supporting the amendment and opposing it. The Liberal Unionist vote of 3–1 against the amendment was therefore decisive. A breakdown by years of service on the Council provides, however, a much more revealing picture as Table 3 below shows:

**Table 3   Voting of Manchester Councillors and Aldermen on Amendment to Seek a Majority on the Ship Canal Board, December 1891**

| Councillors/Aldermen | Seeking L.A. majority | Supporting Company |
|---|---|---|
| Elected before 1880 | 1 | 13 |
| Elected 1880–1885 | 2 | 6 |
| Elected after Oct 1885 | 36 | 22 |

The "popular capitalism camp" was substantially dependent on the old guard, being able to rely on all but one of the pre-1880 cohort and all but two of the 1880–1885 cohort. The role of the Ship Canal Directors in the vote is also revealing, for the three who were most critical of the Board (Harwood, Southern and Thompson) abstained while Mark together with Leech – the shareholders' auditor who saw no conflict of interest in his position – did not hesitate to exercise their vote in favour of the Company. Apparently not wishing to draw attention to the closeness of the vote or perhaps to his own role, Leech omits all reference to the vote on the amendment – which was recorded in detail in the papers and in the proceedings of the Council – and instead claims that the report was adopted by a majority of eleven – a statistic that is recorded nowhere else![51]

The response to the vote was rapid from the other interested parties. The Company's first move was to seek an early meeting with representatives from the Council where

Lord Egerton offered to set up an executive or spending committee to oversee the completion of the Canal, to be chaired by a Corporation director and upon which the four Corporation directors would be in a majority. This arrangement was accepted and the shareholders meanwhile sought to protect their interests by creating their own Association. Again the hand of Leech seems to be evident, for he records that Hilton Greaves, an Oldham cotton spinner and one of the original 1882 supporters, had written to him on 1st December with a suggestion:

> I see that your Corporation had a long meeting yesterday …. I do not in the least regret taking the large number of shares I hold …. It seems to be drifting into the Corporation having much management; this should hardly be so…. What has come of the members of the Consultative Committee who sat on the undertaking in the early part – would it not be well they were called together informally?[52]

Cartoon of Chesters Thompson, a local brewer and leader of the Tory group on the Council.   *MCL*

157

The Canal at Saltpost below Runcorn. This section was open to ships from November 1891. *MCL*

The result was that only six days after the Council vote a preliminary meeting was held, where Reuben Spencer, Managing Director of Platts of Oldham, proposed from the chair that an Association be formed "so that there should be a centre of action should any further difficulty arise, although not to interfere or meddle to the slightest degree with the action of the Board *as now constituted*" (My emphasis). The committee appointed consisted of some of the larger shareholders who had been active from the start, including Hilton Greaves (with a shareholding of £20,000), Alfred Crewdson (£3,000), J. A. Beith (£2,000), and Spencer (£2,000) and was soon talking up the need to protect the interests of the shareholders and their right to "supreme control".[53]

In the Council meanwhile the issue had if anything been inflamed by the vote and the manner in which it had been won. When at the end of January the General Purposes Committee – composed of all members of the Council – was convened at the call of the Mayor it agreed a motion proposed by Gunson that the Town Clerk be instructed to insert a new clause to the Company's Ship Canal Bill giving the Corporation a majority on a Board of fifteen. With this brief the two Sub-Committees responsible for progressing the question of the new Bill on 6th February met jointly with Moulton QC for legal advice. According to Leech "some of the councillors became very offensive in their language towards the Ship Canal directors and had to be called to order".[54] The Mayor was playing a key role in these unfolding events and his laconic two-line summary of their subsequent decision on 12th February not to oppose the Company's Bill provides a further example of his wish to promote the Company's and shareholders' interests at the expense of the Corporation's.

The meeting was in fact held jointly with five of the directors of the Ship Canal – Bythell, Platt, Bailey, Galloway and Leigh – and the minutes make fascinating reading, given the earlier verdict of the General Purposes Committee. After some preliminary skirmishing the question was raised by the Liberal Rhodes and put formally by Leech as to whether the Company – in the event that more than £3 million was needed – would consent to the addition of a new clause giving the Corporation eight of the fifteen directors. Playing for time, the Directors asked that the question be put in writing for the Board to consider and then withdrew for the Committee members to fight it out.

1892 cartoon showing the Ship Canal project tied down by vested interests, commissions, high salaries and waste.
*MCL*

158

Rhodes, supported by Pingstone, a leading figure in the Cooperative Wholesale Society, proposed that the question be formally put to the Directors whereupon an amendment was carried by 9–6 that no petition be put against the Bill. Again those in favour of the amendment were with one exception members of the Special Ship Canal Committee – packed with the old guard with an average of twenty-one years membership of the Council – compared with an average service of only four years for those opposing. When the substantive vote was taken the Liberals moved into line to support, but the Tories were split with 3 voting in favour and 3 of them, the influential Chesters Thompson, Andrews and Williams, abstaining. The *Spy* magazine, which followed Harwood in believing that the Board was paying extravagant salaries to some of the officials and was permitting dubious tendering arrangements, took the view that: "It is only too apparent that the old directors and officials of the Canal Company have sufficient back-door or wine-cellar influence with certain cliques in the Council".[55]

When in August, contrary to all the earlier protestations, it emerged that a further £1.489 million at least was required by the Ship Canal Company to complete the work, the situation caused considerable embarrassment amongst the directors as is evident from a statement made to the Ship Canal Executive Committee by Sir Edward Jenkinson, the London Preference shareholders' nominee on the Board. There was little doubt where he thought blame should rest:

Leader Williams, engineer for the Ship Canal.

There is no question … we have suffered from Bad Engineering … We should have on these works … some competent Deputy Engineer, a younger man than our present Chief Engineer who would be always on the Works … The Chief Engineer should be … at HQ and pulling the strings … Mr Williams for all his good qualities is not the man for this outside work nor has he the time for it.[56]

While the shareholders' and Corporation directors were agreed on the difficulty of replacing Williams and the problem of upsetting him by appointing a strong deputy, there was a direct clash between them over the issue which had been pushed by Gunson and others since December 1891 – who was to control the Board. Writing to Barings in October, Jenkinson was of the view that Harwood was delaying a decision as long as he could in order "to drive us into a corner". He was in close contact with Sir Joseph Lee and the two of them were advising:

that we should take a firm stand against this demand to have control of the Canal until the loan is repaid, and we hope that in this action we may have the strong support of the Preference Shareholders in London …. So before 20 November we must have an alternative scheme ready and have a Bill drafted. We are trying to get a million from Salford …[57]

Over the next few weeks there was a flurry of activity as both sides sought to position themselves most effectively. At the Ship Canal Board meeting on 21st October there was both discussion of the approach to Salford and a report from Samuel Platt that Oldham would be considering the question of a loan five days later. At the Council meeting in Manchester on 28th October it was revealed that the Corporation would be seeking in their Bill to have ten directors out of fifteen but, in answer to a question from Gunson, it appeared that two or three might retire in order for other towns to be represented.[58] On the same day Leech, together with Mark, was advising the Ship Canal Board on the Corporation's position and on 2nd November he again attended the Board meeting – without voting – where a draft letter was agreed which was to be sent to the Mayor (Leech himself!) setting out the Company's new proposals.[59] The full text of the letter appeared in the press on 5th November and revealed that the Company was suggesting an enlarged Board of twenty one, on which the lenders of the £5 million of debentures would have eleven representatives – a majority of one over the shareholders' representatives. It was further indicated that the shareholders would have control over the raising of revenue and that it would be unacceptable for the debenture holders to have voting rights at shareholders' meetings.[60] A second lengthy letter appeared a few days later signed by the ten shareholders' directors, objecting to suggestions that the Corporation had been kept in the dark about Ship Canal affairs and excusing themselves from responsibility.[61]

This was the voice of large scale industrial and finance capital aimed at both a Lancashire and a national audience. Experienced in campaigning and propaganda work, the promoters had won popular support for their movement and persuaded many to invest their capital; but they now faced a tougher challenge – persuading the world that public monies should continue to be pumped in to salvage a private enterprise, while effective control remained in the hands of the men who had piloted the ship onto the rocks. Given the penetration by Ship Canal men of the three councils in Manchester, Salford and Oldham,[62] the strategy to be adopted was now clear. If the other two Councils could be persuaded to provide loans for the Company, then representation on the Board would have to be split *"pari passu* with Manchester ... in proportion to their share in the total advances" – as Manchester had indeed offered in a letter from Leech read to the Board meeting of 28th October, before the proposals of the Company were revealed.[63] Not only would this enable them to limit the influence exercised by a single block of Corporation directors, but it would also result in the election of their own men and make it easier to force through the other terms about the voting rights of the debenture holders. This was the significance of the change from fifteen to twenty-one directors for, under Manchester's proposals, offering two directorships to the other two Councils would still have left them with a majority on the Board.

Putting the Company's plan into action was not however straightforward and it soon became apparent that an alliance of ratepayer and socialist elements might leave the Board vulnerable, with Manchester – which had already indicated it was willing to lend the additional £2 million – left as the sole negotiating partner. The first signs of difficulty came in Oldham where a committee recommendation to lend £250,000 was thrown out by the full Council meeting by a vote of 21–13.[64] Stung into action by this decision, the Mayor and leading aldermen and Ship Canal supporters, including Samuel Platt and Hilton Greaves, decided on the unusual course of calling a ratepayers' meeting to overrule the Council's decision at which the ex-Mayor moved a motion of support. Trading in local loyalties Platt declared – and with less than candour – that "there was a great desire in Manchester that Oldham should assist in the Ship Canal and that they held out the hand of friendship and cordial fellowship".[65] With only Alderman Brierley objecting on the grounds that the rates should not be used for "propping up an aristocratic company like the Ship Canal" the resolution was carried and immediately afterwards the members of the Council assembled and agreed unanimously to proceed with the loan.[66]

In Manchester and Salford meanwhile – where more sophisticated stage management was required – members of the Social Democratic Federation, who had been active in the period of the unemployed agitation in 1885–1886, decided that further funding without turning the Company into a public trust should be opposed and used the opportunity of ratepayers' meetings to put this case. In Manchester Joseph Waddington argued that they must either cease spending the money of overburdened ratepayers or "purchase and municipalise the Ship Canal", but he was quickly marginalised and found no seconder for his motion. Indeed Harwood, who was the main speaker in favour of the proposal for further financial assistance, chose approvingly to describe the public's support as "the unexampled loyalty of the citizens of Manchester in allowing their property to be put in security for an undertaking which, after all, is a private enterprize".[67] Municipalisation was not on his agenda and it is clear that there were no alliances being created between socialists outside the Council and radicals within, although the particular argument being put by Waddington was not such a far step from what Gunson and others had been arguing over the last year.

In Salford, however, the socialists were better organised and as a result were more successful when the issue came into the public arena. The initial meeting of the Council which discussed the issue was held on 28th October, the same day Manchester proposed seeking ten out of fifteen directors. A strong theme was that Salford, where the docks were located, should lend out of a sense of local loyalty in order to put Salford on the world map; and eventually a loan of £1 million was agreed. In the course of the debate however the traditional rivalry across the River Irwell surfaced when Alderman Dickins – unaware of the significance of the manoeuvrings taking place behind closed doors – asked if Salford was being set up "to increase Manchester's representation on the directorate and make Manchester the

masters of the whole situation". With the prospect of only two of their own directors he had gained the impression that "the part Salford would play would be that of the monkey in helping Manchester to take the chestnuts out of the fire". The clear answer to his question – that in fact they were playing the monkey for the Ship Canal Company – did not come until March and was certainly not given in Alderman (and Ship Canal Director) Bailey's cryptic comment that "Dickins' views as to voting power would be kept in view"![68]

When the issue came before a ratepayers' meeting, there was a large attendance of council members, who had voted in favour of the £1 million loan, and a substantial contingent of SDF members led by William Horrocks who had been the prime mover in the 1889 Salford Gasworkers strike. After the Mayor had refused to accept an amendment seeking the formation of a public trust, Horrocks argued that the Corporation should not "bolster up a private company" and that it would be better to spend the money on the "thousands of hungry, starving and ill–clad people" in the borough. When the vote was taken, the loan proposal was rejected by a majority of more than two to one.[69] The Mayor's immediate demand for a poll of the ratepayers provided further opportunities for the SDF to put their views at meetings over the next few weeks, but they were unable to maintain the earlier momentum.[70] When the vote was finally counted and announced on 20th December, it showed a majority in favour of the loan of 13,385 to 3,032.

Specially-built arch at the entrance to Albert Square in Manchester at the 1894 opening of the Ship Canal by Queen Victoria . *CM*

Opening Day, 1st January 1894.

By fast footwork the promoters had been able to secure their plans and were now in a far stronger position to negotiate with the Manchester Corporation. According to Leech, there followed a period in early 1893 of intense negotiation between the Corporation and the Company. Harwood and Lee had fierce disagreements over what had been lodged by the Company as security for the original £3 million loan and there were objections raised by Bythell and other Company directors to their being accused of deception.[71] The key issue remained that of the size and powers of the Corporation's representation on the new Board. When the various Bills finally came before the House of Lords Committee in mid-March, to the surprise of onlookers it was announced that a secret deal had been struck between the Company and Manchester – that while the loan was outstanding, the Corporation was to have a majority of eleven on the Board with the right to elect the Deputy Chairman, but that it would have no voting rights at the shareholders' meetings. On this basis the Corporation was to take powers to loan the full £2 million, and the two other councils decided to withdraw their Bills.

Both Salford and Oldham felt that the Company had broken faith with them. The Mayor of Oldham pointed out that the Chairman of the Company had, as an inducement to them to seek a Parliamentary Bill, expressly promised them a seat on the Board if they advanced £250,000[72] – an offer that was inevitably to bring the Company into conflict with Manchester. Though pilloried by Oldham's QC for "tyrannising" the Canal Company, the Corporation had already advanced twelve times this amount and had indicated from October that it wished to have an absolute majority – indeed as Harwood said in cross examination before the Committee, these were the only terms under which Manchester would advance more money. Leech, in summarising the position, claims that "It was a misfortune that Salford and Oldham had been encouraged to assist", but evades the question of his own role in this. A truer summary of the Company's view can be found in a private letter from Jenkinson to Lord Revelstoke at Barings:

The result is I think very satisfactory... we have got *our* Bill passed... we keep the chairmanship, and Manchester withdraws her claim for voting power at Shareholders' meetings... we have a compact minority of *ten*, against a Corporation majority of *eleven*... of course Salford and Oldham are very sore. They have no doubt been shamefully treated by Manchester and they accuse us of using them to help us in our fight with Manchester, and then throwing them over. In more reasonable moments they will see that we were helpless, and had no choice, but at the same time it is quite true that if we had not used Salford and Oldham we could not have made the terms we have with Manchester.[73]

The log-jam had been broken and from now on the completion of the Canal was comparatively straightforward. In December 1893 the first passage of the Canal from end to end was achieved and on 1st January it was opened for traffic. The formal opening by the Queen was left until May when over a million people came to watch a spectacle that had been promised for over a decade, and at which the Mayors of Manchester and Salford received knighthoods in recognition of their cities' involvement in the scheme. This was not however to put a stop to all controversy for the year because, in the following month, Harwood announced his resignation from the Ship Canal Board of Directors, explaining that he was no longer willing to be party to an enterprise that looked set to be a continuing drain on the rates. His action was regarded by Leech and most of the Liberal councillors as a direct attack on their record, and as

No. 102

## Official Opening
of the
## Manchester Ship Canal
by
# Her Majesty the Queen.

Pass one person only on board the Steamer "Skirmisher," on Monday, May 21st, and on Tuesday, May 22nd 1894.

an honourable gesture by most of the Tories who pressed a vote to delay acceptance of the resignation, which was lost by 29–28 on the casting vote of the Mayor.[74]

The Ship Canal issue was to preoccupy the Corporation for years to come and required the writing off arrears of interest because the undertaking was so slow to bring in sufficient income to provide a dividend for the shareholders. After failing to take entire control of the Canal by a salvage operation in 1891, the Corporation was locked into supporting the scheme and could not thereafter back out. Far from losing their eleven representatives on the Board of Directors after five years – the period it had been said it would take for the loan to be repaid – the Corporation became even more closely entwined in the Scheme in 1904 through the provisions of a special Ship Canal Finance Act, which was passed to deal with a growing financial crisis.[75] By agreeing that its £5 million debentures should be made perpetual and that the rate of interest on them should be reduced from 4½% to 3½%, the Corporation effectively became the Ship Canal Company's bankers – but without real power. It remained in that position with a majority on the Board until 1987, when an agreement on restructuring was reached with Peel Holdings, a property company which had just won a takeover battle for the Ship Canal.

In terms of the initial questions raised at the start of the chapter about the role of the local State, it is clear that the decision of the Manchester Corporation in 1884 to commit itself to supporting the Ship Canal Bill with the proceeds of a two-penny rate against the expressed wishes of key mercantile interests represented an important reinforcement of the dominant position of industrial capital and was the necessary prelude to the substantive rescue role to be played by the local State in the 1890s. Had it not been for the destabilisation threat posed by the agitation over the unemployed, it is likely that the collapse of the 1886 share issue would however have brought an abrupt end to the project. In the event the establishment of the Consultative Committee under the chairmanship of the Mayor, representing

Cartoon of Harwood "letting the cat out of the bag" over the financial mismanagement of the Ship Canal. Many of the older Liberal members of the Council never forgave him for this. *MCL*

# Hail! Hail! Victoria,

## QUEEN OF ENGLAND AND EMPRESS OF INDIA.

**MANCHESTER**

## Ship Canal,

Opened by

**HER MOST GRACIOUS**

**MAJESTY**

QUEEN VICTORIA,

ᴄɴ

Monday, May 21st, 1894,

Accompanied by

THEIR ROYAL HIGHNESSES,

*Prince and Princess*

Henry of Battenburg,

HER DUCAL HIGHNESS

ᴛʜᴇ

**PRINCESS LEININGEN**

And SUITE.

---

The following POEM, written by one of England's Blind Naval Crimean Heroes (**CHARLES H. HUNTLEY**), late of H.M.S. Royal Albert, flagship of Admiral Lord Lyons, Commander-in-Chief of the Black Sea Fleet, and the Honorable Captain F. Egerton, of the Mediterranean Station.

---

BRITANNIA once again is proud to hear the name
 Of Her Majesty, our noble Gracious Queen,
The Empress of India, too, a Monarch kind and true,
 And loved by all her subjects should be seen.
Seven and fifty years you'll own she has reigned upon the throne
 For us, and ruled the nation very well.
Now through Manchester she's been ; in Salford crowned the scene
 In opening of our Mercantile Canal.
Daniel Adamson's good name upon the scroll of fame
 Should be inscribed in gold for evermore.
There's no nation can excel such an ingenious Canal,
 Or boast of such great art and skill I'm sure ;
To Lord Egerton it's true there is much credit due,
 And Alderman Sir John Harwood likewise.
Leader Williams as well, and Directors of Canal,
 In carrying out this marvellous enterprise.
I hope you're pleased you've heard, that knighthood's been conferred ;
 And the laurels they have gone where honour's due.
Sir Anthony Marshall now and Sir William Bailey vow
 For the welfare of us all the best they'll do
Sir Joseph Leigh, M.P., Sir Bosdin Leech, we're proud to see
 The order of merit they have nobly won.

Our hats we ought to raise, the Councillors to praise,
 The Town Clerks for the great work they have done.
Now praise we really should our own chief Malcom Wood,
 Commander Scott, the chief of Salford, too,
Our Soldiers and the Force, and their officers, of course,
 The Fire Brigade and Volunteers so true.
Superintendent Gardiner as well, and his staff upon the Canal,
 A word of praise to them is really due,
The right course he did steer the locks and docks to clear,
 With our jolly tars and jackets of true blue.
I must note one great event of our Superintendent Bent,
 With his little band upon the stand so gay,
And much pleased was the Queen when so many schools she'd seen
 And heard them sing her Anthem on that day.
Through the visit of our Queen let no discord come between,
 Or rude tongue bribe the mind of an honest man.
Those that are not loyal, and do not like our Royal,
 Let them find a better country if they can.
If she were a goddess from above, with all to share her love,
 To please the world she'd have her work to do ;
Let the nation not forget their Monarch to respect,
 And prove to her we're Britons staunch and true.

Poem bringing a focus on Queen and Empire.

the local State, provided the mechanism for reconciling the divisions between these different fractions of capital with Adamson, the personification of an antagonistic industrial capital, being forced out to make way for a much more widely representative Board.

Once the work on the Canal had commenced, the local State became the *de facto* guarantor, but the influx of more radical councillors after 1885 and the growing strength of the Tory Party created a more volatile and unpredictable environment. This was particularly the case in the autumn of 1890 before the November elections, when the Tories were the largest party and a deal was being negotiated with the contractors' executors which was to make the rescue operation inevitable. Though the elections following the boundary changes strengthened the Liberal position, the political dogfighting over the next 30 months, in which cross-party pressure grew for control of the Canal by the Corporation, does reveal the relative autonomy of the local State. Although the overriding need for a £5 million loan was met and all calls for the company to be reformed as a public trust were rebutted, this could only be achieved by a political compromise in which formal control passed to the Corporation with the ceding of a majority on the Board. Undoubtedly this represented a substantially new role for the local State in economic planning but it should be noted that the outcome was seen as "very satisfactory" to the finance capital interests which Rothschilds had drawn into the scheme, as indicated by Jenkinson's letter to Barings (above). Not only had they secured an unprecedented level of public support for a private enterprise, but also ensured an arrangement which maintained their overall *de facto* control of the operation and left the shareholders with any future proceeds from the sale of the underlying equity.

## Notes

1.  Between the years 1892–1895 the rates in the city increased by 26%.
2.  *Ship Canal Gazette*, 13 December 1882, p. 66. Comparative figures for other adjoining Lancashire towns were Bolton £24,000, Rochdale £18,000, Oldham £15,000, and Stockport £8,500.
3.  J. R. Galloway, *The Municipalities of Manchester and Hamburg*, paper to the Manchester Statistical Society, 8 December 1897, pp. 60–61.
4.  N. Poulantzas, *Classes in Contemporary Capitalism*, 1978, pp. 158–9.
5.  P. Saunders, *Urban Politics. A Sociological Interpretation*, 1980, pp. 144–5.
6.  See for instance his remarks from the chair at a very early meeting of the Provisional Committee, Report of Proceedings, 26 September 1882, Manchester Central Library Reference f386 M67, p.28.
7.  S. D. Simon, *A Century of City Government. 1838–1938*, 1938, pp. 357–359.
8.  H. J. Laski (ed.), *A Century of Municipal Progress. 1835–1935*, 1935, p. 310.
9.  Quoted in J. H. G. Archer, "A Civic Achievement: The Building of Manchester Town Hall", in *Transactions of the Lancashire and Cheshire Antiquarian Society*, Volume 8, pp. 9–10, 1982.
10. W. E. Axon (ed.), *An Architectural and General Description of the Town Hall Manchester and Report of Inaugural Proceedings. September 1877*, 1878, p. 61.
11. Sir J. Harwood, *History and Description of the Thirlmere Water Scheme*, 1895, p.182.
12. S. D. Simon, *op.cit.*, pp. 291–294. A small scheme, the Oddfellows Cooperative Building and Investment Company had been established in 1869 with Cllr. Goldschmidt and the Medical Officer of Health as promoters. In 1884 it owned 150 houses. See evidence to the Royal Commission on the Housing of the Working Classes, 1884–5, Evidence of Mr E. Sowerbutts, pp. 517–519, Vol. XXX.
13. G. H. Pownall, *Some Aspects of Local Government*, paper read to the Manchester Statistical Society, 11 November 1896.
14. *Manchester Guardian*, 28 November 1882.
15. *Manchester Examiner and Times*, 22 November 1882, pp. 4–5.
16. *Manchester Guardian*, 30 November 1882.
17. *Manchester Guardian*, 28 November 1882. See also letter from Alderman King on the subject in *Manchester Examiner and Times*, 11 January 1883.
18. *Manchester Guardian*, 22 February 1884; Samuel Ramsbottom Pamphlet, MCL.Reference 386.M80.
19. Ship Canal Rate. Broadsheet Listing of Names, undated, Manchester Central Library Reference 386.M85
20. The controversy excited much correspondence in the press through the Autumn of 1884. See for instance letters to the *Manchester Guardian*, 25 October (H. J. Roby), 27 October (B. Leech), 12 November (H. C. Pingstone); and letter to the *Manchester Examiner and Times*, 26 November (H. Heap).
21. B. Leech, *History of the Manchester Ship Canal*, Volume 1, 1907, p. 81.
22. *Manchester Guardian*, 20 December 1882.
23. See for instance *Ship Canal Gazette* reports of meetings at Warrington (8 November 1882), Ashton under Lyme (27 December); and *Manchester Guardian* reports of meetings at Stockport (24 November), Rochdale (13 January 1883).
24. *Oldham Evening Chronicle*, 24 October 1882. Described as a young man without experience of the Council, James referred specifically in his speech on election to the importance of the Ship Canal. He retired from the Council as soon as the Ship Canal Bill had been enacted (See *Oldham Evening Chronicle*, 8 October 1882).
25. *Ship Canal Gazette*, 15 November 1882, p. 17.

26. *Manchester Guardian*, 3 November 1884, p. 3. Letter from "Ship Canal".

27. *Bolton Chronicle*, 3 January 1883.

28. See for instance letter from J. Cowin, "Our Municipal Elections and our Morals", in *Manchester Courier*, 6 October 1882.

29. *Manchester Courier*, Interior Workings of the Manchester Corporation. Letter dated 22 October 1878 in Pamphlet "Manchester Corporation Proceedings. To Ratepayers of Manchester", 1880, Manchester Central Library Reference 352.042 M14.

30. Manchester Liberal Association, Liberal Union Committee, 17 July 1891.

31. The other two Tories were Charles Moseley, who died in October 1887, and Henry Boddington. See Chapter 4, Note 100.

32. *Manchester Evening News*, 1 November 1890.

33. *Manchester Courier*, 8 November, 1 December 1890.

34. See S. D. Simon, *op.cit.*, p. 397. Lady Simon states inaccurately – as is shown by the figures here – that the Liberal Party was in a majority up to 1890 and that the Tories were in control from then until 1919.

35. *Spy*, 12 March 1892, p. 3.

36. *Spy*, 6 February 1892.

37. *Manchester Guardian*, 7 September 1907, p. 8.

38. See Appendix A for a further discussion of Leech's book. For the best – indeed the only – account of the machinations behind the scenes during this period see the weekly notes and articles which appeared at regular intervals in the satirical magazine *Spy*. Though it was widely read, Leech appears to have taken no cuttings from it.

39. Kelley had originally been put forward by the Labour Electoral Association as a labour candidate for the November 1890 election, but agreed to stand down for the Liberal candidate Robert Gibson. The LEA had been formed by the TUC in 1886 and was closely identified with the Liberal Party. In March 1890 the Manchester and Salford Trades Council had decided to affiliate by a large majority. See L. Bather, *History of the Manchester and Salford Trades Council*, 1956, MA Thesis, University of Manchester.

40. *Spy*, 19 December 1891, p. 8.

41. B. Leech, *op.cit.*, Vol. 2, pp. 84–91.

42. Letter from Samuel Brown to Lees Knowles M.P., 22 April 1891. Collection of Papers on the Manchester Ship Canal in Chetham's Library, Manchester.

43. B. Leech, *op.cit.*, Vol. 2, pp. 93–96.

44. *Spy*, 31 October 1891; 14 November 1891.

45. *Spy*, 21 November 1891, p. 8.

46. B. Leech, *op.cit.*, Vol. 1, p. 101.

47. *City News*, 5 December 1891.

48. *Liverpool Mercury*, 10 December 1891.

49. *Manchester Guardian*, 10 December 1891.

50. There is no known extant copy of the Contract. However we do know from a statement issued by the directors that it did contain at least one extraordinary clause – viz that the Company would advance all plant necessary for the construction of the works, with the contractor agreeing to repay the sum advanced by monthly payments over the length of the four year construction period. The total cost of the plant was £943,000, which would have involved a monthly repayment of £19,645. In April 1889 however, the directors agreed to modify the repayment terms with the result that by November 1890 only £195,000 had been repaid. In the settlement with Walker's executors, the Company had to take over this plant and in so doing effectively commit a further £¾ million of the shareholders' money. For details see *The County Telephone*, 9 May 1891.

51. B. Leech, *op.cit.*, Vol. 2, p. 104.

52. B. Leech, *ibid.*, Vol. 1, pp. 106–108.

53. B. Leech, *ibid.*, Vol. 2, p. 121.

54. B. Leech, *ibid.*, Vol. 2, p. 120.

55. *Spy*. 27 February 1992, p. 12.

56. Reported Statement from Sir Edward Jenkinson at the Executive Committee, 6 September 1892, Baring Brothers and Co. Archive. Ref. HC 3.143.

57. Letter from Sir Edward Jenkinson to Lord Revelstoke, 17 October 1892. Baring Brothers and Co. Archive. HC3.143.

58. *Examiner and Times*, 29 October 1892.

59. Manchester Ship Canal Board Minutes, 28 October, 2 November 1892. Ref.B10/1/3/5.

60. *Manchester Guardian*, 5 November 1892.

61. *Times*, 8 November 1892.

62. A fourth Council, Warrington, was also approached and there were reports of a possible loan of £150,000 to the Company. Links between the directors and this Tory controlled town had never been strong and negotiations collapsed when Warrington, conscious of the track record of the Company, sought to link the loan to the construction of a local dock which the Council would build and control. *Liverpool Daily Post*, 10 November, 12 November 1892.

63. Manchester Ship Canal Company Board Minutes, 28 October 1892.

64. *Evening News*, 10 November 1892.

65. *City News*, 26 November 1892.

66. In a subsequent poll of ratepayers the voting in favour of the loan was 9,805 to 7,451.

67. *City News*, 19 November 1892.

68. *The Salford Chronicle*, 5 November 1892.

69. *Manchester Guardian*, 17 November 1892. See also B. Leech, *op.cit.*, Vol. 1, p. 139.

70. *The Salford Chronicle*, 17 December 1892.

71. B. Leech, *op.cit.*, Vol. 2, pp. 144–153.

72. *Evening News*, 6 April 1893.

73. Letter from Sir E. Jenkinson to Lord Revelstoke, 18 March 1893, Baring Brothers and Co. Archive. HC3.143.

74. The voting showed 20 Liberals, 3 Liberal Unionists and 5 Tories opposing the motion, with 20 Tories supporting it.

75. D. A. Farnie, *The Manchester Ship Canal and the Rise of the Port of Manchester*, 1980, pp. 14–15.

# 8

# CONCLUSION

The initial focus of this study has been on the origins and making of Lancashire's Ship Canal, a giant seaway that was to turn Manchester into the country's fourth largest port. With the subsequent opening in 1896 of Trafford Park, the world's first purpose-built industrial estate and a separately operating company, the Ship Canal scheme generated a substantial increase in the trans-Atlantic trade with the United States and Canada. Furthermore it created the opportunities for a substantial invasion of new, and especially American industries, which were seeking a foothold to exploit new European markets;[1] and with this came new jobs both in engineering in firms like British Westinghouse (later GEC) and Ford Motors;[2] in chemicals and oil in firms like Thomas Hedley (later Procter & Gamble), Shell and Ciba Geigy and food in firms such as Guinness and Kelloggs. By 1903 there were 12,000 working on the Park and during the Second World War a peak of 75,000 was reached, amply justifying the claims of the promoters and the trade unionists, who joined the original Movement, that the Canal would help to diversify the industrial base of the region and bring new jobs. Despite its detractors the project not only represented a vision of modernity and development, but also substantially facilitated the industrial transformation of a region which had hitherto been heavily dependent on the cotton industry. Since the 1880s and 1890s were the peak years for the export abroad of capital by British investors, the commitment to such a low-yielding investment by large-scale manufacturing capital undoubtedly represented a major commitment to the region.

Generating high volumes of traffic and high profits the Suez Canal had had a powerful influence not only on the British Government, which was persuaded to purchase a large shareholding, but also on the popular mind. In the imperial heyday of the 1880s Lancashire's manufacturers sought to emulate its success but, unlike strategically placed Suez, Manchester's "Big Ditch" was not destined to make a permanent impact upon world trading patterns although it did serve a very densely populated industrial region with a huge consumer base. Returning no profit in the first twenty years of its existence – and only modest ones thereafter – the Ship Canal itself owed its continued existence to the support of the local State and the levy imposed upon Mancunians through the rates to pay for the loan. In terms of tonnage shipped through the port it reached its peak of activity in 1955 and declined thereafter.

The development of such a major project is interesting in its own account and because of this has attracted enormous interest from those seeking to describe the growth of the region. All previously published accounts however have concentrated almost exclusively on the physical, engineering and economic aspects and on the Parliamentary campaign. This book has endeavoured to show that the launching and construction of the Canal was a far more complex and subtle operation than has ever been acknowledged and that a

Post card of British Westinghouse, Trafford Park, 1909.

*BTY*

Panoramic view of the Manchester Docks in 1938.  *MSCC*

cumulative process of selective presentation and omission of facts – inspired by a combination of economic, political and academic motives – has served to create a distorted, apolitical and one-dimensional picture. Our understanding of the history of the region has suffered as a result.

But the study has been more than a simple monograph on a piece of regional transport history; it can properly claim the distinction of puncturing beyond repair a 100 year old myth that the Canal was built simply because transport costs were too high for a city in decline. Undoubtedly there were many in Lancashire who *believed* that these costs were excessive, but the evidence does not support the view that this was a critical factor.

In the first instance new perspectives on the urbanisation process in Manchester at the end of the nineteenth century have been opened, filling a gap that is all the more remarkable given the attention that has been paid to developments there in the first half of the century. In this respect and in its consideration of the issue of the unemployed, it bears some comparison with Stedman Jones' study of class relationships in the capital, although the emphasis of *Outcast London* is very distinctly on the demoralised urban poor rather than on the respectable skilled worker.[3] Research has not only pointed up the political dimensions of modernisation and change but also the linkage between the local State and the economy in the process. The City Council has been shown as a key institution to penetrate and control and as having its own political system and infighting. This represents a substantial departure from the orthodox literature on the history of local government which has tended to produce accounts which concentrate on administrative functions, financial arrangements and the linear development of specific services. This suggests that further work elsewhere would yield valuable comparative material.

In exploring wider issues of change in a watershed period of British social and political formation, the Ship Canal story sheds light on the way that industrial Britain was moving at a time of economic and political crisis from a paternalistic and local factory-based system to a more class-conscious urban society. Although the detail contained in the book does not all point in exactly the same direction, in general the 1880s and early 1890s was, as described by Hall and Schwarz, a period of "social transformation and reconstruction".[4] Employers sought to alter the existing customs of the trade and introduced the transition from craft control to modern production and management in the four different sectors of engineering, printing, woodworking and cotton. The local impact of these changes described in this book complements the more general accounts of economic restructuring explored by historians like Saul and Berg.[5]

The study has for the first time drawn detailed attention both to the existence of a cross-class social movement in Lancashire and to its nature and objectives and has demonstrated how the building of this alliance grew out of the political and social tensions of the early 1880s. An imaginative response to problems of depression and unemployment, the Ship Canal scheme was put together initially by Liberals who were seeking to build a Lib–Lab alliance as a way of directing pressure for social and democratic reform. The drawing in of the national leadership of the TUC and of the largest and most powerful trade unions in the country may well be seen as one of the last flings of Lib–Labism but the successful achievement of the alliance's objective – the passage of the 1885 Act – shows that this particular form of industrial–political linkage was still regarded by the participants as having currency up to the middle of the decade.[6]

For a limited period the alliance was able to generate a unique level of cooperation between large-scale manufacturing capital and organised labour, though significantly the assiduous courting of the trade unions by the promoters in this period did not continue in the 1890s, as the Trades Council discovered in 1892 when its request for a meeting with Board members was turned down.[7] Through highly sophisticated campaigning, mobilisation of activists and an array of public relations techniques, the Movement drew in mass support across Lancashire and even further afield. The evidence in support of this argument has highlighted not only the clear linkages with the strategies of the Anti-Corn Law Leaguers, but also the attempt to create a "regional" perspective, uniting the disparate loyalties of the textile towns into a Lancashire voice to be counterpoised to London and wider interests. Although the shifts to national decision-making and class-based politics were already showing the limitations of this approach, the initiative must rank as one of the earliest in Britain seeking to create a regional consensus. It prefigures the strategies adopted in the North East by former coal capitalists in the immediate post-war post-nationalisation period[8] and has close resonances now with the European Community's "Regionalism" emphasis and indeed with Manchester's 1993 Olympic Bid approach – where the local State was incorporated into a development framework shaped and controlled by the private sector.

The public support generated by the campaigning was by any standards phenomenal and gives us a clear indication of the way in which a determined group, backed by the resources of large-scale capital and with access to newspapers, could exploit traditional forms and rituals of solidarity and use for their own purposes the customary vehicles for democratic debate – noticeably newspapers, public meetings and written material. Accounts of this nature which are focused at the local level are extremely valuable for building up a wider picture. Inevitably we are led to ask how far this kind of

Advertisement for Trafford Park Estate.

Bargemen on the Ship Canal – one of a series of powerful illustrations appearing in the *Manchester Guardian* in the early 1900s.
*Chetham's*

169

Arch in Manchester at opening of the Ship Canal by Queen Victoria in 1894. *CM*

moulding of public opinion was typical in Victorian Britain and what this tells us of the nature of urban politics. There is evidence certainly of the buying of influence through the financing of working men's clubs and of bringing trainloads of supporters in support of particular Parliamentary campaigns, but further research in other industrial centres is required to explore the wider question. That examples do not immediately spring to mind should not be taken as evidence that similarities cannot be discovered elsewhere.

A further feature of importance was that the Ship Canal idea was seen as a vibrant and novel symbol for promoting Free Trade principles. McKibbin, in asserting the continuing and strong adherence of the British working class into the twentieth century to the ideology of Free Trade in preference to socialism, underestimates the strong support which was developing in this period for "Fair Trade" policies from those sectors threatened by foreign competition; but his general argument is important.[9] Undoubtedly in Lancashire at this time the Tory-supported clamour for Protectionism, together with a wish to counter the more aggressive influence of socialist ideas, acted as an important stimulus to Free Trade adherents (especially Liberals) to argue the case for the Canal. Though the imagery used was never blatant and at times almost subliminal, the general thrust was not lost on contemporaries, particularly Tory Fair Traders. The eventual completion of the Canal provided a big fillip to the Free Trade standard bearers – as witness the sense of sweet triumph felt by the Liberal Mayor of Salford in sending off a

loaf of sugar to his Manchester counterpart on the day of the Canal's opening.

The Ship Canal idea was however always more than just a Free Trade totem, being rapidly taken up as the instrument for promoting popular capitalism through working class shareholdings – a far more radical economic ideology than Free Trade – which drew its inspiration from the dispersal of ownership that was alleged to have accompanied the development of the Oldham Limited spinning companies. Here again the study has unearthed a significant political-industrial initiative, which has hitherto remained largely invisible but must surely rank as a precursor to the present Tory Government's encouragement of the small shareholder through privatisation programmes and other means. Just as this has been devised to create an analogue of participatory capitalism with a human face, so a significant section of Liberal opinion in Lancashire backed a similar experiment in the years 1882–1886 in order to create at the industrial level a mirror image of the mass democracy being fashioned through electoral reform. It was however an experiment that failed because the conditions of depression and unemployment which inspired the experiment were the very ones that militated against its adoption.

By the time this was clear in late 1886 the political tensions and problems of stabilisation brought to the surface by the rioting of the unemployed on the streets of Manchester and elsewhere – and so effectively fanned by the socialists of the Social Democratic Federation – had created a consensus

170

that the Canal would have to proceed, and if necessary with the backing of public monies against all the existing tenets of economic orthodoxy. These concerns about the dangers of revolutionary change – however illusory they may appear to have been to us now – are the only possible explanation for the sudden conversion to the project of the 23 strong Consultative Committee in late 1886. Moreover the issue of unemployment received ironically a further airing only days after the Canal was opened when a deputation representing 1,000 unemployed was sent to the Mayor of Salford after fighting had broken out at the Docks over the failure to employ local men as labourers and stevedores. Though the *Manchester Courier* pleaded that "the namby-pamby school of sympathisers with all so-called labour agitation will receive scant sympathy from the real working men of Lancashire",[10] the social tensions of a society in which wealth and poverty lay so closely entwined were never far below the surface. Indeed they were reflected in a speech made by the Salford Tory MP Sir Henry Howorth on the day of the Canal's triumphant opening later in the year. He had been struck by seeing in some of the lower streets close by to the procession and the Royal splendour, "in serried rags an enormous mass of faces, which pointed to there being an enormous amount of poverty and misery". Change was sweeping the country bringing power to the masses and in his view "unless they supported and sustained these vast numbers of the poorer workers … danger was inevitable".[11]

Adamson's producer alliance had been one response to these perceived dangers and, in the depression of the early 1880s, had the cutting edge to produce a cross-class movement which won mass working class support. But like the ideology of popular capitalism, the model lost general currency as employers at the workplace showed that they preferred to introduce change and new technology through confrontation and arbitrary exercise of power rather than through cooperation – a process which encouraged men and women (especially in the cotton industry) to see their position more in terms of a class-based analysis of conflicting interests than one where there was a shared community of work between masters and men. The shifts in attitude can be detected in the workplace disputes of the period, particularly in those involving women. They had none of the advantages afforded to male workers in a patriarchal society and increasingly were willing to challenge employers and the structures and practices of a male dominated workplace. The key role they played in the cotton industry from the mid 1880s, which has not been properly recognised, anticipated several of the developments associated with New Unionism at the end of the decade.

By looking at a series of industrial disputes and the changes affecting four different sectors, the study supports arguments that a "new" working class was emerging, bound together by a sense of common identity and independent interest rather than critically divided by place and local loyalty. It was a transformation, as Joyce and McKibbin have argued,[12] which gathered pace with the development of the

Labour Party and with new processes of urbanisation. Notably there was an exodus of the rich from the cities and towns where their wealth had been made and an increasing residential segmentation of the remaining urban population. What this research has particularly drawn attention to is the importance of the transitional period of the 1880s and 1890s in effecting this transformation, and the critical role played by the old craft unions and their members in first bending to the employers' offensive and then acknowledging that their general interests lay more in combining with the semi-skilled and unskilled of the new general unions than in fragile alliances with employers. Because of this a reassessment of the relationship between the old trade union order and the labourist consciousness which was to follow is required.

The North West was the cradle of trade unionism where one in every four trade unionists lived and worked and needs therefore to be studied with close attention by labour historians exploring the development of new unionism at the end of the 1880s and the emergence of the Independent Labour Party in 1893. This is particularly the case with the early 1880s if the charge of periodisation is to be avoided; yet the close involvement of the trade unions in the alliance of the Ship Canal Movement – a central feature in understanding how the craft workers were responding to the employers' offensive in the 1880s – has received no recognition in the literature. The dogged defensiveness of the old craft unions, and of members of the TUC's Parliamentary Committee like James Mawdsley, lacked the glamour associated with the demands of the 1890s, but it was this defensiveness which won space for the wider extension of trade unionism. Moreover, as we have seen, these older craft unions did give active encouragement and support to the less well-organised and unskilled – a point not acknowledged by those who point to the initially hostile reaction that came from the craft unions to the demands from the general and non-craft men.

In a similar way it is no longer possible to accept the judgement of those who have implied either that the City Council's *Lifeboat* operation was an anachronism or that it was merely a heroic example of voluntary civic endeavour. The research has shown that the financial rescue was part of a carefully planned scheme to ensure that the local State was brought into play as soon as it became clear that the efforts of unaided private capital could not achieve the objective of a profit generating scheme. But equally it is clear that while this was an advantage to both small and large-scale investors in protecting the value of their shareholdings, it is also true that the commitment of the State was of great benefit to the trade union and working class fraction of the original alliance, whose dividend was to be found in a wider range of job opportunities. Although there were no emulations of this specific piece of municipal enterprise, there is no doubt that Manchester's involvement was to set the pattern for a much enhanced and more interventionist role to be played by the local State in local infrastructure development and economic planning in the twentieth century.

## Notes

1. F. A. Vanderlip, *The American "Commercial Invasion" of Europe*, 1902.

2. J. Dummelow, *1899–1949. The Golden Jubilee of the Metropolitan-Vickers Electrical Company*, 1949; I. McIntosh, "Ford at Trafford Park: "an Americanised corner of old jog-trot England"", *Manchester Sociology Occasional Papers*, Number 30, 1991.

3. G. S. Jones, *Outcast London. A Study in the Relationship between Classes*, 1971.

4. S. Hall and B. Schwarz, in M. Langan and B. Schwarz (eds.), *Crises in the British State*, 1985, p. 16.

5. S. B. Saul, *Technological Change: The United States and Britain in the Nineteenth Century*. 1970; Berg, M. (ed.), *Technology and Toil in Nineteenth Century Britain*, 1979.

6. P. Joyce, *Work, Society and Politics*, 1980, p. 334.

7. Manchester Ship Canal Company Minutes, 23 August 1892.

8. Benwell Community Development Project, *The Making of a Ruling Class*, 1978, pp. 61–62, 66; M. P. Fogarty, *Plan Your Own Industries*, 1947.

9. R. McKibbin, *The Ideologies of Class*, pp. 31–32. 1991.

10. *Manchester Courier*, 13 January 1894; *Pendleton Reporter*, 13 January 1894.

11. *Pendleton Reporter*, 26 May 1894.

12. P. Joyce, *op.cit.*; R. McKibbin, *op. cit.*

1957 Aerial view of the Docks and Canal at their peak.   *MSCC*

# EPILOGUE

From its inception controversy has followed the Ship Canal scheme and now, in its centenary year, the position has not altered. In the 1880s and 1890s there were disputes about the position of different shareholders, the role of the municipal authorities, the acquisition of land and the rights of the public and private interests associated with the Canal. Claims were also made alleging improper conduct, misleading evidence and dubious financial practice. On one occasion it became clear to the company's astonished shareholders that Marshall Stevens, their former manager, had attempted to buy the racecourse needed for the construction of the new Number 9 Dock for £250,000 and sell it on to them for £1.2 million![1] During the last decade the arguments have ranged over similar ground as competing groups and individuals have sought to gain or maintain control of the company in a period of transition. As shipping activities have declined in the upper reaches, new possibilities have emerged for the extraction of benefit and profits from this major resource.

Behind the arguments lie issues of public importance, for inevitably those who control this unique physical asset – a 36 mile corridor of water and land across a densely populated region – have the opportunity of shaping public policies and influencing the way of life and the livelihoods of thousands of people far beyond the immediate vicinity of the Canal. As the present chairman of the company, Robert Hough recently put it:

> We influence six or seven local authorities, the Mersey Basin Campaign, the Department of Environment. To exercise that kind of control, that kind of dominance – not in an aggressive way of course – well you can't write it off, can you?[2]

A quick retrospect of the events of recent years enables us to see both how the present position has been reached and the options for the future. In the 1960s the long term prospects for the Docks were already looking bleak. As a 1967 Government report, prepared by a committee chaired by Lord Rochdale, tactfully put it: "Manchester labours under great physical limitations and its advantage as an inland port is now less than when the Ship Canal was constructed".[3]

Under managing director Donald Redford imaginative schemes to improve efficiency – including early palletisation, containerisation and roll-on/roll-off operations – helped to stave off the problems up to the mid-1970s, but the respite was only temporary. By 1976 Ellesmere Port at the western end of the Canal, with its own container terminal, was doing more business than Manchester Docks, which was handling less than two million tonnes of cargo per annum. The upper reaches from Runcorn to Manchester were now in long term decline – a message which Redford, by then chairman of the company, spelt out bluntly to shareholders in 1982 as he lamented the loss of the remaining traffic with India and the closure of the Clan Line fleet. "No longer is there any demand for deep sea general cargo vessels in "the heart of the Greater Manchester area".[4] A year later Manchester Liners, whose first ship *Manchester City* had opened up the transatlantic trade with its maiden voyage in 1899, announced that it was to base its operations no longer in Salford but in Ellesmere Port.

The once mighty seaway to the world was becoming little more than a huge drainage system for the area, with the only regular user a weekly boat carrying scrap metal to Northern Spain. The largest single customer on the upper reaches was the North West Water Authority (NWWA) who announced in the same year that it planned to terminate its £1 million contract to carry Manchester sludge to the sea for dumping. A pipeline for sewage extraction was to take its place.[5] Reeling from the collapse in income from shipping activities, the Ship Canal Company responded by announcing in April 1984 its wish to close the upper reaches in 1987 and in so doing set off a train of events which has dominated the last decade. The shift of trade to Europe and the East coast, increased competition from road transport, the high costs of maintaining the Canal round the clock and the growing size of container ships were the reasons for the turnaround in fortunes. Henceforth the Canal Company's property assets were to become the prime focus of attention with Rothschilds Bank and Manchester City Council – the two external bodies which had respectively mounted financial rescues in 1887 and 1892 – playing key roles in the unfolding drama, in which the Ship Canal Company was to pass into the hands of a North West property company, Peel Holdings PLC.

The immediate response to the closure announcement was widespread protest from civic and community bodies, which led to the setting up of a high level steering committee composed of representatives from the local authorities, the Ship Canal Company and NWWA. For the next two years,

the committee was involved in commissioning a series of studies on the commercial, engineering, planning and legal aspects of the Canal. *The Ship Canal Lobby*, as it was called in the press, talked of the possibilities of transforming the Canal into a "multi-purpose waterway for the 21st century".[6] The emphasis was on the needs of the public with Peter Scott, a Greater Manchester councillor and chair of the Steering Committee, expressing the view that a consortium of local authorities was required, which would have to take over responsibility for the Canal after making "appropriate financial arrangements with the Ship Canal Company".[7] In this he was reflecting not only the views of radicals in the 1880s but also the opinions of some Labour councillors in the 1960s – that the best option was for the municipalisation of the undertaking.

When finally the consultants Coopers and Lybrand reported in March 1986, their recommendations, based upon public consultations, were that the upper reaches should remain open for navigation in order to develop a long-term strategy for commercial and leisure uses. The study recognised, however, that the 25 mile stretch from Runcorn to Manchester would never show a commercial profit and proposed a £19 million programme for repairing the basic infrastructure of locks and bridges and for dredging and flood control.[8]

While the Steering Group and public debate focused on the idea of turning the Canal into a 36 mile leisure corridor there were, however, other interests more concerned with the Company's land assets. In the Manchester Docks proper, steps were already being taken in 1981 to persuade Salford City Council to purchase 160 acres of derelict land for £1.6 million, which the Ship Canal Company felt could only be developed with a large injection of public monies. To unlock these reclamation and urban aid grants, which

eventually totalled £25 million for what was to become Salford Quays, the planners struck a deal with a local developer, Ted Hagan of Urban Waterside. The Council would sell him the freehold of nearly 30 acres at a peppercorn price if he could raise £9 million development capital from the private sector – a feat he achieved to the surprise of many. The result of this was the opening of an 8-screen cinema in 1986 and the luxury Copthorne Hotel the following year.[9] Substantial building has also taken place in the area owned by the Council.

The development of the Ship Canal's property assets was starting to feed through into the Company's balance sheet with pre-tax profits rising to £1.5 million in the first half of 1983 compared with £1.9 million for the whole of 1982 and a loss in 1981 of £2.4 million. The potential did not go unnoticed and over the next three years the value of ordinary shares in the company more than trebled. The explanation for this became clear in August 1986, when Highams, an Oldham-based textile firm under the chairmanship of property developer John Whittaker, launched a £37 million takeover bid for the entire Ship Canal Company. As the *Daily Telegraph* explained, "Whittaker's bid has little to do with the waterway at all", but stemmed from his discovery that the company "was sitting on a potential goldmine in the form of 300 acres of open land on the outskirts of the city".[10] The land in question, the Barton Dock Estate at Dumplington, was just five miles to the west of Manchester's city centre – an ideal site for a multi-million pound shopping centre, close to the motorway network and able to draw upon a potential five million customer base within 40 minutes drive.

The resulting battle for the control of the Canal Company and for the development of the Dumplington site has filled the pages of the local and national press for the last eight years. Both the Manchester Corporation directors, who retained a majority on the Board, and the directors nominated by the shareholders initially opposed the bid, on the grounds that the offer of £6.25 a share did not reflect the true asset value of the company. Both sides had to take account of the complex shareholding arrangements which had been set up before the Canal was first opened. Whittaker had over 50% of the shares but the tapered voting structure, geared towards the small shareholder, meant that the holder of 100 shares had 10 votes but the holder of 1,000 shares had only 28 votes. The obvious course for both sides was to parcel up and distribute small packets of shares, so first Highams began door-to-door canvassing round Pennine villagers and then the Ship Canal Board sought the support of Manchester Sunday League footballers – both wishing to create nominee shareholders who would vote in accordance with their wishes.[11]

By March 1987 Highams and Whittaker had gained control of the company but not without antagonising the deposed chairman, Nicholas Berry of Harraps, and other ordinary shareholders who retained 28% of the ordinary shares. They continued to hold out for a higher price, rejecting an offer of £20.70 for ordinary shares in 1988 but finally accepted £25 a share in 1993, with the promise of a top-up payment of £10.50 if final planning permission for the Dumplington site was agreed.[12] In 1991 control of the Ship Canal Company had been transferred to Peel Holdings via Highams, Great Hey Investments and Largs, all part of a network of Whittaker private family companies. Peel was a quoted company, for which in August 1983 Whittaker's financial advisers, N. M. Rothschild the merchant bankers, had arranged a placing of 1.4 million ordinary shares at £2.10 per share. At the time Largs held 67% of the shares of the company.[13] In November 1984 Peel had acquired Bridgewater Estates Ltd and appointed on to its own board as a non-executive director, Donald Redford, who was a former director of Bridgewater and was still chairman of the Manchester Ship Canal Company.

The connection with Rothschilds is interesting because, as the *Financial Times* pointed out, their Manchester Office had "spotted a critical weakness in MSC's share structure that provided a cheap way in. There were then 8 million shares split evenly between ordinaries and preference. The prefs yielded little, so were less than half the price of the ordinaries, which paid reasonable dividends. But each class of share carried equal voting rights".[14] Since, as we have seen, Rothschilds, had been centrally involved in determining the original share and voting structure back in 1887, they were extremely well placed to advise Whittaker from the moment that the Ship Canal Company announced its intentions to close the upper reaches.

Manchester City Council was the other partner in establishing the Canal in the 1890s and, despite Highams achieving in early 1987 a majority of voting shares, the eleven city councillors on the Ship Canal Company retained their control of the Board by virtue of Act of Parliament. For a time Whittaker and the Council appeared locked in dispute over the development of the Barton Dock "shopping city", but in October a deal was announced that the City Council, which was under strong pressure from the Government to reduce their borrowing, would agree to a joint approach seeking new statutory powers to remove the need for a Council majority on the Board. In return it would receive repayment of the original £7 million of loans together with a 49% shareholding, worth about £3 million in a new subsidiary, the Manchester Ship Canal Developments Ltd., which it was expected would be involved in housing developments in East Manchester.[15] The agreement reflected the weakness of the position secured for the Corporation in 1892 when it launched the *Municipal Lifeboat* (see Chapter 7) and allowed Manchester ratepayers only a small share in the greatly enhanced value of the Company's property portfolio.

For the new owners of the company, valued at £160 million according to one estimate, the major concern has been the development of its property interests both in the Salford and Trafford Park sections of the old Docks – where it has been able to take advantage of Enterprise Zone allowances – and at the Barton Dock Estate. In the case of the former, hopes of rapid growth have been hampered by the recession, while at Dumplington the company has been met with opposition not only from rival schemes at Salteye and Carrington, but also from traders and local councils worried that the development of the company's £200 million shopping city would destroy the viability of existing shopping facilities.[16]

The Docks in transition. Grain elevator being demolished in the 1980s. *BTY*

After long delays and two planning enquiries the proposal received planning permission from the Environment Secretary Michael Howard but a consortium of eight Greater Manchester Councils supported by private sector developers decided upon a legal challenge. The High Court decision in October 1993 went against the consortium, but a further appeal is expected in 1994 on the grounds that the decision runs counter to government policies on shopping, transport and the environment as outlined by the new Environment Secretary, John Gummer, at the 1993 Conservative Conference.[17]

Whatever the outcome, we may expect that the development of the company's land assets will continue, but many questions about the Canal itself still remain. The Runcorn end looks healthy at present, showing a profit of about £6 million in the last year, but there is uncertainty about the future of the 23 mile stretch of the upper reaches and no

longer a wider public discussion. Decisions have to be made however if only to maintain the drainage system, for which the company has a statutory responsibility, and undoubtedly public and European funding will be sought for this purpose.

In this centenary year what a fitting and popular tribute to this unique feature of the region it would be if the company, with the backing of the hundreds of bodies involved in the year's events, were to seek support for the idea of turning the Ship Canal into a linear park or national industrial heritage area. As the studies in the mid-1980s have shown, there is substantial potential for wider public and leisure use of the Canal and its designation as a national park would enable the company, public authorities along the Canal and community interest groups to cooperate in shaping its future for the 21st century. What better way could be found to celebrate one hundred years of the People's Canal and the Movement which brought it into existence?

## Notes

1. *Arbitration. Manchester Racecourse Co. Ltd. and Manchester Ship Canal Co.*, 19 February 1901, Manchester Central Library Archive, Misc Item 750/29; *Manchester Guardian,* 22 February 1900. Stevens had been acting for the Trafford Park Estates Company, for whom he was general manager.
2. *North West Business Insider*, January 1994.
3. *Manchester Evening News*, 26 September 1967.
4. Manchester Ship Canal Company, Chairman's Statement to the Shareholders, February 1982.
5. *Guardian*, 16 August 1983.
6. *Manchester Evening News*, 13 July 1984.
7. *Journal of the North West Civic Trust*, Spring 1985.
8. Manchester Ship Canal Steering Committee, *The MSC.*
   *A Strategy for the Future*, 1986.
9. C. M. Law, "From Manchester Docks to Salford Quays: A Progress Report on an Urban Development Project", in *The Manchester Geographer*, 1988.
10. *Daily Telegraph*, August 1986.
11. *Guardian*, 14 January, 15 January 1987.
12. *North West Times*, 7 October 1988; *North West Business Insider*, January 1994.
13. *Guardian*, 3 August 1983.
14. *Financial Times*, 16 July 1993.
15. *Guardian*, 9 September 1987; *City Life*, 23 October 1987.
16. *Manchester Evening News*, 24 August 1989.
17. *Guardian*, 4 January 1994.

Queen Victoria on board *Enchantress*

# Appendix A

## The Treatment of Sources:
## Bosdin Leech's *The History of the Manchester Ship Canal* (1907)

Bosdin Leech, a yarn agent by profession, was in several respects well-equipped for the task of writing a history of the Ship Canal. A councillor in Manchester when the scheme was being first considered in the early 1880s, he became one of its prime movers, acting as auditor for the company, ideologue at public meetings, correspondent with local papers, and intermediary for the company in negotiations with the Corporation. He was a meticulous record-keeper, and much of the material on the Ship Canal which is held by the City's Central Reference Library was donated by him, including some nineteen volumes of newspaper cuttings – an invaluable source of over five million words.

Leech's book is a storehouse of information – which has been eagerly plundered by subsequent writers – but its limitations are very apparent. Written by a man in his seventies who was untrained in writing skills, the book lacks form and structure, jumping from the significant to the trivial without hesitation as the author lurches from one month or year to the next. If there is criticism of his own role, or an account differs from his own, he simply omits all reference. He is also guilty on numerous occasions of lifting sections from his cuttings books and including them verbatim as though written by himself. A lengthy review of the book appeared in the *Manchester Guardian*, written almost certainly by its editor C. P. Scott, who also had an involvement with the project from the early days. A well-argued and informed review, whilst recognizing the value of Leech's book, it does not fail to point out the weaknesses, and stresses that Leech "himself was intimately associated with the affairs of which he treats, and was an eager and militant partisan in the long struggle which he describes. The result is that he does not present a well-conceived, well ordered, and well-proportioned picture."[1] The message, a fair one, is that Leech's account is far from objective and must be interpreted in the light of other factors.

If Leech can be described as approaching his task with a spirit of amateur but committed enthusiasm, Farnie has come with the skills and interests of a professional historian, with a rooted dislike for the *Manchester Guardian* and all it stood for.[2] Through his research into the development and performance of the Port of Manchester, Farnie has done more than any other writer to pinpoint the importance of the Ship Canal, but his history at times takes him off the beaten track on dubious quests.

Farnie is unstinting in his praise for Leech's book and makes the charge that Scott was hostile to the Ship Canal from 1882 to 1886[3] – a view that was put about at the time. Had he attempted to seek its provenance, he would have discovered that the accusation was made by Scott's Tory opponents during his election campaigns of 1886 and 1891, that the *Manchester Guardian* had with caveats given helpful coverage to the scheme, and that the paper's opposition was not to the Canal itself but to the idea of ratepayers rather than private capitalists paying for the scheme. Moreover on several occasions leading supporters had drawn attention to the help Scott had given.

George Hicks, joint auditor of the company with Leech, had first been in touch with Scott in 1876, when the *Manchester Guardian* published a letter and article by Hicks proposing a Ship Canal. In acknowledgement of this debt, Hicks was to write to the paper in the midst of Scott's 1891 campaign with an unequivocal statement:

> Writing with an intimate knowledge of every phase of the movement during its early development, I must in justice to Mr Scott say that he did everything that he could to assist the first promoters by familiarising the public with their ideas. I have always said that we were much indebted to the *Manchester Guardian* for its support 10 years ago, and I know that personally Mr. Scott was very enthusiastic as to the proposed waterway and all the immense advantages to Manchester which would follow its construction.[4]

Farnie's explanation for Scott's attitude is given in a passage which is worth quoting in full:

> His (Scott's) initial hostility was recorded by Leech for the benefit of posterity. Presumably Scott was mortified by the indiscretion of the author in disclosing his opposition to the liberal spirit of the age and in exposing his error of judgement to critical scrutiny. His own hypersensitivity had always led him to shun the publicity which he accorded so freely to others. His vanity may have prompted his ludicrous claim to have been one of the originators of the Canal and may also have been wounded by a personal reflection of the author: "he (Scott) had a flash of genius – such things come to the biggest of fools sometimes [Leech, Volume 1, 324].

The sources, however, when carefully examined and "cleaned" reveal a completely different picture. In a private letter[5] to Scott written five days after Hicks had given a full page interview with the *City News*, Hicks is complaining that Nodal, the editor of the *City News*, had censored material:

... I fully explained to him how important your assistance had been to the cause in 1877, and of the formation of the Consultative Committee in 1886 ... I was much annoyed to find that all reference to you had been taken out and at once called to expostulate with Mr Nodal who seemed under the delusion that you had been the Canal's greatest enemy. I therefore not only repeated what I had told him at our first interview, but also told him, in confidence, of your handsome offer to make the first preliminary survey and give the promoters the benefit of it. This somewhat staggered him but you know his obstinacy.

There is no reason to doubt the truth of this statement which appeared in a letter marked "private and confidential",

and a later comment from Hicks makes it clear that Scott was not keen to have his offer of help made public. The episode in fact tells us nothing about Scott's "hypersensitivity" or indeed about his alleged vanity for Farnie, relying solely on Leech's book, has completely misunderstood the context, and attributed to Leech the remark "he (Scott) had a flash of genius – such things come to the biggest of fools sometimes". The truth is that it was one of Scott's own remarks, a joke against himself, made during his 1886 election campaign when the Tories were spreading the smear about his opposition to the Ship Canal! His witty speech reported in the *Guardian* of 2 July 1886 and carefully pasted into Leech's cuttings book provides the full details.

### Notes

1. *Manchester Guardian*, 7 September 1907, p. 8.
2. D. Farnie, in W. H. Chaloner and B. M. Ratcliffe, (eds.), *Trade and Transport, op.cit.*, p. 209.
3. D. Farnie, *The Manchester Ship Canal and the Rise of the Port of Manchester*, 1980, p. 171.
4. *Manchester Guardian*, 5 October 1891, p. 6.
5. C. Hicks to C. P. Scott, 6 January 1894, C. P. Scott Archive, John Rylands University Library of Manchester.

# Appendix B

## Manchester Councillors and Aldermen by Party, December 1890

| Name | Date Elected | Liberal | Lib/U | Tory |
|------|--------------|---------|-------|------|
| Abbott | 1890 | * | | |
| Aldred | 1887 | * | | |
| Andrews | 1885 | | | * |
| Ashcroft | 1883 | | | * |
| Asquith | 1875 | * | | |
| Bagnall | 1888 | | | * |
| Battersby | 1890 | | | * |
| Batty | 1890 | * | | |
| Bax | 1887 | * | | |
| Birkbeck | 1887 | * | | |
| Boddington | 1881 | | | * |
| Bowes | 1890 | * | | |
| Bradshaw | 1889 | | | * |
| Briggs | 1890 | | | * |
| Brooks, J | 1883 | | | * |
| Brooks, S | 1890 | * | | |
| Butterworth | 1890 | * | | |
| Cardwell | 1887 | | | * |
| Clay | 1882 | | * | |
| Copeland | 1886 | | | * |
| Crosfield | 1890 | * | | |
| Cuff | 1887 | | | * |
| Erwin | 1890 | * | | |
| Estcourt | 1885 | | | * |
| Evans, A | 1876 | * | | |
| Evans, G | 1890 | * | | |
| Fullerton | 1887 | * | | |
| Garlick | 1890 | | | * |
| Gibson | 1882 | * | | |
| Grantham | 1883 | | | * |
| Griffin | 1871 | | | * |
| Gunson | 1885 | * | | |
| Hampson | 1888 | | | * |
| Harwood | 1866 | * | | |
| Heywood | 1843 | * | | |
| Higginbottom | 1890 | * | | |
| Hill | 1890 | | | * |
| Hinchcliffe | 1879 | | | * |
| Holland | 1890 | * | | |
| Holt | 1890 | | | * |
| Hopkinson | 1861 | * | | |
| Hoy | 1882 | * | | |
| Hutt | 1885 | * | | |
| Jennison | 1890 | | | * |
| King | 1856 | | * | |
| Lamb | 1846 | | | * |
| Leech | 1880 | * | | |
| Livesley | 1865 | | | * |
| Lloyd, A | 1880 | * | | |
| Lloyd, R. | 1886 | * | | |

| Name | Date Elected | Liberal | Lib/U | Tory |
|------|-------------|---------|-------|------|
| Mainwaring | 1886 | | | * |
| Mark | 1877 | | * | |
| Marshall | 1882 | | | * |
| McCabe | 1889 | * | | |
| McDougall | 1884 | * | | |
| Milling | 1879 | * | | |
| Milne | 1883 | | * | |
| Morgan | 1890 | | | * |
| Murray | 1885 | * | | |
| Myerscough | 1889 | | | * |
| Needham | 1885 | | | * |
| Norris | 1889 | * | | |
| O'Neill | 1885 | * | | |
| Pingstone | 1885 | | * | |
| Rawson | 1883 | | * | |
| Reade | 1877 | | | * |
| Reynolds | 1890 | | | * |
| Rhodes | 1890 | * | | |
| Richards | 1885 | | | * |
| Roberts, J.F. | 1868 | | * | |
| Roberts, J | 1882 | | | * |
| Robinson, W | 1887 | | | * |
| Robinson, J | 1890 | | | * |
| Rothwell | 1890 | | | * |
| Rowley | 1890 | * | | |
| Royle | 1885 | | | * |
| Rushworth | 1880 | * | | |
| Russell | 1890 | * | | |
| Samson | 1888 | | | * |
| Schofield | 1866 | | * | |
| Schou | 1883 | | | * |
| Shaw | 1871 | | | * |
| Sherratt | 1885 | * | | |
| Simpson | 1889 | | | * |
| Smallman | 1889 | * | | |
| Smith | 1868 | * | | |
| Southern | 1884 | * | | |
| Stanley | 1890 | * | | |
| Tatton, E | 1887 | | | * |
| Tatton, J | 1889 | * | | |
| Tetlow | 1890 | | | * |
| Thompson, J | 1865 | * | | |
| Thompson, S | 1879 | | | * |
| Trevor | 1890 | * | | |
| Tunstall | 1885 | | | * |
| Uttley | 1890 | * | | |
| Vaudrey | 1889 | | | * |
| Wainwright | 1890 | * | | |
| Ward | 1890 | * | | |
| Wells | 1890 | * | | |
| Williams | 1885 | | | * |
| Wilson | 1890 | | | * |
| Windsor | 1876 | | | * |
| Worthington | 1887 | * | | |
| TOTALS | | 49 | 8 | 47 |

Sources: City of Manchester Municipal Handbook and Newspaper Election Reports

# Bibliography

## GENERAL BOOKS

Aldcroft, D. H. (ed.), *The Development of British Industry and Foreign Competition, 1875–1914*, 1968, London.

Armytage, W. H. G., *A. J. Mundella 1825–1897: The Liberal Background to the Labour Movement*, 1951, London.

Ashton, T. S., *Economic and Social Investigation in Manchester 1833–1933*, 1934, London.

Ashworth, W., *Economic History of England, 1870–1939*, 1960, London.

Beer, M., *A History of British Socialism, Volume 2*, 1921, London.

Benwell, C. D. P., *The Making of a Ruling Class*, 1978, Newcastle upon Tyne.

Berg, M. (ed.), *Technology and Toil in Nineteenth Century Britain*, 1979, London.

Bird, J., *The Major Seaports of the UK*, 1963, London.

Briggs, A., *Victorian Cities*, 1963, London.

Brindley, W. H. (ed.), *The Soul of Manchester*, 1929, Manchester.

Brotherston, I. and Windmill, C. (eds.), *Bridging the Years*, 1992, Salford.

Brown, B. H., *The Tariff Reform Movement in Great Britain 1881–1895*, 1943, Oxford.

Cannadine, D. (ed.), *Exploring the Urban Past. Essays in urban history by H. J. Dyos*, 1982, Cambridge.

Challinor, R., *The Lancashire and Cheshire Miners*, 1972, Newcastle upon Tyne.

Chapman, S. D., *The Cotton Industry in the Industrial Revolution*, 1972, London.

Charlton, H. B., *Portrait of a University, 1851–1951*, 1951, Manchester.

Checkland, S. G., *The Rise of Industrial Society*, 1964, London.

Chorley, K., *Manchester Made Them*, 1950, London.

Clapham, J. H., *Economic History of Modern Britain, Vol. 1850–1886,(1932) and Vol. 1887–1914 (1938)*, Cambridge.

Clarke, P. F., *Lancashire and the New Liberalism*, 1971, London.

Clegg, H. A. et al., *A History of British Trade Unions since 1889, Vol. 1, 1889–1910*, 1964, Oxford.

Cole, G. D. H., *A Short History of the British Working Class Movement 1789–1925*, 1925, London.

Cole, G. D. H., *A Century of Cooperation*, 1944, Manchester.

Cole, G. & Postgate, R., *The Common People*, 1946, London.

Cole, M. (ed.), *The Webbs and Their Work*, 1974, London.

Cottrell, P. L., *British Overseas Investment in the Nineteenth Century*, 1975, London.

Crossick, G., *An Artisan Elite in Victorian Society, Kentish London, 1840–1880*, 1978, London.

Daunton, M. J., *Coal Metropolis Cardiff 1870–1914*, 1977, Leicester.

Dugdale, B. E. C., *Arthur James Balfour*, Volume 1, 1936, London.

Elbaum, B. & Lazonick, W., *The Decline of the British Economy*, 1986, Oxford.

Emy, H. V., *Liberals, Radicals and Social Politics, 1892–1914*, 1973, Cambridge.

Farnie, D. A., *The English Cotton Industry and the World Market, 1815–1896*, 1979, Oxford.

Farnie, D. A., *The Manchester Ship Canal and the Rise of the Port of Manchester*, 1980, Manchester.

Finer, H., *Municipal Trading: A study in public administration*, 1941, London.

Fowler, A. & Wyke, T., *The Barefoot Aristocrats. A History of the Amalgamated Operative Cotton Spinners*, 1987, Littleborough.

Fraser, D., *Urban Politics in Victorian England*, 1976, Leicester.

Fraser, P., *Joseph Chamberlain: Radicalism and Empire 1868–1914*, 1966, London.

Fraser, W., *Trade Unions and Society. The Struggle for Acceptance 1850–1880*, 1974, London.

Freeman, T. W. et al., *Lancashire, Cheshire and the Isle of Man*, 1966, London.

Frow, E. & R., *To Make that Future – NOW! A History of the Manchester and Salford Trades' Council*, 1971, Manchester.

Garrard, J., *Leadership and Power in Victorian Industrial Towns 1830–1880*, 1983, Manchester.

Gatrell, V. A. C., "Incorporation and the Pursuit of Liberal Hegemony in Manchester", in Fraser, D., ed., *Municipal Reform and the Industrial City*, 1982, Leicester.

Gray, R. Q., *The Labour Aristocracy in Victorian Edinburgh*, 1976, Oxford.

Habbakuk, H. J., *American and British Technology in the Nineteenth Century*, 1962, Cambridge.

Hamer, D. A., *Liberal Politics in the Age of Gladstone and Rosebery*, 1972, Oxford.

Hanham, H. J., *Elections and Party Management: Politics in the time of Disraeli and Gladstone*, 1959, London.

Harnetty, P., *Imperialism and Free Trade: Lancashire and India in the mid Nineteenth Century*, 1972, Manchester.

Harris, J. R. (ed.), *Liverpool and Merseyside: Essays in the economic and social history of the port*, 1969, London.

Harrison, R., *Before the Socialists. 1861–1881*, 1965, London.

Harrison, R. & Zeitlin, J. (eds.), *Divisions of Labour*, 1985, Brighton.

Harte, N. B., *The Study of Economic History: Collected inaugural lectures 1893–1970*, 1971, London.

Hobsbawm, E. J., *Industry and Empire*, 1969, London.

Hodson, P. M. (ed.), *The MSC: A Guide to Historical Sources*, 1985, Manchester.

Hopwood, E., *A History of the Lancashire cotton industry and the Amalgamated Weavers Association*, 1969, Manchester.

Hyde, F. E., *Liverpool and the Mersey: An economic history of a port 1700–1970*, 1971, Newton Abbot.

Jefferys, J. B., *The Story of the Engineers*, 1946, London.

Jones, G. S., *Outcast London: A Study in the Relationship between Classes in Victorian Society*, 1971, Oxford.
Joyce, P., *Work, Society and Politics*, 1980, London.
Joyce, P., *Visions of the People*, 1991, Cambridge.
Kidd, A. J. & Roberts, K. W., *City, Class and Culture: Cultural Production and Social Policy in Victorian Manchester*, 1985, Manchester.
Kinross, Lord., *Between Two Seas: The Creation of the Suez Canal*, 1968, London.
Kirk, N., *The Growth of Working Class Reformism in Mid Victorian England*, 1985, London.
Lambertz, J., "Sexual Harassment in the 19th Century English Cotton Industry", in *History Workshop Journal*, 1985, Henley-on-Thames.
Langan, M. & Schwarz, B., *Crises in the British State*, 1985, London.
Leventhal, F. M., *Respectable Radical: George Howell and Victorian working class politics*, 1971, London.
Levy, C., ed., *Socialism and the Intelligentsia, 1850–1914*, 1987, London.
Lewis, J. P., *Building cycles and Britain's growth*, 1965, London.
Liddington, J. & Norris, J., *One Hand Tied Behind Us*, 1984, London.
Martin, R. M., *T.U.C. The Growth of a Pressure Group*, 1980, Oxford.
McCord, N., *The Anti-Corn Law League 1838–1846*, 1958, London.
McKibbin, R., *The Ideologies of Class*, 1991, Oxford.
McIntosh, I., *Ford at Trafford Park*, 1991, Manchester.
Mills, W. H., *Sir Charles Macara, Bart. A Study of Modern Lancashire*, 1917, Manchester.
Mills, W. H., ed., *The Manchester Reform Club 1871–1921*, 1922, Manchester.
Moore, R. J., *Liberalism and Indian politics 1872–1922*, 1966, London.
More, C., *Skill & the English Working Class 1870–1914*, 1980, London.
Musson, A. E., *The Typographical Association: Origins and History*, 1954, Oxford.
Owen, D., *The Manchester Ship Canal*, 1983, Manchester.
Pankhurst, E. S., *The Suffragette Movement*, 1931, London.
Pease, E. R., *The History of the Fabian Society*, 1925, London.
Plummer, A., *International Combines in Modern Industry*, 1938, London.
Pollard, S., *A History of Labour in Sheffield*, 1959, Liverpool.
Postgate, R., *The Builders' History*, 1923, London.
Poulantzas, N., *Classes in Contemporary Capitalism*, 1974, London.
Redfern, P., *John T. W. Mitchell. Pioneer of Consumers Cooperation*, 1923, Manchester.
Redfern, P., *The New History of the C.W.S*, 1938, London.
Redford, A., *History of Local Government in Manchester*, 1940, London.
Roberts, B. C., *The Trades Union Congress 1868–1921*, 1958, London.
Robson, R, *The Cotton Industry in Britain*, 1957, London.
Rubinstein, D., *People for the People*, 1973, London.
Rubinstein, W. D., *Men of Property*, 1981, London.
Sandberg, L. G., *Lancashire in Decline*, 1974, Columbus, Ohio.
Sau, R., *Unequal Exchange, Imperialism and Underdevelopment*, 1978, Calcutta.
Saul, S. B., *Technological Change: The United States and Britain in the Nineteenth Century*, 1970, London.

Sharpless, J. B., "Inter City Development and Dependency", in Wirth, J. D. & Jones, R. L., *Manchester and Sao Paulo, Problems of Urban Growth*, 1978, Stanford, California.
Smyth, R. L., *Essays in the Economics of Socialism and Capitalism, 1886–1932*, 1964, London.
Simey, T.S., *The Dock Worker. An Analysis of conditions of employment in the Port of Manchester*, 1954, Liverpool.
Simon, S. D., *A Century of City Government*, 1938, London.
Stevens, T. H. G., *Notes on the Development of Trafford Park*, 1947, Manchester.
Sullivan, D., *Navvyman*, 1983, London.
Thompson, F. M. L., *The Rise of Respectable Society. A Social History of Victorian Britain, 1830–1900*, 1988, London.
Thompson, P., *Socialists, Liberals and Labour. The Struggle for London. 1885–1914*, 1967, London.
Turner, H. A., *Trade Union Growth, Structure and Policy. A Study of the Cotton Unions*, 1962, London.
Ward, J. T. (ed.), *Popular Movements, c1830–1850*, 1970, London.
Watson, G., *The English ideology; studies in the language of Victorian politics*, 1973, London.
Weeks, J., *Sex, Politics and Society. The Regulation of Sexuality since 1800*, 1981, London.
Wigham, E., *The Power to Manage: A History of the Engineering Employers' Federation*, 1973, London.

**CONTEMPORARY BOOKS**

Ashworth, H., *Recollections of Richard Cobden and the Anti-Corn Law League*, 1881, London.
Axon, W. E. A., *An Architectural and General Description of the Town Hall, Manchester*, 1910, Manchester.
Davis, W. J., *The British Trades Union Congress. History and Recollections*, 1910, London.
Ellison, T., *The Cotton Trade of Great Britain*, 1887, London.
Gibbs, H. S., ("H.S.G"), *Autobiography of a Manchester Cotton Manufacturer*, 1887, Manchester.
Harwood, J. Sir., *History and Description of the Thirlmere Water Scheme*, 1895, Manchester.
Leech, H. J. (ed.), *The Public Letters of John Bright*, 1895, London.
Leech, B. T., *History of the Manchester Ship Canal*, 2 Volumes, 1907, Manchester.
Macrosty, H. W., *The Trust Movement in British Industry*, 1907, London.
O'Conor, W. A., *History of the Irish People*, 1886, Manchester.
Rawson, H. (ed.), *Historical Record of the Corporation of Manchester*, 1894, Manchester.
Reade, H. M., *Christ or Socialism – A Human Autobiography*, 1909, London.
Samuelson, J., *Labour-Saving Machinery*, 1893, London.
Shaw, W. A., *Manchester: Old and New*, 3 Volumes, 1890, London.
Slagg, J., *The Cotton Trade and Industry, in The Reign of Queen Victoria*, (ed. T. H. Ward), 1887, London.
Vanderlip, F. A., *The American "Commercial Invasion" of Europe*, 1902, New York.
Watkin, E., *Alderman Cobden of Manchester*, 1891, London.
Webb, S. & B., *The History of Trade Unionism*, 1894, London.
Wood, G. H., *History of Wages in the Cotton Trade*, 1910, London.
Young, T. M., *Manchester & the Atlantic Trade*, 1902, Manchester.

## CONTEMPORARY PAMPHLETS AND BROADSHEETS

*Manchester Corporation Proceedings and Municipal Returns*, 1880.
*Ab-o'th'-yate and the Ship Canal: A dream of 1892*, by Ben Brierley, 1882.
*Facts and Figures in favour of the proposed MSC*, by Mancuniensis, 1882.
*The MSC. Why it is wanted! and Why it will pay!*, by Cottonopolis, 1882.
*The MSC. Reasons why it should be Made*, 1882?
*The MSC Scheme. A Criticism*, by A. Provand, 1883.
*Manchester. A Timber Port*, by Lumber, 1883.
*Manchester on the Sea*, 1883.
*The MSC. A Reply to Mr Provand's adverse criticism*, by A Supporter, 1883.
*MSC. Work going in Outlying Towns*, 1883.
*The Adamsonian Delusion and its influence on the City Council*, 1884.
*MSC. Description of Project now before Parliament*, 1884.
*MSC. Enquiry before the House of Lords. Important Commercial Evidence*, 1885.
*The Rejected Letter: the Working Man as a Shareholder*, by S. Ramsbottom, 1885.
*Interview with Mr Joseph Lawrence*, 1894, (Reprinted from the *Courier*)
*Tourist Guide to Eastham and the MSC*, no date.

## PARLIAMENTARY PAPERS

Census of Population Reports, 1871, 1881, 1891.
Royal Commission on the Housing of the Working Classes, 1884–5. PP. Vol. XXX.
Statistical Tables and Reports on Trade Unions. Board of Trade. 1887–1891.
Royal Commission into the Depression of Trade and Industry. 1886. PP. Vol. XXI.
Royal Commission on Labour. 1891–2. PP. Vols. XXXI–XXXIV.

## NEWSPAPERS, SPECIALISED PERIODICALS, ANNUAL REPORTS ETC.

*Bolton Journal*
*Business History*
*City News*
*Cooperative News*
*Cotton Factory Times*
*CWS Annual Reports*
*Economic History Review*
*Gorton Reporter*
*Illustrated London News*
*Industrial Remuneration Conference Proceedings, 1885*
*Justice*
*Labour Standard*
*Liberal and Radical Year Books, 1887–1890*
*Manchester at the Close of the Nineteenth Century*
*Manchester Courier*
*Manchester Evening Mail*
*Manchester Evening News*
*Manchester Examiner and Times*
*Manchester Faces and Places*
*Manchester Guardian*
*Manchester of Today.* 1888
*Manchester Statistical Society Transactions*
*Mercury Dictionary of Textile Terms*
*Oldham Chronicle*
*Oldham Standard*
*Patricroft and Eccles Journal*
*Rochdale Observer*
*Salford Reporter*
*Social History*
*Ship Canal Gazette*
*Spy*
*The Engineer*
*TUC Annual Reports*
*Typographical Circular*
*Umpire*
*Workmans Times*

## TRADE UNION, EMPLOYER AND OTHER ARCHIVAL MATERIAL

Amalgamated Association of Operative Cotton Spinners Quarterly Reports.
Boilermakers and Iron Ship Builders Monthly Reports.
Cooperative Wholesale Society, Finance Committee Minute Books.
C. P. Scott Archive of Correspondence, John Rylands University Library.
George Howell Archive, Bishopsgate Institute.
Manchester Liberal Association, Minute Books
Manchester Ship Canal, Provisional Committee Minute Books.
Manchester Ship Canal Company, Various Minute Books.
Oldham Masters Letters Book.
Parkyn Papers relating to the MSC, Lancashire County Record Office.
T.U.C. Parliamentary Committee Minute Books.
Typographical Association, Manchester Branch Minute Books.
Tin Plate Workers Society, Manchester Branch Minute Books.
Webb Trade Union Collection of Letters, London School of Economics.
Manchester City Council, Watch Committee Minute Books.
Manchester City Council, Reports of Proceedings.
Baring Brothers and Company Archive, Papers and Letter Books.
The Rothschild Archive (London), Letter Books.

## UNPUBLISHED THESES AND PAPERS

Bather, L., *History of Manchester and Salford Trades Council from 1880*, 1956, Manchester.
Goldberg, G. C., *The Socialist and Political Labour Movement in Manchester & Salford. 1884–1914*, 1975, Manchester.
Morrison, E., *South Salford Branch of the SDF and the Spread of Socialism in Lancashire (1885–1894)*, 1978, Manchester.
Murphy, B., *The Manchester Ship Canal and its Navvies*, 1979, Manchester.
Tyson, R. E., *The Sun Mill Co. Ltd. A Study in Democratic Investment*, 1962, Manchester.
Whitaker, P., *The Growth of Liberal Organisation in Manchester from 1860s–1903*, 1963, Manchester.

# THE PORT OF MANCHESTER

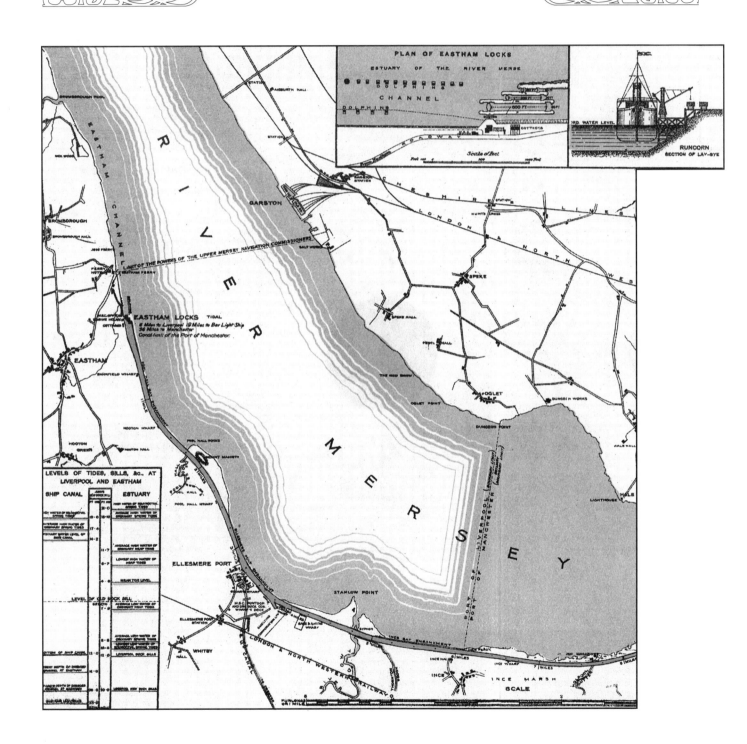

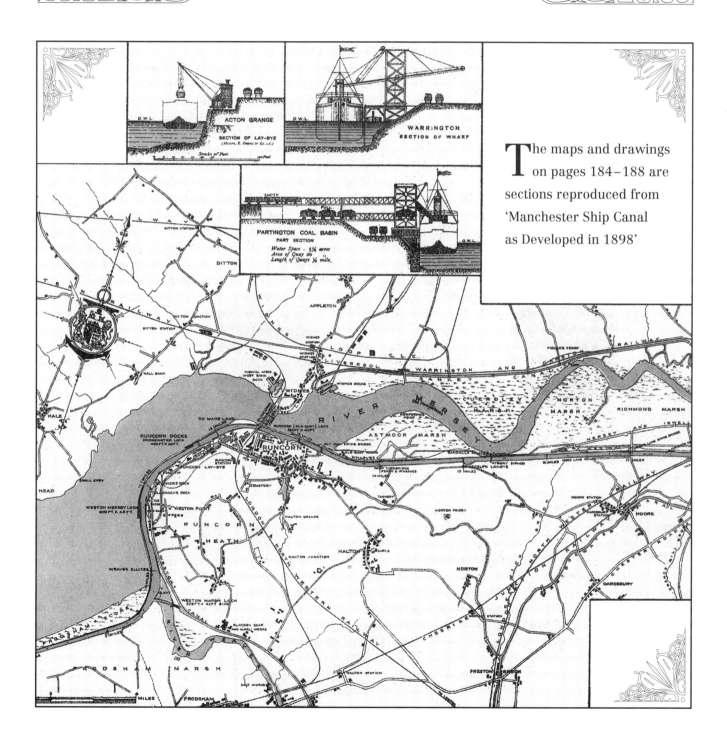

The maps and drawings on pages 184–188 are sections reproduced from 'Manchester Ship Canal as Developed in 1898'

THE MANCHESTER SHIP CANAL is 35½ miles in length, and has been excavated throughout to a depth of 26 feet, which depth is maintained by dredging.

The bottom width at the full depth is 120 feet, with the following exceptions :—

    (a) At the curve at the Weaver Outfall, the width at the full depth is 180 feet; at the bend at Runcorn, approaching the Runcorn Railway Bridge, it is 150 feet.

    (b) For a part of the length between Latchford Locks and Partington Coal Basin (about one mile in all), the bottom width is at present only 80 to 90 feet, and large vessels are not allowed to pass each other on that portion of the Canal.

    (c) From Barton Aqueduct to the Manchester Docks the width is 170 feet.

The Tidal portion from Eastham to Latchford Locks (21 miles) is maintained at a minimum level of 14 feet 2 inches above Old Dock Sill (or 9 feet 8 inches above Ordnance Datum, i.e., mean sea level).

The Fixed Bridges cross the Canal at a minimum height of 75 feet above normal water level.

The principal Docks are at Manchester, and are equipped with Transit Sheds of new design, Steam, Hydraulic, and Electric Cranes, and other appliances for giving quick despatch. There is also a Grain Elevator of the capacity of 40,000 tons.

The Canal Company's Railways convey Traffic between the various loading and discharging berths at the Docks and along the Canal, and are connected with all the Railway systems of the Country.

The Canal and Docks are in direct communication with the whole of the inland navigations of the Country.

The Canal Company receive, warehouse, and distribute all descriptions of traffic, and quote through rates.

The Canal Company have for Sale, or Lease, Plots of Land between Eastham and Manchester, eminently suitable for the erection of works of all kinds, with frontage to the Ship Canal and connection with the principal railways.

Schedules of Charges and further information may be obtained at the Dock Office, Manchester.

1902                 ERNEST LATIMER, *General Superintendent.*

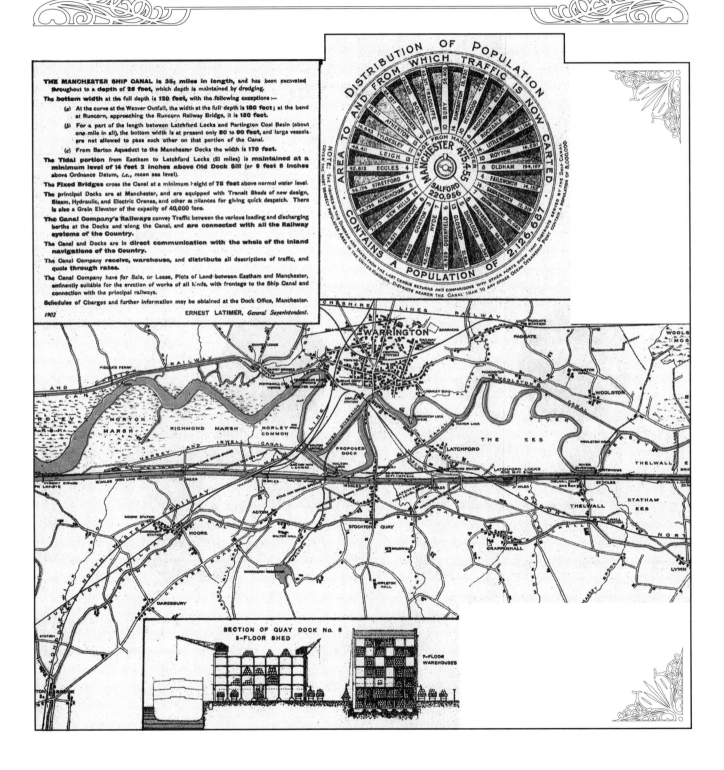

186

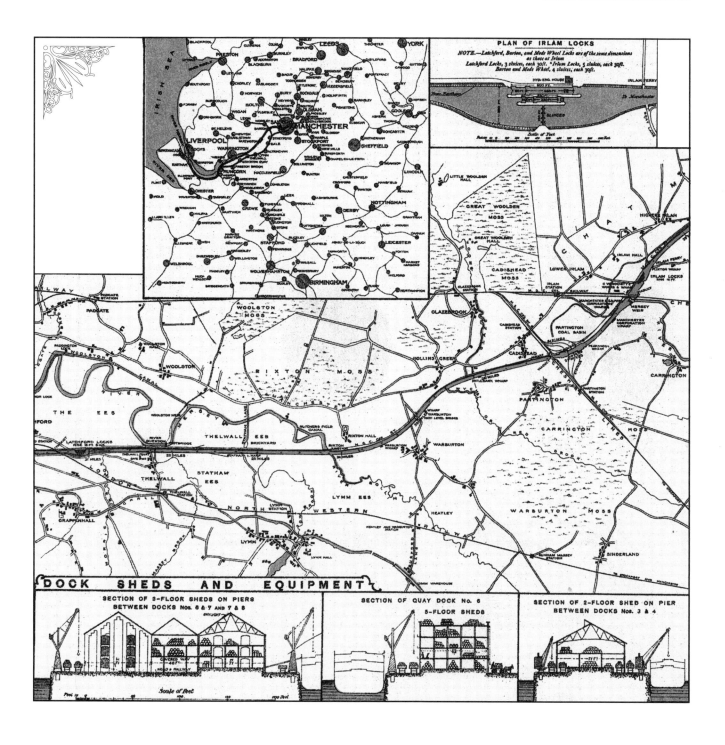

# Index